Reports of the Finance Commissions of India

First Finance Commission*
to the

Twelfth Finance Commission

(THE COMPLETE REPORT)

*The accompanying CD-ROM features
Introduction as well as Summary of Recommendations of the
Reports of all the earlier Finance Commissions (First to the Eleventh)

Also published by Academic Foundation...

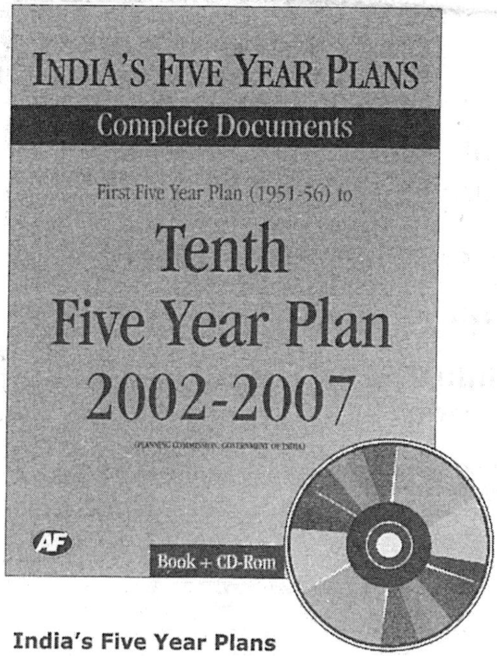

India's Five Year Plans

Complete Documents : First Five Year Plan (1951-56) to Tenth Five Year Plan (2002-2007)

BOOK + CD-ROM

2003 • Hard-cover book (large format) Pp. 222 + CD-Rom • ISBN 81-7188-300-1

Rs. 795 US$ 44.00

For the benefit of the readers and researchers, Academic Foundation has brought out this publication bringing **at one source** *all* the *ten documents* of Five Year Plans (Planning Commission, Govt. of India). While Volume I of the Tenth Five Year Plan, covering : Perspective, Objectives and Strategies, Macro-economic Dimensions, Employment Perspective, Governance and Implementation, Disaster Management, Policy Imperatives and Programmatic Initiatives — is included in this book, the complete Tenth Plan document (in 3 volumes) along with the other nine documents of the earlier Five Year Plans (around 10,000 pages) are given in the accompanying CD-Rom, in order to make the publication handy. Needless to say, the user-friendly CD-Rom offers inbuilt search facility, easy print-out option, along with other usual advantages associated with the digital media.

Book + CD-ROM

REPORTS OF THE FINANCE COMMISSIONS OF INDIA

First Finance Commission*
to the

Twelfth Finance Commission

(THE COMPLETE REPORT)

*The accompanying CD-ROM features
Introduction as well as Summary of Recommendations of the
Reports of all the earlier Finance Commissions (First to the Eleventh)

AF
ACADEMIC FOUNDATION

Academic Foundation
www.academicfoundation.com NEW DELHI

Published in 2005 by
ACADEMIC FOUNDATION
4772-73 / 23 Bharat Ram Road,
(23 Ansari Road), Darya Ganj,
New Delhi - 110 002.

Phones : 23245001, 02, 03, 04.
Fax : 011-23245005
E-Mail : academic@vsnl.com
www : academicfoundation.com

Reports of India's Finance Commissions:
First to the Twelfth Finance Commission
(Book + CD-ROM)
ISBN 81-7188-474-1

Design/Typesetting: Italics India, New Delhi.
Printed and bound in India.

Contents...

The present volume carries complete Report of the Twelfth Finance Commission, except Appendices and Annexures — which are placed in the accompanying CD-ROM that additionally features the essentials, namely, Introduction and the Summary of Recommendations of all the previous reports of the earlier Finance Commissions (First to the Eleventh).

This publication, for the first time, brings together at one source, the invaluable contributions of all the Finance Commissions of India till date — spanning more than half a century of fiscal federalism in India.

Report of the Twelfth Finance Commission

Contents of the CD-ROM...

REPORT OF THE TWELFTH FINANCE COMMISSION

List of Annexures and Appendices available on CD-ROM

ANNEXURES

APPENDICES

List of Abbreviations

ADB	Asian Development Bank
APDRP	Accelerated Power Development and Reforms Programme
APR	Administered Price Regime
ARWSP	Accelerated Rural Water Supply Programme
ATR	Action Taken Report
BCR	Balance from Current Revenue
BE	Budget Estimate
BRAIN	Bihar Revenue Administration Intra Net
C&AG	Comptroller and Auditor General
CENVAT	Central VAT
CPWD	Central Public Works Department
CRF	Calamity Relief Fund
CRSP	Central Rural Sanitation Programme
CSO	Central Statistical Organisation
CSS	Centrally Sponsored Schemes
DDWS	Department of Drinking Water Supply
EFC	Eleventh Finance Commission
ERC	Expenditure Reforms Commission
FC	Finance Commission
FCD	Finance Commission Division
FCI	Food Corporation of India
FPSS	Fiscal Policy Strategy Statement
FRBMA	Fiscal Responsibility and Budget Management Act
FRF	Fiscal Reform Facility
GCS	General Category States
GDP	Gross Domestic Product
GFD	Gross Fiscal Deficit
GIS	Geographic Information System
GSDP	Gross State Domestic Product
GTR	Gross Tax Revenue
GTRR	Gross Tax Revenue Receipts
GST	Goods and Services Tax
HDI	Human Development Index
IATP	Income Adjusted Total Population
IBRD	International Bank for Reconstruction and Development
ICOR	Incremental Capital Output Ratio
IDFC	Infrastructure Development Finance Company
IDA	International Development Association
IIPA	Indian Institute of Public Administration
IMF	International Monetary Fund
IP	Interest Payments
IPE	Infrastructure Professional Enterprises
IPFS	Indian Public Finance Statistics
IRDA	Insurance Regulatory and Development Authority
IRM	Internal Revenue Mobilisation
MH	Major Head
MODVAT	Modified VAT
MOP&NG	Ministry of Petroleum and Natural Gas
MOU	Memorandum of Understanding

MRD	Ministry of Rural Development
MSS	Market Stabilisation Scheme
MSW	Municipal Solid Waste Management
MTFRP	Medium Term Fiscal Reform Programme
MUD&PA	Ministry of Urban Development and Poverty Alleviation
NCCF	National Calamity Contingency Fund
NCCM	National Centre for Calamity Management
NCRC	National Calamity Relief Committee
NELP	New Exploration Licensing Policy
NFCR	National Fund for Calamity Relief
NGOs	Non Governmental Organisations
NIPFP	National Institute of Public Finance and Policy
NIRD	National Institute of Rural Development
NPR	Non-Plan Revenue
NPRE	Non-Plan Revenue Expenditure
NSSF	National Small Savings Fund
OIL	Oil India Ltd.
O&M	Operation and Maintenance
ONGC	Oil and Natural Gas Corporation
ONTR	Own Non-Tax Revenue
OONTR	Other Own Non-Tax Revenue
ORDA	Oilfields (Regulation and Development) Act
OTR	Own Tax Revenue
PEL	Petroleum Exploration License
P&NGR	Petroleum and Natural Gas Rules
PML	Petroleum Mining Lease
PRI	Panchayati Raj Institution
PSC	Production Sharing Contract
PSU	Public Sector Undertaking
RBI	Reserve Bank of India
RD	Revenue Deficit
RE	Revised Estimate
RLB	Rural Local Body
RR	Revenue Receipt
SCS	Special Category States
SEB	State Electricity Board
SFC	State Finance Commission
SGRY	Sampoorna Grameen Rozgar Yojana
SLPE	State Level Public Enterprise
SRTC	State Road Transport Corporation
SSA	Sarva Shiksha Abhiyan
TD	Tax Devolution
TFC	Twelfth Finance Commission
TGR	Trend Growth Rate
TGS	Technical Guidance and Supervision
TOR	Terms of Reference
TRAI	Telecom Regulatory Authority of India
TRR	Total Revenue Receipts
TSC	Total Sanitation Campaign
TUT	Tax Collection from Union Territories
ULB	Urban Local Body
UNDP	United Nations Development Programme
UT	Union Territory
VAT	Value Added Tax
VRS	Voluntary Retirement Scheme
WMA	Ways and Means Advance
ZBB	Zero Based Budgeting

Chapter 1

Introduction

Appointment of the Twelfth Finance Commission

1.1 The appointment of a finance commission by the President is provided for under article 280 of the Constitution of India. The first such commission was constituted on November 19, 1951. The eleven finance commissions, which have preceded the present one, have, through their recommendations, given a definitive shape to fiscal federalism in our country. The present finance commission, which is the twelfth, was appointed by the President of India on 1st November, 2002 under the chairmanship of Dr. C. Rangarajan, the then Governor of Andhra Pradesh. The President also appointed two full-time members, namely, Shri T. R. Prasad, IAS (retd.), former Cabinet Secretary, Government of India and Prof. D. K. Srivastava of National Institute of Public Finance & Policy (NIPFP) and one part-time member, namely, Shri Som Pal, Member, Planning Commission. Dr. G.C. Srivastava, IAS was appointed as the Secretary to the Commission. Later on, he was appointed as Member Secretary, against the vacancy of the fourth Member with effect from July 1, 2003. Consequent upon the resignation of Shri Som Pal from the Commission, Dr. Shankar N. Acharya was appointed as a part-time member with effect from 1st July 2004. The relevant notifications are at annexures 1.1, 1.2 and 1.3.

1.2 The Commission was originally asked to make its report available by the 31st July 2004 covering a period of five years commencing on the 1st April 2005. Subsequently, due to disruption of normal activities on account of preponement of parliamentary election, the President, through his order dated 1st July 2004, extended the tenure of the Commission up to 31st December 2004, but required the report to be made available by 30th November 2004 (notification at annexure 1.4).

Terms of Reference (TOR)

1.3 The President *vide* the notification dated 1st November, 2002 (annexure 1.1) mandated the Commission to do the following:

> "4. The Commission shall make recommendations as to the following matters:-
>
> (i) the distribution between the Union and the States of the net proceeds of taxes which are to be, or may be, divided between them under Chapter I Part XII

of the Constitution and the allocation between the States of the respective shares of such proceeds;

(ii) the principles which should govern the grants-in-aid of the revenues of the States out of the Consolidated Fund of India and the sums to be paid to the States which are in need of assistance by way of grants-in-aid of their revenues under article 275 of the Constitution for purposes other than those specified in the provisions to clause (1) of that article; and

(iii) the measures needed to augment the Consolidated Fund of a State to supplement the resources of the Panchayats and Municipalities in the State on the basis of the recommendations made by the Finance Commission of the State.

5. The Commission shall review the state of the finances of the Union and the States and suggest a plan by which the governments, collectively and severally, may bring about a restructuring of the public finances restoring budgetary balance, achieving macro-economic stability and debt reduction along with equitable growth.

6. In making its recommendations, the Commission shall have regard, among other considerations, to: -

(i) the resources, of the Central Government for five years commencing on 1st April 2005, on the basis of levels of taxation and non-tax revenues likely to be reached at the end of 2003-04;

(ii) the demands on the resources of the Central Government, in particular, on account of expenditure on civil administration, defence, internal and border security, debt-servicing and other committed expenditure and liabilities;

(iii) the resources of the State Governments, for the five years commencing on 1st April 2005, on the basis of levels of taxation and non-tax revenues likely to be reached at the end of 2003-04;

(iv) the objective of not only balancing the receipts and expenditure on revenue account of all the States and the Centre, but also generating surpluses for capital investment and reducing fiscal deficit;

(v) taxation efforts of the Central Government and each State Government as against targets, if any, and the potential for additional resource mobilization in order to improve the tax-Gross Domestic Product (GDP) and tax-Gross State Domestic Product (GSDP) ratio, as the case may be;

(vi) the expenditure on the non-salary component of maintenance and upkeep of capital assets and the non-wage related maintenance expenditure on plan schemes to be completed by the 31st March 2005 and the norms on the basis of which specific amounts are recommended for the maintenance of the capital assets and the manner of monitoring such expenditure;

(vii) the need for ensuring the commercial viability of irrigation projects, power projects, departmental undertakings, public sector enterprises etc. in the States through various means including adjustment of user charges and relinquishing of non-priority enterprises through privatisation or disinvestment.

7. In making its recommendations on various matters, the Commission will take the base of population figures as of 1971, in all such cases where population is a factor for determination of devolution of taxes and duties and grants-in-aid.

8. The Commission shall review the Fiscal Reform Facility introduced by the Central Government on the basis of the recommendations of the Eleventh Finance Commission, and suggest measures for effective achievement of its objectives.

9. The Commission may, after making an assessment of the debt position of the States as on the 31st March 2004, suggest such corrective measures, as are deemed necessary, consistent with macro-economic stability and debt sustainability. Such measures recommended will give weightage to the performance of the States in the fields of human development and investment climate.

10. The Commission may review the present arrangements as regards financing of Disaster Management with reference to the National Calamity Contingency Fund and the Calamity Relief Fund and make appropriate recommendations thereon.

11. The Commission shall indicate the basis on which it has arrived at its findings and make available the State-wise estimates of receipts and expenditure."

1.4 In addition to the above, through a subsequent notification dated 31st October, 2003 (*vide* annexure 1.5), the Commission was asked to make recommendations on the following matters:

"(i) whether non-tax income of profit petroleum to the Union, arising out of contractual provisions, should be shared with the States from where the mineral oils are produced; and

(ii) if so, to what extent."

Administrative Arrangements

1.5 The process of setting up of the administration of the Commission started with the appointment of Dr. V.K. Agnihotri as Officer on Special Duty in the Department of Economic Affairs on 30.06.2002. It took considerable time before the full complement of officers and staff could be put in place. The lists of sanctioned posts and functionaries are at annexures 1.6 and 1.7. It also took a long time for the office accommodation at Jawahar Vyapar Bhavan to be made ready for use.

Golden Jubilee of Finance Commissions of India

1.6 The constitution of the Twelfth Finance Commission coincided with the completion of fifty years of the creation of this institution. In order to have an overview of the efforts made by the earlier commissions in ensuring stability and usefulness of the system of fiscal federalism in the country, a golden jubilee function was organized. It was inaugurated by the President of India, Dr. A.P.J. Abdul Kalam at Vigyan Bhawan in the forenoon of April 9, 2003. The inaugural function was presided over by the then Union Minister of Finance, Shri Jaswant Singh. The occasion was also graced by Shri K.C. Pant, the then Deputy Chairman of Planning Commission as chief guest. Chief ministers and finance ministers of states, secretaries and other officers of the Union and state governments and eminent economists were also present.

1.7 The inaugural function was followed by a conference of the finance ministers of the states and the launching of the official website www.fincomindia.nic.in of the Twelfth Finance Commission by Dr. C. Rangarajan. The website is interactive, dynamic, user friendly and rich in terms of data related to federal finance. Provision has been made to receive suggestions from the public online. A virtual secretariat comprising intranet (FincomNet) for select functionaries has been created and maintained to serve the requirements of the present and future finance commissions. The website is maintained and updated in-house with the technical assistance of the National Informatics Centre.

1.8 On this occasion, the Commission brought out a commemorative volume titled, 'Fifty Years of Fiscal Federalism: Finance Commissions of India', which was released by the Chairman. The commemorative volume has turned out to be a useful compendium of excerpts relating to the composition, terms of reference, approach, recommendations and action taken reports in respect of all the eleven finance commissions. The collection, in one volume, of an otherwise scattered material has served as an authentic document, providing a comprehensive account of how the issues relating to fiscal federalism were handled from time to time.

1.9 In order to draw lessons from the experience of the previous commissions, a brain storming session was organized on 10th April 2003 wherein the chairman and members of previous finance commissions were invited to share their experiences and perception with respect to the intricacies of resource transfers from the Union to the states (list of participants at annexure 1.8).

Major Activities

1.10 Notwithstanding lack of adequately furnished accommodation and dearth of suitable personnel, the Commission started its work immediately after it was formally constituted and the Chairman and the members assumed office. The first formal meeting of the Commission took place on the 16th January 2003 in which the Commission approved the rules of procedure (copy at annexure 1.9).

1.11 The consultation process began with

a meeting of economists and economic administrators on 18.02.2003 at New Delhi. Similar meetings were held at Chennai, Mumbai and Kolkata on 10th March 2003, 17th April 2003 and 8th May 2003, respectively (list of participants at annexure 1.10).

1.12 To benefit from the suggestions of people at large, the Commission issued a press note (annexure 1.11) inviting views from the general public, institutions and organizations on issues related to its TOR. People at large responded to the press note. The list of the respondents is at annexure 1.12.

1.13 To elicit views/ suggestions from the states on the TOR of the Commission, the Chairman wrote letters to chief ministers of the states and to eminent economists. The Member Secretary wrote letters to chief secretaries of the states with a request to furnish the views on TOR and on any issue of concern to them (a copy each of the letters issued are at annexures 1.13 and 1.14). The Commission received memoranda and representations from all the states.

1.14 With a view to getting acquainted with the perspective of the Union ministries on the TOR, the Chairman sought the views/ suggestions of cabinet ministers. The Member Secretary also wrote to the secretaries of departments/ ministries of central government to forward their observations on TOR of the Commission (a copy each of the letters are at annexures 1.15 and 1.16). The Commission received views/ suggestions from many departments/ ministries of central government (list at annexure 1.17).

1.15 Detailed information, data and other inputs relating to Union, state and local body finances were collected from the central and state governments through schedules and write-ups. For this purpose, 57 proformae were designed and 75 topics were selected. A finance commission cell, headed by a dedicated officer, was set up by every state, so as to facilitate smooth flow of information. The Commission was, thus, able to collect a wealth of information, which enabled it to create a sound database for each state. All the information has been stored in the virtual secretariat to ensure its availability to finance commissions in the future.

1.16 In order to gauge the perception of the states relating to their financial requirements and to acquire first hand information about their fiscal performance as also to assess the socio-economic and other infrastructural needs of sub national governments, the Commission undertook visits to states commencing from 25th July, 2003. The schedule of the state visits was interrupted in the beginning of 2004 due to the nation going to polls (Lok Sabha and some of the state assemblies) during February to May 2004. The visits were resumed on 31st May, 2004 and got concluded in the month of July, 2004 (list of participants and itinerary of the state visits are at annexures 1.18 and 1.19). The Commission was warmly received by all the states and the meetings resulted in useful exchange of ideas. The local visits, which formed a part of the overall state visits, gave an opportunity to see and assess the intensity and gravity of the pressing needs of the rural and urban bodies. During the visits, the Commission also interacted with the representatives of local bodies, leaders of various political parties and representatives of trade and industry.

1.17 Meetings with Accountants General of the states preceded the state visits of the Commission. These meetings (list at annexure 1.20) gave an incisive feed back on intricate issues concerning the respective states. The discussions primarily delved on issues relating to revenue and expenditure, vertical and horizontal imbalances at the level of local governments, measures taken for resource mobilization and reforms initiated to inculcate fiscal discipline.

1.18 In order to get inputs from noted economists and administrators in a structured manner, the Commission asked the National Institute of Public Finance & Policy (NIPFP) to organize a seminar on 'Issues before the Twelfth Finance Commission' on 29-30 September, 2003. At the seminar (list of participants at annexure 1.21), several papers were presented which focused on the key concerns in fiscal federalism in India. Some of the papers later appeared in the Economic and Political Weekly (Vol.39, No.26, June 26 – July 2, 2004, pp. 2707-2794). Subsequently, a compilation of all the papers along with experts' comments thereon was published in a volume titled, 'The Dynamics of Fiscal Federalism: Challenges before the Twelfth Finance Commission'.

1.19 The urban municipal bodies form an integral part of the structure of governance at the state-level. Their efficient functioning to meet the requirements of the local residents is crucial and its relevance cannot be relegated. To identify the emerging requirements of the municipalities, the Indian Institute of Public Administration (IIPA), at the behest of the Commission, organized a national seminar on municipal finance on 29-30 December 2003 in New Delhi (list of participants at annexure 1.22). The technical sessions of the seminar highlighted the role of the Twelfth Finance Commission in fiscal decentralisation and brought out the contemporary issues pertaining to municipal finances. The papers presented in the seminar were published by the IIPA in a volume titled, 'Municipal Finance in India: Role of Twelfth Finance Commission'.

1.20 The Commission also took up the initiative to get the National Institute of Rural Development (NIRD), Hyderabad organize a national seminar on panchayati raj finance on 23rd January 2004 (list of participants at annexure 1.23). The discussions threw light on various issues concerning the finances of rural local bodies and outlined the feasible approaches to make the bodies self-sustainable. The proceedings of the seminar have been published by the NIRD.

1.21 With a view to benefit from the insight and research findings of economists, academia and administrators, the Commission awarded 26 studies on a variety of issues related to the terms of reference of the Commission. These included debt sustainability/ debt relief, expenditure management, commercial viability of state electricity boards, revenue implications of value added tax (VAT), tax efforts by the centre and the states and financial status of the irrigation sector, to name a few (complete list of studies commissioned is at annexure 1.24).

1.22 To gain from international experience, the Commission visited USA, Canada and Australia (itinerary at annexure 1.25). The discussions held with national and selected sub-national governments covered issues such as the criteria for inter-governmental transfers, the implementation of the principle of equalization, the sales tax system in Canada, goods and services tax in Australia and Australian reform programme to implement the agreement of centre-state financial relations. During the course of its visit, the Commission interacted with experts from different countries in a workshop organized in Washington (programme of the workshop is at annexure 1.26).

1.23 Workshops on management of solid waste and cost of provision of sewerage, waste water treatment and drainage in urban centers in India were organized by the Infrastructure Professionals Enterprise (P) Ltd. on 2nd July 2004 at India International Centre, New Delhi under the aegis of the Commission. The workshops encompassed brain-storming sessions and presentation of papers on sustainability and viability of waste-to-energy initiatives in India, decentralized waste water treatment in small communities and community waste segregation and composting (list of participants at annexure 1.27).

1.24 In order to assess and evaluate the requirements of central ministries, the Commission held meetings with the Planning Commission and the ministries of finance (departments of economic affairs, expenditure and revenue), railways, defence (departments of defence and defence production & supplies), home affairs (departments of home and border management), health & family welfare (departments of health and family welfare), power, petroleum & natural gas, coal, mines, rural development, urban development & poverty alleviation (department of urban development), chemicals & fertilizers (department of fertilizers), communication & information technology (department of posts), tribal affairs, human resource development (department of elementary education & literacy), law & justice (department of justice), consumer affairs, food & public distribution (department of food & public distribution) and agriculture (department of agriculture & cooperation). A complete list of meetings is at annexure 1.28.

1.25 Eminent personalities from various walks of life met the Chairman, members and Member Secretary at the Commission's office on various occasions and shared their views on different issues. This list of dignitaries, who called on the Chairman is at annexure 1.29.

1.26 A delegation of the Tanzanian Joint Finance Commission, headed by the Chairman, Shri William Shellukindo met the Chairman and Member Secretary and held discussions with a view to learn from Indian experience (composition of delegation at annexure 1.30).

1.27 The Commission held 56 formal meetings in which various issues were deliberated upon. Details are at annexure 1.31. On the suggestion of the Commission, amendments were made in the Finance Commission (Salary and Allowances) Rules, 1951 to make the salary, allowances and perquisites of the members of the Commission at par with those of the members of the Planning Commission. The relevant notification is at annexure 1.32.

Acknowledgements

1.28 We would like to place on record our appreciation of the hard work put in by the officers and staff of the Commission, without which, it would have not been possible for us to prepare this report. We would like to thank the National Informatics Centre and, in particular, Shri Rajiv Prakash Saxena, Senior Technical Director, for assisting us in the computerization of our operations. We also thank the Director of Printing of Government of India and the officers and staff of the Government Press, for printing this report in a short time.

Chapter 2

Issues and Approach

2.1 Article 280 of the Constitution describes the duties of the finance commission, the core of which relates to sharing of central taxes under article 270 and determination of grants for the states as provided for under article 275. The Commission's approach is guided by the mandate of the constitutional provisions and the terms of reference (TOR) contained in the Presidential order constituting the commission. Being the twelfth in the periodic sequence of finance commissions, we have also had the benefit of the views of the earlier commissions on these and related issues [1]. The Commission has duly considered the views of the Union and state governments on the TOR as contained in their respective memoranda. We have taken note of areas where there is convergence, and areas where views differ.

2.2 The Commission has taken cognizance of the prevailing fiscal and macro-economic situation, particularly the need to sustain the growth momentum, while bringing about fiscal consolidation. The revenue deficit of the centre in 2002-03 at 4.4 per cent of GDP was higher by 1.1 percentage points as compared to its level of 3.3 per cent in 1990-91. In the case of the states, the revenue deficit in 2002-03 was 2.3 per cent of GDP, nearly 1.4 percentage points higher than its level of 0.9 per cent in 1990-91. During this period, while the fiscal deficit of the centre declined marginally, that of the states increased.

Design of Fiscal Transfers

2.3 The Commission's endeavour has been to recommend a scheme of transfers that could serve the objectives both of equity and efficiency, and result in fiscal transfers that are predictable and stable. These transfers, in the form of tax devolution and grants, are meant to correct both the vertical and horizontal imbalances. Correcting vertical imbalance relates to transfers from the central government to the state governments taken together, whereas the correction of horizontal imbalance is concerned with the allocation of transfers among the state governments. The vertical imbalance arises since resources have been assigned more to the central government and states have been entrusted with the larger responsibilities. The horizontal imbalance has its roots in the differential capacities and needs of the states as also the differences in the costs of providing services. In India, not only the number of states is large, they differ in various respects such as area, size of population, income, tax base, and mineral and forest resources. Resource gaps may arise because states have inadequate capacities as also because the revenue effort is deficient in relative terms. While the former may need to be taken into account for correcting the horizontal imbalance, the latter should not qualify for such correction.

2.4 In the relevant literature, as also in practice in many federal countries, the concept of 'equalization' is considered to be a guiding principle for fiscal transfers as it promotes equity as well as efficiency in resource use. Equalization transfers aim at providing citizens of every state a comparable standard of services provided their revenue effort is also comparable. In other words, equalization transfers neutralize deficiency in fiscal capacity but not in revenue effort. Under such an approach, transfers should be determined on a normative basis instead of merely filling up gaps arising from the projections of revenues and expenditures based on historical trends. As noted by some of the earlier finance commissions also, there are adverse incentives associated with a 'gap-filling' approach where the case for larger transfers would depend merely on a larger gap in the past without reference to whether available revenue capacity was adequately exploited or whether there was an undue growth in expenditures. The normative approach can effectively neutralize such adverse incentives as states are assessed in terms of revenues that they ought to raise given their respective capacities. Similarly, expenditures are assessed on the basis of needs consistent with an average or minimum acceptable level of service and the relevant cost norms and not driven by the past history of expenditures.

2.5 Two of the well known systems of federal fiscal transfers, viz., Canada and Australia also follow the equalization principle although the way it is defined and the methods by which it is applied are somewhat different in the two cases [2]. In Canada, the objective of equalization has been enshrined in the constitution itself. The Commission had occasion to visit these two countries and study their systems at length. In Australia, the equalization principle has been defined to say that 'States should receive funding ...such that if each made the same effort to raise revenue from its own sources and operated at the same level of efficiency, each would have the capacity to provide services at the same standard'. It is notable that it is only the capacity that is equalized and not necessarily the actual level or standard of service, which would depend on the priorities and allocations among different heads, which remain the prerogative of the states. The way this principle has been applied in Australia, particularly the reference to efficiency, involves detailed assessment of expenditures to take account of the cost disabilities. In Canada, as provided in the constitution, equalization payments are meant to 'ensure that provincial governments have sufficient revenues to provide reasonably comparable levels of services at reasonably comparable levels of taxation'. In Canada, in determining equalization payments, no assessment is made of the expenditure side of the provincial budgets. However, these transfers are complemented by the equally important health and social service transfers, where expenditure requirements are taken into account generally on a per capita basis. The northern territories with large cost disabilities are separately treated under

Territorial Formula Financing. In delineating our approach further, we take up separately aspects of vertical and horizontal dimensions of transfers.

Vertical Dimension

2.6 Vertical transfers refer to the total transfers from the central government to the states. In India, resources are transferred from the central to the state governments through many forms and routes. Among these, the statutory transfers consist of sharing of central tax revenues and grants recommended by the finance commission. These are supplemented by grants from the Planning Commission and discretionary grants from the central ministries. Transfers under the recommendations of the finance commission account for about 65 per cent of the total transfers [see annexure 2.1]. Given the multiplicity of channels of transfers, it is important that the Finance Commission, in making its own recommendations, takes into account the overall volume of transfers. The Eleventh Finance Commission (EFC) recommended an overall share of 37.5 per cent of the centre's gross revenue receipts as transfers to states. In considering the matter further, we have taken into account both the long-term trends in the vertical transfers and their pattern in recent years.

2.7 Fiscal transfers to the states, through all channels, as percentage of the gross revenue receipts of the centre increased from an average of 31.4 per cent in the period of the Sixth Finance Commission to 38.1 per cent for the Seventh Finance Commission. As shown in annexure 2.1, it increased further to 40.3 per cent for the period covered by the Ninth Commission before coming down to 35.8 per cent during the period of the Tenth Finance Commission. This ratio improved to 37.2 per cent during the first two years of the recommendation period of the Eleventh Finance Commission. As percentage of GDP at market prices, fiscal transfers show a decline, falling from the level of about 5 per cent for the period covered by the Eighth Commission to 4.9 and 4.1 per cent respectively for the reference periods of the Ninth and Tenth Finance Commissions. This fall was due mainly to a fall in the ratio of centre's gross tax revenues relative to GDP, which fell from the peak level of 10.6 in 1987-88 to less than 9 per cent at the end of the nineties. In the first two years of the EFC period of recommendation, transfers to the states have remained above 4 per cent of GDP.

2.8 Our approach to formulating a view on the vertical imbalance is to look at the revenues accruing to the centre and the states after the transfers. Table 2.1 gives the share of the revenue receipts of the states in the combined revenue receipts of the centre and the states before and after transfers. It also gives the share of states in the combined revenue expenditure of centre and states after netting out inter-governmental flows. It shows that in terms of access to revenue resources before and after transfers, the position of the centre and states is reversed. In fact, the states get, after transfers, a share in the range of 62-64 per cent of the combined revenue receipts of the centre and states and this share has remained stable. Annexure 2.2 gives the year-wise position since the Seventh Finance Commission. States' share in combined revenue expenditures has also remained stable in the range of 56 to 58 per cent. Annexures 2.3 and 2.4 give details regarding relative shares of the centre and the states in combined

Table 2.1

Share of States in Combined Revenue Receipts and Expenditures

Average*	Revenue Receipts Before and After Transfers		Revenue Expenditures**
	Before	After	
VII FC	35.3	61.4	58.0
VIII FC	34.6	62.0	55.7
IX FC	37.5	64.7	56.9
X FC	38.6	63.0	56.8
2000-01	38.6	63.9	56.0
2001-02	39.3	63.9	58.0
XI FC (Avg. 2 years)	39.0	63.9	57.1

Source (Basic Data): Indian Public Finance Statistics
*Average for years under recommendation period
** net of inter-governmental transfers

revenue and total expenditures, respectively.

2.9 In our view, the overall size of transfers requires to be determined by considering the availability of central revenues after accounting for the relevant expenditure requirements. This in a way represents the supply side of funds in the context of inter-governmental transfers. The demand for funds arises from two considerations: the larger assignment of the responsibilities of the state governments considered together, and the need for ensuring minimum provision of services by the states with less than average fiscal capacities. The supply of transferable funds is influenced by the ability of the central government to raise taxes or prudently borrow or control expenditures. The demand for transfers has been expanding because the low fiscal capacity states are falling behind the average levels of service provisions. The average level of services is low even in the better off states considered against desirable standards. Our key concern is the resolution of these considerations in a manner that is consistent with the best principles of transfers. We take into account the fact that the states receive transfers not only on the basis of recommendations of the finance commissions but also from other channels, which comprise plan grants as well as other grants. The implications of plan size for non-plan expenditures are discussed later in this chapter. Other discretionary grants may be considered relevant only in respect of unanticipated events since finance commission recommendations apply for a period of five years. However, these other grants should not assume a character of large or systematic transfers. In making our recommendations regarding sharing of taxes and grants, we recognize the need to take a holistic view of the transfers from different channels.

Horizontal Dimension

2.10 The horizontal aspect of transfers relates to their *inter se* distribution among states. If, in per capita terms, all states were similar in fiscal capacities and cost conditions, the equalization criterion would be met by equal per capita transfers. The differences in per capita fiscal capacities and differential costs of providing services justify departures from an equal per capita transfer norm. Cost disabilities arise due to factors that are mainly beyond the control of the state like large areas relative to population, hilly terrains, excessive rainfall, and proneness to droughts.

2.11 In combining these considerations into a suitable scheme of transfers, there are both conceptual issues and practical problems. There are two major instruments of transfers: tax revenue sharing and grants. The latter can be unconditional and general purpose or conditional and purpose-specific. In the case of sharing tax revenues, two major considerations are (a) selecting appropriate allocative criteria and their related indicators and (b) determining their relative weights. The key determinant in this exercise is the relative revenue raising capacity of the states. Revenue capacity is often measured, as was done also by some of the previous finance commissions, by GSDP at factor cost even though it is recognized that GSDP is not a perfect correlate of income or fiscal capacity. The Central Statistical Organization (CSO) has furnished to us the comparable estimates of GSDP at factor cost at current prices. The question has been raised from time to time whether GSDP at market prices would serve as a better proxy for income or revenue capacity than GSDP at factor cost. In our view it does. Further, GSDP is an indicator of the domestic product and not of income or consumption. With a view to developing a more suitable macro indicator of fiscal capacity, we also had discussions with the CSO. However, a practical alternative is not readily available. We have, therefore, decided to continue to use the comparable estimates of GSDP as provided by the CSO.

2.12 The two principal modes of fiscal transfers, viz., tax devolution and grants have certain distinguishing features. Tax devolution has a built-in flexibility as it can increase automatically if the central taxes are more buoyant. Conversely, there is a risk, if their buoyancy falls short of expectations. Grants are assured as these are fixed in nominal terms. It is also easier to target grants towards states or sectors. Targeting in the case of devolution is broad and indirect and is limited by the criteria used. Yet all states have expressed a preference for devolution because by definition it is unconditional and comes to the states as a matter of right. In the present scheme of transfers, tax devolution plays a dual role of correcting vertical as well as horizontal imbalance. Grants-in aid are mainly targeted towards achieving a degree of equalization. That is why many of the better-off states assessed to be in revenue surplus do not get article 275 grants. There has also been the question whether such grants can be given as conditional grants although these grants have generally been unconditional. We recognize that grants are the more effective transfer instrument for state-specific and purpose-specific targeting. As such, the transfer instruments available to the finance commission must include tax revenue sharing, assessed gap grants, and grants that may be earmarked for specific purposes like those meant for the local bodies or achieving certain minimum level of services.

2.13 The relative weights to the two forms of the unconditional transfers, viz., tax revenue sharing and assessed gap-grants depend on the extent of the vertical imbalance and the prevailing horizontal imbalance. The latter is linked to the changes in the imbalance in the fiscal capacities of the states. If large horizontal imbalances exist, the horizontal task addressed by tax revenue sharing also becomes relevant.

2.14 Some idea of the prevailing horizontal imbalance may be obtained by comparing the per capita GSDP of the states. For this purpose, a comparison of the three-year average of comparable GSDP over the period 1999-00 to 2001-02 indicates that there are ten states with average GSDP below the all-state average GSDP. These are Arunachal Pradesh, Assam, Bihar, Chhattisgarh, Jharkhand, Madhya Pradesh, Meghaylaya, Orissa, Rajasthan, and Uttar Pradesh. Of these, Arunachal Pradesh and Meghalaya are close to the average. The remaining eight states are the ones with GSDP that is significantly lower than the average, requiring equalization transfers with a view to raising the standard of services upto the average. The newly created states as a result of the bifurcation of Uttar Pradesh, Madhya Pradesh, and Bihar are part of this group. With a view to examining whether the gap has widened, we have compared the growth of per capita GSDP taking the average over 1993-94 to 1995-96 and 1999-00 to 2001-02. It may be mentioned that comparable GSDP data are provided by the CSO only at current prices. Considering the all-state average, the per capita GSDP during this period increased by about 75 per cent. However, for the states at the lower end of the income scale, namely, Bihar, UP, Orissa, Assam, Madhya Pradesh and Rajasthan, the GSDP growth was less than this average. An indication of the increasing gap can also be obtained from the coefficient of variation in per capita incomes. In estimating this, it is relevant to exclude Goa, whose per capita income has increased considerably, but it is an outlier. Comparing 1993-94 with 2001-02, the coefficient of variation has increased by about 2.5 percentage points.

2.15 In our approach, tax devolution has been used, as the earlier commissions have done, both for the vertical and horizontal aspects of transfers. It may be noted that the share of grants in total transfers recommended by the finance commissions has been less than 15 per cent on average over the recommendation period of the commission. Taking the average is relevant because in the case of recent finance commissions, grants in the initial years of the recommendation period have been larger than those in the latter years. The share of grants in total transfers recommended by the finance commissions, from the seventh to the tenth, has respectively been 8.1, 11.1, 13.8, and 10.3 per cent. In this context, in view of the need to ensure a larger role for equalization transfers, we are proposing to increase the share of grants in the total transfers.

Sharing of Central Taxes

2.16 Under article 270, the Commission is required to determine the aggregate and individual shares of the states in the shareable pool of central taxes. The main considerations before the Commission relate to (a) determining the aggregate share of states, (b) specifying criteria that may be used for deciding shares of the individual states, and (c) determining the weights attached to different allocation criteria. In considering the aggregate share of states in the shareable pool, we have examined how the shareable pool of central taxes has changed in the past in its scope and composition and how this may undergo further change in the light of some current and proposed modifications, particularly those related to the taxation of services.

2.17 Prior to the 80th constitutional amendment, two main central taxes were shared with the states, *viz.*, income tax other than corporation tax and the Union excise duties. The sharing of the income tax was mandatory as, under article 270, it had to be shared with the states, while that of the Union excise duties was discretionary, as its sharing was subjected to the phrase "may be divided between the Union and the States" and could be shared if Parliament by law so provided. There were also two tax rental arrangements with the states, where the Union government collected the tax, as it were, on behalf of the states and then distributed the proceeds among the states on principles and shares recommended by the finance commission. These were additional excise duty in lieu of sales tax on textiles, tobacco and sugar, and grant in lieu of the tax on railway passenger fares.

2.18 Following the 80th amendment of the Constitution, all central taxes were brought into a shareable pool and it became mandatory to assign a share from each central tax to the states. The amended article 270 provided for the sharing of all central taxes except taxes under articles 268 and 269 and earmarked cesses, and surcharges under article 271. Only "net proceeds" are to be shared, and as such 'cost of collection' has to be deducted to obtain the net proceeds as prescribed under article 279. The proceeds are to be distributed among the states where the central taxes are "leviable" in "that year". Article 269 has also been amended and it contains only central sales tax and consignment tax, which is not levied. More recently, the Constitution has been amended, and services have been added under the Union List in the Seventh Schedule of the Constitution. Taxation of services has been brought under the purview of article 268 A [3].

2.19 The taxation of services has a bearing on the size of the vertical transfers as it has the potential to impart additional buoyancy to tax revenues [4]. With the 88th amendment to the Constitution, article 268A provides that "Taxes of services shall be levied by the Government of India and such tax can be collected and appropriated by government of India and the states..." It also further specifies that the principles of collection and appropriation will be determined by Parliament. So far, the central government has been levying the service tax on specific services under its residual powers relating to subjects that are not specified in any of the three lists, services being an example. The sharing of this revenue has been on the basis of the recommendations of the finance commission, as applicable to other central taxes. However, revenues from taxation of services that are taxed by the centre under article 268A rather than under article 270 would be excluded from the purview of the finance commission.

2.20 In the 80th amendment, the objective was to construct a pool of all central taxes for sharing so that a holistic view can be taken and both sides could share in the aggregate buoyancy of the central tax revenues. With service taxes having been excluded from the ambit of the re-commendations of the finance commission, the idea of an overall shareable pool of central taxes appears to be in the process of being reversed. While service taxes are likely to prove highly buoyant in the near future, these will not be subjected to sharing with the states under the Constitution, although other statutory arrangements can be made, which can include sharing as well as assignment. It may be noted that hitherto items under articles 268 and 269 were subjects that were generally of inter-state nature with limited revenue importance. These were wholly assigned to the states. In this context, it needs to be stressed that any legislation passed by Parliament with respect to appropriation of service tax proceeds must take care to ensure that the revenue accruing to the states through any proposed changes should not be less than the share that would accrue to them, had the entire service tax proceeds been part of the shareable pool.

2.21 One dimension of transfers relates to their predictability. The finance commission makes recommendations only about the share of states in the central taxes. This implies that the actual amounts are known only when the central taxes are actually realized in the concerned years. The finance commission does provide estimates of the likely amounts of what a state may get as its share in the shareable central taxes. This is then taken into account when grants are determined in absolute amounts. As already noted, predictability is a significant attribute of a robust scheme of transfers. Since devolution of taxes is recommended in terms of shares of central taxes, and the absolute amounts may fall short of these estimates, a suggestion has been made from time to time, and has also been included in many of the states' memoranda submitted to the Commission, that a minimum guaranteed amount under tax devolution should be prescribed. Under the provisions of article 270 only a share for the states in the central taxes is determined. This provides for automatic sharing of the central tax buoyancies. States, however, have a genuine problem if growth in central taxes falls short of expectations. This calls for a certain caution in the projection of central revenues, bearing in mind that such esti-mates of revenue feed into the determin-ation of grants.

2.22 In deciding the different criteria for transfers under tax devolution, our approach has been to keep in mind three sets of considerations, viz., needs, cost disabilities, and fiscal efficiency. Needs refer to expenditures that are required to be made but have not been made due to deficiency in fiscal capacity. In considering the expenditure requirements, merit goods like health and education need to be considered as of prime importance. Cost disabilities refer to the circumstances that lead to higher than average per capita costs for delivering the same level of services at an average level of efficiency. In this case, exogenous causes that are beyond the control of the concerned states like excess rainfall, hilly terrain, and large and remote areas with low density of population may be considered important. Some cost disabilities arise when the size of the state is too small and some minimum expenditure has to be incurred for providing the relevant administrative infrastructure. In a normative approach, fiscal efficiency is implicit because requirements are assessed taking into account only the average revenue effort. However, some explicit incentives have been considered relevant relating to tax effort or other fiscal performance measures so as to raise the average performance itself. These considerations were incorporated in the allocation criteria used by the previous commissions also. While adopting the same criteria, there may be a need for modifying the scheme of weights. These weights will also be affected by the relative importance of the two modes of transfer, namely, tax devolution and grants.

2.23 In the criteria-based distribution of the central taxes, the more recent finance commissions have given considerable importance to the horizontal task of redistribution by giving relatively larger weight to the distance factor, which reflects the difference of the per capita GSDP of a state from the highest per capita GSDP, taken as the average of the three highest per capita GSDPs. The weight attached to this factor reflects the fiscal capacity equalization element of transfers under tax sharing. The better-off states have represented to us that their share has steadily fallen in the overall allocation. We have taken note of this concern. In particular, the share of the better-off states can go down either because the weight to the distance factor has been increased significantly or the inequality among per capita GSDPs, i.e. the fiscal capacities, has increased. Over the period covered by the last four commissions, we find that it is the second factor, which is primarily responsible for this. Since there is some vertical gap even for the richer states, a continuous fall in their tax shares does not appear to be desirable. To some extent, this could be addressed by increasing the aggregate share of the states. However, there are clear limits to the extent to which this could be done. Alternatively, the weights among different criteria could be realigned. To the extent to which this is done, the share of the low fiscal capacity states would be reduced. This would need to be balanced therefore by increasing the equalization content of the grants. Our approach follows this route to a large extent. With an improvement in the buoyancy of the central taxes, this problem will be eased. It may be mentioned that the balancing of resources against responsibilities is qualitatively different now when governments at all levels are nursing large and rising revenue deficits than when the centre and some of the better off states had a surplus. There was a time when some of the states even had a pre-devolution surplus. The task has become progressively more demanding with successive finance commissions. It is in this context that there is a need to emphasize the fiscal efficiency criterion.

Approach to Determining Grants

2.24 In relation to grants, there are two duties cast upon the Finance Commission conjointly by articles 280(3) (b) and 275. Article 280(3) (b) requires the Commission to make recommendations as to the "principles" which should govern such grants-in-aid. Following from article 275(1), specific "sums" are to be recommended to be paid to the states which are assessed to be in "need of assistance". Thus, while article 270 speaks of percentage share, article 275 refers to specific 'sums' and that these grants should be given to states which are in need of assistance.

2.25 Need cannot be taken to mean that any shortfall in revenue relative to expenditure can be met by a corresponding increase in grants. That would only result in the lowering of tax rates in the states in the expectation of expanding the share of the state in the 'common pool' of resources.

Need has therefore to be assessed in relation to norms applied to both revenue effort and the desirable levels of service provision. In this context, the services that should be covered should be limited to the services that can be interpreted as public goods like general administration and law and order and merit goods like education and health services provided by the state governments. Many private goods provided by the state governments do not merit consideration in this context. In considering the expenditure requirements, account can also be taken of particular circumstances of a state that may result in higher per capita costs. This brings us to the issue of suitable principles of assessment.

Principles of Assessment

2.26 This Commission is required to make recommendations regarding sharing of central taxes and grants for a period covering five years from 2005-06 to 2009-10. This, in turn, requires making projections of resources and needs for the centre and for each individual state. Since many of the fiscal variables are related to growth in GDP or GSDP, projections of these variables as also other variables like the interest rate are required. It may be mentioned that such a forecasting mechanism is quite unique to transfers recommended by the finance commission in India. It necessarily follows that the basic data progressively become more dated as we come closer to the later years of the forecast period. Sometimes, critical events like the award of a Pay Commission or the onset of a recession can seriously upset the assumptions on which the recommendations of a finance commission may be made. In other federations, alternative mechanisms have been evolved to cope with the problem of information lag. For example, in Canada, the transfers for any one year remain 'open' for four years and as new data come in, entitlements are reworked on principles that have already been determined. In Australia, there is a five yearly cycle of 'Review' whereby the Commonwealth Grants Commission formulates the methodology of determining the 'relativities', but the calculation is done on an annual basis using latest available data, which are called 'Updates'.

2.27 In the methodology developed by the previous finance commissions, it is the assessment of central finances that indicates availability of funds, and the assessment of state finances that provides the claim on those funds. Para 6(i) and (ii) of the TOR make reference, respectively, to the resources of the central government and the demands on those resources. Resources of the central government have to be assessed on the basis of "levels of taxation and non-tax revenues likely to be reached at the end of 2003-04". The 2003-04 tax and non-tax revenues can therefore serve as the base for assessment of resources for the period from 2005-06 to 2009-10. Para 6(ii) makes reference to the demands on central resources by the central government. Particular reference has been made to expenditure on civil administration,defence, internal and border security, debt servicing and other committed expenditures and liabilities. In making the assessment of central resources and corresponding needs, we have taken into account centre's memorandum and the forecasts.

2.28 In the case of states, a corresponding sub-clause, *viz.*, para 6(iii) of the TOR provides that the assessment of resources for the period 2005-06 to 2009-10 will need to be made on the basis of levels of taxation and non-tax revenues likely to be reached at the end of 2003-04. This is symmetrical to the corresponding consideration for the centre, and gives rise to a similar set of issues. In regard to the needs of the states, particular reference to any specific needs has not been made in the TOR except to the non-salary component of maintenance and upkeep of capital assets and non-wage related maintenance expenditure on plan schemes. Clause 6(iv) specifies the more general consideration in regard to 'the objective of not only balancing the receipts and expenditure on revenue account of *all the States and the Centre*, but also generating surplus for capital investment and reducing fiscal deficit'.

2.29 Although the TOR do not specifically mention that needs of the states should be assessed except in an indirect way, our approach has been to make the assessment in sufficient detail and with the same degree of comprehensiveness as was done by the previous commissions. Our approach to assessments takes into account the need for a normative basis, which encompasses both the revenue and expenditure heads. These assessments also bear a relationship with the overall restructuring plan. In order to meet the requirements of adjustments in the restructuring plan, certain prescriptive parameters have been outlined. These assessments necessarily take into account the additional sub-clause, which makes reference to the taxation efforts of the central government and each state government as against 'targets' and 'potential' in order to improve the tax-GDP and the tax-GSDP ratios respectively for the central and the state governments. The para asking the Commission to suggest a plan for "restructuring of public finances" would also require various measures to augment tax and non-tax revenues beyond levels reached in 2003-04, considered in relation to GDP or GSDP of the individual states.

2.30 Sometimes the issue is raised as to the role of assessment exercises in determining total transfers taking both tax devolution and grants into account. This issue is linked to determination of the appropriate weights to tax devolution and grants in a scheme of transfers. If the relative weight of tax sharing is kept too low, many states would emerge in assessed deficit and would be entitled for grants. There may be some states, which may emerge in pre-devolution surplus and would therefore obtain a share only in the relatively low amounts of tax devolution. Tax devolution should be calibrated to ensure that at least the requirement of minimum vertical transfers is met. The finance commissions in the past have evolved a scheme where a little more than half of the states generally emerge in assessed revenue deficits. Considering entitlements in the *first year* of their respective award periods, 16 out of 25 states emerged in assessed deficit in the case of the Tenth Finance Commission and 15 states emerged in assessed deficit in the case of the Eleventh Finance Commission. All the ten general category states were in assessed deficit. There is also the consideration that the share of tax devolution is very nearly downward rigid. Virtually all states have asked for an upward revision in the share and even the central government's latest memorandum to the Commission effect-ively endorses that idea.

2.31 Grants recommended by the finance commission are largely general and unconditional in nature. But in the case of selected services where minimum standards of service may be considered desirable, it is possible to consider conditional grants. For conditional grants the relevant purposes and associated conditions also need to be specified along with an effective monitoring mechanism. The First Finance Commission had considered the 'principles' of determining grants at length and had opined that both unconditional and specific purpose grants can and should be considered by the finance commission under article 275 read with article 280(3)(b). They had observed [page 91 of their Report]: "We consider that the problem has to be viewed in the larger perspective of securing an equitable allocation of resources among the units. We are, therefore, of the view that the scope of article 275 or article 280(3) (b) should not be limited solely to grants-in-aid which are completely unconditional; grants directed to broad but well defined purposes could reasonably be considered as falling within their scope". The Second Commission had observed that grants-in-aid should be a residuary form of assistance given in the form of general and unconditional grants. However, it also agreed that grants for broad purposes may be given and, in respect of these, states should be under obligation to spend the whole amount in furtherance of the broad purposes indicated. Most of the subsequent commissions had generally agreed to the principles listed by the First Commission but have by and large followed the procedure adopted by the Second Commission. In our view, there is need to ensure that in respect of two areas, viz., education and health including family welfare, states that are below average in terms of per capita expenditures should be brought closer to the average. However, even in these areas, we have not followed a gap-filling approach. The assessed gap covers only the difference that arises due to deficiency in fiscal capacity. It does not take into account the gap, which might be due to deficiency in tax effort or due to a state according a less than average priority in resource allocation to the concerned sector. The precise methodology has been dealt with in chapters 6 and 10.

Interface with Plan Assistance

2.32 The plan assistance is given to the states as consisting of grants and loans. The grant-loan ratio for the states in general is 30:70 whereas for the special category states, this ratio is 90:10. In normal central assistance, 30 per cent is earmarked for the special category states. The expenditure on state plans is met by the balance from current revenues (BCR) from the state budgets, plan assistance in the form of grants and loans by the central government, and borrowing from other sources including the market and those based on small savings. The BCRs for most states have progressively fallen and become negative. In consequence, the financing of the plan, apart from a small contribution of the plan grants from the centre, depends entirely on borrowing by the states. A large plan effectively also means larger borrowing. It becomes therefore necessary that the plan size of every state is linked to the sustainable level of debt.

2.33 There are three links in this process that have a bearing on the tasks assigned to the finance commission. First, as borrowing accumulates as part of the planning process, it gives rise to interest payment liabilities, which are part of the non-plan revenue expenditure.

2.34 Second, the plan process leads either to creation of posts or assets. Once the plan is over, the posts are meant to be carried into the non-plan side of the budget. Assets created in the previous plans also require maintenance expenditure. Both of these increase non-plan expenditure in the form of committed liabilities. The distinction between plan and non-plan expenditures has progressively become blurred as states often continue old plan schemes as part of the new plan so as to show a higher size of the plan. As noted by the previous commissions, notably the tenth and eleventh commissions, the plan, non-plan dichotomy of expenditures results in several in-efficiencies. It is far more important to ensure that assets already created are maintained and yield services as originally envisaged than to go on undertaking commitments for creating new assets. The continued transfer of plan posts on to the non-plan side has also resulted in surplus staff in many sectors, whose salaries must be paid. Surplus staff on the non-plan side is not usually absorbed in the new plan schemes. Considering a larger plan size as more development oriented and ignoring maintenance is not desirable and provides at best an optical illusion of development.

2.35 The third aspect of the interface between plan expenditure and the overall scheme of transfers is even more important. By definition, plan expenditure is 'incremental development expenditure'. It is expected that as a result of the plan intervention, inequalities among states in incomes and services that are publically provided would decrease. If these continue to increase, the horizontal considerations compel finance commission transfers to become more progressive. In this context, it is useful to compare the pattern of inter-state distribution of per capita finance commission (FC) and non-FC transfers consisting of plan grants, external assistance, and other discretionary grants. Relating comparable per capita GSDP with per capita FC transfers for 2001-02, a strong negative relationship is observed. The coefficient of correlation is (-) 0.87 for the general category states excluding Goa. In the case of per capita non-FC transfers for this group of states, the correlation with per capita GSDP turns out to be positive (0.16). This shows lack of progressivity in their distribution. The non-FC transfers become even more regressive when account is taken of the implicit transfers, such as those arising from procurement of food grains by the Food Corporation of India (FCI) largely from some of the better-off states [5]. In the case of special category states, the correlation is positive both for FC and non-FC transfers.

Restructuring of Public Finances

2.36 Like the EFC, this Commission has also been asked to review the state of the finances of the Union and the states and suggest a plan for restructuring public finances with a view to restoring budgetary balance and maintaining macroeconomic stability. Para 5 of the TOR asks for a 'review' of the state of finances of the Union and state governments and a 'plan' for a 'restructuring' of the public finances. In comparison to the terms of reference for the

EFC, the reference to debt reduction and equitable growth is new and emphasizes concern with the growing disparities among states as also accumulation of unsustainable debt. The TOR also mentions certain other factors that should be considered along with para 5. Para 6(iv) talks of the "... objective of not only balancing the receipts and expenditure on revenue account of all the States and the Centre, but also generating surpluses for capital investment and reducing fiscal deficit". Para 9 also stipulates that corrective measures in regard to states' debt may be suggested, consistent with macroeconomic stability and debt sustainability. Clearly, any restructuring plan has to aim at eliminating revenue deficit and bring down fiscal deficit to levels consistent with macroeconomic stability. The reference to capital investment and fiscal deficit in clause 6(iv) also implies that the financing of entire government expenditure, revenue and capital, has to be considered in an integrated framework.

2.37 In understanding the need for restructuring public finances, considering the combined accounts of the centre and states, we take note of five key fiscal trends that cause serious concern. These are: decline in the tax-GDP ratio, large pre-emptive claims of interest payments relative to revenue receipts, high revenue-deficit to GDP ratio, large and unsustainable fiscal deficit to GDP ratio, and falling levels of capital expenditure relative to GDP. Taking the 15-year period from 1987-88 to 2001-02, and comparing three-year averages at both ends, that is for 1987-90 and 1999-2002, we note that

(i) The tax-GDP ratio fell from a level of about 16 per cent relative to GDP by 1.6 percentage points to reach an average level of 14.4 per cent of GDP.

(ii) Interest payments relative to revenue receipts rose by nearly 13 percentage points during this period to reach an average level of 34 per cent of the combined revenue receipts.

(iii) The ratio of revenue deficit to GDP increased by a margin of 3.5 percentage points to reach a level of 6.5 per cent of GDP.

(iv) Fiscal deficit, which was already at a high level of 8.8 per cent of GDP in the late eighties, increased by a margin of 0.7 percentage points. In 2002-03, the combined fiscal deficit was in excess of 10 per cent of GDP.

(v) Capital expenditure relative to GDP fell to the extent of 2.8 percentage points during this period, reaching an average level of 3.3 per cent of GDP.

2.38 The deterioration in the revenue account balance of the centre, states and their combined accounts had started towards the end of the seventies. It was in 1979-80 that the central finances fell into revenue deficit after recording a surplus since 1950-51 in all but two years. The combined account of the centre and states went into revenue deficit in 1982-83, and that of all states in 1986-87. As noted by the Tenth Finance Commission, almost all the states went through three-phase deterioration in the revenue account balance. In the first phase up to 1986-87, non-plan revenue account surplus was larger than the plan deficit and to that extent it yielded an overall revenue balance. During 1986-87 to 1991-

92, the magnitude of plan revenue deficit increased sharply and it became larger than the non plan surplus. Since then, both the plan revenue account and the non plan revenue account have remained in deficit and the deficit has generally been growing in magnitude. Only some of the special category states showed surplus on the plan revenue account. However, this was due solely to the special dispensation for plan assistance where they got ninety per cent as grant credited to their revenue accounts.

2.39 In 1988-89, the base year for the Ninth Finance Commission, the combined revenue deficit of the centre and states was 2.9 per cent of GDP at current market prices. The combined revenue deficits of the centre and states for the corresponding base years for the tenth and eleventh finance commissions were respectively 3.6 per cent of GDP in 1994-95 and 6.3 per cent in 1999-00. In 2002-03, the combined revenue deficit was 6.7 per cent of GDP. The main reasons generally given for this all round fiscal deterioration include the revision of salaries and pensions in the wake of the recommendations of the Fifth Central Pay Commission, erosion in the buoyancy of central indirect taxes, and the high nominal interest rates towards the end of the nineties. Transfers cannot be taken as a means of reducing the revenue deficit for one tier of the government by increasing it for the other. There is a need for improving the position of revenue balance both at the centre and the states.

Sustainability of Fiscal deficits

2.40 In fact, if the central government could borrow without limits, it could also transfer resources without limit. On the other hand, if the state governments could borrow without limits, they can do with minimal transfers. The need for ensuring sustainability of fiscal deficits, however, puts a limit on the borrowing, i.e. fiscal deficit that can be prudently undertaken by the two tiers of governments, considered separately as also together. Sustainable levels of fiscal deficits can be derived with reference to three key parameters: growth rate, ratio of revenue receipts to GDP/GSDP, and the interest rate. The existing level of the debt-GDP ratio also is quite material in the context of sustainability. Prudent levels of fiscal deficit may be determined in relation to growth and interest rates but growth may depend on fiscal deficit and interest rate. Much of this interdependence arises due to the fact that fiscal deficits affect the saving and investment rates of the economy, which in turn affect the growth and interest rates.

2.41 For fiscal sustainability, it is required that a rise in fiscal deficit is matched by a rise in the capacity to service the increased debt. It has been argued that from this angle, borrowing for generation of assets may be justified. Apart from the fact that a little less than 70 per cent of borrowing is presently not being spent on capital assets at least of the physical kind, even where there is capital expenditure, the return on assets is negligible. Even the more indirect return through higher growth to match the growing interest liabilities has not been forthcoming. In fact, the high level of fiscal deficit combined with the rising debt-GDP ratio has led to a fall in the aggregate government demand net of interest payments and pensions. Economists have argued that revenue deficits relative to GDP are equivalent to government dis-savings, which lead to a fall in the overall saving rate unless there is a corresponding rise in the private saving rate. Compared to the levels of domestic saving rate in the mid-nineties, which ranged about 25 per cent in the mid-nineties, there was a clear fall in the rate in recent years where it has been around 22 per cent of GDP.

2.42 Determining the right size of fiscal deficit and the debt in relation to GDP is important for prudent fiscal management. The Tenth Plan has envisaged the average size of fiscal deficit as 6.8 per cent of GDP during the plan period. The Eleventh Finance Commission had suggested fiscal deficit of 6.5 per cent of GDP as the desirable target to be achieved by 2004-05. The macro economic assumptions of the EFC included a growth rate of nominal GDP of 13 per cent with real growth in the range of 7 to 7.5 per cent and an effective rate of interest in nominal terms of 9.8 per cent for the centre and 11 per cent for the states. Since the period in which the EFC formulated its recommendations, one important change relates to a fall in the nominal interest rates. The central government has specified in the rules under its Fiscal Responsibility and Budget Management Act, 2003 (FRBMA), a fiscal deficit target of 3 per cent, which is to be achieved by 2008-09. A view needs to be taken for the aggregate fiscal deficit of the states so that a consolidated fiscal deficit target can be indicated. We have considered this issue in the next chapter.

2.43 The EFC had also set targets for reduction of the level of debt in relation to GDP. The combined debt-GDP ratio of the centre and states was to be brought down by 10 percentage points so as to the reach the level of 55 per cent in 2004-05. There has been considerable slippage in achieving this target. According to Reserve Bank of India's annual report for 2003-04, the combined debt-GDP ratio was 75.7 per cent at the end of 2002-03 with centre's debt-GDP ratio at 63.1 per cent and that for the states at 27.8 per cent of GDP. In these estimates, external debt is taken at historical exchange rates. As discussed in chapter 4, if external debt is evaluated at current exchange rates, an upward adjustment of about 5.6 per cent in the debt-GDP ratio of 2002-03 would be required. The sharp increase in the level of debt relative to GDP has been the consequence of a rise in primary deficits as well as the fact that during the three year-period 2000-2003, the growth rate turned out to be lower than the interest rate. We feel that reduction in the level of primary deficit to GDP would provide the key to controlling the growth of the debt-GDP ratio. This would need to be encouraged by explicit as well as implicit incentives.

Incentives: Explicit and Implicit

2.44 The adoption of a fiscal correction and restructuring plan by the states can be facilitated and induced to some extent by built-in incentives and rewards provided for within the scheme of transfers. We have endeavored to strengthen the incentive and reward mechanism by various elements in the design of transfers. A reward is by definition backward looking in the sense that it links the benefit to past performance. It helps in inducing the desired change to the extent that there is expectation that the reward mechanism will be continued in future. In contrast, an incentive is forward looking in the sense that the benefit is linked to future performance. We recognize that there are several inherent difficulties in including forward looking indicators in the distribution formula. The reward mechanism through indicators of tax effort and fiscal efficiency would continue in our scheme and strengthened. For a forward looking scheme, there are two proposals that can be made in the context of the TOR. These relate to the medium term reform facility and debt relief. These are discussed in subsequent chapters.

Fiscal Consolidation and Institutional Reforms

2.45 Recent experience in fiscal consolidation [6] suggests that institutional reforms, well defined rules, and transparency facilitate fiscal reforms. Institutional reforms should aim at achieving and maintaining fiscal consolidation while leaving enough scope for coping with business cycles through automatic stabilizers as well as discretionary action. Three main ingredients of such reforms relate to formal deficit and debt rules, specification of expenditure rules, and fiscal transparency. The Maastricht Treaty rule of 3 per cent of GDP as the fiscal deficit target and 60 per cent as the desired debt-GDP ratio are well known. In United Kingdom a 'golden rule' of limiting borrowing only to finance capital expenditure has been followed since 1997 as a sustainable investment rule. In other countries like USA, Finland, Netherlands, and Sweden procedural requirements have been used to support expenditure limits. Fiscal transparency has been emphasized in countries like New Zealand, Australia, and the United Kingdom. Fiscal transparency implies being open to public regarding the structure and functions of government. Transparency requires that any policy changes must be introduced with a clear statement of relevance and objectives. Strategies of fiscal consolidation require a longer term focus and the need to promote growth. In this context, the central government's initiative in enacting the FRBMA is a welcome step. Some state governments have also brought about fiscal responsibility legislations. In our view, other states would do well to emulate this example.

Issues of Debt Relief

2.46 Several state governments have asked for debt relief. Some of the previous commissions, notably the tenth and the eleventh, had observed that recommendations regarding debt relief by successive commissions create anticipations about such measures, which has a built-in adverse incentive. Debt relief often underwrites lack of fiscal discipline of the past. It could be unfair and could give significantly adverse signals if the benefit of relief is largest for the state, which was the most profligate in the past. In the literature relating to fiscal federalism, considerable attention has been given to the deleterious effects of a soft budget constraint, which refers to the relative ease with which states can borrow. This also has implications for the assessment of interest payments. If any amount of interest payments liability can be considered as legitimate claim for determining transfers, all normative assessments of current expenditures would be rendered redundant. All that a state would need to do is to borrow more in the current period and generate larger claims for the future. It is imperative that interest payments be assessed normatively and a hard budget constraint be imposed. We have considered the issue of debt relief in the light of these considerations.

2.47 In the context of the question of debt relief, account needs to be taken of the fact that the nominal interest rates have fallen. There are also grounds to believe that the margins that the central government may have charged on its own lending to the states may have been unduly high in the past. It is clear that any debt relief will have to be linked to a desired path of fiscal adjustment including targets for revenue and fiscal deficits. The Planning Commission may also need to ensure that the size of a state plan is consistent with a sustainable level of debt, as the state plans are almost fully financed by borrowing in one form or another.

Decentralization and Transfers to Local Bodies

2.48 Decentralization in governance is considered efficiency augmenting as local representatives are presumed to better understand the preferences, needs, and willingness to finance the provision of the related local goods provided adequate sources were assigned to them. The 73rd and 74th amendments to the Constitution relating respectively to the rural and urban local bodies provided an effective basis for introducing local self governance in the country. Under the Constitution, the duties cast on the state governments included periodic holding of local elections, bring out enabling legislations, specifying the functions transferred to the states along with the sources of revenue, and constituting the state finance commissions at the required intervals.

2.49 The Commission had occasion to listen to the representatives of the local bodies in different states. The emergent picture falls far short of what was envisaged in the two constitutional amendments. States have often been not prompt enough to constitute the state finance commissions with the required regularity. In many instances, after the recommendations are received, decisions have been kept pending. Even grants recommended and earmarked for the local bodies by the earlier finance commission, having been received into the consolidated fund of the state, have not been passed on to the local bodies in certain cases.

2.50 Our approach is to strengthen the basic idea of promoting a fiscal domain for the local bodies as being the key to effective local self-governance. The provision of local goods requires that the link between local service and the responsibility of financing it by the potential beneficiaries is appreciated. Since the local public goods have limited externalities, financing by external sources has considerable problems of adverse incentives that could lead to increasing dependence on transfers from above. The idea can work only if the local bodies are assigned adequate sources of revenue by the states. Various studies do indicate that local bodies have not been enthusiastic about raising revenues. The principle of equalization, extended to the local bodies would mean that while lack of fiscal capacity, at the state level as well as the local level can be made up, lack of revenue effort should not be made up.

Summary and Long Term Perspective

2.51 The system of fiscal transfers in India has run a course of more than fifty years. Apart from the finance commission and the Planning Commission, other institutions like the Inter-State Council and the National Development Council have played a role in providing a framework for centre-state financial relations. In a longer term context, there is a need to emphasize stability in federal relations in general and in the system of transfers in particular. Growing disparities in fiscal capacities and levels of services upset this stability as widening disparities require larger and more progressive transfers. The task of achieving greater equality does not depend on finance commission transfers alone. Transfers by the Planning Commission and those by other central ministries need to play a complementary role that would help reduce these disparities. States also need to give greater attention to policies aimed at accelerating growth and reducing intra-state regional inequalities. It is only when inter-state and intra-state disparities are reduced, that the federal fiscal system would become stable. A coordinated effort is required to reduce inequalities, which would also make the system more stable.

2.52 Some of the basic features of our approach and the resultant modifications in the scheme of transfers considered by us may be summarized as below

(i) Our scheme of transfers provides for larger transfers to correct for the fall in the volume of transfers relative to GDP and to ensure minimum vertical transfers while correcting a larger horizontal imbalance. For this reason, we have suggested that the indicative benchmark for the overall transfers may be raised to 38 per cent of the gross revenue receipts of the central government.

(ii) Our approach to transfers comprising tax devolution and grants is guided by the equalization criterion, determined on the basis of a normative approach. In the case of tax devolution, there is the additional task of ensuring reasonable vertical transfers.

(iii) Increasing imbalance in fiscal capacities of the states adds to the horizontal task of equalization that needs to be performed by fiscal transfers. However, care must be taken that while deficiency in fiscal capacity is redressed; deficiency in revenue effort is effectively discouraged.

(iv) Three main considerations guiding tax devolution are: needs, cost disabilities, and fiscal efficiency.

(v) With a view to ensuring minimum level of services in the case of education and health, we consider conditional grants derived on the basis of a normative approach as relevant. A similar consideration applies to maintenance expenditures.

(vi) There is need to encourage fiscal consolidation both for the centre and the states, which can be facilitated by fiscal frameworks that have institutional basis including rules for deficit and debt and provisions ensuring greater fiscal transparency.

(vii) While a hard budget constraint for

the states is desirable, any debt relief that may be considered would need to be linked to monitorable achievements in regard to fiscal consolidation.

□□

Endnotes

[1] The Commission brought out a volume summarizing the terms of reference of the previous finance commissions and their observations on "Issues and Approach" in a commemorative volume on the occasion of celebrating 50 years of fiscal federalism in India.

[2] A review of the transfer systems in Canada and Australia and relevant comparisons with the Indian system are drawn in C. Rangarajan, and D.K. Srivastava, "Fiscal Transfers in Canada: Drawing Comparison and Lessons", Economic and Political Weekly, Vol. 39, No.19, May, 2004, and "Fiscal Transfers in Australia: Review and Relevance to India", Economic and Political Weekly, Vol. 39, No.33, August, 2004.

[3] This constitutional amendment would become effective from the date of notification.

[4] The recently completed report of the Task Force appointed by the Union Ministry of Finance, in the context of achieving the FRBMA targets, estimates that the service tax may have a buoyancy of more than 5 in the period 2005-06 to 2009-10 in their reform scenario.

[5] The recently published World Bank Report (Macmillan, 2004) on State Fiscal Reforms in India provides a discussion of implicit transfers to states and their implications for the overall progressivity of transfers.

[6] World Economic Outlook, IMF, 2001 contains a review of some recent experiences in fiscal consolidation.

Chapter 3

Trends in Central and State Finances

3.1 In this Chapter, we have looked at some of the salient trends in central and state finances, particularly for the period since the initiation of economic reforms in the early nineties. Fiscal reforms, constituting a key element of the economic reforms, entailed significant changes in the regime of direct as well as indirect taxation during this period. The nineties also witnessed other momentous changes having a bearing on central and state finances. One critical development, following the recommendations of the Fifth Central Pay Commission, was the revision of the salaries of the central government employees. States, one after another, as if under a domino effect, agreed to implement comparable salary scales for their employees. Towards the latter half of the nineties, some of the highest nominal interest rates were witnessed, until inflation and interest rates began to fall. In the first few years of the new decade, as already discussed in the preceding chapter, the economy smarted under a severe recession, with some of the lowest nominal and real growth rates in recent years with the year 2002-03 also witnessing a severe drought. In 2000, the system of fiscal transfers also underwent a phase change when, the eightieth amendment to constitution, with the objective of facilitating tax reforms and broad-basing tax-sharing arrangements, provided for the sharing of all central taxes with limited exceptions, replacing the earlier arrangement of sharing only the income tax and the Union excise duties.

3.2 Arguably, the six years from 1997-98 to 2002-03, have had a debilitating impact on government finances. The first three years, put finances under pressure because of the salary revision and high interest rates, and the next three years, due to low growth and severe drought. With a view to providing a background to formulating our views on vertical and horizontal imbalances and the overall scheme of fiscal transfers, we have examined the salient trends in (a) central finances, (b) aggregate state finances, and (c) finances of individual states in a comparative perspective.

Trends in Central Finances

3.3 In analyzing the trends in central finances, we have focused on indicators of revenue receipts, particularly tax revenues, expenditure, in aggregate and in terms of broad categories, and debt. We examine first, however, the profile of fiscal imbalance, as it provides a summary view of the net outcome of the performance of various revenues and expenditures.

Centre: Profile of Fiscal Imbalance

3.4 We look at three indicators of fiscal imbalance: revenue deficit, fiscal deficit, and primary deficit. Revenue deficit indicates the extent to which current receipts are not able to cover revenue expenditures necessitating borrowing to finance current, not-asset building, expenditure. It represents government consumption expenditure that requires to be financed by capital receipts. These capital receipts, apart from a small portion of non-debt capital receipts, consist of net borrowing, which is called fiscal deficit. The primary deficit is equal to fiscal deficit, which represents net inflow of borrowed funds, minus interest payments, which represent outflows in the form of transfer payments. Primary deficits accumulate into debt, unless offset by an excess of GDP growth rate over interest rate. One related measure, namely, the ratio of revenue deficit to fiscal deficit, indicates the extent to which borrowing is used for current expenditures.

3.5 Table 3.1 provides the profile of different indicators of fiscal imbalance in respect of central finances from 1990-91. In comparing fiscal deficit since 1990-91, one adjustment requires to be made for figurer prior to 1999-00, when lending to the states on account of small savings was not channeled through the public account of National Small Savings Fund (NSSF) and constituted part of centre's fiscal deficit. After this adjustment, as given in Table 3.1, the fiscal deficit of the centre, first declined from 6.6 per cent in 1990-91 to 4.1 per cent in 1996-97. It started rising from 1997-98 to reach a level of 6.2 per cent of GDP in 2001-02. After that, there is a fall in centre's fiscal deficit relative to GDP. A similar profile is observed in the case of revenue deficit, which, after declining from 3.3 per cent of GDP in 1990-91 to 2.4 per cent in 1996-97, rose steadily to 4.4 per cent in 2001-02. The year 2002-03 witnessed an improvement in fiscal deficit to 5.9 per cent of the GDP due to a reduction in primary deficit, although the revenue deficit

Table 3.1
Centre:Profile of Fiscal Imbalance

(Per cent of GDP)

Year	Fiscal Deficit	Revenue Deficit	Primary Deficit	Ratio of Revenue to Fiscal Deficit(%)
1990-91	6.61	3.26	2.83	49.36
1991-92	4.72	2.49	0.65	52.72
1992-93	5.33	2.76	0.72	51.73
1993-94	6.43	3.81	2.15	59.21
1994-95	4.74	3.06	0.39	64.60
1995-96	4.23	2.50	0.02	59.16
1996-97	4.11	2.38	-0.24	58.01
1997-98	4.81	3.05	0.50	63.45
1998-99	5.14	3.85	0.67	74.78
1999-00	5.41	3.49	0.75	64.55
2000-01	5.69	4.08	0.93	71.74
2001-02	6.18	4.39	1.47	71.06
2002-03	5.87	4.37	1.10	74.36
2003-04 RE	4.77	3.60	0.27	75.59

Source: Central Budget Documents and Indian Public Finance Statistics, 2002-03
Figures for 2003-04 are revised estimates
Fiscal deficit figures exclude states' share against small savings.
Primary deficit is derived by netting interest payments from fiscal deficit.

continued almost at the same level as 2001-02. The situation seems to have improved in 2003-04 (RE), with the fiscal deficit and the revenue deficit declining to 4.8 and 3.6 per cent of GDP, respectively.

3.6 The most persistent deterioration is observed in the ratio of revenue deficit to fiscal deficit, which, by indicating the extent to which borrowed resources are used for current expenditures, shows the 'quality' of fiscal deficit. In 1990-91, this ratio was about 50 per cent. It increased steadily to 75 per cent in 1998-99. Thereafter, there was some improvement, but the ratio again increased back to the level of 75.6 per cent in 2003-04, indicating that three-fourth of borrowing has been used for current consumption in some years.

3.7 The outstanding liabilities of the centre, including the public account liabilities of the NSSF, after declining from 55.3 per cent of GDP in 1990-91 to 51.2 per cent in 1998-99, rose to 63.1 per cent in 2002-03. The liabilities as a percentage of GDP, however, declined marginally to 62.6 per cent in 2003-04 and are again expected to rise to 63.96 per cent of GDP at the end of 2004-05. However, in order to make changes in debt more consistent with fiscal deficit, it is useful to consider centre's debt after adjusting for lending to states through the NSSF against which the central government has equivalent assets in the form of securities issued by the state governments. If this is done, centre's debt from 51.2 per cent in 1998-99 would be shown to increase to 57.2 per cent in 2002-03, implying a rise of 6 percentage points. Thereafter, it is estimated to fall to about 53 per cent of GDP in 2004-05, when GDP growth rate once again became higher than the interest rate, and since the centre has been able to extinguish some of its own liabilities to the NSSF and others, on the basis of the repayments it obtained from the states under the debt swap programme. It may be noted that these estimates of debt include external debt that is evaluated at historical exchange rates. The adjustment required when external debt is evaluated at current exchange rates is discussed in Chapter IV.

Centre's Gross Tax Revenues

3.8 With fiscal consolidation, as one of the core objectives of economic reforms, the direct taxes, both personal and corporate income taxes, were rationalized. The number of rate categories as well as the marginal income tax rates were substantially reduced. The main central commodity taxes, i.e., Union excise duties and customs duties also underwent salient changes. In the case of customs duties, there were drastic reductions in the tariff rates across the rate categories including the peak rates. Reforms also entailed reduction in the rate categories and exemption regimes. In the case of Union excise duties, the principle of taxing the value added was adopted, first in the form of modified VAT (MODVAT) and later as central VAT (CENVAT). The impact of these reforms on direct and indirect taxes was diametrically opposite. While the direct taxes showed, even with the lower rates, a rising tax-GDP ratio, this ratio for the indirect taxes kept sliding down. The indirect taxes had a larger share in the total tax revenues of the centre and the fall in the indirect tax to GDP ratio could not be compensated by a rise in the direct taxes. As a result, the overall central tax-GDP ratio fell. Chart 3.1 shows the pattern of change in direct and indirect tax revenues of the centre relative to GDP from 1970-71, with a view to highlighting the reversal of the roles that these two types of taxes have played over the years. Prior to reforms, not only the indirect taxes contributed more, these steadily rose as percentage of GDP, while the direct taxes remained stagnant at about 2 per cent of GDP. After the nineties, the indirect taxes relative to GDP started falling, but in terms of their overall contribution, these are still higher than that of the centre's direct taxes.

3.9. Table 3.2 gives, relative to GDP, revenues from the four major central taxes, namely, corporation tax, income tax, customs duty, and Union excise duties. Considering the gross receipts from the central taxes, the tax-GDP ratio of the centre declined from 10.1 per cent in 1990-91 to 8.8 per cent in 2002-03. The major contributor to this decline was customs duty, which, relative to GDP, halved from 3.6 per cent in 1990-91 to 1.8 per cent in 2002-03. This, as already mentioned, has been on account of a phased reduction in import duty rates in the wake of WTO commitments and to become globally competitive. More serious was the decline in the ratio of excise duty collections to GDP by 1 percentage point during the same period from 4.3 per cent of GDP to 3.3 per cent. The direct tax revenues grew from 1.9 per cent of GDP in 1990-91 to 3.4 per cent in 2002-03, but the loss in the revenue from customs and excise duties did not get fully compensated, resulting in the lower tax-GDP ratio.

3.10 The main reason, among others, for the fall in the revenues from Union excise duties relative to GDP, is the reduction in the average tax rates without a compensatory rise in the tax base. With the rise in the share of service sector in GDP, it is neither feasible nor desirable to augment the ratio of domestic indirect taxes relative to GDP without fully incorporating services in the tax base. The service sector, which accounts for more than fifty per cent of GDP, has been subjected to taxation since 1994 and the scope of service tax has been

Chart 3.1

Centre's Tax-GDP Ratios: Direct to Indirect (1970-71 to 2002-03)

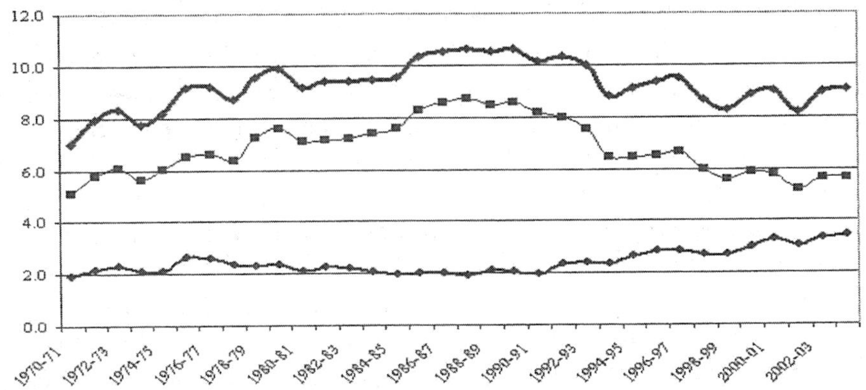

expanding, but the collection from service tax remains at levels below 0.5 per cent of GDP.

3.11 The composition of centre's gross tax revenues has changed in a fundamental way, as indicated in Table 3.2, in favor of corporation tax and income tax. The share of corporation tax increased from 9.3 per cent of centre's gross revenue receipts in 1990-91 to 24.7 per cent in 2003-04 RE, implying an increase of 15.4 percentage points. During the same period, the increase in income tax was 6.5 percentage points, which in 2003-04 RE accounted for 15.8 per cent of centre's gross revenue receipts. The fall during the period was 16.5 and 6.4 percentage points in customs duties and Union excise duties, respectively. It is almost point to point that the larger loss in customs duties was made up by the rise in corporation tax, and that in the Union excise duties was made up by a corresponding rise in revenues from the income tax.

Table 3.2

Major Taxes of the Centre: Performance since 1990-91

(Per cent of GDP)

Year	Corporation tax	Income Tax	Customs Duties	Union Excise Duties	Total Central Tax Revenues (Gross)
1990-91	0.94	0.95	3.63	4.31	10.12
1991-92	1.20	1.03	3.41	4.30	10.31
1992-93	1.19	1.06	3.18	4.12	9.97
1993-94	1.17	1.06	2.58	3.69	8.82
1994-95	1.36	1.19	2.65	3.69	9.11
1995-96	1.39	1.31	3.01	3.38	9.36
1996-97	1.36	1.33	3.13	3.29	9.41
1997-98	1.31	1.12	2.64	3.15	9.14
1998-99	1.41	1.16	2.34	3.06	8.26
1999-00	1.58	1.32	2.50	3.20	8.87
2000-01	1.71	1.52	2.28	3.28	9.03
2001-02	1.60	1.40	1.76	3.18	8.20
2002-03	1.87	1.49	1.82	3.33	8.76
2003-04r	2.27	1.45	1.78	3.33	9.20
Year	**As percentage of Centre's Gross Tax Revenues**				
1990-91	9.27	9.34	35.85	42.58	
1991-92	11.66	9.99	33.04	41.73	
1992-93	11.92	10.58	31.86	41.31	
1993-94	13.28	12.04	29.30	41.85	
1994-95	14.98	13.03	29.02	40.46	
1995-96	14.82	14.02	32.15	36.13	
1996-97	14.42	14.16	33.28	34.95	
1997-98	14.38	12.28	28.87	34.45	
1998-99	17.06	14.08	28.28	37.03	
1999-00	17.87	14.94	28.19	36.04	
2000-01	18.93	16.84	25.21	36.33	
2001-02	19.57	17.11	21.53	38.79	
2002-03	21.35	17.04	20.74	38.06	
2003-04r	24.71	15.80	19.36	36.24	

Source(Basic Data): Central Budget Documents and Indian Public Finance Statistics

Centre: Non Tax Revenues

3.12 The non tax revenues of the centre, which mainly comprise interest receipts, dividends from public sector undertakings (PSUs) and banks and receipts from economic services, rose from 2.11 per cent of GDP in 1990-91 to 2.98 per cent in 1992-93, but have not shown any significant increase after 1999-2000. The non tax receipts as a percentage of GDP have varied from 2.75 per cent in 1999-00 to 2.97 per cent in 2001-02, after which a declining trend is observed, mainly on account of a fall in interest receipts, as a result of the debt-swap scheme and a softening interest rate regime.

Centre: Trends in Expenditures

3.13 The total expenditure of the central government, comprising revenue and capital expenditure, after witnessing some fall relative to GDP in the first half of the nineties, started rising in 1997-98. It declined as a proportion of GDP from 18.5 per cent in 1990-91 to 14.7 per cent in 1996-97, rising thereafter to 16.8 per cent in 2002-03. The quality of expenditure has also witnessed deterioration over the years as the share of capital expenditure declined from 5.6 per cent of GDP in 1990-91 to 3.0 percent in 2002-03. The total expenditure was expected to increase to 17.1 per cent of GDP and capital expenditure to 4.02 per cent in the revised estimates for 2003-04. If, however, the prepayment of the centre's loans to NSSF from debt-swap receipts is excluded, the total expenditure would be 15.4 per cent and capital expenditure, 2.3 per cent. Revenue expenditure as a percentage of GDP declined from 12.9 per cent in 1990-91 to 11.6 per cent in 1996-97 and rose thereafter to 13.8 per cent in 2002-03.

3.14 Interest payments, subsidies, pensions and defence revenue expenditure account for 60 to 65 per cent of revenue expenditure. Interest payments form the single largest component of revenue expenditure, accounting for about 35 per cent of revenue expenditure. As a proportion of centre's revenue receipts, these accounted for about 51 per cent of centre's revenue receipts in 2002-03. Since then this ratio has come down to about 45 per cent in 2004-05 BE. With lower nominal interest rates in recent years, the average cost of market borrowings has witnessed a declining trend since 2000-01. Its effect on the total interest burden of the centre is not distinctly visible due to the growth of outstanding debt. However, in 2003-04 the debt-GDP ratio showed a fall as a result of prepayment based on repayments by the states under the debt swap arrangements.

3.15 Table 3.3 also gives details of some other major expenditures of the centre. Considering three year period averages over 1990-93 and 2000-03, Table 3.3 indicates that interest payments increased by about 0.6 percentage points of GDP, and pensions, by about 0.2 percentage points. Capital expenditure, on the other hand fell by a little less than 3 percentage points of GDP. Although subsidies show a decline, there is a need to prune these further. Table 3.4 gives more details on centre's explicit subsidies.

3.16 The main subsidies provided by the centre are food and fertilizer subsidies. More recently, the central government had also agreed, as part of the plan for dismantling the administered price regime (APR), to provide subsidies for kerosene and cooking

Table 3.3

Trends in Central Government Expenditures

(Per cent of GDP)

Year	Revenue Expenditure	Interest Payments	Pensions	Subsidies	Capital Expenditure	Total expenditure
1990-91	12.93	3.78	0.38	2.14	5.59	18.52
1991-92	12.60	4.07	0.37	1.88	4.46	17.06
1992-93	13.76	4.61	0.45	1.78	4.44	18.20
1993-94	12.59	4.28	0.39	1.35	3.92	16.51
1994-95	12.06	4.35	0.36	1.17	3.81	15.87
1995-96	11.77	4.21	0.36	1.07	3.23	15.01
1996-97	11.62	4.35	0.37	1.13	3.08	14.69
1997-98	11.84	4.31	0.45	1.22	3.40	15.24
1998-99	12.43	4.47	0.58	1.36	3.61	16.04
1999-00	12.86	4.66	0.74	1.26	2.53	15.39
2000-01	13.30	4.75	0.69	1.28	2.29	15.58
2001-02	13.21	4.71	0.63	1.37	2.67	15.88
2002-03	13.75	4.77	0.59	1.76	3.02	16.77
2003-04 (RE)	13.09	4.49	0.55	1.61	4.02	17.11
Average(1990-93)[A]	**13.09**	**4.15**	**0.40**	**1.93**	**4.83**	**17.92**
Average(2000-03)[B]	**13.42**	**4.74**	**0.64**	**1.47**	**2.66**	**16.08**
B-A	**0.32**	**0.59**	**0.24**	**-0.46**	**-2.17**	**-1.85**

Source (Basic Data): Central Budget Documents

gas for a limited period before phasing these out. Various studies have shown that many of these subsidies are ill-targeted and inefficiency promoting. In recent years, as shown by Table 3.4, the food subsidies have grown sharply rising from a level of 4.8 per cent of centre's revenue receipts in 1996-97 to 10.4 per cent in 2002-03. The volume of food subsidies depends, among other factors, on the difference between the procurement and carrying costs of food grains and the issue price for the public distribution system. While the procurement prices involve an income subsidy to the farmers, the carrying costs are dependent on the level of previous stocks as well as operational inefficiencies and wastages. The carrying costs have increased enormously since 1997-98, partly because of higher interest costs and partly due to higher salaries and wages in the FCI operations. Food subsidy has also become an indirect instrument of resource transfer to the states, depending on the location of the FCI procurements. Clearly, through this mechanism, the government is attempting to target multiple goals with a single instrument. Two changes, among other subsidy reforms, would help. First, the central government should develop a separate instrument for income support to farmers and make it more broad based in terms of coverage of crops than focusing it primarily on just producers of wheat and rice. Secondly, procurement policies should be more decentralized, with part of procurement being handled by the state governments. This would help reduce handling and operational costs and also make the indirect transfers more evenly distributed across states.

3.17 There has been a fall in the fertilizer subsidies relative to centre's gross revenue receipts, but ideally these should be reduced further. The fertilizer subsidies have undergone some reforms in recent years.

The fertilizer subsidies arose because of administered prices for purchase of fertilizers by the farmers and a retention price scheme in the case of indigenous urea fertilizer, which allowed a guaranteed return on net worth. The amount of subsidies depends on the difference between the consumer's and the retention price, and the level of production. There are subsidies also for imported urea fertilizers and sale of decontrolled fertilizers with concession to farmers. Fertilizer subsidies are input based and the benefits of the subsidy accrues more to farmers who use larger amounts of fertilizers and who also have more resources for the other complementary factors of production including water. As such, it is difficult to control and target the incidence of the benefit of the subsidy. Secondly, in so far as it relates to domestic production, it subsidizes inefficiencies of production. There is a clear need to develop an alternative instrument so that the volume of subsidy is small and its benefits better targeted. The present mechanism needs to be phased out as soon as possible.

Table 3.4

Explicit Subsidies Relative to Centre's Revenue Receipts

(per cent)

Year	Food	Fertilizer	Others	Total
1990-91	4.45	7.98	9.67	22.11
1991-92	4.32	7.85	6.39	18.56
1992-93	3.78	7.82	3.01	14.60
1993-94	7.31	6.02	1.99	15.31
1994-95	5.58	6.32	1.08	12.98
1995-96	4.88	6.12	0.50	11.50
1996-97	4.80	6.00	1.47	12.27
1997-98	5.90	7.41	0.54	13.85
1998-99	6.09	7.76	1.94	15.78
1999-00	5.20	7.30	1.00	13.49
2000-01	6.26	7.16	0.51	13.93
2001-02	8.69	6.26	0.55	15.50
2002-03	10.43	4.75	3.59	18.78
2003-04[RE]	9.58	4.48	2.93	17.00

Source (Basic Data) :Centre's Budget Documents

Centre: Some New Initiatives

3.18 Among others, three initiatives in recent years by the central government are quite important. These can play a significant role in reversing the fiscal deterioration witnessed since the late nineties. First, the central government enacted a Fiscal Responsibility and Budget Management Act, 2003 (FRBMA). The Act requires the central government to take appropriate measures to reduce the fiscal deficit and revenue deficit, so as to eliminate the latter by 2007-08 and thereafter build up an adequate revenue surplus. The target date for this has since been modified to 31st March, 2009 through the Finance Act, 2004. In terms of the Rules made under the Act, the fiscal deficit is required to be reduced to 3 per cent of GDP by 31st March, 2009. The enactment of the FRBMA provides an institutional framework and binds the government to prudent fiscal policies. For this reason, it is important that the targets set for the various fiscal parameters in the Act and the Rules are not relaxed. This will set an example for the states also. Secondly, the central government has brought about pension reforms by introducing a new pension scheme meant for new entrants to government service. Although this scheme may initially increase the expenditure on pensions, as the centre will have to make contributions to the pension fund, it will prove to be beneficial in the long run. Thirdly, the central government brought out a debt swap scheme, which has benefited the state governments and, in some way, also the central government. The states have been able to swap their high cost debt to the centre with low cost market borrowings. These additional recoveries have enabled the centre to repay some of its own high cost debt to the NSSF, among others.

3.19 In summary, the following are the main features in regard to the trends in the finances of the centre:

1. After declining in the mid-nineties, the fiscal deficit of the centre in 2001-02 was 6.2 per cent, only marginally lower than its level in 1990-91. In 2003-04 RE and 2004-05 BE, the fiscal deficit relative to GDP has shown a decline.
2. The revenue deficit relative to GDP shows a similar time profile. Having risen to a historical peak of 4.4 per cent, it is slated to come down to 2.5 per cent of GDP in 2004-05 RE. The ratio of revenue deficit to fiscal deficit has been progressively deteriorating until 2003-04 RE, when it amounted to 75.6 per cent.
3. Although centre's gross tax revenues fell from a level of 10.3 per cent of GDP in 1991-92 to 8.2 per cent in 2001-02, amounting to a fall of 2.1 percentage points, it has started improving since then.
4. The composition of central tax revenues has progressively tilted towards corporation tax and income tax. The Union excise duties still account for the single largest source of tax revenue, amounting to about 36 per cent of centre's gross tax revenues.
5. On the expenditure side interest payments and pensions relative to GDP increased during the period under review, and the burden of adjustment has mainly fallen on capital expenditure, which fell by about 2.2 percentage points during 2000-03 compared to average level during 1990-93.

The central government has taken an important step in enacting the FRBMA. It is vital that the revenue and fiscal deficit targets of the Act and the Rules are not modified and the centre sets an example for the states.

Trends in Aggregate State Finances

3.20 State finances, in their aggregate account, had only occasionally shown small revenue deficits until 1986-87. From 1987-88, state finances at the aggregate level have always been in revenue deficit. The magnitude of the deficit relative to GDP has also increased over the years since then, as state after state, rich and poor, small and large, special category and general category, increasingly slid into revenue deficit. Only a few special category states showed surplus on revenue account, but this arose from the composition of plan assistance, being ninety percent in the form of grants, adding to revenue receipts, although meant for capital expenditure, and did not signify any fiscal health.

3.21 As mentioned earlier, the six years from 1997-98 to 2002-03, have been the worst in the history of state finances. The first half of this period, saw one of the sharpest increases in the salary bill of state government employees, when as shown elsewhere in this Report, the average per employee salary increased by close to 60 per cent in a span of three years. This was also the period when central transfers, relative to GDP, fell and states were engaged in exemption-proliferating tax competition leading to a fall in the level of own tax revenue relative to GDP.

3.22 Unable to adjust their expenditure downwards, states depended more and more on borrowing to finance their revenue expenditures in a period when the nominal interest rates hit a peak. While the states finances smarted under these multiple pressures, the economy, as discussed in the preceding Chapter, went into a recession, showing some of the lowest real and nominal growth rates in the first three years of the new decade. The impact of these changes, being felt in a short span of six years, was swift and debilitating. In no other stretch of six years of the fiscal history of the states, has there been a rise of more than 10 percentage points in the debt-GDP ratio as the one, which occurred in this period where the ratio of outstanding debt to GDP increased from 21 per cent in 1996-97 to 31 per cent in 2002-03. We have analyzed below, focusing on the period 1993-03, the trends in state finances, in the aggregate as well as in a comparative perspective across states.

All-States: Contours of Fiscal Imbalance

3.23 We look at three indicators of fiscal imbalance: revenue deficit, fiscal deficit, primary deficit. Table 3.5 shows that for the states considered together the revenue deficit as percentage of GDP, comparing the averages over 2000-03 and 1993-96 was higher by a margin of 1.9 percentage points, and the fiscal deficit, by a margin of 1.5 percentage points. The primary deficit relative to GDP had reached a peak in 1999-00, but has since evinced a decline. In fact, in 1999-00, both revenue deficit and fiscal deficit had reached a peak at 4.64 and 2.82 per cent of GDP, respectively. As mentioned earlier, the outstanding debt to GDP ratio increased from 21 per cent in 1996-97 to 31 per cent in 2002-03. Comparing the average over 2000-03 with that of 1990-93, the increase amounted to about 9.4 percentage points.

Table 3.5

Aggregate State Finances: Alternative Deficit Indicators

(per cent of GDP)

Year	Revenue Deficit	Fiscal Deficit	Primary Deficit	Rev. Def. /Fisc Def.	Debt./GDP
1993-94	0.45	2.35	0.52	19.05	21.79
1994-95	0.69	2.72	0.79	25.55	21.40
1995-96	0.73	2.59	0.76	28.06	21.00
1996-97	1.31	2.77	0.90	47.37	21.00
1997-98	1.23	2.94	0.93	42.01	21.73
1998-99	2.61	4.31	2.24	60.48	23.02
1999-00	2.82	4.64	2.34	60.87	25.20
2000-01	2.61	4.16	1.69	62.60	27.42
2001-02	2.68	4.09	1.41	65.49	29.37
2002-03	2.29	3.94	1.14	58.09	31.15
Averages					
1993-96[A]	0.62	2.55	0.69	24.22	21.79
2000-03[B]	2.53	4.07	1.41	62.06	31.15
[B]-[A]	1.90	1.51	0.72	37.84	9.36

Source (Basic Data): State Finance Accounts

3.24 The ratio of own tax revenues to GDP for all states fell from 5.3 percent to 4.9 per cent in 1998-99 and was at 5.1 percent in1999-00. There was a substantial improvement in 2000-01 as most states agreed to the implementation of floor rates in sales tax and to reduce and rationalize various exemptions. In 2002-03, the states' own tax revenues as percentage of GDP had improved to 5.5 per cent. Comparing the 2000-03 average with that of 1993-96, there was an improvement of 0.17 percentage points. In the case of own non-tax revenues, there has been a downward slide. It fell from 1.6 per cent of GDP in 1993-94 to 1.2 per cent in 2001-02. Comparing the 2000-03 average to that of 1993-96 average, there is a fall of 0.3 percentage points in the own non tax revenues of the states.

3.25 In the period under review, the Finance Commission's transfers relative to GDP were the lowest in 1998-99 and 1999-2000 at 2.4 per cent and 2.5 per cent respectively. There has been an improvement since. In the case of non-Finance Commissions' transfers, the fall was even more significant. In 1993-94, non-Finance Commission transfers accounted for about 2 per cent of GDP. These fell to below 1.3 per cent in the period sine 1998-99. Together, the Finance Commission and non-Finance Commission transfers from the centre fell by about 0.44 percentage points comparing the 2000-03 average with that of 1993-96. Taking these revenue flows together, the aggregate revenue receipts of the states as percentage of GDP were the lowest in 1998-99 at 9.8 per cent. Comparing the two period averages of 1993-96 and 2000-03, there has been a fall of little less than 0.6 percentage points in the total revenue receipts of the states.

Table 3.6

Aggregate State Finances: Main Fiscal Indicators

(per cent of GDP)

Year	Own Tax Revenues	Own Non-Tax Revenues	Finance Commission Transfers	Non- Finance Commission TransfersReceipts	Total Revenue
1993-94	5.30	1.59	3.05	2.02	11.96
1994-95	5.31	1.55	2.86	1.55	11.27
1995-96	5.20	1.51	2.90	1.30	10.91
1996-97	5.01	1.47	2.94	1.29	10.71
1997-98	5.14	1.43	2.90	1.33	10.80
1998-99	4.93	1.26	2.44	1.17	9.81
1999-00	5.09	1.38	2.50	1.29	10.26
2000-01	5.46	1.37	3.02	1.20	11.04
2001-02	5.32	1.19	2.84	1.28	10.63
2002-03	5.52	1.23	2.80	1.22	10.77
Average					
1993-96[A]	5.27	1.55	2.94	1.62	11.38
2000-03[B]	5.44	1.26	2.88	1.23	10.81
[B]-[A]	0.17	-0.29	-0.05	-0.39	-0.57

Source (Basic Data): State Finance Accounts

Aggregate State Finances: Expenditure Trends

3.26 Table 3.6 shows the main trends in the all-state revenue expenditures focusing on interest payments and pensions as well as the aggregates of plan and non-plan revenue expenditures. In contrast to the trends in revenue receipts, almost all expenditure categories show perceptible increases during the period under review. These increases are particularly sharp in the case of interest payments and pensions. As far as interest payments are concerned, these rose from about 1.8 per cent in 1993-94 to 2.8 per cent in 2002-03 showing a rise of 1 percentage point in a span of 10 years. In the case of pensions also, there has been a sharp rise. In 1993-94, relative to GDP, pensions amounted to 0.6 per cent. These rose to 1.24 per cent in 2002-03, showing a rise of more than 100 per cent. Both these heads of expenditure account for transfer payments. With their claims rising in this manner, the required adjustments led to fall in plan revenue expenditure, which was at the level of 2.2 per cent of GDP in 1993-94. By 2002-03 it had fallen to a level of 1.8 per cent.

3.27 It is on account of interest payments and pensions that the total revenue expenditure increased from 12.4 per cent in 1993-94 to 13 per cent in 2002-03. Comparing the period averages of 1993-96 and 2000-03, there has been a rise of 1.34 percentage points of GDP. At the aggregate level, total revenue expenditure of all the states was at its lowest at 11.6 per cent of GDP in 1995-96. Thereafter, it increased steadily to reach a level of 13.7 per cent in 2000-01, after which it came down to 13.1 per cent in 2002-03. The increase during 1998-2001 can be attributed to the large increases in salaries and pensions due to their revision following the

Table 3.7

Aggregate State Finances: Expenditure Indicators

(per cent of GDP)

Year	Total Revenue Expenditure	Interest Payments	Pension	Plan Revenue Expenditure	Non-Plan Revenue Expenditure
1993-94	12.41	1.82	0.61	2.22	10.19
1994-95	11.96	1.92	0.63	2.06	9.91
1995-96	11.63	1.83	0.66	2.01	9.63
1996-97	12.02	1.87	0.72	2.10	9.93
1997-98	12.03	2.01	0.77	1.93	10.10
1998-99	12.41	2.07	0.93	1.99	10.43
1999-00	13.08	2.30	1.16	1.87	11.21
2000-01	13.65	2.48	1.24	1.91	11.74
2001-02	13.31	2.68	1.26	1.85	11.46
2002-03	13.06	2.80	1.24	1.81	11.24
Average					
1993-96[A]	12.00	1.86	0.63	2.09	9.91
2000-03[B]	13.34	2.65	1.25	1.86	11.48
[B]-[A]	1.34	0.79	0.62	-0.24	1.57

Source (Basic Data): State Finance Accounts

recommendations of the Fifth Central Pay Commission. Within the overall revenue expenditure, the non-plan component increased steadily from 9.6 per cent in 1995-96 to 11.7 per cent in 2000-01, after which it has been coming down.

3.28 Among the factors that have contributed to the deterioration of the state finances, a reference must be made to subsidies. Bulk of the subsidies provided by the states is implicit rather than explicit. Implicit subsidies arise when services are provided at prices that do not recover costs. Low user charges have been a universal phenomenon. Budgetary support to the power sector in particular has been an important source of drain in states where explicit subsidy for this purpose has been provided for in the budgets. However, several states do not provide subsidy, even though electricity boards may be suffering losses. Subventions received by the power sector from the state governments are estimated to be 32.8 per cent of commercial losses in 2003-04, according to the Tenth Plan document. A reform of the power sector aimed at reducing losses will be an important step in improving state finances.

3.29 The main trends relating to the aggregate state finances, comparing the average over 1993-96 with that of 2000-03 may be summarized as follows:

1. Revenue deficit of the states rose from 0.62 per cent of GDP in 1993-96 to 2.53 per cent in 2000-03, implying an increase of 1.9 percentage points.
2. Fiscal deficit of the states increased from 2.55 per cent during 1993-96 on average to about 4 per cent of GDP, implying a rise of about 1.5 percentage points.
3. Within the period from 1996-97 to 2002-03, the debt-GDP ratio of the states increased by a massive margin of 10 percentage points of GDP, rising from 21 per cent of GDP in 1996-97 to 31.2 per cent in 2002-03.
4. The own tax revenues of the states showed an increase from 5.3 per cent of GDP during 1993-96 on average to 5.5 per cent during 2000-03. But own non-tax revenues as also the central transfers relative to GDP fell during this period. The fall in transfers was mainly on account of non-Finance Comm-ission transfer.
5. On the expenditure side interest payments and pensions increased. In the case of interest payments, the rise amounted to 0.79 percentage points, rising from 1.86 during 1993-96 to 2.65 during 2000-03. In fact, if only end years 1993-94 and 2002-03 are compared, the increase is a clear one percentage point of GDP. Pensions rose by 0.62 percentage points comparing the averages for the two periods under review.

State Finances: A Comparative Perspective

3.30 In this section, we look at the relative performance of individual states in a comparative perspective. For this purpose, we have focused on the following variables: own tax revenue, revenue and capital expenditures, interest payments and pensions, revenue and fiscal deficits, and outstanding liabilities. Comparisons are made for two three-year period averages, 1993-96 and 2000-03. All variables are taken as percentages to the respective GSDPs of the states. States other than the eleven special category states (SCS) are referred to as the general category states (GCS). States of Uttar Pradesh, Madhya Pradesh, and Bihar are taken as undivided states for purposes of comparison for the entire period.

Contours of Fiscal Imbalance: Inter-State Comparison

3.31 As mentioned earlier, the aggregate revenue account of the states went into deficit in 1987-88. During the nineties, some of the individual states were still in revenue surplus. Among the general category states, Andhra Pradesh went into revenue deficit in 1994-95, Gujarat and Haryana in 1995-96, and Goa, at the top end of income scale, also went into revenue deficit in 1997-98. As shown in Table 3.8, the largest revenue deficit on average during 1993-96 was that of Orissa at 2.0 per cent of GSDP followed by Punjab, Uttar Pradesh, and West Bengal. The deficits of these states rose persistently. In the period 2000-03, there were no states of the general category showing a revenue surplus. The magnitudes of their revenue deficits were higher and their relative position had also changed. The highest revenue deficit relative to GSDP was now that of West Bengal at 5.5 per cent followed by Punjab, Orissa and Rajasthan. Among the special category states, Arunachal Pradesh, Meghalaya, and Sikkim continued to show a surplus. The deterioration in the case of general category states, comparing the 2000-03 average with that of 1993-96, was 2.33 percentage points of all-state GSDP of the general category states.

3.32 The difference between period averages of 1993-94 and 2000-03 shows that the largest deterioration in the revenue deficit to GSDP ratio was that for West Bengal followed by Orissa, Rajasthan, and Punjab. Thus, revenue deficit became high relative to GSDP for high income states like Punjab, middle income states like West Bengal, and low income states like Orissa. In fact, the states which did not show any perceptible deterioration during this period were Bihar with an increase in the revenue deficit to GSDP ratio of only 0.04 percentage point and Haryana with an increase of 0.56 percentage point.

3.33 Table 3.8 shows that the fiscal deficit among the general category states was the highest during 1993-96 in the case of Orissa, Rajasthan, Punjab, Uttar Pradesh, West Bengal, and Andhra Pradesh. During 2000-03, Orissa had become the highest fiscal deficit state among the general category states followed by West Bengal, Punjab, Rajasthan, Gujarat, and Uttar Pradesh. The average deterioration over these two periods was the largest in the case of West Bengal followed by Gujarat and Orissa.

Debt-GSDP Ratios: Comparative Position of States

3.34 Relative to all-State GSDP, as shown in Table 3.9, the outstanding liabilities had increased by nearly 12 percentage points from 1993-96 average of 24.86 per cent to the 2000-03 average of 36.7 per cent. Among the general category states, Orissa had the highest debt-GSDP ratio during 2000-03 at 63.7 per cent followed by 47 per cent for Uttar Pradesh, 46.7 per cent for Punjab, 44.9 per cent for Rajasthan, and 42.7 per cent for West

Table 3.8

Comparative Performance of States: Revenue and Fiscal Deficits

(Per cent of GSDP)

	Revenue Account [Deficit (-)]			Fiscal Account [Deficit(-)]		
States	**1993-96[A]**	**2000-03[B]**	**[B-A]**	**1993-96[C]**	**2000-03[D]**	**[D-A]**
Arunachal Pradesh	24.28	1.76	-22.51	1.48	-12.70	-14.18
Assam	-0.01	-1.90	-1.88	-2.38	-3.73	-1.34
Himachal Pradesh	-1.56	-7.28	-5.72	-6.70	-11.41	-4.71
Jammu & Kashmir	4.56	-1.82	-6.38	-3.85	-8.28	-4.44
Manipur	6.07	-2.46	-8.53	-3.02	-6.06	-3.04
Meghalaya	3.32	0.84	-2.48	-3.20	-5.28	-2.08
Mizoram	7.53	-9.07	-16.60	-5.82	-17.79	-11.96
Nagaland	-0.19	-2.12	-1.93	-5.26	-7.97	-2.71
Sikkim	8.10	11.30	3.20	-8.26	-3.42	4.84
Tripura	2.57	-0.61	-3.18	-4.04	-7.20	-3.15
Total: SCS	**1.96**	**-2.53**	**-4.49**	**-3.64**	**-7.04**	**-3.40**
Andhra Pradesh	-0.51	-2.03	-1.51	-3.16	-4.57	-1.41
Bihar	-1.83	-1.87	-0.04	-2.85	-4.52	-1.67
Goa	1.44	-2.44	-3.89	-2.30	-4.68	-2.38
Gujarat	0.10	-4.66	-4.75	-1.82	-5.74	-3.93
Haryana	-0.75	-1.32	-0.56	-2.50	-3.69	-1.19
Karnataka	-0.07	-2.21	-2.15	-2.71	-4.37	-1.65
Kerala	-1.18	-4.17	-2.99	-3.32	-5.13	-1.81
Madhya Pradesh	-0.61	-2.05	-1.44	-2.16	-3.94	-1.78
Maharashtra	-0.09	-3.09	-3.00	-2.16	-4.12	-1.96
Orissa	-2.00	-4.91	-2.91	-4.63	-7.84	-3.21
Punjab	-1.88	-4.53	-2.66	-4.37	-6.14	-1.77
Rajasthan	-1.09	-3.87	-2.78	-4.51	-6.05	-1.54
Tamil Nadu	-0.71	-2.50	-1.78	-1.99	-3.75	-1.77
Uttar Pradesh	-1.77	-2.98	-1.21	-4.04	-5.07	-1.03
West Bengal	-1.53	-5.47	-3.95	-3.18	-7.31	-4.13
Total: GCS	**-0.86**	**-3.19**	**-2.33**	**-2.93**	**-4.97**	**-2.04**
All States	**-0.72**	**-3.15**	**-2.43**	**-2.96**	**-5.08**	**-2.12**

Source (Basic Data): State Finance Accounts

Bengal. The highest deterioration during the period under review was that for Orissa at 27.5 percentage points followed by West Bengal at 19.5 percentage points, Gujarat at 16.9 percentage points, and Rajasthan at 16.6 percentage points.

3.35 The special category states had a high debt-GSDP ratio during 1993-96, the highest being that for J&K at 58 per cent, followed by 53.7 per cent for Sikkim. These ratios also increased sharply during the late 1990s. During 2000-03, the debt-GSDP ratio for Mizoram was as high as 85 per cent followed by 63.2 per cent for Sikkim, 61.8 per cent for Himachal Pradesh 56 per cent for J&K and 54.8 per cent for Arunachal Pradesh. The largest deterioration, comparing the period averages under review, was for Mizoram at 32.3 percentage points of its GSDP, followed by 19.8 percentage points, for Himachal Pradesh and 18.3 percentage points for Arunachal Pradesh, relative to their respective GSDPs.

Table 3.9

Outstanding Debt Relative to GSDP: State-wise Position

(Per cent)

States	1993-96[A]	2000-03[B]	Col.[B-A]
Arunachal Pradesh	36.48	54.82	18.34
Assam	31.40	34.75	3.35
Himachal Pradesh	41.95	61.79	19.84
Jammu & Kashmir	58.01	55.99	-2.02
Manipur	38.16	47.88	9.72
Meghalaya	24.12	38.68	14.56
Mizoram	53.05	85.29	32.25
Nagaland	42.71	49.91	7.20
Sikkim	53.65	63.24	9.59
Tripura	38.77	38.11	-0.67
Total:SCS	**39.68**	**47.17**	**7.48**
Andhra Pradesh	21.86	29.93	8.07
Bihar	36.80	44.35	7.55
Goa	41.64	33.54	-8.10
Gujarat	21.07	37.92	16.85
Haryana	19.85	28.02	8.17
Karnataka	19.62	27.27	7.65
Kerala	27.27	37.58	10.32
Madhya Pradesh	19.95	30.42	10.47
Maharashtra	15.63	27.11	11.48
Orissa	36.21	63.68	27.47
Punjab	34.55	46.66	12.10
Rajasthan	28.28	44.88	16.60
Tamil Nadu	18.87	26.16	7.29
Uttar Pradesh	33.94	46.94	13.00
West Bengal	23.26	42.73	19.47
Total: GCS	**24.12**	**36.06**	**11.94**
All States	**24.86**	**36.65**	**11.79**

Source (Basic Data): State Finance Accounts

Comparative Performance of States: Own Tax Revenues

3.36 The single positive feature in this otherwise depressing narrative of state finances was the performance of states in regard to their own tax effort. Table 3.10 shows that the tax-GDP ratio increased, considering the two period-averages over 1993-96 and 2000-03, for the groups of special category and general category states, and all the individual states except a few. The overall increase over the period-averages under review for the states as a whole was 0.67 percentage points for all states relative to the all-state GSDP, 0.66 for the SCS and 0.69 for the GCS group, relative to their respective group-GSDPs. The only exceptions in terms of individual states, where the tax-GDP ratio declined in terms of their 2000-03 averages are Goa, Karnataka, Kerala, and West Bengal, although while the first three went from high to less high, West Bengal had a somewhat lower tax-GSDP ratio even in the 1993-96 period. Among the SCS group, only Manipur has shown a decline in tax-GSDP ratio.

Table 3.10

Own Tax Revenues: Comparative Performance of States

States	Average OTR/GSDP (%)			Buoyancy
	1993-96 [A]	2000-03 [B]	[B-A]	1993-03
Arunachal Pradesh	0.55	1.47	0.91	2.543
Assam	3.69	4.58	0.90	1.326
Himachal Pradesh	4.87	5.08	0.21	1.043
Jammu & Kashmir	3.11	4.51	1.40	1.443
Manipur	1.44	1.21	-0.23	0.842
Meghalaya	3.02	3.26	0.23	1.089
Mizoram	0.59	0.97	0.38	1.608
Nagaland	1.18	1.19	0.01	0.980
Sikkim	3.44	4.58	1.15	1.303
Tripura	1.95	2.19	0.24	1.105
Total:SCS	**3.30**	**3.96**	**0.66**	**1.226**
Andhra Pradesh	5.90	7.30	1.40	1.271
Bihar	3.71	4.46	0.75	1.290
Goa	7.91	6.46	-1.45	0.806
Gujarat	7.51	7.71	0.20	1.010
Haryana	7.22	8.30	1.09	1.205
Karnataka	8.53	8.33	-0.19	0.969
Kerala	8.45	8.11	-0.34	0.946
Madhya Pradesh	4.91	6.45	1.53	1.452
Maharashtra	6.64	7.76	1.12	1.221
Orissa	3.93	5.81	1.87	1.639
Punjab	6.88	7.13	0.25	1.061
Rajasthan	5.50	6.48	0.98	1.231
Tamil Nadu	8.40	9.00	0.60	1.110
Uttar Pradesh	4.76	5.88	1.12	1.318
West Bengal	5.46	4.26	-1.20	0.690
Total: GCS	**6.26**	**6.95**	**0.69**	**1.143**
All States	**6.12**	**6.79**	**0.67**	**1.141**

Source: State Finance Accounts

3.37 During 2000-03, the highest tax-GSDP ratio was that for Tamil Nadu at 9.0 per cent of GSDP, and the lowest for West Bengal at 4.26 per cent, among the general category states. Chart 3.2 shows the tax-GSDP ratios of the general category states along with Assam. States are arranged in ascending order of per capita comparable GSDP (average over 1999-2002). A logarithmic trend line has also been shown. The pattern does show a positive relationship, and would have been even better, but for the exceptions of Punjab and Goa at the higher income end, West Bengal, in the middle range, and Assam and Bihar, at the lower per capita GSDP end. These states, in terms of the tax-GSDP ratio have performed below the par set by other states in their neighborhood in terms of the level of per capita GSDP.

3.38 Table 3.10 shows the buoyancy of own tax revenues of the states with respect to their respective per capita GSDPs, which indicates the extent of increase in own tax revenues following a one per cent change in per capita comparable GSDP, taking the latter as a macro indicator of the tax base. The tax-buoyancy has been estimated over the period 1993-2003. If the states with a low tax-GSDP ratio have a high buoyancy, they would find improvement in their tax-GSDP ratios over time. If the tax-buoyancy is less than 1, the tax-GSDP ratio would fall over time. Subject to adjustment for levels of per capita GSDPs, it would be desirable if states at the lower end of the chart show higher buoyancy. In this sense, the states at the lower to middle income ranges, with the exception of West Bengal, do show an improving picture.

Comparative Performance of States: Expenditures

3.39 In respect of revenue expenditures relative to GSDP levels, comparing

Chart 3.2

State's Own Tax Revenues Relative to GSDP (2000-03)

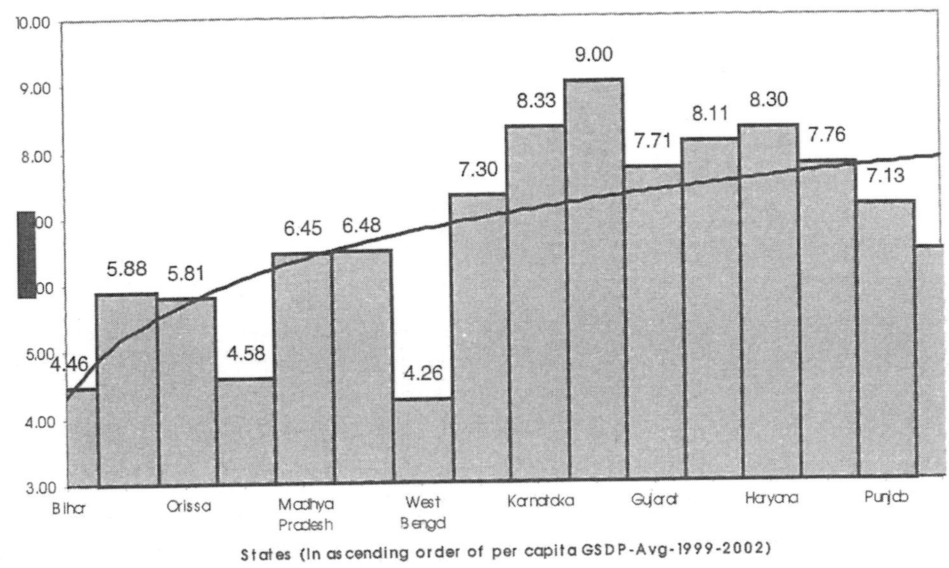

averages over the two periods, viz., 1993-96 and 2000-03, Table 3.11 shows a general upward trend. The corresponding ratio for capital expenditure, however, shows a change in the reverse direction. For the SCS group, there is an increase of 1.4 percentage points between the two period averages. Among the general category states, the largest increase in the ratio of revenue expenditure to GSDP are in respect of Gujarat (5.9 per cent) and Orissa (5.7 per cent). The states where this increase is least are Goa (0.1 per cent) and Haryana (0.4 per cent). The main reason for the increase in revenue expenditure in relation to GSDP can be attributed to the increases in salaries and pensions during the period as well as on account of an increasing debt servicing burden.

3.40 Looking at the levels of revenue expenditures relative to GSDP, the average for 2000-03 indicates that for the SCS group the ratio is about 10 percentage points higher than that for the general category states. In this group, Orissa has an exceptionally high ratio at 22.2 per cent. At the lower end, we have Haryana at 13.5 per cent and Maharashtra at 14.1 per cent, which are the only states below 15 per cent.

3.41 Expectedly, the increase in revenue expenditure has led to a fall in capital expenditure with special category states displaying the larger reduction in capital expenditure to GSDP ratio between 1993-96 and 2000-03, comparing group to group. In the GCS group, Orissa has the highest level of capital expenditure at 3.2 per cent in 2000-03 while Kerala has the lowest at 1.1 per cent.

3.42 Table 3.12 shows comparisons over the two period-averages under review for two other important ratios, namely, interest

Table 3.11

States: Comparative Trends in Expenditure

(Per cent of GSDP)

	Revenue Expenditure			**Capital Expenditure**		
States	**1993-96[A]**	**2000-03[B]**	**[B-A]**	**1993-96[C]**	**2000-03[D]**	**[D-A]**
Andhra Pradesh	13.47	15.56	2.08	3.87	2.93	-0.94
Bihar	16.50	18.11	1.60	1.04	2.67	1.63
Goa	17.11	17.25	0.13	3.86	2.33	-1.54
Gujarat	12.52	18.37	5.85	2.37	2.43	0.06
Haryana	13.06	13.45	0.39	2.33	2.52	0.18
Karnataka	13.96	15.33	1.36	3.08	2.44	-0.64
Kerala	14.93	16.11	1.18	2.23	1.07	-1.16
Madhya Pradesh	13.29	16.74	3.45	1.90	2.37	0.47
Maharashtra	10.68	14.10	3.42	2.56	1.47	-1.09
Orissa	16.49	22.22	5.74	2.83	3.23	0.40
Punjab	12.75	15.33	2.59	2.65	2.11	-0.54
Rajasthan	15.43	18.06	2.63	3.89	2.30	-1.59
Tamil Nadu	13.95	15.60	1.66	1.85	1.51	-0.34
Uttar Pradesh	14.28	16.78	2.50	2.63	2.23	-0.40
West Bengal	11.80	15.02	3.23	1.78	1.94	0.16
General Category	**13.33**	**16.05**	**2.72**	**2.51**	**2.12**	**-0.38**
Special Category	**26.27**	**27.66**	**1.40**	**5.71**	**4.69**	**-1.03**
All States	**13.94**	**16.67**	**2.72**	**2.66**	**2.26**	**-0.40**

Source: State Finance Accounts

payments relative to total revenue receipts and pension expenditures relative to GSDP. In the absence of adequate availability of non-debt resources, many states relied on increased borrowing to finance the upward revision of salary scales and pensions during 1997-2000. Consequently, the debt servicing burden of states as typified by the interest payments to TRR ratio has increased to unsustainable levels. Among SCS group, IP-TRR ratio is the highest for Himachal Pradesh at 28.8 per cent during 2000-03. This state has registered the largest increase in this ratio at 12.9 percentage points over 1993-96. The increase in debt servicing burden has affected the GCS group more than the special category states. West Bengal has registered the largest increase in IP-TRR ratio in 2000-03 over 1993-96 at 24.0 percentage points. As a consequence, its IP-TRR ratio at 44.3 per cent during 2000-03 is the highest among all states. Punjab follows next at 38.5 per cent. A consistently high level of this ratio for this state during the nineties is reflected by the fact that its IP-TRR ratio was the highest at 32.1 per cent during 1993-96. Orissa and Rajasthan have also shown large increases in their IP-TRR ratios at 13.5 and 13.2 percentage points, respectively between the two periods. During 2000-03, Karnataka, undivided Madhya Pradesh, and Tamil Nadu have displayed lower levels of the IP-TRR ratios at about 18 per cent.

3.43 The phenomenal growth of pension liabilities consequent upon the revision of

Table 3.12

State Expenditure Trends: Comparative Profile

(Per cent of GSDP)

	Int. Payment/TRR			Pension Exp./GSDP		
States	**1993-96[A]**	**2000-03[B]**	**[B-A]**	**1993-96[C]**	**2000-03[D]**	**[D-A]**
Andhra Pradesh	14.07	22.37	8.30	1.01	1.49	0.48
Bihar	21.78	24.92	3.14	1.01	2.82	1.82
Goa	14.21	19.50	5.29	0.55	1.28	0.74
Gujarat	15.18	24.59	9.41	0.60	1.25	0.65
Haryana	15.26	23.35	8.09	0.54	1.10	0.56
Karnataka	12.08	18.07	6.00	0.92	1.42	0.50
Kerala	17.61	27.34	9.73	1.72	2.57	0.85
Madhya Pradesh	13.34	18.36	5.02	0.67	1.17	0.50
Maharashtra	11.93	20.75	8.82	0.36	0.88	0.52
Orissa	22.39	35.85	13.46	0.68	2.21	1.53
Punjab	32.13	38.51	6.38	0.64	1.62	0.98
Rajasthan	17.38	30.57	13.19	0.73	1.91	1.18
Tamil Nadu	11.98	18.61	6.63	0.93	2.11	1.19
Uttar Pradesh	22.30	28.27	5.97	0.54	1.21	0.67
West Bengal	20.34	44.33	23.98	0.61	1.44	0.83
General Category	**16.70**	**25.40**	**8.70**	**0.72**	**1.51**	**0.80**
Special Category	**13.41**	**16.98**	**3.57**	**1.11**	**2.39**	**1.28**
All States	**16.37**	**24.57**	**8.20**	**0.73**	**1.56**	**0.83**

Source: State Finance Accounts

pay scales, shows, as indicated by Table 3.12, that during 2000-03, pension liabilities as a percentage of GSDP were higher than the corresponding average over 1993-96 by 1.28 percentage point for the general category states and by 0.8 percentage points for the special category states. During 2000-03, pension expenditures relative to GSDP varied from 1 per cent to 3 per cent across all states. Among the general category states, the increase in terms of percentage points, in the ratio of pension expenditures to GSDP, was the highest for undivided Bihar (1.82), Orissa (1.53), Rajasthan (1.18) and Tamil Nadu (1.19).

3.44 In summary, in the context of evaluating the comparative performance of states in a period when they had to face the impact of the salary and pension revisions and other macroeconomic developments, some major features, comparing 1993-96 to 2000-03 averages, may be highlighted as below:

1. The revenue deficit to GSDP ratio, over the period, showed the largest increase for West Bengal, followed by Orissa, Rajasthan and Punjab. Bihar showed the least deterioration. In the case of fiscal deficit also, the largest deterioration was for West Bengal, Punjab, Rajasthan, Gujarat, and Uttar Pradesh. This list of states does indicate that the level of GSDP alone was not responsible for the deterioration and other aspects of fiscal management may have been important.
2. During 2000-03, among the general category states, Orissa had the highest debt-GSDP ratio at 63.7 per cent, followed by Uttar Pradesh at 47 per cent, Punjab at 46.7 per cent, Rajasthan at 44.9 per cent, and West Bengal at 42.7 per cent.
3. During 2000-03, the highest tax-GSDP ratio was for Tamil Nadu at 9 per cent of GSDP, and the lowest for West Bengal at 4.26 per cent. The level of GSDP does show a positive impact on the tax-GSDP ratio, but Goa and Punjab at the higher income end, West Bengal in the middle income range, and Assam and Bihar at the low income end show lower performance than what might be expected if the per capita GSDP was taken as a determinant.
4. In terms of revenue expenditure relative to GSDP, comparing the two period averages, the largest increases are those for Gujarat and Orissa, and the lowest increases are for Goa and Haryana.
5. In terms of pension expenditures, the largest increase relative to GSDP, comparing the two period-averages, are for Bihar, Orissa, Rajasthan, and Tamil Nadu.

The presence of several high and middle income states in several indicators of performance, which have shown deterioration, does indicate that while robust resource bases are important for fiscal health, the quality of fiscal management is also equally important.

Concluding Observations

3.45 We have seen that the period during 1997-98 to 2002-03 , the finances both of the central and the state governments suffered serious adverse effects due to one time events like the increase in salaries and pensions and macroeconomic factors that affected interest rates and growth rates. In a way, the states finances suffered a larger shock because they had by far a large base of government employees, faced higher interest rates including those charged by the central government, and also partook in sharing the impact of a fall in centre's tax-GDP ratio, which had resulted in a noticeable fall in the level of transfers. In fact, the lower than expected growth during 2000-03 resulted in less than anticipated tax devolution in the first three years of the award period of the Eleventh Finance Commission.

3.46 It is worth taking note of the fact that government finances and macroeconomic performance should not be viewed in isolation but rather as interdependent and integrally linked. In a way, by nursing large revenue deficits, the centre and the states contributed to a fall in the aggregate government savings to GDP ratio which, although partially compensated by a rise in the households savings relative to GDP set in motion a vicious cycle of falling growth rates, decreasing transfers, increasing borrowings, rising interest payments, and worsening revenue deficit. We have examined these issues in the next Chapter, in the context of macroeconomic stability and the need for restructuring government finances.

□□

Chapter 4

Restructuring Public Finances

4.1 This Commission has been asked under clause 5 of the TOR to "review the state of finances of the Union and the States and suggest a plan by which the Governments, collectively and severally, may bring about a restructuring of the public finances restoring budgetary balance, achieving macroeconomic stability and debt reduction along with equitable growth". A similar term of reference, addressed for the first time to the Eleventh Finance Commission (EFC), had made reference to budgetary balance and macroeconomic stability. The plan for restructuring is now required to also address the objectives of debt reduction and equitable growth.

4.2 Some other parts of the TOR have a bearing on the plan for restructuring. Para 6(iv) makes reference to the "...objective of not only balancing the receipts and expenditure on revenue account of all the States and the Centre, but also generating surpluses for capital investment and reducing fiscal deficit". Para 6(v) emphasizes the need for raising the tax-GDP ratio for the centre and tax-GSDP ratios for the states. In the context of debt reduction, Para 9 stipulates that corrective measures in regard to states' debt may be suggested, consistent with macroeconomic stability and debt sustainability. We have endeavoured to develop an integrated framework for restructuring public finances to address these interrelated objectives.

4.3 Referring to the issue of budgetary imbalance, the EFC had observed that revenue deficits have become 'malefic fixtures' in the central and state budgets and that a restructuring of public finances was called for to steer public finances away from the 'self-perpetuating spiral of debt and deficit'. The EFC went on to draw up a fiscal adjustment programme for the central and the state governments that was meant to eliminate revenue deficit of the states and reduce centre's revenue deficit to 1 per cent of GDP by 2004-05. The overall fiscal deficit target was set at 6.5 per cent of GDP with centre's target being 4.5 per cent, and that for the states, 2.5 per cent. The combined debt to GDP ratio was to be reduced to 55 per cent. The ratio of interest payment to revenue receipts for the centre was targeted to be brought down to 48 per cent within a period of five years and to 35 per cent in the long run. The target for the states in this case was set at 18 per cent.

4.4 The fiscal adjustment called for achieving these targets required raising the combined tax-GDP ratio to 17.7 per cent with centre's tax-GDP ratio at 10.3 per cent. The aggregate revenue receipts to GDP ratio in the EFC's plan for restructuring were to be brought close to 20 per cent. On the expenditure side, with reference to the combined revenue expenditure, a reduction of 2.37 percentage points of GDP was planned with a corresponding increase in capital expenditures of a marginally higher magnitude. Evidently, there has been considerable slippage in achieving these targets by both levels of governments. Although the 2004-05 accounts data would become available only later, as per 2002-03 data, the combined revenue deficit of the centre and states was about 6.7 per cent and the debt-GDP ratio was about 76 per cent of GDP [1]. While failure in achieving the stipulated targets to some extent was due to deficiency in revenue effort and slackness in expenditure control, there was also a slowdown in economic growth during the first three years of the EFC reference period. The nominal growth rates in respect of GDP at current market prices in the four years during 2000-01 to 2003-04 were 7.9, 9.2, 8.2 and 12.3 per cent. The EFC had assumed a trend nominal growth rate of 13 per cent. If centre's fiscal deficit finally turns out, as estimated in the budget for 2004-05, to be 4.4 per cent of GDP, it would be fractionally lower than what was stipulated by the EFC.

4.5 There has been some notable improvement in the institutional environment that can support fiscal reforms. The central government has enacted a Fiscal Responsibility and Management Act (FRBMA) in 2003, which had, under its rules, set the target for eliminating revenue deficit by 2007-08, and reducing fiscal deficit to 3 per cent of GDP. The July 2004 budget has ensured that the target year is shifted to 2008-09.. The states of Karnataka, Kerala, Tamil Nadu, Punjab, and Uttar Pradesh have enacted fiscal responsibility legislations. Many states have drawn up their medium term reform programs with specific monitorable targets in the context of the Medium Term Fiscal Reform Facility instituted on the basis of EFC's recommendations. We note that these changes are likely to contribute to more effective and transparent fiscal management.

4.6 Restructuring public finances aimed at macroeconomic stabilization and achieving revenue account balance requires a broad analytical framework. The impact of the size and composition of government expenditure on growth, inflation, interest rate and the external account has to be considered in a framework that takes into account relevant inter relationships and feedbacks. The structure of public finances relates, apart from other features, to the size and composition of expenditure. Government expenditure as a proportion of GDP is smaller in India in comparison to many other countries. Getting the right size and the right composition of government expenditure with a view to facilitating achievement of highest attainable growth rates, and meeting governments' social obligations including poverty reduction and provision of health and education should be considered integral to any plan for restructuring public finances. This requires increasing public spending in social and economic infrastructure for accelerating growth while reducing the overall fiscal imbalance.

Views of the Central and State Governments

4.7 In their memoranda as also in their discussions with the Commission, most state governments have acknowledged the need for restructuring public finances. Some states have suggested that monitoring of the progress of restructuring should be done by an independent agency and not by the central government. Several specific suggestions were made by them. Some of the more commonly expressed suggestions are listed below.

(i) In regard to plan assistance, the states have suggested that the grant-loan ratio in the case of general category states be modified from the present 30: 70 to 50:50. In some suggestions, the ratio of 70:30 has also been suggested. In the case of the special category states, the suggestion in some cases is to raise the grant component to 100 per cent instead of the present 90:10 ratio;

(ii) In lending by the central to the state governments, a floating interest rate should be used, and the states should be allowed greater access to the market;

(iii) All centrally sponsored schemes should to be transferred to the states along with funds;

(iv) The distinction between plan and non-plan expenditure should be abolished as it leads to unbalanced prioritization of financial resources that ignores the need for maintenance expenditures;

(v) In the State Fiscal Reform Facility, there should be no withholding of assessed gap grants;

(vi) There is a need to restructure state level public enterprises;

(vii) Following the constitutional amendments regarding rural and urban local bodies, there has been greater demand for resources by them, and states have come under tremendous financial pressure. Any restructuring should take a view covering all the three tiers of governments.

(viii) Review of tax assignment should include the assignment of services to the states.

4.8 The central government, in its memorandum, referred to the report of the Task Force appointed in the context of the FRBMA, which has a bearing on issues related to restructuring of central finances. The Task Force has recommended a path of adjustment that emphasizes a revenue-led, front loaded fiscal consolidation, which augments capital expenditure relative to GDP. Similar views are also expressed in the fiscal policy strategy statement brought out along with the 2004-05 budget as required under the FRBMA. In formulating our programme for restructuring of public finances, we have taken note of the views, both of the central government and the state governments.

Growth and Macroeconomic Stability

4.9 Macroeconomic stability refers to the capacity of the economy to keep close to levels of output consistent with full employment while inflation is also contained within acceptable limits. In practice, there may be structural rigidities that keep the economy below full employment on a long term basis. Issues of stabilization are, therefore, considered with reference to growth of 'potential' or trend levels of output. Measurement of potential output requires that cyclical variations are removed to identify the level of output along its long term path. In a period of recession, real output may fall below potential output. In a period of expansion, inflation may exceed its long term levels. Both departures constitute a threat to stability. The objective of stabilization is to keep the economy growing close to its long term growth path while also keeping the inflation rate within acceptable limits.

4.10 In a stable situation, the economy would have a built-in capacity to return to its long term path. In the context of fiscal policy, this capacity is provided by automatic stabilizers. Automatic stabilizers exist if the structure of public finances is such that the responsiveness of taxes is larger than that of expenditures following a change in nominal output. Thus, in an inflationary situation, taxes will withdraw more from the expenditure stream than what increased government expenditures would put in, and there will be a net contraction in aggregate expenditures, thereby dampening the cycle. In a recessionary situation, government expenditures contribute more to the expenditures than taxation withdraws, thereby reducing the impact of recession. If automatic responses are not adequate, discretionary fiscal interventions are called for to bring about stabilization. The Reserve Bank of India [2] in its Report on Currency and Finance for 2001-02, had estimated that the elasticity of receipts of the combined government sector is 1.07 whereas that for combined non-interest expenditure is 1.06. Since the difference in the two response coefficients is small, automatic stabilizers in India may be weak. Effective discretionary action is therefore required for stabilization.

4.11 In considering the issue of growth with stabilization, there is a need to examine (a) whether potential output along its growth path remains persistently below full employment levels, and (b) whether actual output in any given year is above or below the growth path of potential output. In both cases, the structure of public finances and the management of fiscal policy have a role to play. When the long run growth path is below full employment levels, it is desirable to design public finances to remove the structural constraints such as supply bottlenecks and bring potential output closer to full employment levels. In this context, the structure of government expenditure, particularly the share of capital expenditure and its allocation becomes important. In regard to the second issue, in achieving stabilization, the management of aggregate government demand in response to the cyclical movements of potential output along its growth path becomes relevant.

4.12 The manner of financing government expenditures also affects stabilization and growth. Governments have to resort to borrowing, i.e. fiscal deficit to the extent their expenditures are not covered by the revenue and non-debt capital receipts. Excessive dependence on domestic market borrowing can push the interest rates, while excessive dependence on borrowing from the central bank can unduly accelerate the inflation rate. The use of external borrowing under certain circumstances can put pressure on the exchange rate. Fiscal deficit also needs to be viewed as consisting of two components: a structural or long term component and a cyclical component reflecting deviation from the long run average. The cyclical or the temporary component of fiscal deficit may be used to stabilize fluctuations around the trend growth of output. Fiscal deficits in India are pre-dominantly structural in nature and the cyclical component is small in magnitude [3].

4.13 Our fiscal reform strategy centers on growth. Growth depends, among other factors, on the rate of investment which, in turn, depends on the saving rate. The saving rate depends, among other factors, on government's revenue deficit, which amounts to government's net dis-saving. In other words, the aggregate saving rate, consisting of the saving rate of the household sector, the private corporate sector, and the government sector, remains less than what is potentially achievable as long as government is contributing negatively, i.e., drawing upon the saving of the private sector to finance consumption expenditure. We review below the long term profile of growth, as well as that of the saving-investment rates, focusing on the experience of the nineties, with a view to highlighting the deleterious effects of government dis-savings on growth.

4.14 Chart 4.1 depicts the growth rates derived of trend levels of output along with actual annual growth of GDP at factor cost at constant 1993-94 prices from 1950-51 to 2002-03. The analysis is with reference to GDP at factor cost with a view to focusing on the performance in respect of growth of output. Indirect taxes net of subsidies are fiscal instruments that take GDP at factor cost to GDP at market prices. The trend growth has been estimated by using a statistical filter [4]. Chart 4.1 shows that a long term cyclical path has been followed by output where the trend growth fell from a little below 4.5 per cent to about 3.3 per cent in the early seventies, after which there was a rise bringing the trend growth to levels above 6 per cent in the mid-nineties. It is the fall in the trend growth rate to below 5 per cent since then that should be our primary current concern.

Chart 4.1

Growth Rates of Actual and Trend GDP at Constant Prices

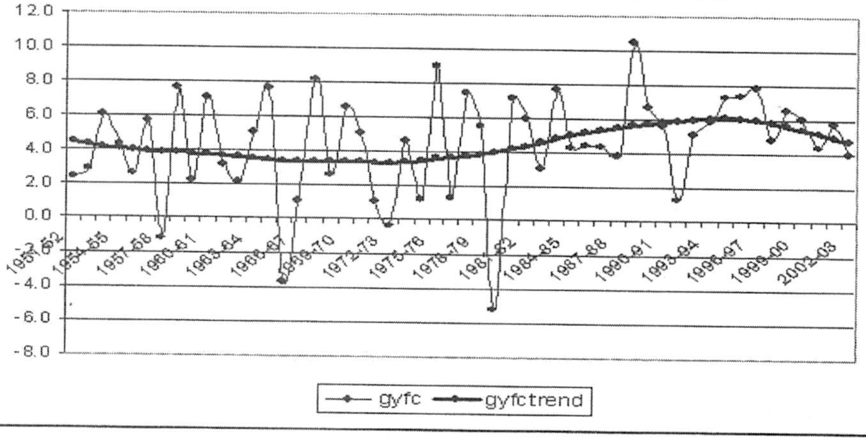

4.15 It may also be seen that the amplitude of variation from trend growth rate has come down in the late nineties. A corresponding analysis of actual and trend inflation rates indicates that the trend inflation rate during 1999-00 to 2002-03 has come down marginally below 5 per cent, although actual inflation rate was even lower remaining below 4 per cent. These clearly were signs of recession that had continued until 2002-03. Table 4.1 gives the actual, trend, and the residual components of growth and inflation from 1990-91 to 2002-03. Following the strong recovery of agriculture in 2003-04 and the upturn in industry in both 2003-04 and 2004-05, the overall growth rate during 2003-04 and 2004-05 is estimated to be above 8 per cent and 6 per cent, respectively. To achieve a growth rate of above 7 per cent on a sustained basis, the investment rate has to increase to levels equal to or above those achieved in the mid-nineties. The saving rate also has to go up correspondingly.

4.16 Table 4.2 gives the saving rate of the household, private corporate, and the public sector. Table 4.3 provides the rate of gross domestic investment for private and public sectors. Looking at the public sector saving rate, it is clear that it became negative in 1998-99 and the magnitude of negative savings went on increasing until 2001-02. Within it, dis-saving of the government, consisting of administrative and departmental enterprises showed a sharp deterioration from 1.7 per cent of GDP in

Table 4.1

Growth and Inflation Rates: Trends and Actuals

(per cent)

Year	Actual growth in output*	Trend$ growth in output	Deviation from trend growth	Actual inflation rate**	Trend inflation rate	Deviation from trend inflation rate
1990-91	5.57	5.83	-0.26	10.50	9.65	0.85
1991-92	1.30	5.90	-4.60	13.81	9.46	4.35
1992-93	5.12	5.98	-0.86	8.72	9.15	-0.43
1993-94	5.90	6.06	-0.16	9.59	8.75	0.84
1994-95	7.25	6.10	1.15	9.43	8.27	1.16
1995-96	7.34	6.08	1.26	9.03	7.75	1.28
1996-97	7.84	6.00	1.84	7.44	7.21	0.23
1997-98	4.79	5.85	-1.06	6.67	6.68	0.01
1998-99	6.51	5.66	0.85	7.94	6.17	1.77
1999-00	6.06	5.45	0.61	3.94	5.70	-1.76
2000-01	4.37	5.21	-0.84	3.49	5.30	-1.81
2001-02	5.78	4.98	0.80	3.88	4.98	-1.10
2002-03	3.98	4.74	-0.76	3.46	4.72	-1.26

Source (Basic Data):National Accounts Statistics

* **Output refers to GDP at factor cost.**

** **Inflation refers to implicit price deflator of GDP at factor cost.**

$ **Trend is calculated using Hodrick-Prescott filter covering 1950-51 to 2002-03 data.**

1996-97 to 6.2 per cent in 2001-02. The aggregate saving rate had peaked in 1995-96 at 25.2 per cent. In 1998-99, it reached its lowest level in recent years at 21.5 per cent. Correspondingly, the investment rate had peaked in 1995-96 and reached its lowest level in recent years at 22.6 per cent in 1998-99. The three years in the mid-nineties provide some evidence for the kind of saving and investment rates required for a 7 plus growth. The three years covering 1994-95 to 1996-97 had an average investment rate of about 26 per cent and domestic saving rate of about 24.7 per cent. In contrast during 2000-01 to 2002-03, the investment rate on average was 23.6 per cent and the average saving rate was 23.8 per cent. There has been a persistent fall in public investment in the nineties. The rate of gross domestic capital formation in the public sector fell from an average of 10.1 per cent of GDP during 1985-1990 to 5.7 in 2002-03. Since private investment was increasing up to the mid-nineties, it made up for the fall in the public sector investment. However, after 1995-96, the private corporate sector investment also fell.

4.17 There are four main features that can be highlighted in comparing the growth-saving-investment profile of the mid-nineties with that of the first three years of the new decade.

i. In the mid-nineties, the average growth of GDP at factor cost was 7.5 per cent per annum, which fell to an average of 4.7 per cent during 2000-03;

ii. The public sector saving rate fell during this period from an average level of 1.8 per cent to -2.3 percent of GDP, amounting to a fall of 4.1

Table 4.2

Gross Domestic Saving at Current Prices as per cent of GDP

(per cent)

Year	House-hold	Private corporate Sector	Private Sector (2+3)	Public Sector	Total (4+5)
1	2	3	4	5	6
Average (1985-86 to 1989-90)	16.03	1.96	17.99	2.39	20.38
1990-91	19.33	2.67	22.00	1.10	23.10
1991-92	16.96	3.11	20.07	1.97	22.04
1992-93	17.51	2.67	20.18	1.59	21.77
1993-94	18.42	3.48	21.90	0.63	22.53
1994-95	19.68	3.48	23.16	1.66	24.82
1995-96	18.19	4.93	23.12	2.03	25.15
1996-97	17.05	4.47	21.52	1.67	23.19
1997-98	17.63	4.17	21.80	1.33	23.13
1998-99	18.77	3.74	22.51	-0.99	21.52
1999-00	20.88	4.35	25.23	-1.04	24.19
2000-01	21.93	4.12	26.05	-2.31	23.74
2001-02	22.74	3.46	26.20	-2.75	23.45
2002-03	22.65	3.41	26.06	-1.85	24.21

Source (Basic data): National Income Accounts, CSO

percentage points;

iii. The public sector investment fell by 1.9 percentage points from an average level of 7.8 percent of GDP to 5.9 per cent and the overall investment rate fell by 2.2 percentage points from an average level of 25.8 per cent to 23.6 per cent. The corporate investment fell from a high of 9.8 per cent of GDP in 1995-96 to 4.8 per cent in 2002-03;

iv. The excess of gross domestic investment over gross domestic saving between the two periods, showing the extent of reliance on current account deficit, fell from 1.4 percentage points to -0.2 percentage points.

4.18 For increasing and sustaining the growth rate at 7 per cent, an aggregate investment rate of 28 percent is required on the assumption that the incremental capital-output ratio (ICOR) is 4. The Tenth Plan had envisaged an average investment rate of 28.4 per cent to attain a growth of 8 per cent by assuming a lower ICOR. Such levels of total investment would require increasing levels of both public and private investment relative to GDP. The restructuring plan suggested by us, as detailed later in this chapter, provides for a tangible increase in government investment and savings relative to GDP.

Issues of Equitable Growth

4.19 In considering the issue of equitable

Table 4.3

Gross Capital Formation at Current Market Prices as per cent to GDP

(per cent)

Year	Public sector	Private corporate	Household	Private sector (3+4)	Total (2+5)	Errors& omissions	Adjusted total (6+7)
1	2	3	4	5	6	7	8
Average (1985-86 to 1989-90)	10.11	4.33	8.83	13.16	23.27	-0.56	22.71
1990-91	9.34	4.13	10.60	14.73	24.07	2.23	26.30
1991-92	8.82	5.66	7.45	13.11	21.93	0.62	22.55
1992-93	8.55	6.46	8.78	15.24	23.79	-0.17	23.62
1993-94	8.24	5.61	7.40	13.01	21.25	1.84	23.09
1994-95	8.71	6.91	7.76	14.67	23.38	2.62	26.00
1995-96	7.66	9.58	9.29	18.87	26.53	0.37	26.90
1996-97	7.03	8.05	6.69	14.74	21.77	2.71	24.48
1997-98	6.61	7.97	7.99	15.96	22.57	2.02	24.59
1998-99	6.58	6.39	8.41	14.80	21.38	1.20	22.58
1999-00	6.94	6.46	10.26	16.72	23.66	1.67	25.33
2000-01	6.29	5.06	11.27	16.33	22.62	1.73	24.35
2001-02	5.83	4.88	11.60	16.48	22.31	0.83	23.14
2002-03	5.68	4.80	12.34	17.14	22.82	0.45	23.27

Source (Basic data): National Income Accounts, CSO

growth, we look at three of its manifestations. Inter-state disparities in levels and growth of per capita GSDP indicate disparities in fiscal capacity. Disparities in per capita government expenditures, particularly those in priority sectors like education, health, and water supply and sanitation indicate how lower fiscal capacities translate into differences in governments' fiscal intervention in the provision of services. By examining the inter-state pattern in the human development index, we look at the disparities in some of the relevant outcomes that may be influenced by fiscal intervention among other factors.

4.20 Table 4.4 shows trend growth rates of GSDP at 1993-94 prices. In general, the higher income states have grown at higher rates. There are some significant changes between average growth rates in the eighties and the nineties. In the case of Punjab and Haryana, growth has come down although Punjab has the highest per capita GSDP considering the average over 1999-00 to 2001-02. Among the poorer states, cases where the growth rates fell in the nineties as compared to the eighties are Assam, Bihar, Orissa, Uttar Pradesh, and Rajasthan.

4.21 Table 4.5 presents summary indicators of disparity in comparable per capita GSDP over 1993-94 to 2001-02. The ratio of minimum GSDP per capita (that of Bihar) and maximum GSDP per capita (which, after excluding Goa, has pertained to either Maharashtra or Punjab in different years) decreased from 30.5 in 1993-94 to 26.1 in 1995-96, after which the ratio improved until 1998-99. It again declined reaching a level of 26.5 per cent in 2001-02. In the weighted coefficient of variation also there is some reduction

Table 4.4

Trend Growth Rates of GSDP at Constant Prices (1993-94): State Series#

	1980-81 to 1989-90	1990-91 to 2001-02		1980-81 to 1989-90	1990-91 to 2001-02
Andhra Pradesh	5.35	5.60	Madhya Pradesh.*	4.02	4.81
Arunachal Pradesh	8.14	4.68	Maharashtra	5.64	6.27
Assam	3.50	2.53	Manipur	5.12	5.35
Bihar*	4.60	3.79	Meghalaya	4.94	5.81
Goa	4.79	8.40	Orissa	5.01	4.21
Gujarat	5.05	7.20	Punjab	5.44	4.66
Haryana	6.21	4.72	Rajasthan	6.01	5.85
Himachal Pradesh	4.70	6.09	Tamil Nadu	5.18	6.26
J & K**	2.80	4.89	Tripura	5.29	8.94
Karnataka	5.36	7.17	Uttar Pradesh*	4.80	3.84
Kerala	3.16	5.51	West Bengal	4.70	6.93

Source(Basic data): CSO

* **These states were divided in 2000. Data relate to the combined states.**

** **Upto 2000-01**

\# **Pertains to State GSDP series**

witnessed after 1995-96; and it rose again after 1999-2000. The Gini coefficient, given in Table 4.5, reflects income inequality assuming that all persons within a state are located at the mean income for that state. It therefore captures inter-state inequality and not intra-state inequality [5]. The Gini coefficient shows progressive increase in income disparity till 1999-00, except in 1996-97. Thereafter, it has shown a decline. It may, however, be noted that the value of the Gini coefficient lies between 0.1917 and 0.2173.

Table 4.5

Disparity in Per Capita GSDP

	Ratio of minimum to maximum Per capita GSDP* (per cent)	Coefficient of variation (per cent)	Gini coefficient #
	Weighted**		
1993-94	30.527	34.549	0.19170
1994-95	29.697	35.031	0.19262
1995-96	26.107	37.892	0.20719
1996-97	27.586	36.781	0.20708
1997-98	28.282	35.933	0.20853
1998-99	30.018	35.898	0.21062
1999-00	28.899	37.417	0.21732
2000-01	28.233	37.638	0.21034
2001-02	26.534	37.877	0.21016

Source (Basic Data): CSO

*** excluding Goa;**

**** weighted by population**

 # Relates to 14 states, i.e. Assam and the general category states excluding Goa; Gini coefficient is calculated with respect to state GSDP series at constant 1993-94 prices. For 2000-01 and 2001-02, the divided states are clubbed together to maintain comparability.

4.22 The inter-state pattern of per capita government expenditures, particularly in social and economic services shows the prevailing disparities in respect of publically provided services. Table 4.6 shows per capita average state government expenditures over the period 1998-99 to 2000-01 in general, social, and economic services. In the general services, interest payment, pensions, and lotteries are excluded. The larger states are considered here focusing on the general category states except Goa but including Assam. Within the social sector expenditures, per capita expenditures on education, health, and water supply and sanitation are also shown. States are arranged in ascending order of per capita GSDP. The general pattern is that states with low per capita GSDPs also have low per capita expenditures. However, there are several exceptions. The ratio of minimum to maximum expenditure and that of minimum to mean expenditure indicates that in the case of general category states, the minimum expenditure is only 30 per cent of maximum expenditure, excluding Goa, and it is 60 per cent of average expenditure. In the case of social services the minimum per capita expenditure is 36 per cent of the maximum and 47 per cent of the mean. The corresponding relations for economic services are 16 per cent and 34 per cent. In the case of education, the minimum to mean ratio is 57 per cent. The corresponding figures are 41 per cent and 34 per cent for health and water supply and sanitation. These figures cover both non-plan and plan revenue expenditures.

4.23 The Planning Commission prepares estimates of state wise index of human development (HDI). This is available for

Table 4.6

Per capita expenditure on General, Social & Economic Services

(Rs.)

States	1998-99 to 2000-01			1998-99 to 2000-01		
	GEN	SOC	ECO	EDN	HTH	WSS
Bihar	189.1	474.0	204.9	311.1	50.9	19.1
Orissa	224.2	931.2	406.5	463.1	94.7	56.2
Uttar Pradesh	267.5	555.8	324.9	340.4	63.4	20.0
Assam	334.4	929.9	369.3	615.2	92.2	59.2
Madhya Pradesh	235.6	781.3	469.0	344.5	86.2	63.4
Rajasthan	265.4	1020.7	405.0	545.3	128.3	111.5
West Bengal	262.4	958.2	392.6	512.3	136.8	42.5
Andhra Pradesh	255.8	1004.1	634.3	411.7	118.2	57.7
Kerala	318.2	1254.8	716.5	713.3	172.3	52.3
Karnataka	279.2	1083.9	755.8	558.3	135.7	60.3
Tamil Nadu	336.4	1240.9	685.3	651.5	154.4	38.3
Gujarat	274.6	1331.3	1285.7	664.4	154.3	39.0
Haryana	320.9	1145.4	902.4	587.6	122.1	102.1
Maharashtra	624.4	1276.1	647.7	730.9	131.7	79.7
Punjab	533.6	1220.5	733.9	716.3	221.1	55.0
coeff of variation	36.88	25.24	45.95	26.30	34.93	45.11
Min/Max	0.30	0.36	0.16	0.43	0.23	0.17
Min/Mean	0.60	0.47	0.34	0.57	0.41	0.34

Source: **State Finance Accounts**

Key: **GEN = General services excluding interest payments and pensions.**

SOC: **Social services; ECO: Economic services; EDN=Education; HTH=Health; WSS= Water supply and sanitation. States are arranged in Order of per capita GSDP; Bihar,U.P., and M.P.are taken as undivided states**

1981 and 1991. The UNDP office in Delhi prepared, for the benefit of the Commission, the HDI for 2001[6]. According to these estimates the lowest ranked state is Bihar, followed by Uttar Pradesh, Orissa, and Madhya Pradesh. There is a clear positive relationship, as expected, between per capita GSDP and the HDI. At the same time, states, which have provided more in terms of per capita budgetary expenditures on health and education, have ranks that are higher than their relative position in the ranking of per capita GSDP. This is so also for the special category states. Based on the relative ranking of an index of infrastructure [7], the states have also been grouped into five categories, as shown in Table 4.7. While the HDI reflects access to social services, the infrastructure index reflects access to physical infrastructure. Together, these capture two different dimensions of disparities. It is notable that while the special category states do better in the HDI, their position in terms of access to infrastructure is a major handicap. For the low income states like Bihar and Rajasthan, both HDI and the infrastructure index show a handicap.

Table 4.7

States Grouped According to Selected Indicators

Human Development Index	Infrastructure Index
High Goa, Kerala, Maharashtra, Mizoram	**High** Goa, Maharashtra, Punjab
High Middle Gujarat, Manipur, Nagaland, Punjab, Sikkim, Tamil Nadu	**High Middle** Gujarat, Haryana, Kerala, Tamil Nadu
Middle Andhra Pradesh, Arunachal Pradesh, Haryana, Himachal Pradesh, Meghalaya, Karnataka, Tripura, West Bengal, Uttaranchal	**Middle** Andhra Pradesh, Karnataka
Lower Middle Assam, Chhattisgarh, J &K, Jharkhand, Rajasthan	**Lower Middle** Himachal Pradesh, Madhya Pradesh, Orissa, U.P., Uttaranchal,West Bengal
Low Bihar, Madhya Pradesh, Orissa, Uttar Pradesh	**Low** Arunachal Pradesh, Manipur, Meghalaya, Jharkhand, Mizoram, Nagaland, Assam, Chhattisgarh, Sikkim, Tripura, J&K, Bihar, Rajasthan

Source: UNDP for HDI and IDFC for Index of Infrastructure

4.24 Levels of income and its growth depend on many factors that include states' own efforts and policies, the inter-state distribution of private capital, domestic and foreign, and the inter-state pattern of the benefit of central investment and current expenditures. In some respects, the increasing globalization and market orientation may result in increasing the relative flow of funds towards the more developed states partly because of the pro-active policy stance and partly because of the availability of infrastructure facilities. Much of the required correction has to come from the distribution and allocation of plan funds. On our part, besides building into the devolution formula appropriate criteria in the scheme of transfers, we have also recommended grants, based to some degree on the application of the equalization principle to expenditures on education and health. The benefit would accrue mainly to the states, which have relatively lower ranks in the HDI.

Trends in Combined Government Finances

a. Fiscal Imbalance

4.25 We have examined the main trends in the combined government finances over the 15-year period from 1987-88 to 2001-02. The reference to the period in the late eighties highlights changes from peak levels of tax-GDP ratio as also peak past levels of fiscal deficit. Fiscal imbalances as indicated by revenue, fiscal, and primary deficits, which were at high levels at the end of the eighties, showed improvement in the mid-nineties, but deteriorated since then. As indicated by annexure 4.1 and chart 4.2, revenue and fiscal deficits as percentage of GDP were higher in 1999-2002 on average as compared to their levels in the late eighties. Revenue deficit shows the most persistent deterioration, increasing by more than double, from the average of 3 per cent of GDP in 1987-1990 to 6.7 per cent in 1999-2002. It had declined to 3.2 per cent in 1995-96, after which it steadily climbed up.

4.26 In the case of fiscal deficits, there is a deterioration of 0.7 percentage points. At the end of the eighties, the average level of fiscal deficit was 8.8 per cent of GDP, which increased to 9.5 percent in 1999-2002. However, there was an improvement in the mid-nineties. In 1996-97, fiscal deficit had fallen to 6.3 per cent of GDP. The primary deficit was 4.9 per cent of GDP on average at the end of the eighties. It fell to 1.1 per cent in 1996-97, after which it deteriorated but the average over 1999-2002 was still lower than that in 1987-1990. Thus, the primary deficit as percentage of GDP was lower by 1.2 percentage points as compared to its average level in 1987-1990. The ratio of revenue to fiscal deficits indicates the 'quality' of fiscal deficit by highlighting the proportion of government borrowing that does not lead to creation of assets, which can give returns in the future to service the borrowing. This ratio has increased from about 34 per cent at the end of the eighties to 68 per cent on average during 1999-2002. This underlies a major weakness in the profile of government finances, indicating that a progressively larger share of borrowing is being spent on consumption. The main reasons given for the fiscal deterioration after the mid-nineties include the revision of salaries and pensions in the wake of the recommendations of the Fifth Central Pay Commission, erosion in the buoyancy of central indirect taxes, and the high nominal interest rates towards the late nineties combined with a fall in the inflation rate in subsequent years. The fall in the nominal interest rates towards the end of the nineties has however had some beneficial effects on expenditures.

b. Trends in Combined Revenues and Expenditures

4.27 Table 4.8 shows the structural

Chart 4.2

Revenue, Fiscal, and Primary Deficits as per cent of GDP

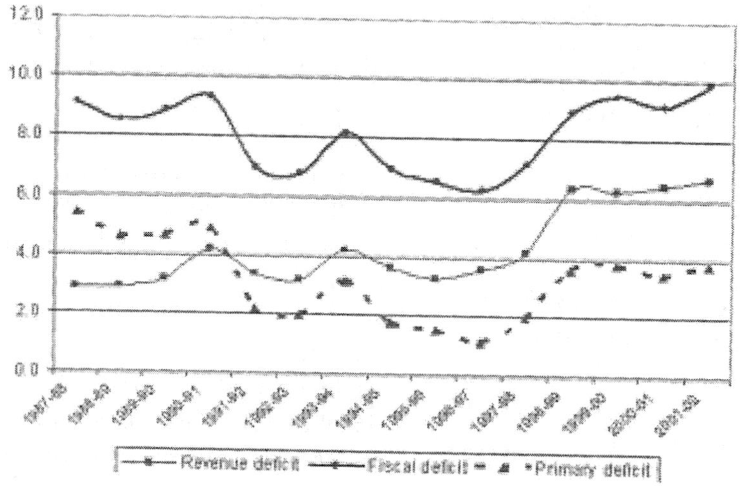

changes in some of the major heads of the combined revenues and expenditures of the central and state governments after netting out all intergovernmental flows. The aggregate tax-GDP ratio fell from a level of 16 per cent of GDP towards the end of the eighties to about 14.4 per cent, i.e. a fall of 1.6 percentage points. The fall in the ratio of total revenue receipts was of the same order indicating that there was no perceptible change in the contribution of non-tax revenues relative to GDP. In the case of revenue expenditure, the average revenue expenditure increased from 21.7 per cent of GDP to 23.6 percentage points showing a rise of 1.8 percentage points. This was mainly accounted for by the increase in interest payments relative to GDP, which increased from 3.9 to 5.8 per cent. Capital expenditure fell by 2.8 percentage points, from 6.1 to 3.3 per cent of GDP on average during 1999-2002.

4.28 The size and composition of tax revenues are of major importance in the structure of government finances. An examination of the evolution of the tax-GDP ratio since 1950-51 indicates that starting from a level of 6.3 per cent of GDP in 1950-51, the tax-GDP ratio steadily increased to 16.1 per cent in 1987-88. Much of this increase was due to growth in indirect taxes. In 1950-51, indirect taxes amounted to 4 per cent of GDP whereas the direct taxes accounted for 2.4 per cent of GDP. Since then indirect taxes increased to a peak level of 14 per cent in 1987-88 whereas direct taxes remained less than 3 per cent until 1994-95. As a result of tax reforms, the indirect taxes relative to GDP started coming down whereas that of direct taxes started increasing. But the magnitude of increase in the direct taxes was less than the fall in indirect taxes. In consequence, the overall tax-GDP ratio fell from its peak in 1987-88 to 14.4 per cent in 2001-02. Table 4.9 shows decade-wise buoyancies of direct and indirect taxes for the central and state governments. The buoyancy of central direct tax revenues, except for the seventies, was less than 1 until the eighties. It was with the direct tax reforms in the nineties, which included widening of the tax base and reduction in tax rates, that the buoyancy picked up to reach a level of 1.3 for the period 1990-91 to 2001-02. The central indirect taxes followed a reverse course.

Table 4.8

Structural Changes in Combined Finances of Central and State Governments

(Per cent to GDP at Market Prices)

	Tax revenues	Interest payments	Capital expenditure	Revenue Receipts	Revenue expenditure	Interest payments to revenue receipts (per cent)
Average (1987-88 to 1989-90)[I]	16.0	3.9	6.1	18.7	21.7	21.0
Average (1999-00 to 2001-02)[II]	14.4	5.8	3.3	17.1	23.6	34.0
(II-I)	**-1.6**	**1.9**	**-2.8**	**-1.6**	**1.8**	**13.0**

Source (Basic data): Indian Public Finance Statistics

Maintaining a buoyancy of more than 1 until the end of the eighties, their buoyancy with respect to GDP fell significantly below 1 in the nineties. This followed from the reduction in the tax rates of both Union excise duties, and even more sharply in the case of the customs duties. Given the higher weight of central indirect taxes, the overall tax-GDP ratio fell. The buoyancy of state indirect taxes also fell in the nineties although it remained higher than that of the central indirect taxes. The decade-wise buoyancies of state indirect taxes show a noticeable decline in the eighties and nineties although these have remained higher than 1.

c. Growth in Debt: Centre and States

Table 4.9

Decade-wise Buoyancies of Central and State Tax Revenues

	1950-51 to 1959-60	1960-61 to 1969-70	1970-71 to 1979-80	1980-81 to 1989-90	1991-92 to 2001-02	1950-51 to 2001-02
Central Taxes: Gross Revenues						
Direct	0.94	0.96	1.18	0.94	1.30	1.09
Indirect	1.65	1.24	1.30	1.20	0.72	1.16
Total	**1.38**	**1.15**	**1.27**	**1.14**	**0.89**	**1.14**
States Own Tax Revenues						
Direct	-8.43	3.61	-6.32	-8.20	-4.34	-2.46
Indirect	1.41	1.37	1.37	1.11	1.02	1.23
Total	**1.39**	**1.17**	**1.35**	**1.11**	**1.02**	**1.17**
Total Tax Revenues						
Direct	1.05	0.79	1.16	0.96	1.26	1.03
Indirect	1.55	1.29	1.33	1.16	0.86	1.19
Total	**1.38**	**1.16**	**1.30**	**1.13**	**0.93**	**1.15**

Source (Basic data): Indian Public Finance Statistics and National Income Accounts

Direct taxes in the case of states contribute a negligible share in total tax revenues. Negative buoyancy implies a fall in absolute terms.

4.29 The combined debt-GDP ratio of the central and state governments at the end of 2002-03 was about 76 per cent of GDP, subject to some qualifications. First, the government budget documents give the centre's external debt as evaluated at the historical exchange rates, i.e. exchange rates in the years in which the debt was incurred. Since the exchange rate has depreciated over the years, it makes a difference if external debt is evaluated at the current exchange rates. This difference was as large as nearly 11 per cent in 1991-92. However, over the years, this difference has steadily come down. In 2002-03, if external debt is evaluated at the current exchange rates, about 5.6 per cent would need to be added to the debt-GDP ratio. This would take the combined debt-GDP ratio in 2002-03 to 81.6 per cent. The second qualification is that in accounting for the liabilities of the state governments, certain liabilities of reserve funds and deposits are not included. In 2002-03, about 3.4 percentage points of GDP needs to be added on this account, taking the overall debt-GDP ratio to 85 per cent. These figures do not include contingent liabilities, which amount to more than 11 per cent of GDP.

4.30 Even if we focus on the more conventional budgetary figure of debt without these qualifications, it is striking how the growth in debt-GDP ratio has accelerated since 1996-97 when it was 56.3 per cent, which was only marginally above the EFC's stipulated target. During the period of 1995-96 to 2002-03, the combined debt-GDP ratio rose from 56.3 per cent to 76 per cent in 2002-03, i.e. an increase of a little less than 20 percentage points in a span of 6 years. This is an unprecedented increase in the growth of the debt-GDP ratio in such a short span of time. One way of looking at the source of increase in the debt-GDP ratio during this period is to decompose the increase in terms of the contribution of cumulated primary deficits and that of the differential between growth and interest rates [8]. For three consecutive years, viz., 2000-01, 2001-02, and 2002-03, the nominal growth rate fell below the effective interest rate. In these years, instead of absorbing the impact of primary deficits, the growth-interest differential, being negative, worked in the reverse by adding to the debt-GDP ratio. For the period 1996-97 to 2002-03, therefore the excess of growth over interest could not absorb any part of the impact of cumulated primary deficits, the benefit in the first three years being negated by the opposite effect in the latter three years. The entire increase therefore was due to accumulation of primary deficits, which remained unabsorbed by any excess of growth over interest rates.

4.31 High levels of debt-GDP ratio result in high interest payments relative to revenue receipts. Since interest payments are committed expenditures, revenue deficits are bound to increase when revenue receipts to GDP ratios remain sluggish. This has the effect of lowering the saving rate on the one hand and increasing the fiscal deficit on the other to maintain primary expenditures. Eventually, these changes have the potential of developing into a spiral of rising fiscal deficits, debt, interest payments, revenue deficits, and back to a higher fiscal deficit. This gives rise to the issue of sustainability of debt.

Fiscal Deficit and Debt: Issues of Sustainability

4.32 Government debt is the outcome of accumulation of borrowing that is used to finance fiscal deficits. If the revenue account is balanced, the entire fiscal deficit would be spent on capital expenditures. Such investment can provide direct as well as indirect returns. The direct returns are in the form of interest receipts or dividends. The indirect returns arise when government investment stimulates growth, which results in higher revenue receipts. Debt becomes a problem when the increase in revenue receipts, whether direct or indirect, is not adequate to cover the interest liabilities that are required to service the debt. When large interest payments, remaining uncovered by an increase in revenue receipts, result in growing revenue deficits, the portion of fiscal deficit that is used for revenue expenditures becomes progressively larger and any revenue increases linked with increased expenditures remain small. Eventually, debt becomes unsustainable.

4.33 While the views of economists differ, the circumstances under which debt, and its increment, i.e. fiscal deficit, become unsustainable have been discussed extensively in the relevant literature. There are three main theoretical perspectives, namely, neo-classical, Ricardian equivalence, and Keynesian. Depending on circumstances and the relevant theoretical perspectives, fiscal deficit may be bad, indifferent, or good. The neo-classical view considers fiscal deficits detrimental to investment and growth, while in the Keynesian paradigm, it constitutes a key policy prescriptive. Under Ricardian equivalence fiscal deficits do not really matter except for smoothening the path of adjustment to expenditure or revenue shocks. While the neo-classical and Ricardian schools focus on the long run, the Keynesian view emphasizes the short run effects.

4.34 In the neoclassical perspective, fiscal deficits will have a detrimental effect on growth if the reduction in government saving, which is equivalent to revenue deficit [8], is not fully offset by a rise in private saving. Besides affecting the overall savings, when there is a net fall in the saving rate, there will be pressure on the interest rate which may crowd out private investment, and therefore adversely affect growth. The neo-classical economists assume that markets clear so that full employment of resources is attained. The Keynesian view argues, particularly when there are unemployed resources, that an increase in autonomous government expenditure, whether investment or consumption, financed by borrowing would cause output to expand through a multiplier process. The traditional Keynesian framework does not distinguish between alternative uses of the fiscal deficit as between government consumption or investment expenditure, nor does it distinguish between alternative sources of financing the fiscal deficit through monetization or external or internal borrowing. Although there is no explicit budget constraint in the analysis by Keynes, subsequent developments that do incorporate the budget constraint show that, as a result, some of the Keynesian conclusions are weakened. In Ricardian equivalence, fiscal deficits are viewed as neutral in terms of their impact on growth. The financing of budgets by deficits amounts only to postponement of taxes. The deficit in any current period is exactly equal to the present value of future taxation that is required to pay off the increment to debt resulting from the deficit. Since government spending must be paid for, whether now or later, the present value of spending must be equal to the present value of tax and non-tax revenues. If household spending decisions are based on the present value of their incomes that takes into account the present value of their future tax liabilities, fiscal deficits would not have an impact on aggregate demand.

4.35 The relevance and applicability of these alternative analytical frameworks depend on the empirical characteristics of a given economy as also the initial conditions. It depends particularly on the saving behavior of the household sector. If consumers are myopic or liquidity constrained, aggregate consumption becomes very sensitive to changes in disposable incomes, and the Keynesian prescriptions may be more applicable. If individuals are rational, fully informed and motivated by altruistic behavior, Ricardian equivalence may have some validity. In general it has been argued that for short term demand management, Keynesian prescriptions apply and for long term growth, the neo-classical view should be considered relevant. The critical difference in these alternative perspectives comes from how the saving of the private sector is affected by the existence of fiscal deficit of a given order. If fiscal deficits are meant to largely finance revenue deficits, there would be a fall in government savings. To some extent, this fall may be offset by an increase in the private savings as their wealth in terms of holding government bonds increases with an increase in fiscal deficit. The latter effect is often much smaller than the former effect [10], and there is a fall in the overall saving rate.

4.36 A review of the performance of different sectors in terms of the saving-investment balance provides one approach to determining the levels of permissible fiscal deficit. In India, it is the household sector that has surplus savings that are absorbed by the private corporate and government sector. These surplus savings are their savings in the financial form. Table 4.10 gives a perspective on the surplus saving of the household sector that is available for use in other sectors. The financial savings of the household sector were roughly of the same order since 1993-94, being in the range of 10-11 per cent of GDP with small variations. Comparing

Table 4.10

Sector-wise Balance in Saving and Investment (per cent to GDP)

(per cent points)

Year	Deficit Sectors		Surplus sector	Difference
	Pub sector	Private corporate sector	Saving of house-hold sector in financial assests	Excess of investment over saving
	Ip-Sp	Ic-Sc	Sh-Ih	I-S
Average(1985-86 to 1989-90)	7.72	2.37	7.20	2.33
1990-91	8.23	1.47	8.73	3.20
1991-92	6.85	2.56	9.51	0.52
1992-93	6.97	3.79	8.73	1.85
1993-94	7.61	2.14	11.03	0.56
1994-95	7.05	3.43	11.92	1.17
1995-96	5.63	4.65	8.90	1.75
1996-97	5.36	3.58	10.35	1.30
1997-98	5.28	3.80	9.64	1.46
1998-99	7.57	2.65	10.36	1.05
1999-00	7.98	2.11	10.62	1.14
2000-01	8.61	0.94	10.66	0.61
2001-02	8.58	1.42	11.14	-0.32
2002-03	7.54	1.39	10.30	-0.92

Source (Basic data): National Income Accounts, CSO

the trend since 1995-96, it is apparent that the public sector has been absorbing a larger part of the financial savings of the household sector. The demand for this surplus by the private corporate sector came down from 4.65 per cent of GDP in 1995-96 to 1.4 per cent in 2002-03. That is why there was no pressure on the interest rates in the late nineties. Once the private sector demand picks up, a growth augmenting scenario would emerge only if the government is able to reduce its revenue deficit. Only then would the interest rates also remain benign. Further, if the government is able to eliminate its revenue deficit, and increase its savings and capital expenditures, demand for private investment would be further strengthened. Studies have shown that government investment in infrastructure crowds-in private investment.

4.37 Questions have been raised whether government debt in India has become unsustainable as it has been rising faster than GDP. For fiscal sustainability, it is required that a rise in fiscal deficit is matched by a rise in the capacity to service the increased debt. It has been argued that from this angle, borrowing for generation of assets may be justified. Apart from the fact that a little less than 70 per cent of borrowing is presently not being spent on capital assets, even where there is capital expenditure, the return on assets is negligible. Even the more indirect return through higher growth to match the growing interest liabilities has not been forthcoming. In fact, the high level of fiscal deficit combined with the rising debt-GDP ratio has led to a fall in the current government expenditures net of interest payments and pensions.

4.38 Considering that borrowing is often the easier option than raising revenues, attempts are often made to set predetermined targets for borrowing to provide an exogenous benchmark for the policy makers. The Maastricht Treaty, for example, has two convergence conditions for the members of the European Monetary Union:(i) country's overall budget deficit for each fiscal year must be equal to or below 3 per cent of the GDP and (ii) a country's stock of public debt must be equal to or less than 60 per cent of the GDP. In the U.K., a 'golden rule' is being followed since 1997 whereby fiscal deficit is kept equal to government investment. In India, also there have been attempts to tie down fiscal deficits to some target levels. The EFC had suggested a fiscal deficit of 6.5 per cent of GDP as the desirable target to be achieved by 2004-05. The Tenth Plan has envisaged the average size of fiscal deficit as 6.8 per cent of GDP during the plan period. The FRBMA targets for the central government have provided a target for fiscal deficit at 3 per cent of GDP be achieved by 2008-09.

4.39 The targets for revenue and fiscal deficits are essential ingredients of a restructuring program. Like the central government, similar targets would need to be fixed for the states, jointly and individually. These targets need to take into account an underlying growth scenario along with levels of interest rates and other macroeconomic parameters. In fixing such targets, it is useful to take into account the determinants of debt dynamics. In this analysis, growth in the debt-GDP ratio depends on two factors: (a) primary deficit to GDP ratio and (b) the excess of growth over interest rate. If growth rate is equal to interest rate, debt relative to GDP would be the outcome of accumulated primary deficits only. However, as long as growth rate is higher than interest rate, it absorbs some of primary deficits being translated into higher debt relative to GDP. On the other hand, if interest rate exceeds growth rate, the debt-GDP ratio would increase as a result of both factors. One critical limitation is that the nominal growth rate (g) and the nominal interest rate (i) cannot in reality be taken as exogenous. In particular, increasing levels of fiscal deficit, particularly when these are for investment, can increase the growth rate while high levels of fiscal deficit can put pressure on interest rates, particularly when the household savings in the financial form are not adequate to cover the demand for those savings from the government leaving enough for the private corporate sector. Using the equation of debt dynamics, under certain assumptions, conditions can be derived that stabilize debt and fiscal deficit relative to GDP. It is assumed that the nominal growth rate (g) and the nominal effective interest rate are given and exogenous. The relevant conditions state [11] that:

(a) The debt-GDP ratio will be stabilized at a level b* where b*= p (1+g)/(g-i).

(b) The fiscal deficit to GDP ratio will be stabilized at f* where f*= p.g/(g-i).

4.40 Indicating the ratio of revenue receipts to GDP indicated by (r), these conditions could be written equivalently, in terms of the ratio of interest payments to revenue receipts (ip)* instead of primary deficit, as follows [12]:

(a) The debt-GDP ratio will be stabilized at a level b* where b*= (ip)*r (1+g)/ i.

(b) The fiscal deficit to GDP ratio will be stabilized at f* where f*= (ip)*r.g/ i.

In the case of states, the ratio of revenue receipts to GSDP and that of interest payment to revenue receipts differ widely across states. Revenues accrue to the states also as transfers. It is more useful to cast the debt-sustainability conditions in terms of the ratio of interest payments to revenue receipts although the two sets of conditions are equivalent.

4.41 In the present Indian context, the FRBMA has fixed a fiscal deficit target for the central government at 3 per cent of GDP. Using relations (a and b), which imply [b*=f*(1+g)/g], it is seen that for this level of fiscal deficit and a nominal growth rate of 12 per cent, the debt-GDP ratio will eventually be stabilized at 28 per cent. At present, the centre's debt-GDP ratio is close to 53 per cent, with external debt measured at historical exchange rates, and not taking into account that part of the NSSF liabilities against which there are assets in the form of state securities and also excluding the Market Stabilization Scheme (MSS) liabilities against which an equal amount of cash balance is held. Since the fiscal deficit target is given by the FRBMA, as long there is an excess of growth over interest rate, a primary deficit can be maintained in the stabilization phase. For a combination of 12 per cent nominal growth rate and 7 per cent interest rate, this would be equal to 1.25 per cent of GDP. We think that a combined fiscal deficit target, relative to GDP, of 6 per cent would be consistent with the availability of savings of the household sector in financial assets, which is of the order of 10 per cent, the desirable level of current account deficit, and the requirements of the corporate sector and the non-departmental public sector undertakings. The transferable savings of the household sector of 10 per cent of GDP combined with an acceptable level of current account deficit of 1.5 per cent would be adequate to provide for a government fiscal deficit of 6 per cent, an absorption by the private corporate sector of 4 per cent, and by non-departmental public enterprises of 1.5 per cent of GDP. When the revenue deficit becomes zero, the entire fiscal deficit would lead to an augmentation of investment with the total investment as percentage of GDP touching a level in the range of 28 to 30 per cent. Of this total, the household sector could invest about 12 per cent of GDP, the private corporate sector, about 8 per cent of GDP, and the public sector, about 8 to 10 per cent of GDP.

4.42 Limiting the combined fiscal deficit at 6 per cent of GDP is also necessary to bring down the ratio of interest payments to revenue receipts from the very high levels of almost 50 per cent in 2002-03 for the centre, 26 per cent for the states, and 37 per cent on their combined account. In the proposed plan for restructuring government finances, these are to be brought down by 2009-10, respectively, to 28 per cent for the centre, 15 per cent for the states, and 22 per cent, on their combined accounts.

4.43 Given the desirability of 6 per cent of GDP as the overall fiscal deficit, as the centre has already fixed a target for its own borrowing at 3 per cent of GDP, a similar level of fiscal deficit for the states considered together can be permitted. Thus, the borrowing of the public sector including the non-departmental enterprises could be of the order of 7.5 per cent. The corresponding debt-GDP ratio for the combined account is set at 56 per cent, with external debt measured at historical exchange rates, which is close to the actual level of combined debt relative to GDP at the end of 1996-97. Targets for individual states can be determined in terms of the ratio of interest payments to revenue receipts by using the conditions specified in para 40. This is discussed in detail in appendix 4.1.

4.44 It may be noted that there is a difference between stabilizing the debt-GDP ratio at the existing levels and stabilizing them at lower levels consistent with sustainability or desirable debt-GDP ratios derived from some considerations of optimality. In fiscal consolidation, two phases can be distinguished: adjustment phase and stabilization phase. In the adjustment phase, the debt-GDP ratio will steadily fall as primary deficit follows a path of adjustment so that the fiscal deficit target of 6 per cent is achieved. After the debt-GDP ratio has fallen to the desirable levels, primary deficit and fiscal deficit will be stabilized.

4.45 Keeping in view these considerations, we recommend that

(i) The overall debt-GDP ratio on the combined account (with external debt measured at historical exchange rates) may be targeted to be brought down to 56 percent of GDP over a period of time. Since the level is estimated to be as high as 81 percent of GDP at the end of 2004-05, it should be brought down to at least 75 per cent by the end of 2009-10.

(ii) The level of combined interest

payments relative to revenue receipts should be brought down from 34 per cent in 2004-05 to 22 per cent in 2009-10, and eventually to about 17 per cent.

(iii) The system of on-lending by the centre to the states should be phased out. The long term goal for the centre and state for the debt-GDP ratio should be 28 per cent each. Their fiscal deficit to GDP ratio targets should be 3 per cent each.

Fiscal Adjustment: 2005-10

4.46 In this section, we discuss the contours of fiscal adjustment up to 2009-10. Clause 3 of the FRBMA provides that the central government shall lay in each financial year before both houses of Parliament, three statements relating to (i) Medium Term Financial Policy Statement (ii) Fiscal Policy Strategy Statement, and (iii) Macroeconomic Framework Statement, which shall contain an assessment regarding (a) growth in GDP (b) fiscal balance of the Union government as reflected in the revenue balance and gross fiscal balance, and (c) external sector balance of the economy as reflected in the current account balance in the balance of payments. The 2004-05 budget estimates the central revenue deficit at 2.5 and fiscal deficit at 4.3 per cent of GDP. As part of the requirement of the FRBMA, one set of forecasts covering the period up to 2006-07 has been presented to both houses of Parliament as part of the medium term fiscal strategy statement. In the meanwhile, the central government appointed a Task Force for the implementation of the FRBMA to draw up the medium term fiscal framework to achieve the FRBMA objectives. The Task Force forecasts cover the period up to 2008-09 and relate to a base scenario that is premised on the continuance of existing trends and a reform scenario that proposes certain basic changes in the framework of indirect taxation in the country. The central government has given to the Commission its own memorandum and forecasts and also referred the Task Force Reform Scenario forecasts by extending these upto 2009-10.

a. Task Force Forecasts

4.47 The Task Force has come out with a plan of restructuring central finances. This plan also has significant implications for state finances. The salient features of the Report of the Task Force may be summarized as below:

i. Vide article 268A, the power to tax services has been vested in the central government.

ii. The value-added in the case of goods beyond manufacturing is in the nature of trade arising from wholesaling or retailing, which can be considered as a service. The centre is therefore entitled to tax this value added.

iii. States are not entitled to tax services as the subject is in the Union list. However, under article 268 A the taxation of services can be assigned fully or partially to the states.

iv. A 'grand bargain' can then be proposed to the states whereby they may agree to participate in a national Goods and Services Tax (GST), which can be levied at the rate of 20 per cent, of which the centre will levy 12 per cent and states can levy 8 per cent.

4.48 As per the estimates provided by the Task Force, these changes will have significant revenue implications. The base scenario assumes a buoyancy of 1.87 for direct taxes and 0.74 for indirect taxes, which include taxation of services under the present laws. These result in considerable improvement in the ratio of centre's gross tax revenues to GDP, which rises from 9.2 per cent of GDP in 2003-04 to 10.7 in 2008-09, showing an improvement of 1.5 percentage points. Even after this margin of improvement, the FRBMA target is not met, with revenue deficit at 1.66 per cent of GDP in 2008-09. In the reform scenario also, the core adjustment comes from a substantial improvement in the ratio of gross tax revenues of the centre to GDP taking it above 13 percent in 2008-09. In relation to Task Force's recommendation of GST under a 'grand bargain', several issues have been raised in the related discussions.

i. The legal status of centre's power to tax value added of goods interpreting as services has been questioned. It is a matter that can lead to legal issues, once the actual legislation is made and notified.

ii. The 12: 8 ratio of in favor of the centre can increase the vertical imbalance in the system, particularly because stamp fees, registration duties and sales tax on works contracts will be merged under the GST. The states will also lose the autonomy to fix rates, which is the essence having autonomy over tax bases.

iii. Aspects of inter-state taxation of services raise additional problems. Some have argued for the need for a negative list of taxes that have an inter-state character. The proposal of a clearing house mechanism to address issues of inter-state taxation and settlement of rebate claims and counter claims may run into a variety of practical problems.

iv. Inefficiencies will increase, if decisions to spend are totally divorced from decisions to tax.

v. The status of divisibility of the tax on services will remain open-ended as these will not be subject to sharing under article 270, and therefore, under the recommendations of the finance commission.

4.49 In our view, the proposal of a comprehensive GST is an attractive one, and should be pursued. However, the relevant legal and administrative aspects should be extensively discussed, particularly with the states. The implementation of a state-level VAT would facilitate its introduction in due course. However, even without this radical change, it should be possible to raise the tax-GDP ratio adequately. It may be noted that the central budget for 2004-05 is predicated on the gross central tax revenue to GDP ratio rising by 1 percentage point in one year.

b. Statements under FRBMA

4.50 A Macro Economic Framework Statement providing an overview of the economy and that of the central finances was presented for the first time to Parliament along with the 2004-05 budget. The Medium Term Fiscal Policy Statement gives rolling targets until 2006-07. It projects tax revenues based on the assumption of average annual growth rate of 12 per cent in GDP in nominal terms. Under this assumption, gross tax revenues of the centre is expected to grow by an average 22 per cent per annum based on an average annual growth of 26 per cent in direct taxes and 19 per cent in indirect taxes. The implied buoyancy for direct taxes therefore is equal to 2.15 and that of indirect taxes is equal to 1.58. The tax revenues as proportion of GDP are targeted to increase from 10.2 per cent in BE 2004-05 to 11.1 per cent in 2005-06. It is argued that since 1991, reforms have sought to reduce tax rates, simplify procedures, reduce litigation, cast the tax net wider and generally increase voluntary compliance. The Fiscal Policy Strategy Statement (FPSS) notes that the financing of fiscal deficit is now almost entirely domestic. It also notes that there are some discernible moderation in growth of public expenditure. It speaks of restructuring of subsidies so that benefits are usurped by those not intended to be the beneficiaries of these subsidies. The FPSS conveys the commitment of the government to gradually move towards integrated taxation of goods and services and bring down custom tariff to levels prevailing in ASEAN countries.

c. *Fiscal Adjustment*

4.51 In considering a plan for restructuring, generally a base scenario is constructed, which reflects the likely outcomes on the assumption that prevailing fiscal trends would continue in future. In comparison, the reform scenario presents a path of corrections. In our analysis, as a result of the FRBMA, and also following from our own recommendations, the existing trends cannot continue. As such there would no relevance in drawing up a base scenario. Instead, we will focus on a core reform scenario and consider alternative paths of adjustments around this reform scenario. Table 4.11 indicates the salient differences in the macroeconomic scenario before and during the period 2005-10. The fiscal deficit is to be reduced to 6 per cent on the combined account of the centre and the states, and revenue deficit is to be reduced to zero. This enables increase in the aggregate saving rate as well as an increase in government capital expenditure as percentage of GDP. In consequence, as the aggregate investment rate increases, growth is stabilized at above 7 per cent. It is assumed that, at the margin, nominal interest rates will remain at the present levels, which would imply a continuing fall in the average interest rate for the centre and the states. As fiscal deficits are reduced and inflation is kept under control, there will be no pressure on the interest rate to rise.

Table 4.11

Macro Economic Scenario: Current and Forecast Period

(per cent to GDP)

	2004-05 (estimates)	2009-10 (projections)
GDP Growth (constant prices) (per cent p.a.)	6.5	7.0
Inflation Rate (per cent p.a.)	6.0	5.0
Saving Rate	24.0	26.0
Investment Rate	24.5	27.5
Current Account Deficit	-0.5	1.5
Fiscal Deficit	8.9	6.0
Revenue Deficit	4.5	0.0
Government Capital Expenditure	5.6	6.6

4.52 The plan for restructuring relies both on augmenting revenues and restructuring expenditures. The main elements in this programme are increases in the tax revenues and capital expenditures relative to GDP while attaining targeted reductions in revenue and fiscal deficits both for the centre and the states. Table 4.12 shows, for the combined revenue account of the central and state governments that more than 60 per cent of the adjustment comes from the revenue side. The quantum of increase in the tax-GDP ratio is stipulated to be 2.0 percentage points. The increase in the overall revenue to GDP ratio is close to 3.0 percentage points. On the expenditure side, the fall in combined revenue expenditure to GDP ratio is 1.7 percentage points. Even though total expenditure falls, primary expenditure increases as capital expenditure relative to GDP increases by about 1 percentage point. As revenue deficit is eliminated, the entire fiscal deficit supplemented by non-debt receipts in the form of loan recoveries and disinvestment proceeds can be used for capital expenditures. Since the targeted combined fiscal deficit is 6 per cent, capital expenditure would be higher than 6 per cent of GDP. We have provided a small amount as disinvestment proceeds. We expect that the actual amounts would be larger, and accordingly capital expenditure could be higher than what is stipulated.

4.53 Our plan of debt restructuring involves consolidation of the debt of the states to the centre, to be repaid in a specified number of years. It is also suggested that the central government should progressively reduce its intermediation in state borrowing. Where it is essential, as in the case of external assistance, it should be done through a public account. If on-lending to states remains part of centre's fiscal deficit, the 3 per cent fiscal deficit target would prove to be too narrow. As centre stops on-lending to states, the repayments made by the states become available to the centre to meet its capital expenditure targets. States

Table 4.12

Summary of Suggested Restructuring: Combined Finances

Combined Finances	2004-05	2009-10	Adjustment 2009-10 minus 2004-05	Average Adjustment per year
Tax Revenue	15.6	17.6	2.0	0.40
Non tax Revenues	2.5	3.4	0.9	0.18
Total Revenue Receipts	18.1	21.0	2.9	0.58
Interest Payment	6.1	4.5	-1.6	-0.31
Total Revenue Expenditure	22.6	21.0	-1.7	-0.33
Capital Expenditure	5.6	6.6	1.0	0.20
Total Expenditure	28.3	27.6	-0.7	-0.13
Primary Expenditure	22.2	23.1	0.9	0.18
Revenue Deficit	4.5	0.0	-4.5	-0.90
Fiscal Deficit	8.9	6.0	-2.9	-0.57
Primary Deficit	2.8	1.5	-1.3	-0.26
Int. Payment/ Rev. Receipts	33.7	21.6	-12.1	-2.42
Outstanding Liabilities	80.8	74.5	-6.3	-1.26

should be allowed to borrow the repayment amount from the market in addition to its net borrowing requirement according to the stipulated path of fiscal deficit in the plan for restructuring state finances.

4.54 Table 4.13 provides a summary of suggested restructuring separately for the central and state finances. In respect of tax revenues, both central and state taxes show improved tax-GDP ratios in 2009-10, the

Table 4.13

Summary of Suggested Restructuring of Central and State Finances

	2004-05	2009-10	Adjustment 2009-10 minus 2004-05	Average Adjustment per year
Central Finances				
Gross Tax Revenues	9.7	10.9	1.2	0.24
Tax Revenue(Net to centre)	7.2	7.9	0.8	0.16
Non Tax Revenues	2.2	2.2	0.0	0.01
Total Revenue Receipts	9.4	10.2	0.8	0.17
Interest Payment	4.2	2.8	-1.3	-0.26
Total Revenue Expenditure	11.9	10.2	-1.7	-0.33
Capital Expenditure	3.0	3.5	0.5	0.10
Total Expenditure	14.8	13.7	-1.2	-0.23
Primary Expenditure	10.7	10.8	0.2	0.03
Revenue Deficit	2.5	0.0	-2.5	-0.50
Fiscal Deficit	4.5	3.0	-1.5	-0.29
Primary Deficit	0.3	0.2	-0.2	-0.03
Int. Payment/ Rev. Receipts	44.5	28.0	-16.6	-3.32
Debt(end-year adj liabilities)	53.0	43.7	-9.3	-1.86
State Finances				
States' Own Tax Revenues	5.9	6.8	0.8	0.17
Tax Revenues	8.4	9.7	1.3	0.25
Own Non-tax Revenues	1.2	1.4	0.2	0.03
Non Tax Revenues	3.2	3.5	0.3	0.07
Total Revenue Receipts	11.6	13.2	1.6	0.32
Interest Payment	2.9	2.0	-0.9	-0.18
Total Revenue Expenditure	13.6	13.2	-0.4	-0.08
Capital Expenditure	2.6	3.1	0.5	0.10
Total Expenditure	16.2	16.3	0.1	0.01
Primary Expenditure	13.3	14.3	1.0	0.20
Revenue Deficit	2.0	0.0	-2.0	-0.40
Fiscal Deficit	4.5	3.0	-1.5	-0.30
Primary Deficit	1.6	1.0	-0.6	-0.12
Int. Payment/ Rev. Receipts	24.9	15.0	-10.0	-1.99
Debt(end-year adj liabilities)	30.3	30.8	0.6	0.11
Memo:				
States' interest payments to centre	0.9	0.3	-0.7	-0.13

Note: **Combined non-tax revenues are defined as centre's non tax revenue plus states' own non-tax revenue minus interest payments from states to centre.**

margin of improvement being larger for the centre. On the expenditure side, in both cases, capital expenditure increases and interest payments fall as percentage of GDP. In both cases, the fiscal deficit targets have been kept at 3 per cent of GDP, with centre's on-lending to states being minimized or discontinued altogether. Where it is unavoidable, it should be done through a public account rather than through the consolidated fund of India. We discuss below the various dimensions of the proposed restructuring.

Dimensions of Restructuring

4.55 We recommend a multi-dimensional restructuring of government finances aimed at both the qualitative and quantitative aspects of managing government finances. In particular, the proposed restructuring covers the following areas:

i. Taxation reforms aimed at building up non-distortionary and revenue-elastic system of taxation with tax rates that are low, limited in number of rate categories, and stable;

ii. Non-tax revenues where user charges, as a short term objective, ensure recoveries of current costs, and aim at full recovery of costs measured at acceptable efficiency levels in the longer run, in the case of services where there is no clear cut case for subsidization and ensure rates of return on investment that covers the average cost of borrowing;

iii. Expenditure restructuring relating to both its size and sectoral allocations aimed at removing inefficiencies arising from misallocations, design and implementation of schemes, and delivery of services;

iv. Rationalizing subsidies by reducing their overall volume, increasing their transparency by making them explicit, and improving their targeting;

v. Public sector restructuring where, apart from natural monopolies and strategic reasons, there is a strong case for reducing government's involvement;

vi. Fiscal transfer system where equalizing transfers are given much greater weight and extended to local bodies;

vii. Suggesting a reformed role for the plan process;

viii. Strengthening the role of local bodies to become a more effective instrument in the delivery of local public goods;

ix. Role of the central government in intermediating loans for the states including the need to specify annual ceiling of borrowing for each state and implementing a hard-budget constraint; and,

x. Suggesting institutional frameworks including ceiling on debt and deficits and mechanisms for their monitoring through state level fiscal responsibility legislation.

Revenue Restructuring

4.56 In considering revenue restructuring, we recognize that the fall in the tax-GDP ratio of central commodity taxes has been only partially mitigated by the rise in the central direct taxes. This has adversely affected the finances of both central and state governments. However, some of these changes might have been efficiency-augmenting by reducing cascading of taxes. Large tax bases and low rates, limited rate categories, absence of tax cascading, minimum exemptions, and absence of tax barriers in inter-state trade would characterize a desirable system of taxation of goods and services. Such a system should also be harmonized across states so that competitive reduction of tax rates can be avoided. Where tax related decisions of the central government affect the tax bases of the state governments and vice versa, such as in the case of sales tax and Union excise duties, there is need for vertical coordination in using common tax fields. Implementation of state level value added tax (VAT) and removal of tax-related barriers to an integrated country-wide market like the central sales tax would therefore strengthen the efficiency effects of tax reforms.

4.57 States initiated tax reforms somewhat later than the centre. In particular, they reduced the rate categories in the case of sales taxes, reduced exemptions, and introduced floor rates. There were tangible revenue benefits after these changes. Efforts have been underway for some time now under the guidance of the empowered committee of the state finance ministers to facilitate the implementation of state level VAT. In his speech introducing the 2004-05 budget, the Union Finance Minister made reference to 'broad consensus among the states to implement VAT' and that 'April 1, 2005 has been set as the date for implementation'. If the state level VAT is implemented from this date, this would further reduce distortions due to cascading. We recommend that the tax rental arrangement regarding the additional excise duty items, viz., textiles, tobacco and sugar should be formally revoked and these items should be integrated into the overall design of state VAT. Any ceiling of 4 per cent should not be there, and in fact the relevance of the entire mechanism of declared goods should be reexamined. Taxation of services has, however, remained fragmented and piecemeal. If state level VAT is implemented by the states, the question as to how state tax revenues would be affected individually and in the aggregate becomes important, particularly so, as the beginning of the changed system coincides with the recommendation period of this Commission. With the objective of formulating a view on the likely impact of the State-VAT on revenues, we had commissioned two studies [13], one related directly to the revenue-impact of VAT, and the other on the revenue potential of tax reforms at the state level, which takes into account the interdependence of the state and central tax revenues. These studies have affirmed that, properly designed, the state level VAT should prove to be revenue augmenting over the medium to long term. If there are any losses, these are likely to be transitory. The implementation of state level VAT would be facilitated, and its revenue performance improved, if a centralized institutional mechanism for compilation and exchange of information relevant to production, consumption, and dealer-wise flow of goods and services within and across states, is established. We understand that the central government is examining a suitable mechanism by which the states can be compensated for such transitory losses. It may be mentioned that for augmenting revenues, most commodities should be placed under the proposed core rate of 12 per cent. The states may be given the option to use a higher rate, if desired. A very small number of goods, under well enunciated principles, should be put under the proposed lower rate category of 4 per cent. The central sales tax should be quickly phased out.

4.58 In our restructuring plan, the tax-GDP ratio goes up by 2 percentage points with both centre and states contributing to it. For the states, the adoption of the VAT is likely to be revenue-augmenting in the medium to long term. If there is a fall in revenues for some states, it is likely to be small and temporary. We consider that this change would add to growth and shift resources to some extent towards the consuming states. These changes thus will have both vertical and horizontal benefits. The vertical benefit would be due to augmentation of the tax base as distortion related inefficiencies are reduced. The horizontal benefit will accrue from the fact that consuming states will gain more in relative terms. It is important to resolve the issue of taxation of services following the 88th amendment to the Constitution. Since the service tax has been put under article 268A, the sharing of its revenues with the states will be taken out of the purview of the finance commission. This may not have been the best among possible options for dealing with this subject. As matters stand, the centre can assign certain services to the states for collecting and retaining the revenues, but the tax will be levied by the centre. As already indicated earlier, it is necessary to ensure that the revenue accruing to the states, under the new arrangement should not be less than the share that would accrue to the states, had the entire service tax proceeds been part of the shareable pool. We have made this assumption in the proposed scheme of tax devolution.

Non Tax Revenues

4.59 Non tax revenues consist of a heterogeneous mix of sources encompassing interest receipts on loans given by the governments, dividends on equity investment, and user charges and tariffs for services provided by the governments. Non-tax revenues have remained stagnant relative to GDP contributing around 3 per cent of GDP in the combined revenues of the centre and states. In the context of goods and services that are private in nature, the principle of cost recovery should apply, and where costs are not meant to be recovered fully, explicit subsidies should be provided. The management of government finances in such a way would impart the necessary transparency and improve the efficacy of fiscal intervention. In the context of interest receipts and dividends, the issue is linked to the reform of public enterprises, and the question of user charges is linked to subsidies. Where royalties are payable, these should be on ad valorem basis. Our restructuring plan proposes a tangible increase in the non-tax revenues relative to GDP.

Expenditure Restructuring

4.60 In restructuring expenditures, there is need to make reference to the basic objectives of government intervention in economic activities, as also to the basic objectives for assignment of responsibilities as between central and sub-national governments. It is also important to relate government expenditures to outcomes in terms of the quality, reach, and impact of government services. This would be facilitated if governments focus more on their primary responsibilities rather than spreading resources thinly in many areas where the private sector can provide the necessary services. The primary role of government is to provide public goods like defence, law and order, and general administration. This represents one kind of market failure. The role of governments extends to merit goods and services with large positive externalities like education and health. The services should be assigned to the central government if the scope of public goods is nation-wide like defence. The services get assigned to state governments if the scope of the public good is limited to regions or if externalities are more local in character like the health services. Admittedly there may be many examples of benefit spillovers, some of which can be internalized to the state level decision makers by a suitable scheme of grants. There is a felt need to examine whether the central government is not partaking in many responsibilities that legitimately belong to the domain of the states. Governments at both levels have also stepped into the provision of many private goods, which adversely affects the quantum and quality of service in regard to public and merit goods. Two key elements of restructuring government expenditures relate to augmentation of capital expenditure relative to GDP, focused on infrastructure and a reduction of central government's expenditures on subjects listed as state responsibilities.

From Expenditures to Outcomes

4.61 The conventional budget exercises have focused on allocation of resources to different heads, without taking into account how these government expenditures get translated into outputs and outcomes. Outputs are the direct result of government expenditure and outcomes are the final results. Thus, in the context of education, opening a new school or appointing a new teacher is an output and reduction in the rate of illiteracy is an outcome. Issues of efficiency require consideration whether the same outcome can be achieved at lower costs and whether the same costs can produce better outcomes. A critical part of budgetary reforms must include information on the relationship between expenditures and the corresponding performance in producing real results as in determining the size of the budget and its allocation among different heads. Although in the past there have been attempts at introducing performance budgeting, such endeavors have receded in importance. There is need to bring back performance budgeting as an integral part of the preparation and evaluation of budgets, both for the centre and the states. Thus, the management of public expenditures should be guided by economy, efficiency, and effectiveness.

Subsidies

4.62 Budgetary subsidies can be explicit or implicit. When subsidies are explicitly stated in the budget it adds to transparency in expenditure management. According to the Discussion Paper brought out by the Ministry of Finance in 1997, there are many hidden subsidies in the budget. These arise because the costs of providing these are not recovered from the users or beneficiaries. In the case of merit goods like education and health, subsidization may be desirable. But the desired extent of subsidization should be clearly worked out. Various studies [14] have highlighted that government subsidies, measured as un-recovered costs in the public provision of private goods, are large in volume, amounting to 13 to 14 per cent of GDP. In many instances, subsidies promote or subsidize inefficiencies. Subsidies are often wasted as these do not reach the intended beneficiary. The Discussion Paper brought out by the Ministry of Finance in 1997 did highlight many of these problems and suggested a course for subsidy reforms that included reducing their volume, eliminating input-based subsidies, making these subsidies explicit, and improving their targeting. The Expenditure Reforms Commission also examined food and fertilizer subsidies at length and suggested an agenda of reforms. Some changes were introduced in the regime of subsidization of fertilizers. In spite of these efforts, the volume of subsidies in the central budget has remained large. It accounted for about 18 per cent of centre's gross revenue receipts in 2002-03. Some of the earlier commitments for reducing subsidies, particularly in areas of fertilizers and petroleum, should not be diluted. The centre should draw up a programme for containing the growth in subsidies. In the case of states, a large part of the subsidization process remains hidden as cost of services keep increasing, while recoveries as proportion of costs become less and less. There is a clear need to link user charges with costs. The determination of user charges for a variety of private services provided by the governments should be supervised by an autonomous regulatory commission, which can protect both the interests of the consumer and the revenues of the government.

Government Salaries

4.63 Many states have represented to the Commission that salaries and allowances have tended to converge with those of the central government and that they find it difficult to implement a salary structure that is different from that of the centre. The problems have become acute for some states as the share of salaries in their total expenditure is very large. The initial conditions for the states differ because in the past their salary scales were different from the centre and they also followed different recruitment policies. If salary structures across the states are allowed to converge, the number of employees in a state also needs to follow some comparable norms in relation to the size of population, fiscal capacity, and other relevant considerations. The per employee salary expenditure may still differ because of the composition of the workforce. Normalization can be done in respect of the total salary bill relative to their fiscal capacities. The salary burden is already heavy and at the minimum, the ratio of salaries to revenue expenditure net of interest payments and pensions must not be allowed to increase. It should be progressively brought down to levels prevalent in 1996-97. Appendix 4.2 provides a discussion of the relative profile of employment and salary bills of the government. It can be seen that expenditure on salaries relative to revenue expenditure excluding interest payments and pensions has gone up from 35 per cent in 1996-97 to 42 per cent in 1999-00. The EFC had recommended that there is no need to appoint Pay Commissions as a routine at the interval of 10 years. It also recommended that states should be consulted while appointing a new Pay Commission. We agree with these recommendations.

Pension Reforms

4.64 Pension payments constitute an important component of committed expenditures in the central and state budgets. The central government has taken steps for pension reforms, particularly in respect of new appointments. A defined contribution pension scheme was introduced by the central government with effect from January 1, 2004 for central government employees recruited on or after that date, (except armed forces, in the first stage) replacing the existing defined benefit pension system. The central government has also initiated the process for bringing out legislation for the appointment of an independent pension regulatory authority, which can ensure proper investment of pension funds. The pension fund regulator will have the responsibility of regulating, promoting and ensuring the orderly growth of the pension funds. The pension liabilities in the case of the states account for a larger share of its revenue receipts. This share may increase further in view of the increasing longevity and the number of appointments in the late sixties and early seventies, when the size of state governments was expanding. State governments need to take up initiatives similar to those of the central government for pension reforms. This would also be facilitated by the appointment of a regulator.

From Unproductive to Productive Capital Expenditure

4.65 In the proposed restructuring plan, the level of capital expenditure, on the combined account of the centre and the states relative to GDP, is set to rise to about 7 per cent of GDP by 2009-10. We have indicated that this capital expenditure is meant for administrative departments and departmental enterprises. Separate borrowing limits have been prescribed for non-departmental enterprises. The increase in capital expenditure is for augmenting investment and building physical assets for the various publically provided services aimed at promoting growth and improving the quality of services provided by the central and state governments. It is not meant for covering losses of non-departmental public enterprises, by contributing to their share capital, or for servicing debt arising from off-budget borrowing.

Restructuring the System of Fiscal Transfers

4.66 Fiscal transfers from the centre to the states take place through finance commission, Planning Commission, and the central ministries. The over all system of fiscal transfers suffers from many inadequacies and deficiencies, which arise due to segmentation of transfers as well as within each segment of the transfers. We suggest a scheme of reforms that can be implemented over a period of time in respect of the different channels of transfers.

a. Finance Commission Transfers

4.67 The system of transfers should be guided by equalization, which is consistent with equity as well as efficiency. To some extent the exercise of using a normative approach is constrained by information lags. The data on population pertains to 1971. By the time the recommendation period of this Commission is over, it will be out of date by nearly 39 years. Even the data on GSDP, which serves as indicator of revenue base, will be dated by about 8 years by 2009-10. In a context where disparities are increasing, the transfers system could become regressive by the time actual transfers take place even when transfers are designed to be progressive under an equalization approach with respect to data used. It is difficult to see the relevance of 1971 population census data when population of all states was about 54 crore, when 2001 census puts the population of all states at more than 100 crore. This is out-of date by nearly 100 per cent. We recognize that the implicit objective is to penalize states, which have done less well in comparative terms in controlling population growth. But population growth is the outcome of the birth rate, the death rate, and net migration. It would be better to state the objective in the TOR and leave the principle by which it is implemented in the transfer mechanism for the finance commission to decide. The information lag problems would be finally overcome when the finance commission determines the formula and the weights of transfers, which holds for 5 years, but actual shares are updated every year by application of the most recent data. This is the method of 5-yearly review and annual updates followed in Australia. The major concerns relating to finance commission transfers have been discussed in detail in the earlier chapter.

b. Planning Commission Transfers

4.68 In the case of plan assistance, the proportion between grants and loans at 30: 70 for the general category states and 10:90 for the special category states has a counterpart in the interest rate charged by the central government on the plan loans to the states, which has been, in the past, sometimes, 300 to 400 basis points higher than the cost of funds to the centre. In other words, plan grants are not really interest-free grants. Over the time, these are recovered back in the form of higher interest receipts. Plan grants should be given as genuine grants and states may be encouraged to borrow from the market directly. Such a change would require delinking of grants from loans in plan assistance. This would facilitate determination of grants according to needs and loans according to capacities. The plan size of each state needs to take into account the sustainable level of debt and the capacity to borrow from the market.

4.69 A restructuring plan must include reforms relating to the planning process. Part of the distortion in the structure of expenditure derives from the distinction between plan and non-plan expenditures. It is inefficient to show preference for creating new assets or undertaking new schemes being part of the plan, while sacrificing maintenance of already created assets. As a result, there remain many incomplete projects/schemes not yielding services on one side, and ill-maintained and fast depreciating assets, on the other. Over the time, plans have become more scheme-oriented rather than project-oriented, so that assets that could provide returns to service the debt that was used to finance plan expenditures are neither being created nor maintained.

4.70 In the case of centrally sponsored schemes also there should only be the grant element and no loans linked to grant. A state should be given its total entitlement of grants and allowed to select its own mix of centrally sponsored (CS) schemes floated by different ministries, within the limit of the total grant. The CS schemes would then start competing among themselves and pressure would come on the ministries to design schemes that are in demand. This would do away with the present supply-driven approach where schemes are characterized by large numbers, duplication, and lack of monitoring. The CS schemes have been the subject of study by many committees. The general consensus has been towards reducing their number, but the follow-up action has been weak.

Restructuring Debt

4.71 In 2002-03, the central government brought out a debt-swap scheme to facilitate the state governments to swap their high cost debt owed to government of India with additional market borrowings and a part of current small saving transfers. During 2002-03, the state governments swapped Rs. 13766 crore with 20 per cent of small saving share and additional market borrowings. During 2003-04, according to provisional data, loans amounting to Rs. 46211 crore have been swapped with 30 per cent of small saving transfers and additional market borrowings. The central government has used the receipts under the debt-swap scheme to repay its liabilities to the National Small Savings Fund (NSSF). This has the effect of bringing down centre's overall debt as well as its effective interest rate. During 2004-05, additional debt swap amounting to Rs. 43887 crore has been envisaged.

4.72 The total liabilities of the government of India according to receipts budget of 2004-05 are shown as Rs.1985866 crore. These include liabilities in the public account of NSSF against loans to the state governments and Rs. 60000 crore worth of market stabilization scheme (MSS). The MSS funds are not available to the government for current expenditures and are held as cash with RBI. Against the lending to the states from the NSSF, states have issued special securities. Adjusting for these two amounts from the asset side, the outstanding liabilities of the central government at the end 2004-05 are estimated to be about 53 per cent of GDP. There has been a fall in centre's liabilities relative to GDP because of the redemption of special securities issued to the NSSF based on the debt-swap programme for the states.

4.73 At the same time, the central government should phase out its intermediation in borrowing by the states. Where necessary, this should be managed through a public account. However, there is a need to determine borrowing limits for each state taking into account borrowing from all sources including small savings and states public accounts and reserve funds. The prescribed borrowing limit on states' aggregate fiscal deficit in our restructuring plan is 3 per cent. In their case also, revenue deficits should be brought to zero by 2008-09. Once stabilized, these deficit rules should be taken to apply over the medium term with some changes to take into account the cyclical pattern.

4.74 Our suggested debt restructuring

programme for the states as detailed in chapter 12 will have two components: a consolidation of all state debt to the centre outstanding at the end of 2004-05 at an interest rate of 7.5 per cent to be repaid in 20 years, and a debt relief scheme linked to achievement in reducing revenue deficits. We are proposing that as a precondition for availing the benefit of the scheme, all states should enact a fiscal responsibility legislation, that provides for eliminating revenue deficit in the respective states no later than 2008-09, incorporates annual targets for reduction of fiscal and revenue deficits, and presents to the respective legislatures a consolidated growth and fiscal strategy statement along with their budgets. As the states are increasingly exposed to the markets for borrowing, their fiscal positions would be increasingly assessed by the markets. They may be forced to pay higher than average interest rates to cover additional risk if the public finances are not evaluated to be robust by the assessment of the market. We are relying therefore on two mechanisms for fiscal correction: self evaluation under the Fiscal Responsibility Act and exposure to market. These in our view may prove to be effective instruments of fiscal discipline without compromising the autonomy of the states.

Public Sector Reforms

4.75 As pointed out by the Eleventh Finance Commission, large amounts of capital is locked up in the public sector showing extremely low returns in relation to the average cost of funds to the government. As per available information, 109 central public sector companies were running in losses. The problem is particularly acute in the case of the states. Out of 1003 state level public enterprises (SLPEs), 599 SLPEs are reported to be either non-functioning or running into losses. Not only the returns on government investment are non-existent or low, but also a large number of SLPEs fail to finalize their accounts. The total amount of investment in respect of the SLPEs, where accounts were finalized, was estimated to be Rs. 2,38,220 crore at the end of 2000-01. Many states have, however, taken steps for closing down many of the SLPEs and for disinvestment in others. This process should be further strengthened. In the period of restructuring, that is 2005-10, state governments should draw up a programme that includes closure of almost all loss making SLPEs. Reforms of state electricity boards and transport enterprises are being taken up separately. By the end of 2009-10, states should have a small but viable set of SLPEs.

Fiscal Frameworks for Reforms

4.76 In the nineties many countries around the world were able to achieve fiscal consolidation, attaining primary surpluses. Widespread reforms including debt ceilings and deficit targets have strengthened fiscal frameworks. Expenditure rules and transparency in the fiscal management has also been emphasized in these fiscal frameworks. Evaluations of these fiscal consolidation efforts [15] have identified certain factors that account for reliable and durable adjustments. Accordingly, fiscal consolidation is more likely to be successful when based on cuts in expenditure, particularly when undertaken by countries with high levels of debt. Widespread reforms in fiscal frameworks require institutional reforms aimed at achieving and maintaining fiscal consolidation, while leaving room for fiscal policy to respond to business cycles through automatic stabilizers and policy actions.

4.77 Recent institutional reforms can be classified into three broad groups: formal deficit and debt rules, expenditure limits, and transparency. The main examples of this approach are European countries bound by the Maastricht Treaty as supplemented by the Stability and Growth Pact. The U K since 1997 has operated a Golden Rule whereby borrowing is done only to finance capital spending and the limit on net debt is 40 per cent of GDP over a cycle. Several countries have deficit and debt rules at the sub national level. In the US, all but two states have laws requiring balanced budgets and limiting the states to raise debt. Nine provinces and territories of Canada have fiscal rules with balanced budgets requiring them to take on debt only for the purpose of financing investment projects. Canada has also focused on instituting a rigorous expenditure review process. Debt ceiling can serve as a useful adjunct to deficit rules. In practice debt ceilings have been driven not by calculations based on theory, but run by the concern about reducing high debt levels and are thus generally chosen on the basis of the experience of the individual countries. The main criticism of the deficit rules in general and balanced budget rules in particular is that they are invariant and therefore tend to be pro-cyclical. This is a more important consideration for national governments as compared to sub national governments. For this reason the deficit rules in the national government have increasingly been defined in terms of a cyclically adjusted deficit measures or as an average over the economic cycle. Thus these rules allow the operation of domestic stabilizers and to some extent also provide room for discretionary policy within the cycle.

4.78 Transparency in fiscal management has been emphasized by countries like New Zealand, Australia and the U K. The key elements in this approach are an explicit legal basis, elaboration of guiding principles of fiscal policy, requirement that objectives are clearly stated, emphasis on the need for a long term focus to fiscal policy, and fiscal reporting to the public. The UK, US, and New Zealand have enacted legislations for transparency which require statements providing the objectives for deficits and debt. The US places relatively greater emphasis on expenditure and deficit rules. Expenditure rules typically emphasize ceilings on specific areas of expenditure like discretionary expenditure as opposed to non discretionary expenditure and in some cases with respect to particular programmes. Thus, three structural changes can help restore the fiscal health in India, namely, (i) legislative enactments that can restrict fiscal imprudence and set targets such as those relating to fiscal and revenue deficits, debt, and rules for expenditure cuts contingent on specified conditions, (ii) transparency requirements in fiscal management, which help a better understanding of the fiscal health of a government by its citizens and their representatives, and (iii) exposure to market discipline, particularly in raising debt.

Summary

4.79 Our approach to restructuring requires determined and coordinated effort by the central and state governments. It emphasizes fiscal corrections in a macroeconomic framework with a medium term perspective. It endorses the view that most of the changes in taxation and fiscal framework should be completed by 2005-06, and course corrections should be undertaken on the basis of quarterly and annual reviews. The core strategy of fiscal restructuring, recommended by us, centers on raising the trend rate of growth. This can be done by enhancing the savings ratio, which requires large reduction of government dis-savings. This, in turn, requires elimination of revenue deficit at both levels of government. However, we recommend increase in government investment aimed at infrastructure. The specific suggestions made by us are summarized below.

i. The suggested reform strategy has to aim for strengthening growth by increasing public sector saving and government's capital expenditures relative to GDP. This would require reducing the share of revenue deficit in fiscal deficit, which itself should fall.

ii. The macroeconomic scenario that serves as the framework for fiscal corrections is characterized by 7 per cent real growth on average and 5 per cent inflation rate.

iii. Fiscal correction requires increasing, by 2009-10, the combined tax-GDP ratio to 17.6 per cent, primary expenditure to a level of 22 per cent of GDP, and capital expenditure to nearly 7 per cent of GDP.

iv. In the context of debt and fiscal deficit, keeping in view the FRBMA targets and the related sustainability requirements, we consider that:

(a) With a combined fiscal deficit of 6 per cent of GDP and a nominal growth rate of 12 per cent per annum, the system will converge to a combined debt-GDP ratio of 56 percent. The present level is as estimated to be as high as 81 percent of GDP, with external debt measured at historical exchange rates. This should, at a minimum, be brought down to 75 per cent by the end of 2009-10.

(b) With the system of on-lending being brought to an end over time, the long term goal for the centre and state for the debt-GDP should be 28 per cent each. Their fiscal deficit to GDP ratio targets may be fixed at 3 per cent of GDP each. In both cases, revenue deficit should be eliminated by 2008-09.

(c) Under the assumptions of revenue to GDP ratios, eventually the centre's interest payment relative to revenue receipts would reach about 28 per cent by 2009-10. In the case of states, the level of interest payments relative to revenue receipts would fall to about 15 per cent by 2009-10.

v. As part of the proposed fiscal adjustment, revenue deficit relative to GDP for the centre and the states, for their combined as well as individual accounts should be brought down to zero by 2008-09. This is already provided in the centre's FRBMA.

vi. States should follow a recruitment and wage policy, in a manner such that the total salary bill relative to revenue expenditure net of interest payments and pensions does not exceed 35 per cent.

vii. We recommend that each state should enact fiscal responsibility legislation. This has been stipulated as a precondition for availing the debt-relief scheme as recommended by us in a later Chapter. This legislation should, at a minimum, provide for

(a) eliminating revenue deficit by 2008-09;

(b) reducing fiscal deficit to 3 per cent of GSDP or its equivalent defined as ratio of interest payment to revenue receipts;

(c) bringing out annual reduction targets of revenue and fiscal deficits;

(d) bringing out annual statement giving prospects for the state economy and related fiscal strategy;

(e) bringing out special statements along with the budget giving in detail number of employees in government, public sector, and aided institutions and related salaries.

□□

Endnotes

[1] This includes external debt evaluated at historical exchange rates.

[2] Reserve Bank of India, Report on Currency and Finance, 2000-01, pages IV-12 to14.

[3] According to an estimate by RBI (op. cit.), the cyclical deficit has ranged between a deficit of 0.12 per cent of GDP and a surplus of 0.21 per cent of GDP during the nineties. The structural fiscal deficits have been in the range of about 10 per cent of GDP in the recent years.

As in [2].

[4] We use the Hodrick – Prescott (HP) filter to derive the trend output in real terms and the price deflator. Given a series **y**, the H-P filter computes the smoothed series **s** of **y** by minimizing the variance of **y** around **s** subject to a penalty that constrains the second difference of **s**. The penalty parameter controls the smoothness of the series **s**. The larger the penalty parameter, the smoother is the series. With very large values of the parameter, the smoothed series approaches a linear trend. We have used a value of 100 for this parameter, which is generally recommended in the case of annual series.

[5] Ahluwalia in his article "Economic Performance of States in Post-Reforms Period" (EPW, 2000) lists the necessary qualifications in interpreting estimates of Gini Coefficient, assuming population of a state is centered on the mean income of that state.

[6] Prepared by Dr. Sita Prabhu and her associates at UNDP's India office.

[7] Prepared by IDFC for the benefit of the Finance Commission by Prof. TCA Anant of the Delhi School of Economics and Mr. Nirmal Mohanty of the IDFC.

[8] The standard specification of the equation describing debt dynamics with discrete time periods is given by equation (1) $[b_t = p_t + b_{t-1} \{(1+i_t)/(1+g_t)\}]$. As discussed in Rangarajan and Srivastava (2004), writing $z_t = b_t - b_{t-1}$, equation (1) can also be written as

$$z_t = p_t - b_{t-1} [(g_t - i_t)(1+g_t)^{-1}]$$

or $$p_t = z_t + b_{t-1} [(g_t - i_t)(1+g_t)^{-1}]$$

Summing up over any two benchmark years 1 and T, we have

$$\Sigma p_t = \Sigma z_t + \Sigma b_{t-1} [(g_t - i_t)(1+g_t)^{-1}] \quad (t=1,\ldots, T)$$

The term $A1 = \Sigma z_t / \Sigma p_t$ (t=1,...,T) shows the extent to which the cumulated primary deficits translate into accumulation of debt. On the other hand, the term

$$A2 = \Sigma b_{t-1} [(g_t - i_t)(1+g_t)^{-1}] / \Sigma p_t \quad (t=1,T)$$

shows the extent to which the impact of cumulated primary deficits is absorbed by the excess of growth over interest rate.

[9] Discussions with CSO have confirmed that subject to some statistical adjustments, net savings of administrative departments and

departmental enterprises and the combined revenue deficit of the central and state governments are equivalent.

[10] Muhleisen (1997, IMF Staff papers) had estimated that for each increase of 1 percentage point in public saving, there is reduction of 0.25 percentage points in private savings. This relationship would hold in the reverse as well.

[11] Let D= end-period outstanding debt, Y = GDP at market prices, g = growth rate, i = effective interest rate, P = primary deficit, F = fiscal deficit, and I = interest payment. The relevant period is indicated by the subscript t. The debt-GDP ratio is given by b and the primary deficit to GDP ratio is given by p. Thus, $b_t = D_t/Y_t$, and $p_t = P_t/Y_t$.

By definition,

$D_t - D_{t-1} = F_t$

or, $D_t - D_{t-1} = P_t + I_t$ ...(a)

We can write, $I_t = i\, D_{t-1}$, and $Y_t = Y_{t-1}(1+g_t)$

Dividing (a) by Y_t, we have

$b_t - b_{t-1}[1/(1+g_t)] = p_t + i_t b_{t-1}[1/(1+g_t)]$

or, $b_t = p_t + b_{t-1}\,[(1+i_t)/(1+g_t)]$ ...(b)

or, $b_t - b_{t-1} = p_t - b_{t-1}[1-(1+i_t)/(1+g_t)]$

or, $b_t - b_{t-1} = p_t - b_{t-1}[(g_t-i_t)/(1+g_t)$ ...(c)

Thus the long run equilibrium value of $b_t = b_{t-1} = b^*$ is given by

$b^* = p\,(1+g)/(g-i)$ ... (d)

Correspondingly, $f^*=p.g/(g-i)$ ...(e)

Thus, given the values of i and g, for any targeted level of primary deficit to GDP ratio(p), the stabilized debt-GDP ratio is given by (d), and the corresponding fiscal deficit to GDP ratio which will ensure that f* is remains constant year after year is given by (e). It is also implicit by (d) and (e) that the relationship between b* and f* is given by

$f^*=b^*.g/(1+g)$ ...(f)

[12] The interest payment to revenue ratio (IP_t/RR_t) can be derived as below.

$IP_t = i.B_{t-1} = ib_{t-1}Y_{t-1}$

As debt is stabilized $b_t=b_{t-1}=b^*$

$IP_t = i.[p(1+g)/(g-i)]Y_{t-1}$ or $i.p/(g-i)]Y_t$ [since $Y_{t-1} = Y_t/(1+g)$]

The revenue receipts can be written as $RR_t = r.\,Y_t$

Thus $(ip)^* = IP_t/RR_t = i.p/r(g-i)$ or $p/(g-i) = (ip)^*r/i$

Further, since with stabilization $b_t = b_{t-1}$, it is implied that $B_t = B_{t-1}(1+g)$

Then fiscal deficit can be written as $F_t = B_{t-1}g$

Or $f_t = b_{t-1}g/(1+g)$

Or $f^* = b_t\, g/(1+g) = p.g/(g-i)$

We can then write

Using $f^* = (ip)^*r\, g/i$ ...(g)

And $b^* = (ip)^*\, r(1+g)/\, i$ ... (h)

Accordingly, $f^*/b^* = g/(1+g)$

[13] One study was undertaken by the National Institute of Public Finance and Policy, which focused on two states,

namely, Andhra Pradesh and West Bengal. The other study was done by the Foundation for Public Finance and Policy, which looked into the question of vertical externality in taxation.

[14] Government of India brought out a Discussion Paper on Government Subsidies in India in 1997.

[15] World Economic Outlook, 2001, IMF.

□□

Chapter 5

Union Finances: Assessment of Revenue and Expenditure

5.1 According to the terms of reference (TOR), in making recommendations on transfers to states in the form of tax devolution and grants, the Commission shall have regard, among other considerations, to the resources of the central government for the five years commencing on 1st April, 2005 on the basis of levels of taxation and non-tax revenues likely to be reached at the end of 2003-04. The Commission is, further, required to take into consideration (a) the demands on the resources of the central government, in particular, on account of expenditure on civil administration, defence, internal and border security, debt servicing and other committed expenditures and liabilities, (b) the objective of not only balancing the receipts and expenditure on revenue account of the centre, but also generating surpluses for capital investment and reducing fiscal deficit, and (c) the taxation efforts of the central government as against targets, if any, and the potential for additional resource mobilization in order to improve the tax-GDP ratio. Related to these considerations is para 5 of the TOR, which requires us to review the finances of the central and state governments and suggest a plan for restructuring of the public finances restoring budgetary balance, achieving macro-economic stability and debt reduction along with equitable growth.

5.2 As in the case of earlier finance commissions, the central government's memorandum and forecast have provided the basis for our assessment of the finances of the centre during the reference period (2005-2010). We held detailed discussions on the subject with the senior officials of the Ministry of Finance and various central ministries before formulating our approach. We have taken note of the fiscal responsibility legislation enacted by government of India, that has implications for the projection of revenues and expenditure. The Fiscal Responsibility and Budget Management Act, 2003 (FRBMA) came into force on 26th August, 2003 and rules thereunder were notified on 2nd July, 2004. In terms of the Act, the centre's revenue deficit was required to be eliminated by 31st March, 2008. The rules under the Act further require the central government to reduce the revenue deficit by an amount equivalent to 0.5 per cent or more of GDP at the end of each year beginning with 2004-05. The fiscal deficit is to be reduced by 0.3 per cent or more of GDP at the end of each financial year beginning with 2004-05, so that it is brought down to 3 per cent of GDP in 2008. The Finance Act, 2004 has shifted the targets fixed for 31st March,

2008 with respect to the revenue deficit and the fiscal deficit to 31st March, 2009.

5.3 After the FRBMA was passed, the central government set up a Task Force for drawing up a medium-term framework for fiscal policies to achieve the objective of the FRBMA and to formulate annual targets indicating the path of adjustment as well as the required policy measures. The report of the Task Force, presented to the central government in July 2004, was made available to us. Besides, we had the benefit of meeting the chairman of the Task Force. The Task Force has presented two scenarios for the future – the baseline scenario and the reform scenario. The base line scenario assumes that the four years from 2005-06 till 2008-09 will prove to be similar to recent years in terms of progress on policy and administration. It does not assume any major new tax reforms. The projections in the baseline scenario indicate that, under this scenario the targets prescribed in the FRBMA with regard to the revenue and fiscal deficits will not be achieved. The second scenario, which the Task Force calls the reform scenario, incorporates substantive reforms in taxes and follows the principle of a revenue led and front loaded fiscal consolidation. The adoption of the suggested reforms is expected to help the achievement of the required fiscal corrections for eliminating revenue deficit and reducing fiscal deficit.

5.4 The FRBMA requires that three statements, namely, a macro-economic framework statement, a fiscal policy strategy statement and a medium-term fiscal policy statement containing three-year rolling targets for prescribed fiscal indicators and the underlying assumptions, be placed before the Parliament every financial year. The first such set of statements was placed in the Parliament in July, 2004 alongwith the budget of 2004-05. We note that the rolling targets in the medium-term fiscal policy statement correspond to the projections made in the reform scenario of the report of the Task Force. While we have considered the statements laid in the Parliament and the suggestions made in the report of the Task Force (although the recommendations are still to be accepted by the central government), we have made our own assessment of the feasibility of implementing the suggested reforms during our award period. Our assessment of the resources of the centre has, therefore, been made in the light of the considerations mentioned in our terms of reference and in consonance with the restructuring programme outlined by us in chapter 4. We have also been guided by the targets in regard to revenue and fiscal deficits and the minimum annual adjustments prescribed under the FRBMA and the rules framed thereunder.

Memorandum and Forecast of the Central Government

5.5 The central government submitted its memorandum to the Commission in September, 2003. A number of statements containing item-wise projections of revenues and expenditures were also forwarded to us from time to time by the Ministry of Finance, spelling out assumptions and growth rates adopted for various items. The forecast of the summary position of the finances of the central government containing the projections of revenue and fiscal deficits was made available to the Commission in September,

2004. We were informed that the forecast of the summary position, though submitted after a medium-term fiscal policy statement was laid in Parliament, did not factor in the budget estimates of 2004-05 or the targets under the FRBM Act/rules. It was, however, consistent with detailed statements submitted to us earlier, projecting large revenue and fiscal deficits for 2009-10. However, in a meeting with us, the senior officials of the Ministry of Finance indicated that the implementation of the measures recommended by the Task Force under the reform scenario will be necessary for achieving the targets prescribed in the FRBM Act/rules with regard to the revenue and fiscal deficits.

5.6 In the memorandum, the central government has urged the Commission to take due note of the centre's commitments and strike a balance between the requirements of the Union and the states while determining the quantum of transfer from the centre to the states. The Commission was also urged not to view the share of central taxes and the grants under article 275 in isolation but calibrate these transfers taking into account the overall resource transfers from the centre to the states.

5.7 The central government expressed concern on the inability of the centre and the states to apply fiscal corrections with a view to reducing deficits and ultimately generating surpluses which can be gainfully deployed in sectors that need large infusion of public resources in order to achieve the policy goals and objectives of the government. The central government's memorandum further states that in accordance with the provisions of the FRBMA, the central government is required to take appropriate measures to reduce the fiscal deficit and revenue deficit, so as to eliminate revenue deficit by March 31, 2008 (since extended to March 31, 2009) and thereafter build up adequate revenue surplus. This mandatory requirement on the part of the central government needs to be taken into account by the Finance Commission while making its recommendations. In view of the large revenue deficit of the centre and the states, as also the low level of tax-GDP ratio, fiscal consolidation together with enhancement of the tax-GDP ratio is imperative for the period 2005-10. In this context, the memorandum further states that "this has to be done to reduce the combined fiscal deficit of the centre and states to 3 per cent of GDP by the year 2009-10, keeping in view the consideration that central government fiscal deficit is required to be brought down to 2 per cent by March, 2008 and thereafter revenue surplus is required to be generated".

5.8 The memorandum, while indicating the trends in central government's expenditure, has drawn our attention to the inflexibility of non-plan expenditure comprising *inter alia*, interest payments, defence expenditure, subsidies, pensions, and transfers to states. These together pre-empt over 100 per cent of total revenue receipts of the central government. It has also been stated that Union taxes are not expected to be particularly buoyant because of reduction in rates and continuation of exemptions. The Commission has been urged to take the sluggish growth of tax revenue into account together with the commitments on the expenditure side. Our attention has also been drawn to the possible reduction in customs duties on account of the WTO commitments.

5.9 With regard to the value added tax (VAT), which is expected to be implemented from April, 2005, the central government has stated that the introduction of VAT should lead to a net gain in revenue resources, but a compensation mechanism for three years has been thought of as a measure of 'comfort' to the states. Details of the possible revenue loss and the likely quantum of compensation have not been made available to us.

5.10 The central government has urged the Commission to review the level of user charges which form part of non-tax revenue of the government and make suitable recommendations with a view to boosting non-tax revenues of the centre and states. It has been suggested that international experience in this regard may be drawn upon especially in emerging areas like those in the telecom sector. It has been mentioned that the auction of radio spectrum in the case of this sector has fetched billions of dollars in revenues in countries like the U.K., Germany etc. and its levy in the Indian context may merit attention of the Commission.

5.11 Referring to the need for capping the level of guarantees given by state governments, the central government has stated that in so far as the central government is concerned, efforts will be made to limit fresh guarantees to 0.5 per cent of GDP each year, as provided for in the FRBMA. The central government has also stated that in the light of the tight fiscal situation of the centre and the external macro-economic imperatives of containing centre's fiscal deficit and debt, there should be a gradual reduction in devolution to states. Given the likely levy of sales tax by states on sugar, tobacco and textiles and the availability of collection of service tax by states on items to be specified, the Commission may also review the maximum level of overall transfers from centre to states and prescribe a ceiling that is lower than that recommended by the Eleventh Finance Commission.

5.12 In a subsequent submission dated 9th August, 2004, which in many ways differs from the earlier memorandum, the central government has suggested that in respect of the share of states in the net proceeds of taxes, the Commission may take a view consistent with National Common Minimum Programme objectives (*which, inter alia, states that the share of states in the single divisible pool of taxes will be enhanced*) and after taking into account the following considerations:

(i) under the eighty-eighth Constitutional amendment, "Taxes on Services" are to be excluded from the single, divisible pool of central taxes/duties;

(ii) the centre is presently discharging a number of expenditure obligations pertaining to subjects/areas in the State list, both through plan transfers and non-plan transfers/expenditures; and

(iii) demands on the resources of the central government and statutory requirements of eliminating revenue deficit of the centre as stipulated in the FRBMA and rules framed thereunder.

A statement containing the fiscal projections for 2009-10 under the reform scenario of the Task Force was also provided along with this submission suggesting that the Commission may make its own assessment in this regard as the Task Force recommendations are based on comprehensive tax reforms and the suggested measures are still to be adopted by the government.

5.13 We have considered the various submissions of the central government: the memorandum dated 1.9.03, the statements of revenues and expenditures submitted from time to time, the statement forwarded in August, 2004 containing fiscal projections for 2009-10, and the statement on the summary position of the finances of the central government submitted in September, 2004. Giving due consideration to these submissions and taking into account the imperatives of the FRBMA as modified by the Finance Act, 2004, we have prescribed a fiscal adjustment path for meeting the FRBMA objectives. In doing so, our attempt has been to maintain an appropriate balance between augmentation of revenue and compression of non-priority expenditure for fiscal consolidation.

Reassessment of the Base Year : 2004-05

5.14 The assessment of the centre's resources needs to be done in two stages. The first step is to arrive at the revenues and expenditure for the base year 2004-05. For this purpose, we have broadly accepted the budget estimates of 2004-05 with some modifications in the revenue receipts and expenditure of the centre. On the suggestion made by the officials of the Ministry of Finance during discussions, we have scaled down the estimate of corporation tax from Rs.88436 crore to Rs.80436 crore on the ground that the Budget Estimates include a one-time estimated collection of arrears to the extent of Rs.8000 crore. This adjustment is only for the purpose of further projections and does not imply that the estimates will not be realized in the base year. The estimate of income tax has been brought down from Rs.50929 crore to Rs.47929 crore consequent to the amendment brought about in the original scheme of securities transaction tax. The base year figures of Union excise duties have also been revised downwards as the budget estimates (Rs. 109199 crore) did not seem achievable in the context of the performance in recent years as also the trend of collections in the current year which indicates that only 34 per cent of the estimate could be realized till September, 2004. We have, therefore, reassessed the base year estimates as Rs. 103557 crore based on the average growth in revenue during 1999-2000 to 2003-04 (RE). The estimate of education cess had also to be adjusted in accordance with the above modifications. Another item in BE 2004-05 that has been reassessed by us is the interest receipts from states. This appeared to be on the higher side, if the central government loans shown as outstanding against the states on 31.3.04 in the Receipts Budget, 2004-05 is kept in view. We have, accordingly, revised the figure of Rs. 29982 crore indicated in the Budget Estimates 2004-05 to Rs. 23164 crore applying a 12 per cent rate of interest on the loans outstanding on 31.3.04. We have had to make corresponding adjustments in the plan revenue expenditure and minor adjustments with a view to retaining the revenue deficit at 2.5 per cent of GDP and fiscal deficit at 4.5 per cent close to the budget estimates. For the remaining items of revenues and expenditure, the BE

2004-05 figures have been adopted by us. However, while computing the outstanding debt of the government of India in the base year, we have excluded the borrowings of Rs. 60000 crore under the Market Stabilization Scheme as these are to be held as cash balance and investments in special securities of states under NSSF as the latter would be serviced by the state governments.

5.15 The recovery of loans from states in the year 2004-05 indicated in the budget documents incorporates a debt-swap of Rs. 11000 crore. This has been retained in our reassessment, although we have separately been informed that the total debt-swap expected to take place during the year is nearly Rs. 46000 crore and a swap of around Rs. 29300 crore has already been effected. The adjustments in this regard are, however, expected to be made at the stage of working out the revised estimates for 2004-05.

Revenue Receipts : 2005-10

Tax Revenues

5.16 The next step is to make an assessment for the period 2005-10. In the central government's forecast, the income tax and corporation tax were assumed to grow at 20 per cent per year during the Commission's award period. Customs duties and service tax were both assumed to grow at the rate of 10 per cent per annum. The projection of Union excise duties was done using a double log regression with index of industrial production (manufacturing) as the independent variable, assuming an average growth of index of industrial production at 6.6 per cent for the period 2004-05 onwards. This translated into an annual growth rate of 10.47 per cent in Union excise duties.

5.17 Compared to these projections, the statement laid by the central government before the Parliament under the FRBMA estimates that during the period 2004-05 to 2006-07, gross tax revenues will grow at an average of 22 per cent per annum based on an assumed average annual growth of 26 per cent in direct taxes and 19 per cent in indirect taxes. The tax-GDP ratio of the centre is projected to rise from 9.2 per cent in 2003-04 RE to 10.2 in 2004-05, 11.1 in 2005-06 and 12.1 in 2006-07. We find that these estimates correspond to the projections in the reform scenario of the Task Force on the implementation of the FRBMA. In our view, the implementation of the tax reforms will take time as it involves far reaching changes, which require the consent of the states. We have, therefore, assessed the tax revenues for the future taking into account the additional resource mobilization possible under the present scenario. We feel that service tax would have a much higher buoyancy than projected by the central government because of significant growth in the services sector. We have also followed the principle that the centre should improve upon its past performance by ensuring better tax compliance and utilizing the scope for mobilizing additional revenues effectively, particularly where service tax is concerned.

5.18 Accordingly, our estimates of tax revenues have been derived by applying growth rates computed on the basis of buoyancy norms for individual taxes. The nominal GDP has been assumed to grow at 12 per cent per annum which, in our view, is realistic in the backdrop of the growth in nominal GDP in the last 2-3 years The buoyancy of each of the major taxes has been worked out on the basis of the growth rates from 1999-2000 to 2003-04 (RE) and the scope for additional resource mobilization. We have accordingly used a buoyancy of 1.7 for corporation tax, 1.4 for income tax, 0.6 for customs, 0.9 for Union excise duties and 1.75 for service tax during our award period. For the remaining taxes, namely, wealth tax and taxes of UTs, the average of the growth rates from 1999-2000 to 2003-04 (RE) have been used.

5.19 Our projection of the tax revenues of the centre entails an improvement in the tax-GDP ratio by 0.92 percentage points by 2009-10 over 2004-05 (reassessed) levels but 1.68 percentage points over 2003-04 (RE) figures. The improvement projected by us is modest compared to the reform scenario of the Task Force as well as that envisaged in the medium-term fiscal policy statement of the central government and is, therefore, more likely to be achieved. This facilitates a realistic estimation of tax devolution to states and subsequently grants.

5.20 The eighty-eighth Constitutional amendment envisages exclusion of service tax from the single divisible pool and lays down the manner in which service tax is to be shared. We have, however, for the purpose of our projections treated it as a part of the divisible pool as at present, since the necessary notification on the amendment has not yet been issued. As already indicated in chapter 2, the implications of this may, therefore, be factored in by the central government while issuing the notification in this regard.

Non-Tax Revenues:

5.21 The principal components of the non-tax revenue are interest receipts, dividends and profits, receipts from the petroleum and telecom sectors and different user charges levied by the central government. The central government's projections with regard to non-tax revenues in respect of most of the items are based on the average rate of growth obtaining over the years 1997-98 to 2001-02. The interest receipts have been projected to grow at the same rate at which overall non-tax revenues have grown during 1997-98 to 2001-02. Similar assumptions have been made in respect of items for which the rate of growth has been seen to fluctuate widely. The receipts on account of dividends and profits have been projected to increase by 4 per cent per year.

5.22 Interest receipts accrue to the central government mainly on the loans given to states, public sector undertakings (PSUs) and the railways. In the central government's memorandum, the declining trend of the share of interest receipts in total non-tax revenues has been noted. It has been further mentioned that in the current regime of softening of interest rates and implementation of debt-swap arrangements, its share in non-tax revenues is likely to decline further. Taking into account the fact that central loans to states to the extent of Rs.114000 crore would have been swapped by 2004-05 and loans to states are expected to be granted in 2004-05 at lower rates of interest, we have projected interest receipts from states by factoring in the interest receipts actually due from past loans during our award period and allowing for continuation of the present interest rate regime with regard to future central loans to states. As regards interest receipts from public sector undertakings, we have been informed that the centre has been supporting many sick PSUs for meeting their immediate needs of salary payment and for covering their gap in resources. The exercise in restructuring of sick PSUs has reduced the revenue streams of the Government on account of foregoing of loan/interest payments, conversion of loan into equity, write-off etc. Our analysis of the returns from PSUs based on data in the Public Enterprises Survey shows extremely low returns varying from 4 to 6 per cent from 1999-2000 to 2001-02 on loans given to PSUs. In our view, this is an area in which greater discipline is called for and the centre should ensure reasonable returns on loans given to PSUs. We have, accordingly, assumed an average return of 10 per cent per annum on outstanding loans to PSUs during our award period.

5.23 Based on the recommendations of the eighth report of the Railway Convention Committee, the railways are expected to pay interest in the form of dividend at the rate of 7 per cent on the entire dividend paying capital, except the capital cost of residential buildings which carries a dividend of 3.5 per cent. Dividend concessions are given to the railways in the form of subsidy from general revenues in respect of unremunerative branch lines, ore lines and in respect of some other specified areas. We find that the projections made by the Ministry of Railways for dividend payment are based on the prescribed rate of dividend payment as recommended by the Railway Convention Committee. We have, therefore, accepted the projections made by the Ministry of Railways in regard to interest receipts from railways. We, however, urge that the dividend concessions given to railways be reviewed at regular intervals not exceeding three years to ensure a rational and properly targeted subsidy.

5.24 As far as the receipts on account of dividends and profits are concerned, we have projected the dividends from PSUs on the basis of the trend growth rate from 1993-94 to 2003-04 keeping in view the fact that disinvestment as earlier planned may not take place. Profits from RBI/Banks have been projected to grow at the rate of 12 per cent from 2005-06 onwards in keeping with the growth rate of nominal GDP. The Comptroller and Auditor General's Report on PSUs (2003) has pointed out that a number of profit making PSUs do not declare dividends, although instructions have repeatedly been issued by the Ministry of Finance that all profit making PSUs should declare a minimum dividend of 20 per cent either on equity or on post-tax profit, whichever is higher. For PSUs in oil, petroleum, chemical and other infrastructure sectors, the prescribed figure for dividend declaration is 30 per cent of post-tax profit. We feel that the government of India needs to take concrete steps to ensure reasonable returns from PSUs on account of dividends.

5.25 Receipts from economic services also contribute significantly to the non-tax revenues of the centre. Our projections for various receipts under economic services are based on norms regarding their potential for generating resources. We notice that the telecom receipts of the centre have shown a marked increase in the last decade as a result of revenue sharing arrangements with the telecom service providers We expect the central government to move towards alignment of license fees to the cost of regulation and administration of the Universal Service Obligation. The auction of radio spectrum is another area where the exchequer may be able to derive fresh non-tax revenues. We find that the Task Force has recommended that the Ministry of Finance should work with TRAI to explore these issues and identify mechanisms through which the spectrum can be effectively auctioned to telecom and computer industry service providers. The government of India should exploit the potential of auction of spectrum for additional revenue generation. In the meantime, keeping the historical growth and scope in regard to license fee alignment in view, we have assumed an annual growth of 20 per cent in telecom receipts. Similarly, keeping in view the scope for additional royalty and the resources generated due to the license fee for the right to exclusive exploration of oil and gas in a particular region, we have provided for an annual growth of 15 per cent in petroleum receipts. The receipts from the remaining economic services have also been projected to grow at 15 per cent per annum. In the case of user charges, which accrue by way of UPSC/SSC examination fees, receipts from stationery, printing, cantonment and defence lands, visa and immigration fees etc., we feel that realignment to cover costs will result in increased revenues and the centre should move towards that objective. Pending a rationalization of user charges, we have projected the remaining items of non-tax revenues on the basis of past growth rates.

5.26 In terms of our projections, the total non-tax revenues of the centre as a percentage of GDP are not expected to grow substantially and will reach 2.45 per cent of GDP in 2009-10 as compared to 2.21 per cent as per our reassessment of 2004-05. The gross revenue receipts of the centre are expected to rise from 12.16 per cent of GDP in 2004-05(reassessed) to 13.33 per cent of GDP in the terminal year of our award period, an increase of 1.17 percentage points. The centre's net revenue receipts will similarly rise from 9.55 per cent of GDP in 2004-05 (reassessed) to 10.39 per cent in the terminal year of our award period.

Non-plan Revenue Expenditure: 2005-10

5.27 Interest payments, defence revenue expenditure, subsidies and pensions form the major component of revenue expenditure of the central government and constitute almost 80 per cent of the total non-plan revenue expenditure. In making projections for various items of non-plan revenue expenditure, the central government has generally used the average rate of growth in each major head over a four-year period (1997-98 to 2001-02). In the case of some of the items, however, the average rate of growth of non-plan expenditure over the four-year period has been used. For projecting plan expenditure, the growth rate indicated in the base line scenario of the Task Force report has been adopted.

5.28 Like the Eleventh Finance Commission, we have, in our forecast, adopted different rules for projecting different items of non-plan revenue expenditure. Our projection of interest payments is based on the assumption of continuation of the present interest rate regime. We find that the effective interest rate on the centre's outstanding debt as on 31.3.04 is 8.56 per cent. The weighted average cost of market borrowings during 2003-04 has been 5.74 per cent. We, therefore, estimate that by 2009-10 the effective interest rate on outstanding debt will decline to 7 per cent. Accordingly, for arriving at interest payments, the outstanding debt of the centre has first been worked out based on the adjustment path prescribed by us for fiscal deficit and thereafter, a declining effective interest rate has been applied such that the effective rate in 2009-10 is 7 per cent.

5.29 With regard to the expenditure on pensions, we found that the growth in the past few years has been erratic (varying between 0.4 per cent and 6.01 per cent) resulting in an average annual growth rate of 1.87 per cent. We find that the growth assumed in BE 2004-05 is 3.65 per cent. The projections of the Ministry of Finance indicate a growth rate of 4 per cent per annum which, we feel, is reasonable taking into account the annual revision of dearness relief and the annual accretion to the number of pensioners The new pension scheme introduced by the central government is not likely to have a significant impact on the pension bill during our reference period. We have, therefore, allowed for an annual growth of 4 per cent in expenditure on pensions during our award period.

5.30 The projection of defence revenue expenditure made by the Ministry of Finance assumes an annual growth of 9.10 per cent. The Ministry's memorandum mentions, *inter alia*, that the need of defence preparedness and the acquisition of modern armaments for the three Services is likely to add to the commitments of the central government in the area of defence spending in the years ahead. The Ministry of Defence has separately stressed before us the 'need-based' requirement of the three Services as reflected in its long-term perspective plans. Its projections imply a steep rise of 52 per cent in defence revenue expenditure in 2005-06 and thereafter, a growth rate ranging from 8.3 to 10.96 per cent. Similarly, in defence capital expenditure, a 37 per cent growth over 2004-05 levels has been sought in 2005-06 after which defence capital expenditure is expected to grow at rates ranging from 7.3 to 10.8 per cent. We have considered the suggestions of the Ministry of Defence. While we appreciate the perceptions of the Ministry of Defence, these need to be viewed in the overall context of the resource position of the central government and various demands on its resources. We further feel that defence spending should have a bias towards capital expenditure and have, therefore, projected defence revenue expenditure based on past growth rates after allowing for some increase. Considering that the defence revenue expenditure has grown at an average rate of 5.38 per cent annually from 1999-2000 to 2003-04 (RE), we feel that an annual growth of 6.5 per cent in defence revenue expenditure for the purpose of forecast during our award period is reasonable. The increase in capital expenditure as a percentage of GDP estimated by us later is expected to take care of the additional requirements of capital expenditure on defence.

5.31 Subsidies form an important component of the centre's expenditure. In addition to food and fertilizer subsidy, the central government has, since 2002-03, been incurring substantial expenditure on petroleum subsidy, despite the decision to dismantle the administered price mechanism in the petroleum sector. The central government's memorandum states that there does not appear to be any likelihood of the subsidy bill getting reduced in spite of "exhortation/pronouncements" on this account. A fairly low growth in the expenditure on subsidies has, however, been projected by the centre based on the inputs of the concerned Ministries. In the context of subsidies, attention needs also to be paid to the recommendations of the Expenditure Reforms Commission (ERC), the implementation of which would ultimately result in savings. It is further seen from the medium-term fiscal policy strategy statement that the central government intends to take up an intensive review of the operational aspects of the subsidies and restructure them so that the benefits are not usurped by those not intended to be the beneficiaries of these subsides. Our projection of subsidies reflects to a great extent these policy decisions. Keeping in view these initiatives, we have held constant the food subsidy at Rs. 22000 crore per year during 2005-10 as against the BE 2004-05 figure of Rs. 25800 crore on the consideration that the BE 2004-05 levels include some arrears which are not likely to be repeated during our award period. It may be noted that the Task Force Report has assumed that the food subsidy would decline by 5 per cent per year. In regard to petroleum subsidy, we have assumed that it would be phased out by 2007-08. Fertilizer subsidy has been frozen at BE 2004-05 levels during our award period in the light of ERC's recommendations and the recent decision to carry out a review of subsidies. Other subsidies have similarly been held constant at BE 2004-05 levels. Consequently, in our reassessment, subsidies as a percentage of GDP would decline from 1.40 per cent in the base year to 0.66 per cent in the terminal year of our award period.

5.32 As per our terms of reference, we are required to consider the demands on the centre on account of expenditure on internal and border security. The average annual growth in expenditure on police from 1999-2000 to 2003-04 (RE) has been 7.04 per cent. The central government's memorandum has pointed out that in the present internal security environment, it is likely that expenditure on central police forces will increase rapidly in the coming years. The likelihood of raising additional battalions of police to meet the needs of internal security has also been mentioned. The Ministry of Home Affairs. in its submissions to the Commission has highlighted the need for higher allocations not only for recurring expenditure but also on account of certain new initiatives. In view of this, we have provided for an annual growth of 7.5 per cent for the expenditure on police.

5.33 The remaining major items of non-plan revenue expenditure of the central government are broadly divided into Other General Services, Economic Services and Social Services. Salaries constitute a major portion of these expenditures, particularly of Other General Services. Although the Eleventh Finance Commission had segregated the salary and non-salary components of such expenditure and projected these at differential growth rates, we have taken into account the recent trends and projected each of these items based on the composite growth rates after making our own assessment of the expenditure under these heads. Accordingly, the Other General Services and Social Services have been assumed to grow at the rate of 5 per cent while Economic Services have been allowed to grow at a higher rate of 7.5 per cent annually during our award period.

5.34 In the context of the expenditure of the central government on salaries, it is necessary again to refer to the reports of the ERC covering 38 ministries/departments. The ERC studied the working of all ministries/departments and considered whether their activities needed to be carried out by the government and whether these could be tackled more effectively through other methods. After a detailed scrutiny, the ERC recommended abolition of around 42000 posts in the government. Although the ministries and departments were required to implement the recommendations of the ERC, the pace of implementation has been slow. According to the information collected from various ministries by the Commission, only 9833 posts have so far been abolished. Information on the amount of savings which has accrued to government as a result of this is incomplete. Available figures place the annual saving at Rs. 68.21 crore. An attempt was also made by the Commission to ascertain the likely savings that would have accrued to government, had the ERCs recommendations been implemented in full. Although the information is again incomplete due to many ministries/departments being unable or unwilling to make their estimation, it appears that at least an additional sum of Rs. 250 crore could have been saved annually by full implementation. For rationalizing the centre's expenditure on salaries, there is a need to implement all the recommendations of the Expenditure Reforms Commission immediately. There is also a need to have periodic reviews of the functions carried out by various ministries in order to ensure that activities which are not necessary in the current context are not continued.

5.35 The residual categories of non-plan revenue expenditure include expenditure of the union territories (UTs), postal deficit and grants-in-aid to foreign governments etc. Postal deficits have been projected on the basis of the forecast of the Department of Posts showing a declining trend during our award period. Other expenditures including expenditure of the UTs and other non-plan revenue expenditure have been projected by us on the basis of average annual growth rates from 1999-2000 to 2003-04 (RE).

5.36 In making our projections on various items of non-plan revenue expenditure, we have not factored in the compensation that may be payable to states for revenue losses arising from the introduction of VAT with effect from 1.4.2005 and reduction in the central sales tax rate. The central government would, therefore, have to find resources to provide for this compensation separately, should the need arise.

Plan Revenue Expenditure: 2005-10

5.37 We have made an analysis of the plan revenue expenditure of the centre with particular reference to plan grants to states. In this context, a criticism often leveled against the central government is that it interferes in the states' priorities through the mechanism of centrally sponsored/central plan schemes on subjects, which are entirely in the State List or substantially handled by the states though in the Concurrent List. We, therefore, analyzed the demands on the resources of the central government on account of expenditure on subjects which are in the State/Concurrent List. Our study reveals that on an average 9.6 per cent of the total expenditure of government of India is in respect of subjects which are in the State

List. This has a plan component of 7.4 per cent and a non-plan component of 2.2 per cent. Similarly, on an average 9.4 per cent of the total expenditure of government of India is in respect of subjects which are in the Concurrent List. This has a plan component of 3.8 per cent and a non-plan component of 5.6 per cent. The centre incurs a substantial expenditure on its ministries/ departments to administer such schemes. In pursuance of the objective of rationalizing the central plan and centrally sponsored schemes (CSSs) by way of convergence, weeding out or transfer to the states, the Planning Commission carried out a zero based budgeting (ZBB) exercise for all the central ministries/departments in the terminal year of the Ninth Plan. As a result of this exercise, the Planning Commission recommended that out of a total of 360 CSSs in operation, 48 schemes may be weeded out, 161 schemes may be merged into 53 schemes and the remaining 135 schemes may be retained. This implied that 188 CSSs were to be carried forward to the Tenth Plan. In respect of 2247 central sector schemes, the ZBB exercise carried out by the Planning Commission resulted in recommendations for weeding out 539 schemes, merger of 1019 schemes into 233 schemes and retention of remaining 689 schemes, thereby implying carrying forward of 922 central plan schemes to the Tenth Plan. The Tenth Five Year Plan document emphasizes the need to continue this ZBB exercise as a regular feature and recommends that states should also be encouraged to carry out such reviews of their schemes.

5.38 For projecting plan revenue expenditure, we have followed the methodology used by the Eleventh Finance Commission of working it out as a residual keeping in view the targets laid down for revenue deficit and after arriving at non-plan revenue expenditure. Compared to the average annual growth of 13.76 per cent in plan revenue expenditure of the centre from 1999-2000 to 2003-04, our projections imply a higher growth in plan revenue expenditure except in the first year of the award period. Plan grants to states form a major component of the plan revenue expenditure of the centre. Based on the methodology of the Eleventh Finance Commission, plan grants to states have been worked out by us as a residual of the ceiling on overall fiscal transfers recommended by us deducting the amounts recommended as tax devolution and grants-in-aid to state governments.

Revenue Expenditure : 2005-10

5.39 On the basis of our projections, the total revenue expenditure of the centre is expected to decline from 12.05 per cent of GDP in 2004-05 (reassessed) to 10.39 per cent in 2009-10.

Overall Fiscal Transfers

5.40 Apart from tax devolution and grants, fiscal transfers to states also include devolution of funds through centrally sponsored schemes, block plan grants and other discretionary transfers The Eleventh Finance Commission had looked at the revenue transfers to states between the period 1979-80 to 1997-98 and had suggested that the centre's fiscal transfers to the states should be around 37.5 per cent of the gross revenue receipts of the central government. We have reviewed the matter. Keeping in view the slight increase recommended by us in states' share in central taxes and the need to sustain the resource transfers for Plan, we estimate that the total transfers from the centre to states would be 38 per cent of the gross revenue receipts of the centre. This is in keeping with the indicative ceiling we have suggested.

Capital Receipts and Expenditure: 2005-10

5.41 Our terms of reference require us to consider the objective of not only balancing the receipts and expenditures on revenue account of the centre but also generating surpluses for capital investment and reducing fiscal deficit. We have factored in the target of bringing down the fiscal deficit to 3 per cent of GDP by 2009, as laid down in the rules under FRBMA. We have maintained it at 3 per cent of GDP in the terminal year of our award period. The capital receipts of the centre comprise recovery of loans and advances, disinvestment receipts and borrowings. For projecting recovery of loans from state governments, we have taken into account the actual recoveries due from state governments and provided for recovery of additional loans expected to be granted during 2005-10 on the basis of a 20 year repayment schedule with a moratorium of 50 per cent on half the repayment in the first five years. Recovery of other loans is based on the profile from 1999-2000 to 2003-04 (RE). As far as disinvestment receipts are concerned, we have accepted the projections of the central government which indicate that the receipts would be Rs. 4000 crore per annum during our award period.

5.42 The estimates of capital expenditure during our award period have been worked out as a residual keeping in view the targets for fiscal and revenue deficits and the expectations in regard to non-debt capital receipts. The projections made by us indicate an increase in capital expenditure as a percentage of GDP by 0.66 percentage point by the terminal year of our award period as compared to the base year figures. This compares well with the corresponding increase from 1999-2000 to 2004-05, which has been of the order of 0.44 percentage points if we exclude the payments to NSSF met out of debt-swap receipts.

Statements Containing Projections: 2005-10

5.43 The revenue and expenditure projections based on the above reassessment of central finances for the period 2005-06 to 2009-10 along with item-wise details are given in annexure 5.1. In chapter 12, we have devised a scheme of debt relief for states as a result of which the centre's interest receipts and capital receipts will decline during our award period. After factoring in the impact of the component of the debt relief applicable to all states and assuming a success rate of fifty per cent in respect of debt write-off related to fiscal performance, we have made revised projections as indicated at annexure 5.2. These projections also take into account the impact of our recommendation regarding the disintermediation by the centre as far as loans to states are concerned. As such, we have assumed that additional central lending to states will come down to half of 2004-05 (BE) levels in 2005-06 and will be phased out by 2009-10. We have also assumed that the interest rates charged will be aligned to the marginal cost of borrowing by the centre.

As a result of the debt relief recommended by us, while the centre's tax-GDP ratio remains unaffected, the gross revenue receipts will be 13.13 per cent of GDP in 2009-10 compared to 13.33 in terms of the figures in annexure 5.1, net revenue receipts will be 10.20 per cent compared to 10.39 while revenue expenditure will be 10.20 per cent of GDP compared to 10.39, the impact being felt on plan revenue expenditure. Capital expenditure will reach 3.47 per cent of GDP in 2009-10 compared to 3.63 per cent otherwise. The targets under the FRBMA are, however, expected to be met in terms of both the projections.

□□

Chapter 6

State Finances: Assessment of Revenue and Expenditure

6.1 In making recommendations regarding tax devolution and grants-in-aid to the states, it is necessary to assess the revenues and expenditures of states for the period 2005-10. In this context, para 11 of the terms of reference (TOR) requires us to prepare state-wise estimates of receipts and expenditure. While carrying out this exercise, the Commission, under para 6 of TOR, has to consider the resources of the state governments and their taxation efforts, the need for balancing the revenue account of the states, maintenance of capital assets and completed plan schemes, and ensuring commercial viability of irrigation and power sectors.

Basic approach

6.2 Assessment of states' revenues and expenditures requires to be guided by a normative approach, which serves to ensure inter-state equity and avoids adverse incentives. No state can obtain a larger share than what is warranted by the deficiency of its fiscal capacity. Similarly, a state should not expect expenditure not justified by normative considerations to be taken into account in the assessment. We have, however, recognised that it is not possible to apply fully the normative principle because of the heterogeneity of the states with respect to various dimensions affecting capacities and costs, and problems related to the availability of relevant data. In our projections for the receipts and expenditure of the states during the forecast period 2005-10, we have relied on the fiscal data of 1993-2003 as contained in the finance accounts, as well as on the revised and budget estimates for 2003-04 and 2004-05 respectively. The projections of revenue and expenditure were also obtained from each state for the period 2005-10. While seeking these projections, it was indicated to the states that these should broadly conform to the objectives being pursued under their Medium Term Fiscal Reform Programme (MTFRP).

6.3 Table 6.1 shows, in aggregate, a comparison of past period data for certain broad fiscal parameters with the projections received from the states, while state-wise details of projections are furnished in annexure 6.1.

6.4 The pre-devolution deficit, in aggregate, is seen as coming down from a level of 4.5 per cent of GDP in 2002-03 to 4 per cent in 2004-05 (BE), and finally to 3.8 per cent in 2009-10. However, the reduction over 2004-10 is driven entirely by the projected compression in non-plan revenue

Table 6.1

Comparison of Past Fiscal Data with Projections made by the States

(Rs. crore/per cent)

Item	1993-94 (Actuals)	2002-03 (Actuals)	2004-05 (B.E)	2009-10 (States' projection)	2005-10 (States' projection)
1. Own Revenue Receipts	59081 *(6.9)*	166484 *(6.7)*	215941 *(7.0)*	328482 *(6.0)*	1391002 *(6.3)*
2. Non-Plan Revenue Expenditure	87552 *(10.2)*	277630 *(11.2)*	340444 *(11.0)*	534054 *(9.8)*	2315499 *(10.5)*
3. Pre-devolution deficit (1 – 2)	-28471 *(-3.3)*	-111147 *(-4.5)*	-124503 *(-4.0)*	-205572 *(-3.8)*	-924497 *(-4.2)*
4. GDP (Current prices)	859220	2469564	3104857	5471819	22091645

Figures in parentheses are percentage of GDP.
GDP at current prices for 2004-10 has been projected by the Finance Commission.

expenditure to the tune of 1.2 percentage point of GDP, which is substantially offset by projected reduction in own revenue receipts going down by 1 percentage point of GDP over this period. A fall in own revenue receipts as a percentage of GDP can not help in achieving the objective of restructuring the overall public finances aiming at a healthier fiscal situation.

6.5 We, therefore, decided to make our own assessment of the revenue and expenditure for each state. Our macro approach has been guided by the overall objective of restructuring the public finances of the states outlined in Chapter 4. Norms have been used for making projections for each of the 28 States in the forecast period. This was a two-step process. In the first step, revenue and expenditure for the base year 2004-05 were estimated. Some corrections in the base year were necessary, as accepting the budget estimates may amount to endorsing laxity in expenditure or inefficiency in raising revenues on the part of the states. Thereafter, revenue and expenditure were normatively projected for 2005-10 in consonance with the overall goals of fiscal restructuring.

Gross State Domestic Product

6.6 The Gross State Domestic Product (GSDP) provides an indication of the fiscal capacity of a state government to raise revenues. GSDP levels also give an idea of the level of expenditure required to pursue the chosen trajectory of economic growth. One of our first tasks, therefore, has been to project the GSDP of each state during the forecast period.

6.7 The time series data on comparable levels of nominal GSDP at factor cost were provided upto 2001-02 for each state by the Central Statistical Organisation (CSO). The non-comparable nominal GSDP series received individually from each state was available up to 2002-03. The growth rates for 2002-03, available from the states' series, were applied on the GSDP of 2001-02 of the comparable series to obtain comparable nominal GSDP for 2002-03 for each state. The next step was to project nominal GSDP for 2003-04 and thereafter upto 2009-10. Since the nominal growth rate of aggregate GSDP has been marginally lower than that of GDP, the ratio of aggregate GSDP's trend growth rate (TGR) to that of GDP was obtained for the period 1993-2002. This ratio was applied on 12.25 per cent growth rate adopted for GDP in

2003-04. This yielded a figure of 11.1 per cent nominal growth rate for aggregate GSDP for 2003-04. For arriving at the state-specific nominal growth rates, the average annual growth rate of each state's comparable GSDP was worked out for the period 1997-2002 and proportionately adjusted in a manner that in the aggregate, the nominal GSDP growth rate came to 11.1 per cent. These state-specific growth rates were applied on the 2002-03 levels to arrive at 2003-04 levels for each state. In a similar manner, state-specific growth rates were derived for 2004-05 and applied on the estimated 2003-04 levels to arrive at state wise nominal GSDP estimates for 2004-05. It may be noted that for 2004-05, the projected nominal GDP growth rate of 12 per cent yielded a growth rate of 10.9 per cent for aggregate GSDP.

6.8 In the forecast period 2005-10, the annual nominal growth rate of GDP has been projected at 12 per cent. For the purpose of GSDP projections, the same growth rate (i.e., 12 per cent) has been adopted for aggregate GSDP in order to achieve the overall goals for restructuring the states' finances. In conformity with the view expressed in the Tenth Five Year Plan document that GSDP should grow at different rates for reducing regional inequalities, we have prescribed an annual nominal growth rate of 12.8 per cent for states projected to achieve average real annual growth rate of 8 per cent and above in the Tenth Plan document. Similarly, 12 per cent and 11 per cent nominal growth rates have been prescribed for states expected to achieve a real annual growth rate between 8 per cent and 7 per cent and below 7 per cent respectively during the Tenth Plan. Annexure 6.2 gives the state-wise growth rates of GSDP. The annual nominal growth rate of aggregate GSDP then works out to 12 per cent during the forecast period 2005-10.

Own Tax Revenues

6.9 Our approach to projecting own tax revenues of states was guided by para 6(iii) of TOR, which reads, "In making its recommendations, the Commission shall have regard, among other considerations, to the resources of the state governments for the five years commencing on 1st April 2005, on the basis of levels of taxation and non-tax revenues likely to be reached at the end of 2003-04". Para 6(v) further stipulates that the Commission should take into account the taxation efforts of each state government as against targets, if any, and the potential for additional resources mobilization in order to improve the tax-GSDP ratio.

6.10 The own tax revenues of states consists of sales tax, excise, stamp duty and registration fee, motor vehicles and passenger tax, and others. The Tenth Finance Commission had projected each of these categories separately for each state. The Eleventh Finance Commission, however, reasoned that possibilities of substitution among different tax streams made it more desirable to project own tax revenues as one omnibus group. We are in agreement with the view expressed by the Eleventh Finance Commission.

6.11 In keeping with the TOR, the improvement in the tax-GSDP ratio became the underlying principle for projecting own tax revenues of states. This was achieved by first adjusting for the under-utilisation of taxable capacity in the base year for some states, and then by further improving its utilisation through prescriptive levels of tax buoyancy specific to each state.

Base year estimates

6.12 The TGR of own tax revenue (OTR) has been estimated for each state for the period 1993-2003 and applied on their respective 2002-03 levels (the latest year for which accounts figures are available) to arrive at the TGR-based estimates for the base year 2004-05. For the six bifurcated states, the same TGR has been used for the parent and the successor states, which was obtained from their combined accounts for the period 1993-2003. The TGR so determined has been applied on the separate accounts of 2002-03 for the bifurcated states to arrive at the TGR based estimates of 2004-05. Thereafter, the TGR based estimate of OTR of each state has been compared with its respective budget estimates of 2004-05 and the higher of the two chosen as the initial estimates for the base year. The initial estimates were next expressed as a ratio to GSDP for each state, and the averages of this ratio for special and general category states were computed separately for 2004-05.

6.13 For the purpose of normative assessment, at least partial adjustment for under-utilization of taxable capacity in the base year 2004-05, was deemed reasonable for states where the ratio of OTR to GSDP was below the respective category average. Specifically, for the purpose of normative base year estimation in respect of below average states, we increased the initially estimated tax-GSDP ratios by 30 per cent of their distance from the respective group average of the special and general category states. Having determined the normative OTR/GSDP ratio of each state in this manner, this was applied on the estimated GSDP level of 2004-05 to arrive at the base year adjusted level of OTR in absolute (rupee) terms. This has resulted in adjusted own tax revenue aggregated for all states bearing a ratio of 5.9 per cent to national GDP in the base year.

Projections for forecast period

6.14 We have incorporated an increase of a little less than 0.9 percentage point in the aggregate OTR as a percentage of GDP over the forecast period, i.e., from 5.91 per cent in the base year to 6.75 per cent in the terminal year. This is in accordance with the plan for restructuring government finances. The increase in OTR/GDP ratio implies that aggregate OTR should grow at an annual rate of 15 per cent in the forecast period. Keeping this in view, prescriptive buoyancy levels of 1.1, 1.2, 1.25, 1.3 and 1.35 were assigned to individual states as detailed in annexure 6.2. While assigning prescriptive buoyancies to the individual states, the impact of the introduction of VAT was assumed to be revenue neutral, if not revenue augmenting.

6.15 For assigning the prescriptive buoyancies, the following factors have been taken into consideration:

(i) Average OTR/GSDP ratio achieved in 2000-03.

(ii) Improvement in OTR/GSDP ratio in 2000-03 over 1993-96.

(iii) Average per capita GSDP for 1999-2002.

A state, for example, was prescribed a higher buoyancy if its recent OTR/GSDP ratio as well as its improvement over time were relatively low, provided its per capita income was relatively high. The assigned buoyancy was multiplied by the projected state-specific GSDP annual growth rate to arrive at annual growth rate of OTR for each state, which was then applied on the base year estimates to generate OTR levels in the forecast period. Annexure 6.2 indicates the projected GSDP growth rates of states during the forecast period.

Own Non-Tax Revenues

6.16 Unlike OTR, own non-tax revenues (ONTR) have not been treated as one omnibus category since these included receipt items which have little in common with each other. Major receipt items under ONTR, therefore, have been projected individually. In view of the data constraints, the remaining items were clubbed under one residual category and a uniform norm was applied for the projection period. The items projected are as follows:

- (i) Interest receipts and dividends
- (ii) Royalty
- (iii) Receipts from forestry and wildlife
- (iv) Other miscellaneous general services and lotteries
- (v) Irrigation receipts
- (vi) Other own non-tax revenues

Interest Receipts and Dividends

6.17 Interest receipts accrue to states against institutional and non-institutional loans given by the state governments. Institutional lending is mainly to state level public sector undertakings (PSUs), which include state electricity boards (SEBs), state road transport corporations (SRTCs) and other commercial and promotional enterprises. Non-institutional loans are extended mostly to government employees. It was found that the effective rate of return on outstanding loans was extremely low at around 2 per cent in 2002-03 for all states put together. This was much lower than the cost at which the state governments borrow. In particular, SEBs and SRTCs routinely defaulted in interest payments and loan repayments. Similar was the case for dividends as well, where the average rate of return was even lower at 0.6 per cent in 2002-03.

6.18 Para 6(vii) of the TOR mentions the need to ensure commercial viability of public sector enterprises, including power projects, through means such as adjustment of user charges and relinquishing of non-priority enterprises through privatization or disinvestment. We have assumed a 7 per cent return on outstanding loans and advances and 5 per cent on equity, to be achieved in a graded manner by the terminal year of the forecast period. For this purpose, the amount of loans and advances as on 1.4.2005 and equity level as on 1.4.2003 have been kept constant throughout the forecast period.

Royalty

6.19 Under this head, royalty from minerals, coal and petroleum has been considered. We took note of the fact that the power to revise the rates of royalty in most of the cases vests in the central government. Government of India has not been revising the royalty rates as regularly as provided for. This is particularly true of coal and lignite. We recommend that since royalty is an important source of revenue for some of the states, the rates of royalty should be fixed on an ad valorem basis.

6.20 For projecting this revenue stream, we took a view that since the states did not have the power to revise the royalty rates, the best that can be expected is that revenue under this head will keep pace with inflation. The average of three years 2002-05 was compared with 2004-05 (BE), and the higher of the two was adopted as the base year figure, and an annual growth rate of 5 per cent was applied to project the figures for 2005-10.

Receipts from Forestry and Wild Life

6.21 The receipts under this head do not show a clear trend for any of the states. The Supreme Court has placed restrictions on the exploitation of forest wealth, which has a consequential impact on states' revenues. In this case, the average revenue of three years 2002-05 was compared with 2004-05(BE) and the higher of the two adopted as the base year estimate, and held at that level for the forecast period.

Receipts from Other Miscellaneous General Services and Lotteries

6.22 The items under this head include sundry receipts not included under any other major head. Due to unpredictability of receipts under this head, it was considered best to take the average of three years 2002-05 as the base year estimate, on which an annual growth rate of 5 per cent was applied in the forecast period. Net positive lottery receipts were averaged for 2000-03 (2001-03 for bifurcated states), and held constant at that level in the forecast period.

Receipts from Irrigation

6.23 Para 6(vii) of TOR refers to the need for ensuring commercial viability of irrigation projects. It was, therefore, decided that for projecting receipts under this item, the principle of recovery of current costs be adopted explicitly. Irrigation receipts in 2004-05 (BE), which have been adopted as the base year estimates, were 32.3 per cent of non-plan revenue expenditure on irrigation for all states put together. This recovery rate was considered very low. Without higher rates of cost recovery, the maintenance of irrigation network would suffer seriously. Accordingly, in the assessment of irrigation receipts, cost recovery rates of 50 per cent in 2005-06, 60 per cent in 2006-07, 70 per cent in 2007-08, 80 per cent in 2008-09 and 90 per cent in 2009-10 have been prescribed in relation to the maintenance expenditure on utilised potential projected for the major, medium and minor irrigation projects in the forecast period.

Other Own Non-Tax Revenues

6.24 The receipts under other own non-tax revenues (OONTR) form a residual category after excluding the items mentioned above from total own non-tax revenues, and these largely represent the flows from various user charges. This residual item was dis-aggregated into general, social and economic services. While doing so, receipts under the head "Elections" from general services were excluded, because election expenditure has been projected on a net basis separately. Similarly, receipts from dairy, power and transport were also excluded from economic services. These exclusions from the economic services were in keeping with our stand of not allowing implicit subsidies for departmentally run commercial activities. Thus the adjusted OONTR (service-wise) was obtained for each state for the period 1993-2003 (actuals), 2003-04(R.E) and 2004-05 (B.E). Next, service-wise TGR for the period 1993-2003 was computed for each state and applied on 2002-03 levels to arrive at the initial estimates for 2004-05. For bifurcated states, combined accounts were used to estimate the trend growth rate, which has been applied on their respective accounts of 2002-03 to generate the initial estimates. These initial estimates have been compared with 2004-05(BE) and the higher of the two taken as the base year estimates. On these estimates, 12.5 per cent annual rate of growth has been applied for general services and 25 per cent annual growth rate for both social and economic services in the forecast period, reflecting the need for the states to achieve a greater degree of cost recovery in these services.

Non-Plan Non-Finance Commission Grants

6.25 These are mainly discretionary grants provided by various ministries of government of India. Since these are non-finance commission (non-FC) grants on the non-plan side, it is necessary to take a view about their levels in the forecast period. The Eleventh Finance Commission had taken the average of the latest three years as the base year estimates and applied an annual growth rate of 10 per cent in the forecast period. Since there is no firm basis for projecting these grants in view of their discretionary nature, these are best excluded from the base year assessment of both receipts and expenditure. The average of these grants for the period 2000-03 for each state was taken as the base year level. These were excluded from the base year estimates of non-plan revenue receipts. Correspondingly, since the break-up of expenditure against these grants was not available, an amount equal to the base year estimate of the non-FC grants has been deducted from the base year estimates of "Other general services" under non-plan revenue expenditure.

Expenditure: Non-Plan Revenue Expenditure

6.26 In projecting non-plan revenue expenditure (NPRE), an approach similar to that for non-tax revenues has been followed and item wise projections made, wherever possible. In other cases, items have been clubbed under some broad categories either for want of adequate information or for the purpose of applying category-wise norms. Further, while our aim in general has been to achieve some compression in the growth of non-plan revenue expenditure in a normative manner, we also believe that certain components of this expenditure deserve to be encouraged. These components are education, health and maintenance of roads and buildings. We have provided for a more liberal treatment of these components as compared to other components of NPRE while projecting expenditure.

6.27 Before undertaking the projection exercise, certain adjustments are required in the NPRE data series for the period 1993-2005. The grants as well as expenditure relating to calamity relief have been excluded because this item is projected separately in chapter 9. In the case of local bodies, grants have been excluded from revenue receipt side, but the expenditure on local bodies has been retained on NPRE side. In our view, separate recommendations on local body grants should serve as additional grants over and above those embedded in the deficit grants. Expenditure relating to sinking fund provisions, booked under the head "appropriation for debt avoidance", has also not been considered as it would be inappropriate to allow this expenditure to be met out of deficit grants. Next, all contra-entries have been excluded, which figure in equal magnitude both under non-tax revenues and under non-plan revenue expenditure without having any net impact on the states' deficits. Under this head, interest payments embedded in irrigation expenditure, with a contra-entry under interest receipts, figured prominently. Further, adjustments for "transfer to/from funds" have been made to neutralize the impact of under-statement or over-statement of expenditure. This involved deducting those "transfer to fund" expenditures from respective functional heads, where these have been booked but not translated into actual cash outflows. Similarly, those "transfer from fund" receipts have been added to respective functional heads where actual cash outflows took place without the corresponding budgetary allocation. Expenditure on lotteries has also been excluded as it has been taken to the receipt side on net basis. Further, expenditure on elections has been excluded as the receipts under elections have not been considered in our data series, and because net expenditure on elections has been projected separately.

6.28 These adjustments have made the assessment of NPRE data comparable across states. Further, we have deleted all identified subsidies, including those for power, transport and dairy sectors, by excluding the non-plan revenue expenditure and receipts under these heads. All the above adjustments provided an adjusted NPRE series for each state. Consequently, the base year estimates also did not include these items listed above for exclusion.

6.29 The adjusted series excluded subsidies relating to power, transport, dairy and food. It was felt, however, that some subsidy was needed to ensure adequate outreach of the public distribution system in the remotest corners of a state. Therefore, an annual provision for food subsidy at the rate of Rs.10 per capita per year has been made for each of the states in the forecast period. The amount of food subsidy for each state is indicated in annexure 6.3.

6.30 The adjusted non-plan revenue expenditure of each state has been analysed under four broad categories viz., general services, social services, economic services, and compensation and assignment to local bodies. Within these categories, certain important items have been taken up individually for projection. These items include interest payments and pension payments under general services; education, health, and maintenance of buildings under social services, and maintenance of irrigation projects and roads under economic services. After making separate projections for these items, the remaining items were clubbed under "Other General Services", "Other Social Services" and "Other Economic Services" on which specific norms were applied for projection.

Compensation and assignment to local bodies was projected independently. In addition to these four broad categories, the expenditure relating to transfer of committed plan liabilities at the end of the Tenth Plan to the non-plan revenue expenditure side has also been projected.

Interest Payments

Base year assessment

6.31 It was felt that the interest payments, as budgeted by the states for 2004-05, could not be accepted because it would amount to accommodating excessive borrowings by some states, which would not be fair to those states, which have borrowed more prudently. For assessing the interest payments in the base year, the ratio of interest payments to total revenue receipts (IP/TRR) (net of lotteries) has been estimated for each state for the year 2002-03, and group averages worked out for special and non-special category states. For states with ratios higher than the respective group averages, only 80 per cent of the excess was allowed to be retained. Thereafter, the reduced ratios of such states and unadjusted ratios of the remaining states were applied on respective state's TRR to arrive at the corrected level of interest payments for 2002-03. On the corrected levels of each state, 10 per cent annual growth has been applied to arrive at the base year estimates for 2004-05. This growth rate was the same as employed by Eleventh Finance Commission to project interest payments in their forecast period, 2000-05.

Projections for forecast period

6.32 Interest payments have grown at an annual rate of 18.2 per cent during the period 1993-2003 for all states combined. There has been a fall in the nominal interest rates in recent years, and the states have also been able to benefit from the debt-swap programme of the central government. Taking into account the strategy for restructuring state finances, the growth rate of interest payments for all states taken together was pegged at 7.5 per cent per annum. Using this level as the bench mark, general category states were assigned differential growth rates, namely 6.5 per cent, 7.5 per cent and 8.5 per cent for projecting their interest payments. States having IP/TRR ratio above 30 per cent in 2003-04 (RE) were assigned lower growth rate of 6.5 per cent, because these states have a very heavy burden of interest payment on account of excessive borrowings in the past, and this burden needs to be reduced in the forecast period. States with IP/TRR ratio between 23 per cent and 30 per cent were assigned a growth rate of 7.5 per cent, and those below 23 per cent were assigned a growth rate of 8.5 per cent during the forecast period. All special category states were assigned a growth rate of 7.5 per cent, except one which was assigned a rate of 6.5 per cent due to its excessively high debt burden. Thereafter, state-specific growth rates have been applied on the base year estimates for projecting the interest payments during 2005-10. This was compared with the state's own projection, and the lower of the two adopted.

Pension Payments

6.33 In projecting pension payments, our effort was to make minimum departure from the existing trends, given the inability of the states to influence the pension profile in the short or medium term. Accordingly, 2004-

05 (BE) figures have been adopted as the base year estimates for pension payments. Thereafter, the annual growth rate of pension payments in the forecast period has been worked out. Our analysis of states' aggregate pension payments revealed a growth rate of 23.9 per cent for the period 1993-2003. Since this period included the period of upward revision of pensions on account of Fifth Pay Commission's recommendations, it was decided to look at the growth of pension payments in the recent years. The states' aggregate pension payments have grown at a rate of 14.8 per cent and 8.7 per cent in 2003-04 and 2004-05 respectively. We have adopted an annual growth rate of 10 per cent and applied it on the base year estimates of each state to generate pension payment levels in the forecast period. It may be noted that this rate being higher than the rate of inflation, factors in the increase in the number of pensioners during 2005-10.

General Education and Health

6.34 As already pointed out earlier, we have allowed for expenditure restructuring in favour of these two sectors. This has been reflected both in providing higher growth rate for non-salary component in projecting the expenditure in this chapter, as well as in providing additional grants-in-aid for these sectors as discussed in Chapter 10. For estimating the base year figures, the TGR for 1993-2003 was applied on the figures for 2002-03 to arrive at the corresponding number for 2004-05. This was compared with the budget estimates for 2004-05 and lower of the two taken as base year estimates.

6.35 Thereafter, the growth rates to be used during the forecast period have been determined. In the case of education, it has been found that for the states as a whole, roughly 85 per cent of the non-plan revenue expenditure consisted of salaries, while the corresponding figure for health was about 75 per cent. In general, we have been providing only 5 per cent growth rate in salaries so as to ensure that salaries are held constant in real terms. While this norm has been followed for the health sector, a slightly higher growth rate of about 6 per cent was adopted for the salary component in education sector in order to factor in the additional recruitment of teachers, which would be necessary to achieve the goals of Sarva Shiksha Abhiyan. Separately, a high growth rate of 30 per cent in the non-salary part of these two sectors has been provided. Combining the growth rates of salary and non-salary components with their respective weights as above, a composite growth rate of 9.5 per cent for general education (major head 2202) and 11.5 per cent for health (major heads 2210 and 2211) was obtained. These growth rates were applied to each state. The projected expenditure for these two sectors (excluding expenditure relating to additional grants-in-aid provided separately in chapter 10) for 2005-10 is indicated in annexures 6.4 and 6.5.

Maintenance of Irrigation Works

6.36 We have obtained the norms for maintenance of irrigation works (major heads 2701 and 2702) from the Ministry of Water Resources. Normative expenditure requirements of Rs.600 per hectare for utilised potential and Rs.300 per hectare for unutilised potential of major and medium irrigation projects in the base year 2004-05 were indicated to us. In the case of minor irrigation works, the Ministry suggested a norm of Rs.400 per hectare in 2004-05 for utilised potential. The Eleventh Finance Commission had, however, taken a view that the maintenance norms for minor irrigation works should be half of those for major and medium projects. We decided to follow the practice of the Eleventh Finance Commission and adopted a rate of Rs.300 per hectare in 2004-05 for utilised potential of minor irrigation. It was decided to ignore the unutilised potential of minor irrigation works as being insignificant. For special category states, a step up of 30 per cent has been applied on the maintenance norms, as suggested by the Ministry. State-wise utilised and unutilised potential as reported by the Planning Commission at the end of the Ninth Plan have been taken for working out maintenance expenditure. For each state, the norm based estimates for 2004-05 have been compared with that of 2004-05 (B.E), and the higher of the two estimates adopted as the base year estimates. This was felt necessary to provide larger provision for maintenance. On the base year estimates so worked out, 5 per cent annual rate of growth was applied to generate projected levels in the forecast period. Annexures 6.6 and 6.7 indicate the projected level of maintenance expenditure on major & medium and minor irrigation schemes during the forecast period.

Maintenance of Roads and Buildings

6.37 The TGR for non-plan revenue expenditure for maintenance of roads and bridges (major head 3054) and for buildings (major heads 2059 and 2216) for the period 1993-03 (combined TGR in the case of bifurcated states) was ascertained under the relevant major head and applied, subject to a minimum of 5 per cent, on 2002-03 levels of respective states to generate the initial estimates for 2004-05. These initial estimates have been compared with 2004-05 (BE), and the higher of the two adopted as the base year estimates. Here also, the minimum TGR of 5 per cent and the choice of the higher of the TGR-based estimates and budget estimates reflected the need to provide adequately for maintenance. On the base year estimates, an annual growth rate of 5 per cent has been applied to generate projected levels in the forecast period. Annexures 6.8 and 6.9 indicate the projected levels of maintenance expenditure of roads and buildings in the forecast period. These expenditures do not include the expenditure corresponding to additional grants-in-aid being provided separately in chapter 10.

Other General, Other Social and Other Economic Services

6.38 For each state and for each of these three services, the lower of the TGR-based estimates of 2004-05 and budget estimates was adopted as the base year estimates. While doing so, the minimum value for TGR was taken as 7.5 per cent. For the bifurcated states, the TGRs of the combined states have been derived for each of the services, but applied on their respective 2002-03 levels to arrive at the TGR-based estimates for 2004-05.

6.39 The next task was to arrive at state-wise, service-specific annual growth rates of expenditure in the forecast period for these three service categories. Within each service category, we have adopted a uniform growth rate for non-salary expenditure for all the states, and a varying salary growth rate for different states as explained below. For non-salary expenditure, 7 per cent annual growth rate has been adopted for all the states under 'Other General services' and 10 per cent both for 'Other Social Services' and 'Other Economic Services'.

6.40 The annual growth rates to be assigned for the salary component under each of the three services, varied across the states depending upon their respective levels of salary intensities ("salary intensity" of a major head being defined as the percentage of non-plan salary expenditure to NPRE under that head). The objective was to discourage increases in salary expenditure for those states, which already had a high salary intensity under a particular service category. Thus, under 'Other General Services', states with salary intensities of 85 per cent and above formed the sub-group with the highest salary intensity and were assigned the lowest annual growth rate of 4.5 per cent for the salary component. Similarly, states with a lower salary intensity in the range of 75 per cent to 84 per cent were assigned a salary growth of 5 per cent, and other states were assigned a salary growth of 5.5 per cent. The non-salary component of "Other General Services" was to grow normatively at 7 per cent for all states, as already mentioned above. By combining the two components, the composite growth rate for "Other General Services" as a whole was obtained for each sub-group.

6.41 Under 'Other Social Services', states with salary intensities of 45 per cent and above formed the highest salary intensity sub-group, 44 per cent to 30 per cent formed the middle intensity sub-group and below 30 per cent, the lowest intensity sub-group. The sub-group wise salary growth rates were combined with the uniform non-salary growth rate of 10 per cent to arrive at composite growth rates for each sub-group.

6.42 Under 'Other Economic Services', states with salary intensity of 65 per cent and above constituted the top sub-group, those between 64 per cent and 50 per cent, the middle sub-group and below 50 per cent, the lowest sub-group. These growth rates were combined with the non-salary growth rate of 10 per cent to yield the composite growth rates for each sub-group.

6.43 Thus, for all the states, nine composite growth rates were worked out, three for each of the three services. For each service, the appropriate composite growth rate for a given state was applied on its base year estimates to generate the forecast levels. The resultant composite growth rates and the states corresponding to these rates are indicated in annexure 6.10.

6.44 The net expenditure on elections (major head 2015 – minor head 0070-02) has been estimated broadly on the basis of the projections furnished by the states. However, wherever such projections of any state exceeded the net expenditure incurred by that state on elections during 2000-05 by more than 50 per cent, this has been brought down. The net expenditure estimated for each state has been distributed over the period of five years 2005-10, with a major share being earmarked for the years in which elections are due. These projections relating to elections have been added to the expenditure under "Other General Services" (as estimated in the preceding para) for the purpose of overall projection of NPRE for each state.

Compensation and Assignment to Local Bodies

6.45 The expenditure under this item (major head 3604) represents the explicit grants-in-aid provided by the states to their local bodies. As this expenditure stream did not show a clear trend, we took the average of 2000-03 (in case of bifurcated states, 2001-03) and applied an annual growth rate of 10 per cent, to arrive at the base year estimates, assuming that the average is centred at 2001-02. In the forecast period, an annual growth rate of 12.5 per cent was applied on the base year estimates. This is a comparatively high rate of growth, as compared to other items of expenditure, and this is in keeping with our emphasis on increased funding for local bodies.

Transfer of Committed Plan Liabilities

6.46 On the completion of a five year plan period, states are expected to transfer the committed liabilities associated with completed plan schemes to the non-plan side. This arrangement helps the states in funding such liabilities from sources other than central plan assistance. Consequently, central plan assistance becomes available for funding new schemes of the state governments. Para 6(vi) of TOR requires us to take into consideration the non-wage related maintenance expenditure on plan schemes to be completed by 31st March, 2005. Since the transfer of plan schemes to the non-plan side is normally expected to take place at the beginning of Eleventh Plan, we have factored in this consideration from 2007-08 onwards.

6.47 The information obtained on committed liabilities transferred to the non-plan side at the beginning of Tenth Plan was not found to be reliable. Our intention was to estimate these transfers as a percentage of plan revenue expenditure, and apply the same proportion to the projected plan revenue expenditure of states in 2006-07, the terminal year of the Tenth Plan, in order to estimate the committed liability to be transferred in the last three years of our forecast period. Most of the states could not provide us with this information and the ones that did, showed varying proportion of transfers. We, therefore, decided to use the proportion adopted by the Eleventh Finance Commission for general category states. Thus, 30 per cent of the plan revenue expenditure in 2006-07 has been proposed for transfer to non-plan side in the next year for the general category states. Further, even though the Eleventh Finance Commission did not provide for any such transfer in the case of special category states, we have assumed a transfer of 10 per cent of their plan revenue expenditure to non-plan side.

6.48 For working out the plan revenue expenditure in 2006-07, we applied 5 per cent annual growth rate on the plan revenue expenditure of 2004-05(BE) of each state to obtain the level of 2006-07. Of this, 30 per cent has been provided as transfer to non-plan revenue expenditure side in 2007-08 for general category states, and 10 per cent for special category states. We decided on a lower proportion for special category states as the Planning Commission allows them to divert 20 per cent of central plan assistance for meeting non-plan expenditure. Thereafter, the level of committed liabilities estimated for 2007-08 was grown at an annual rate of 7.5 per cent in the remaining two years of the forecast period. Annexure 6.11 indicates the expenditure relating to transfer of committed liabilities in the forecast period.

Summary of Assessment

6.49 The result of this detailed exercise, indicating our assessment of the revenue, expenditure and pre-devolution non-plan revenue deficit of each state for each year of the award period, is furnished in annexure 6.12. Table 6.2 indicates the summary of the results for all states combined.

Table 6.2

Pre-devolution Non-Plan Revenue Account of Aggregate States, 2005-10

(Rs. crore/per cent)

Item (1)	States' Projections (2)	Our Projections (3)	Difference (3-2) (4)
i. Own Revenue Receipts	1391002 *(6.3)*	1653661 *(7.5)*	262659 (1.2)
ii. Non-Plan Revenue Expenditure	2315499 *(10.5)*	1879298 *(8.5)*	-436201 (-2.0)
iii. Pre-devolution gap (i - ii)	-924497 *(-4.2)*	-225637 *(-1.0)*	698860 *(3.2)*

Figures in parentheses are percentage of GDP.

As compared to the states' projections of own revenue receipts at 6.3 per cent of GDP, the assessment by this Commission has placed it at 7.5 per cent, an increase of 1.2 percentage points. The reduction in NPRE, however, has been somewhat larger at 2.0 percentage points. The compression of the pre-devolution gap from 4.2 per cent of GDP to 1.0 per cent has resulted from the normative assessment of revenues and expenditure.

Salient features of normative assessment

6.50 Own Tax Revenues: In conformity with the plan for restructuring state finances, the tax-GDP ratio, considering all states, has been raised by a little less than 0.9 percentage point over the forecast period. This has been achieved by a two-step process. In the first instance, the tax-GSDP ratio of those states, for which this ratio is lower than their respective group average, has been partially corrected in the base year. In the second step relating to projection for the forecast period, differential buoyancies have been assigned to the states in a manner so that the objective of overall improvement in the tax-GDP ratio is achieved.

6.51 Own Non-Tax Revenues: Wherever possible, the projection of own non-tax revenues have been linked to associated costs. Thus, the projections of interest receipts and dividends are based on recovering some part of the borrowing costs. Similarly, cost recovery norms have been used for projecting irrigation receipts by making these recover a substantial part of maintenance expenditure. For projecting user charges under general, social and economic services, the growth rates employed have been fixed at a higher level than the growth rates used for projecting their corresponding expenditure. Thus, the principle of cost recovery adopted for projecting own non-tax revenues has resulted in reducing the subsidies implicit in the budgetary provisions.

6.52 Non-Plan Revenue Expenditure: Our approach has been to attempt compression of the growth rate of NPRE in general, while encouraging higher growth in expenditure in areas relating to education, health, maintenance of roads and maintenance of buildings. This has been captured in the following manner:

(i) Interest payments: The overall objective has been to bring down the burden on this count, and not provide fully for interest payments arising from large scale borrowings by some of the states in the past while computing the deficit grant. For this purpose, corrections in the base year have been made for those states whose ratio of interest payments to total revenue receipts is higher than the average. Further, for projections in the forecast period, an average growth rate of 7.5 per cent has been adopted, as against the average growth rate of 18.2 per cent during 1993-2003.

(ii) Pension payments: In determining pension payments, keeping in view the inability of the states in influencing this expenditure stream in the medium term, budget estimates for 2004-05 have been adopted as the base year figure, and a growth rate of 10 per cent adopted in the forecast period, broadly in line with recent growth rate.

(iii) Education and health sectors: Our objective has been to encourage higher expenditure in these sectors. In the projections here, we have assigned the normal growth rate of 6 per cent and 5 per cent in the salary component of education and health sectors respectively, but a much larger growth rate of 30 per cent in the non-salary components. The revenue deficit grants have been worked out accordingly. Being conscious of the fact that application of liberal norms for education and health expenditure does not guarantee that larger funds would flow to these sectors, we have given additional grants-in-aid separately for these two sectors in line with the equalisation principle to some of the states, as discussed in chapter 10.

(iv) Maintenance of irrigation works: The projections have been worked out largely on the basis of norms obtained from Ministry of Water Resources. The expenditure norms adopted by us in the base year are Rs.600 per hectare for utilised potential and Rs.300 per hectare for unutilised potential of major and medium irrigation schemes. A norm of Rs.300 per hectare has been adopted for minor irrigation schemes. The projections have been worked out on the basis of an annual growth rate of 5 per cent.

(v) Maintenance of roads and bridges: The approach followed by us is similar to that for health and education sectors. We have encouraged larger expenditure for maintenance of roads and bridges by providing separate additional grants as discussed in chapter 10. For computation of revenue deficit grant, however, we have decided to adopt the normal expenditure figures, with a 5 per cent growth rate in the forecast period.

(vi) Other general, other social and other economic services: These items were considered appropriate for expenditure compression in terms of growth rate, particularly their salary part. Thus, in the base year, we took the lower of the TGR-based estimates and the budget estimates. For purposes of projection, the salary component was held constant in real terms by assigning an average nominal growth rate of only 5 per cent. The non-salary part is to grow normatively at 7 per cent for other general services, and 10 per cent for the remaining two services.

(vii) Compensation and assignment to local bodies: We have encouraged the expenditure on local bodies in two ways. Firstly, we have excluded local body grants given on central finance commission's recommendations from the receipt side of the states, but we have not excluded an equal amount from the expenditure side. This would result in a higher normative revenue deficit for the states. Secondly, we have assumed a larger annual growth rate of 12.5 per cent during the projection period on expenditure relating to compensation and assignment to local bodies.

(viii) Transfer of committed plan liabilities: 30 per cent of the plan revenue expenditure in 2006-07 for general category states, and 10 per cent in the case of special category states, has been transferred to the non-plan revenue expenditure side in 2007-08, which would help the states in taking up new plan schemes.

Chapter 7

Sharing of Union Tax Revenues

7.1 In accordance with article 280 (3) (a) of the Constitution and para 4(i) of the TOR, the Twelfth Finance Commission is required to make recommendations as to the distribution between the Union and the states of the net proceeds of taxes which are to be, or may be, divided between them under chapter I of part XII of the Constitution and the allocation between the states of the respective share of such proceeds.

Constitutional Provisions

7.2 Prior to the enactment of the Constitution (Eightieth Amendment) Act, 2000, the sharing of the Union tax revenues with the states was in accordance with the provisions of articles 270 and 272, as these stood then. While article 270 provided for the compulsory sharing of the net proceeds of the income tax (excluding corporation tax), article 272 permitted for sharing of the net proceeds of Union duties of excise (excluding duties of excise on medicinal and toilet preparations), if Parliament by law so provided. Consequently, the principles adopted for revenue sharing differed between the two taxes significantly.

7.3 The eightieth amendment of the Constitution altered the pattern of sharing of Union taxes in a fundamental way. Under this amendment, article 272 was dropped and article 270 was substantially changed. The new article 270 provides for sharing of all the taxes and duties referred to in the Union list, except the taxes and duties referred to in articles 268 and 269, respectively, surcharges on taxes and duties referred to in article 271 and any cess levied for specific purposes. The basis for this change was the alternative scheme of devolution recommended by the Tenth Finance Commission. There is considerable merit in the change, as it gives greater freedom and flexibility to the centre in pursuing the tax reforms in an integrated manner and enables the states to share the aggregate buoyancy of central taxes. The Eleventh Finance Commission was the first to take these changes into account, while recommending the share of the states in the divisible pool.

7.4 Another Constitutional amendment that is of relevance to Centre-State fiscal relations is the eighty eighth amendment, enacted in January, 2004 through the Constitution (Eighty Eighth Amendment) Act, 2003. This is relating to service tax and will come into effect from a date, which is yet to be notified. This amendment provides for a specific entry in the Constitution to authorize levy of service tax. The central government has been imposing and collecting this tax as a residual item under entry no. 97 in the Union list and the net proceeds thereof are distributed between the centre and the states as per article 270 of the Constitution on the recommendations of the finance commission. As per the eighty eighth amendment (annexure 7.1), taxes on services are to be levied by the central government and the net proceeds of such taxes are to be collected and appropriated by the centre and the states in accordance with such principles of collection and appropriation as may be formulated by Parliament, by law. Further, in the Seventh Schedule to the Constitution, an item, 'Taxes on services' is to be inserted in the Union list under entry no. 92C, thereby assigning the power to tax services clearly to the central government. A new article 268A, has been inserted, whereby service tax is to be taken out of the divisible pool of central taxes and consequently out of the jurisdiction of the finance commission.

Evolution of the Sharing Process

7.5 As noted above, prior to the eightieth amendment of the Constitution, only two central taxes were shareable, non-corporate income tax and Union excise duties. In addition, there is a tax rental arrangement between centre and states with respect to additional excise duties *in lieu* of sales tax on three commodities. A brief review of sharing of the two taxes is given below.

Income Tax

7.6 By the time the First Finance Commission was constituted, the share of states in the 'net proceeds' of income tax had already been fixed at 50 per cent. The First Finance Commission raised the share to 55 per cent owing to increase in the number of states. The second, third and fourth finance commissions raised the share gradually to 60, 66.67, and 75 per cent respectively, to compensate for the non-inclusion of corporate income tax and surcharge (annexure7.2). The Fifth Finance Commission did not raise the share, but recommended inclusion of advance tax collections and arrears thereof in determining the proceeds of income tax during a financial year. The Sixth Commission raised it to 80 per cent, as the arrears of advance collections were not available any more. The Seventh Commission further increased the share to 85 per cent in response to the grievance of the states that the centre had raised the Union surcharge as a revenue measure rather than for meeting any specific Union purposes, thus depriving the states of a share in the increased revenue[1]. While the eighth and ninth commissions did not alter the position, the Tenth Finance Commission felt that the authority that levies and administers a tax should have a significant and tangible interest in its yield and accordingly revised the share of the states in the proceeds of income tax downward to 77.5 per cent, but increased the share in the net proceeds of the Union excise duties to protect the level of overall devolution to the states.

Union Excise Duties

7.7 At the time of the First Finance Commission, there were 12 important commodities subject to Union excise duties in 1951-52. The First Finance Commission felt that it was advisable to share the excise revenue from a select number of commodities of common consumption that yielded sizeable revenue for distribution.

Accordingly, the Commission recommended sharing of the excise on three commodities – tobacco (including tobacco products), matches and vegetable products and the share was fixed at 40 per cent[2]. The Second Finance Commission increased the number of commodities for sharing the excise duty revenue to 8 but reduced the share to 25 per cent. While the coverage of commodities was expanded by the third and fourth commissions, the share was reduced to 20 per cent. The fifth and sixth commissions, while keeping the share at 20 per cent, extended the shareable excise duties to special and auxiliary duties as well. The Seventh Finance Commission doubled the share with a view to reducing the elements of grants-in-aid[3]. The Eighth Commission increased the share by adding additional 5 per cent, which was to be distributed among the deficit states. The Ninth Commission, in its second report, retained the share at 45 per cent for distribution among the deficit states. The Tenth Commission further raised the share of the states to be 47.5 per cent with 7.5 per cent distributed among the deficit states.

Sharing in Aggregate Central Taxes

7.8 The Tenth Finance Commission in its alternative scheme of tax devolution suggested that instead of sharing of individual taxes, the states may have a share in the total net proceeds of all central taxes excluding surcharges and cesses. In determining the share of the states in the total net proceeds of the central tax revenues, the Commission distinguished between shares in income tax, basic excise duties and grants *in lieu* of tax on railway passenger fares as a proportion of central tax revenues (S1) on the one hand, and the share of additional excise duties *in lieu* of sales tax in respect of items covered by tax rental arrangement on the other (S2)[4]. The Commission observed that the average value of S1 had been 24.32, 22.22 and 24.3 per cent during the five-year-periods 1979-84, 1984-89 and 1990-95 respectively, and that of S2 at 2.96, 3.22 and 2.95 per cent. Having regard to these values, the commission recommended that the share of states in the gross receipts of central taxes should be 26 per cent, and until the tax rental arrangement is terminated, a further share of three per cent in the gross tax receipts of the centre to compensate for the additional excise duties *in lieu* of sale tax.

7.9 The Eleventh Finance Commission, while considering the issue of vertical devolution of the central tax revenues, reviewed the past trends in the aggregate share of states in the net proceeds of all Union taxes and duties, excluding surcharge and cesses during the last two decades[5]. It was observed that the share of the states in all Union taxes and duties (worked out on the basis of share of all states in the Union excise duties and income tax recommended by successive finance commissions) fluctuated between 26.17 per cent (in 1988-89) and 31.79 per cent (in 1993-94). The year-to-year fluctuations had been significant even within the devolution period covered by the same finance commission, largely due to fluctuations in the rates of growth of income tax and Union excise duties, the only taxes shared with the states before the eightieth amendment to the Constitution.

7.10 After completing the assessment of the central resources and state finances for the period, from 2000-01 to 2004-05, the Commission recommended that the share of the states be fixed at 28 per cent of the net proceeds of all taxes and duties referred to in the Union list, except the taxes and duties referred to in articles 268 and 269, and the surcharges and cesses, for each of the five years starting from 2000-01 and ending in 2004-05.

7.11 The Eleventh Finance Commission further noted that as a consequence of the amendment, which *inter alia* deleted article 272, additional excise duties levied under the Additional Excise Duties (Goods of Special Importance) Act, 1957, had become part of the revenue receipts of the central government and were shareable with the states. It was felt that there was a need for a review of the earlier arrangement and pending such a review, the commission recommended that 1.5 per cent of all shareable union taxes and duties be allocated to the states separately and its *inter se* distribution among the states may be done in the same manner as the distribution of 28 per cent of the net proceeds. If any state levied and collected sales tax on the commodities covered under this Act, it would not be entitled to any share from this 1.5 per cent. This brought the total tax devolution recommended by the Eleventh Finance Commission to 29.5 per cent of the net proceeds of all shareable central taxes and duties.

Trends in Vertical Sharing

7.12 At this stage, it may be useful to examine the historical trends in the transfers from centre to states through major channels in India. As can be seen from Table 7. 1, over the period covered by the seventh to eleventh finance commissions, the award period-wise average ratio of total transfers to central government gross revenue receipts had remained around 38 per cent during the seventh and eighth finance commission periods. It went up to 40 per cent during the Ninth Finance Commission period.

Table 7. 1

Transfers from Centre to States as Percentage of Gross Revenue Receipts of the Centre: Finance Commission Period Averages

Year	Finance Commission Transfers			Other Transfers			Total Transfers (4+7)
	Share in Central Taxes	Grants	Total Transfers through Finance Commission (2+3)	Grants through Planning Commission	Non-plan Grants (Non-statutory)	Total Other Transfers (5+6)	
1	2	3	4	5	6	7	8
VII FC	22.39	1.96	24.35	12.11	1.66	13.77	38.11
VIII FC	20.25	2.52	22.77	13.56	1.54	15.10	37.86
IX FC	21.37	3.42	24.79	14.48	1.06	15.54	40.33
X FC	21.40	2.34	23.75	10.57	0.63	11.19	35.79
XI FC (first two years)	20.93	5.20	26.13	10.39	0.82	11.21	37.20

Source: Union Government Finance Accounts and Revenue Receipts are from Central Government Receipts Budget (Various issues).

Note: In 1997-98, an amount of Rs 7,594 is on account of VDIS, which is included in non-plan grants to the states in the Finance Accounts. Since it should logically form part of the tax devolution, this amount is taken out from the non-plan grants and added to the Finance Commission transfers.

Thereafter, it came down steeply to 35.8 per cent during the Tenth Finance Commission period. During the first two years of Eleventh Finance Commission award period it has shown a rise to 37.2 per cent.

7.13 The finance commission transfers have accounted for about 60 to 70 per cent of total central transfers to states and have also shown variation over time. The average ratio to the gross revenue receipts of the centre for the Seventh Finance Commission period was 24.4 per cent. It went down to 22.8 per cent during the Eighth Commission. It rose to 24.8 per cent during the Ninth Commission and declined to 23.8 per cent during the Tenth Commission period. During the first two years of the Eleventh Finance Commission period, however, the average ratio was 26.1 per cent (Table 7. 1). Of particular interest are the finance commission transfers through tax devolution. The ratio of the tax devolution component to centre's gross tax revenue has been stable at around 21 per cent during the last three finance commissions.

7.14 The aggregate share of states in the net proceeds of all Union taxes and duties, excluding surcharges and cesses, during the last two decades has varied between 26.2 per cent (1988-89) and 31.8 per cent (1993-94) (annexure 7.3). The finance commission award period average has varied from a low of 27.3 per cent to a high of 28.8 per cent. This ratio is stipulated to be 29.5 per cent by the Eleventh Finance Commission.

Views of the Central Government

7.15 The central government in its memorandum of September 2003, has stated that in the light of the tight fiscal situation of the centre and the external macroeconomic imperatives of containing central fiscal deficit, there should be a gradual reduction in devolution to states. With the additional availability of revenues through collection of service tax on specified items, states' mobilization of revenue will increase to the detriment of the centre. Further, the centre has agreed in principle to allow the states to levy sales tax on sugar, tobacco and textiles. The central government has, therefore, urged that the tax devolution may be kept to a maximum of 28 per cent of the net proceeds of the shareable taxes, with the additional 1.5 per cent of the net proceeds being distributed as long as additional excise duty *in lieu* of sales tax on sugar, textiles and tobacco continues.

7.16 The memorandum also stated that in the event of abolition of additional excise duty, the states would regain the right to levy sales tax and would compensate themselves for the 1.5 per cent revenue loss resulting from the termination of the tax rental arrangement. The memorandum also referred to the fiscal responsibility legislation, which makes it obligatory for the centre to rein in the level of deficit and debt and suggested that the Commission may review the maximum level of overall transfer from centre to states and prescribe a ceiling lower than what was recommended by the Eleventh Finance Commission, that is, 37.5 per cent of the gross revenue receipts of the centre.

7.17 In a subsequent communication on August 9, 2004, the central government urged the Commission to take a view consistent with the National Common Minimum Program objectives and after taking into account the following considerations:

i) Under 88th Constitutional amendment, "Taxes on services" are to be excluded from the single, divisible pool of central taxes/duties [*vide* article 270 of the Constitution].

ii) Centre is presently discharging a number of expenditure obligations pertaining to subjects/areas in the state list, both through plan transfers and non-plan transfers/expenditures.

iii) Demands on the resources of the central government and statutory requirement of eliminating revenue deficit of the centre as stipulated in the Fiscal Responsibility and Budget Management Act and rules framed thereunder.

7.18 The National Common Minimum Program, while dealing with the subject of centre-state relations, has observed that "the share of states in the single, divisible pool of taxes (be) enhanced"[6].

7.19 With regard to the adverse impact on the states in the event of centre's revenue projections remaining unfulfilled, it has been stated in the communication that the basic rationale of creating a single, divisible pool of Union taxes is to ensure that both the centre and the states share the buoyancy. Partaking a share in positive buoyancies also implies acceptance of sharing of negative buoyancy.

Views of the States

7.20 In their memoranda, states have, almost unanimously, sought an increase in the total share of central taxes. A large number of states such as Chhattisgarh, Rajasthan, Tripura, Meghalaya, Mizoram, and Uttar Pradesh have asked for raising the tax share to 33 per cent. A share of 40 per cent has been suggested by Bihar, Jharkhand, Gujarat, Himachal Pradesh, Karnataka, Orissa and Goa. The states of Arunachal Pradesh, Andhra Pradesh, Assam, Haryana, Nagaland, Punjab and Tamil Nadu have sought as much as 50 per cent share. The arguments advanced by the states for seeking a higher share can broadly be summarized as follows.

i) It was resolved on the basis of a consensus in one of the meetings of the Standing Committee of the Inter-State Council that, to begin with, the divisible portion of the central taxes should be raised to 33 per cent.

ii) The suggestions for including all the taxes in the divisible pool emanated, *inter alia*, out of the pleadings for higher share of central taxes, but the share fixed by the Eleventh Finance Commission at 29.5 per cent of net central tax revenues has not resulted in increased devolution.

iii) Government of India has accepted the recommendations of the Expenditure Reforms Commission and if these recommendations are implemented, there will be considerable economy of expenditure and it would be possible for the central government to provide increased share in central taxes.

iv) A decision has been taken by the Government of India to transfer centrally sponsored schemes along with funds to the states and this transfer could be effected in the form of higher share of central taxes.

v) It would be possible for the central government to reduce its expenditure further by dispensing with many of the departments, which deal with subjects that are exclusively in the state list and do not pursue or implement any important national policy.

vi) Central tax collection has not been in accordance with the estimates of the Eleventh Finance Commission, as a result of which the states have not received amounts due to them.

vii) Some of the states desire that service tax should be in the state list or it should be collected by the centre and transferred to the states.

viii) As regards surcharges, states have expressed the view that in case a surcharge / cess is continued for a long period (beyond one or two years), it should be integrated with the basic tax and counted towards the shareable taxes.

ix) The concept of 'net' proceeds, instead of 'gross' proceeds of Union taxes, does not provide any incentive to the Union to reduce the collection cost. The cost of collection of the Union taxes, which was only 0.67 per cent of the gross tax revenue in 1980-81, has gone up to 1.06 per cent of the gross tax revenue. Some states desire that the devolution should be on 'gross receipts' and not on 'net receipts' basis.

x) Over the years, the non-tax revenue of the Union has increased significantly. In 1980-81, non-tax revenue was only 24 per cent of the total revenue receipts of the Union. It grew to almost 30 per cent in 1999-2000. The non-tax revenue is non-shareable and hence, the Union government is now financially better equipped and there is a scope for higher devolution to the states.

7.21 Some states desire that at least 30 per cent of the states' share in the divisible pool should be earmarked for distribution amongst the Special Category States [Assam, Himachal Pradesh, Jammu & Kashmir and Manipur]. Some of the states, notably Assam, Jammu & Kashmir, Kerala, Manipur and Tripura have suggested that the finance commission may indicate a minimum amount that must be transferred by the central government to the states. States have also referred to the shortfall in the revenues of the central government as compared to the projections of the Eleventh Finance Commission and suggested that such difference during the award period be made good either by providing for a minimum guaranteed devolution based on the Twelfth Finance Commission's assessment of states' share or by giving grants-in-aid to the extent of the difference. Another demand of the states pertains to the tax on railway passenger fares, shared earlier by the states on the basis of the state's contribution to the earnings. After the repeal of the Railway Passenger Fares Act, 1957 in 1961, the states had been getting compensation for the repealed tax on the basis of non-suburban passenger earnings from traffic originating in each state. It has been suggested that either (a) the practice of compensating the states for repealed Act should be continued or (b) the Act may be reintroduced and the states should be allowed to collect taxes on fares on behalf of the Union and keep the proceeds.

Recommendations Regarding Vertical Devolution

7.22 While determining the share of the states in the divisible pool of central taxes, it is necessary to look at the level of overall transfers relative to centre's gross revenue receipts, the relative balance between tax devolution and grants, and feasible redistribution that can be undertaken in the *inter se* share of states in tax devolution. As mentioned earlier, many states have asked for increasing the share of states in the shareable pool from 29.5 per cent to 33 per cent. Some states have even suggested a figure of 50 per cent. We consider that if the share of states is increased, the redistributive content in the *inter se* distribution will have to be increased significantly by altering the weights among the distribution criteria so as to be consistent with the equalization objective. However, for this purpose, grants provide a more effective mechanism. We have, therefore, used grants to a larger extent as an instrument of transfers. At the same time, we recommend that the share of the states in the net proceeds of shareable central taxes be raised from 29.5 per cent to 30.5 per cent. For this purpose, additional excise duties *in lieu* of sales tax on textiles, tobacco and sugar are treated as part of the general pool of central taxes. If, however, the tax rental arrangement is terminated and if states are allowed to levy sales tax (or VAT) on these commodities without any prescribed limit, the share of the states in the net proceeds of shareable central taxes will be 29.5 per cent. According to estimates available from the budget papers, additional excise duties *in lieu* of sales tax constituted about one per cent of the shareable taxes in 2003-04 and 2004-05 (BE). The recommended increase can be accommodated easily by the central government by rationalizing the centre's participation in areas that are directly the responsibility of the states. We have treated the service tax as shareable. This is, in fact, the current position. The position will change after the eighty eighth Constitutional amendment is notified. In that situation, as indicated in Chapter 2, any legislation that is enacted in respect of service tax must ensure that the revenue accruing to a state under the legislation should not be less than the share that would accrue to it, had the entire service tax proceeds been part of the shareable pool. Further, as suggested earlier, the indicative amount of overall transfers to states in central gross revenue receipts, which was fixed at 37.5 per cent by the Eleventh Finance Commission, may be fixed at 38 per cent.

Horizontal Sharing

7.23 As regards the determination of the *inter se* shares of the states, the basic aim of the finance commission transfers in the past has been to (i) to correct the differentials in revenue capacity and cost disability factors inherent in the economies of states and (ii) to foster fiscal efficiency among the states. The criteria used in the past for these purposes can be grouped under: (a) factors reflecting needs, such as population and income measured either as distance from the highest income or as inverse; (b) cost disability indicators such as area and infrastructure distance; and (c) fiscal efficiency indicators such as tax effort and fiscal discipline. (annexure 7.4).

7.24 Over the past few finance

commissions, the distributive criteria have converged towards the following. Among the need factors, population and income distance have gained acceptance; among the cost disability factors, area and infrastructure index distance have tended to be the preferred indicators; and among the fiscal efficiency factors, tax effort and fiscal discipline as measured by the ratio of own tax revenue to revenue expenditure, are regarded as appropriate.

Views of the States on Horizontal Sharing

7.25 States in their memoranda have expressed their desire for the continuation of the use of population as a factor, with weights suggested varying from 5 per cent (Rajasthan) to 88 per cent (Gujarat) [annexure 7.5]. Bihar, Jharkhand, Karnataka preferred retaining a 10 per cent weight, while many states wanted a higher weight. On the use of income distance criterion, states have suggested weights ranging from 10 per cent (Tamil Nadu and Haryana) to 70 per cent (Assam). Andhra Pradesh, Karnataka and Maharashtra desire 25 per cent weight while Jharkhand and Uttar Pradesh want the weight to be 62.5 and 50 per cent, respectively. Many states have asked for continuation of 'area' as a factor with weights ranging from 5 per cent (Haryana and Karnataka) to 20 per cent (Rajasthan). Also, states have suggested retaining of the tax effort and index of fiscal discipline criteria. The suggested weights for tax effort range from 5 per cent (Rajasthan, Tripura, Maharashtra and Jharkhand) to 40 per cent (Tamil Nadu). The suggested weights for fiscal discipline range from 5 per cent (Karnataka, Maharashtra and Rajasthan) to 10 per cent (Andhra Pradesh, Bihar, Kerala, and Punjab). Andhra Pradesh, Assam, Haryana, Kerala, Maharashtra, Rajasthan and Uttaranchal prefer the same weight for both the criteria. Jharkhand and Karnataka prefer a smaller weight to fiscal discipline than tax effort. Chhattisgarh, Tamil Nadu and Tripura have recommended only tax effort, while Punjab has recommended only fiscal discipline.

Criteria and Weights

7.26 As per the formula used by the Eleventh Finance Commission, the share of each state in tax devolution was determined by the following criteria and relative weights: population (10 per cent), income distance (62.5 per cent), area (7.5 per cent), index of infrastructure (7.5 per cent), tax effort (5 per cent) and fiscal discipline (7.5 per cent)[7]. We have examined each of these criteria and the weights assigned and have suggested changes, where necessary.

Population

7.27 Population (annexure 7.6) is the basic indicator of need for public goods and services and as a criterion, it ensures equal per capita transfers across states. The weight attached to population has varied substantially over time. Looking at the recent periods, during the seventh and eighth finance commissions, the weight attached to population varied between 22.5 per cent and 25 per cent. This weight was reduced to 20 per cent by the Ninth Commission and further to 10 per cent by the Eleventh Commission. We feel that a strong case exists for increasing the weight and have fixed it at 25 per cent.

Per capita Income Distance

7.28 Among the criteria used for correcting differential fiscal capacities and for enabling poorer states to meet better the needs for public goods and services, per capita income distance appears to be the preferred indicator. It imparts progressivity in distribution. The Fifth Finance Commission, while using this criterion, recommended that a portion[8] of the shareable Union excise duties be distributed among the states "whose per capita income is below the average per capita income of all states in proportion to the shortfall of the states' per capita income from all states' average, multiplied by the population of the state"[9]. The Sixth Commission followed the distance method for all states with no cut-off point for eligibility. In this method, the distance of per capita income of each state from the per capita income of the state which had the highest per capita income was measured. This value was then multiplied by the population of each state. In this method, the distance in the case of the state with the highest per capita income would be zero, but various commissions have adopted a method by which this state is also given a share on the basis of a notional distance between the per capita income of that state and that of the next highest per capita income state. The eighth and ninth commissions have used this method[10]. The tenth and eleventh finance commissions, while following this method, have used the average of the top three states with highest per capita incomes for measuring the distance. In all the cases, the commissions had taken the average GSDP for three years in order to even out year-to-year variations.

7.29 For determining the state-wise income distance index, we considered the average per capita comparable GSDP of each of the 28 states for the last three years, 1999-2000, 2000-01 and 2001-02 (annexure 7.7) provided by the Central Statistical Organization (CSO). Following the tenth and the eleventh finance commissions, the average of the top three states with highest per capita income, namely Goa, Punjab and Maharashtra was taken to compute the income distance of each state. For the top three states, the notional distance was assigned by taking their distance with the per capita income of the fourth highest ranked state, namely Haryana. We have assigned a weight of 50 per cent to the income distance criterion. This criterion combined with the criterion of population, representing together the needs and deficiency in fiscal capacity, will thus have a combined weight of 75 per cent.

Area

7.30 The use of 'area' of a state as a criterion for determining its share emanates from the additional administrative and other costs that a state with a larger area has to incur in order to deliver a comparable standard of service to its citizens. It should be noted that the use of 'area' as a criterion in the formula can also be interpreted as inverse of population density multiplied by population[11]. It should be recognized, however, that the costs of providing services may increase with the size of a state, but only at a decreasing rate. At the other end, even the smaller states may have to incur certain minimum costs in establishing the framework of governmental machinery. The Tenth Finance Commission provided for a floor level of 2 per cent and a ceiling of 10 per cent in the measurement of the area. The Eleventh Finance Commission also followed the same procedure. We have also assigned a minimum 2 per cent share for states with their area share smaller than 2 per cent. But, we have not fixed an upper ceiling of 10 per cent, as there is only one state (Rajasthan) which marginally exceeds 10 per cent. States that are assigned 2 per cent minimum share are: Goa, Haryana, Himachal Pradesh, Kerala, Manipur, Meghalaya, Mizoram, Nagaland, Punjab, Sikkim, Tripura and Uttaranchal (annexure 7.8). We have assigned a weight of 10 per cent to the area criterion.

7.31 Another cost disability criterion used by the last two commissions was the index of infrastructure, as an indicator of the relative availability of economic and social infrastructure in a state. This index was inversely related to the share. We find that the infrastructure index distance criterion is correlated with the income distance criterion. More importantly, our attention was drawn to the fact that this index is better used in an ordinal way. For these reasons, we have dropped the index of infrastructure as a criterion.

Tax Effort

7.32 As observed by the Tenth Finance Commission, measurement of tax effort on a comparable basis among the states is not a straightforward exercise, because tax effort must be related to some notion of tax potential and there are differences in the nature and composition of tax bases among the states. Given the data constraints, the Tenth Commission had used per capita GSDP as a proxy for the aggregate tax base. Tax effort was measured by the ratio of per capita own tax revenue of a state to its per capita income. The Commission felt that there was a need to provide for an adjustment for states with poorer tax bases. If the tax effort ratio as defined above is weighted by the inverse of per capita income, it would imply that if a poorer state exploits its tax-base as much as a richer state, it gets an additional positive consideration in the formula. The Eleventh Finance Commission, while considering the tax effort index, reduced the weight of inverse of per capita income from 1 to 0.5. We have adopted the same practice, but have raised the weight given to the tax effort criterion to 7.5 per cent, as the need for fiscal consolidation has become more urgent. The tax effort criterion is worked out by taking the three-year average (1999-2000, 2000-01 and 2001-02) of the ratios of own tax revenue to comparable GSDP (annexure 7.9) weighted by the square root of the inverse of the per capita GSDP.

Fiscal Discipline

7.33 The index of fiscal discipline was proposed by the Eleventh Finance Commission with a view to providing an incentive for better fiscal management. The Eleventh Finance Commission adopted improvement in the ratio of own revenue receipts of a state to its total revenue expenditure, related to a similar ratio for all states, as a criterion for measurement. The ratio so computed was used to measure the improvement in the index of fiscal discipline in a reference period, in comparison to a base period. For the base period, the Commission took the average for the three-year period from 1990-91 to 1992-93 and for the reference period that from 1996-97 to 1998-99. It may be noted that such an improvement can be brought about by higher own revenues or lower revenue expenditure or a combination of the two. The comparison of the performance of a state with the all state performance reflects the consideration that, if the performance of the states is deteriorating in general, the state that accomplishes a relatively lower deterioration is rewarded. Similarly, if all revenue balance profiles are improving, the state where improvement is relatively more than average is rewarded relatively more. While retaining the index of fiscal discipline criterion we have computed it using the base period from 1993-94 to 1995-96 and the reference period from 2000-01 to 2002-03 (annexure 7.10) and kept the weight at 7.5 per cent.

7.34 Table 7. 2 shows the criteria and the weights, thus assigned for *inter se* determination of shares of states.

Table 7. 2

Criteria and Weights

Criteria	Weight (per cent)
Population	25.0
Income Distance	50.0
Area	10.0
Tax Effort	7.5
Fiscal Discipline	7.5

Recommendations regarding Horizontal Devolution

7.35 We have tried to evolve a formula that balances equity with fiscal efficiency. Equity considerations, however, dominate, as they should, in any scheme of federal transfers trying to implement the equalization principle. In view of the above considerations, we recommend that the states should be given a share as specified in the Table 7. 3 in the net proceeds of all the shareable Union taxes (excluding service tax, as it is not leviable in Jammu & Kashmir) in each of the five financial years during the period 2005-06 to 2009-10.

Table 7. 3

***Inter se* Shares of States**

State	Share (per cent)
Andhra Pradesh	7.356
Arunachal Pradesh	0.288
Assam	3.235
Bihar	11.028
Chhattisgarh	2.654
Goa	0.259
Gujarat	3.569
Haryana	1.075
Himachal Pradesh	0.522
Jammu & Kashmir	1.297
Jharkhand	3.361
Karnataka	4.459
Kerala	2.665
Madhya Pradesh	6.711
Maharashtra	4.997
Manipur	0.362
Meghalaya	0.371
Mizoram	0.239
Nagaland	0.263
Orissa	5.161
Punjab	1.299
Rajasthan	5.609
Sikkim	0.227
Tamil Nadu	5.305
Tripura	0.428
Uttar Pradesh	19.264
Uttaranchal	0.939
West Bengal	7.057
All States	**100.000**

7.36 As mentioned above, service tax is presently not leviable in the state of Jammu & Kashmir, and its proceeds are, therefore, not assignable to this state. We have worked out the share of each of the remaining 27 states in the net proceeds of service tax and these will be as indicated in Table 7. 4. If in any year, this tax becomes leviable in the state of Jammu & Kashmir, the share of each state including that of Jammu & Kashmir would be in accordance with the percentages given in Table 7. 4.

7.37 If in any year during the period 2005-10, a tax under Union is not leviable in a state, the share of that state in that tax should be put to zero and the entire proceeds should be distributed among the remaining states by proportionately adjusting their share.

Table 7. 4

Share of States other than Jammu & Kashmir in the Service Tax

State	Share excluding J&K (per cent)	State	Share excluding J&K (per cent)
Andhra Pradesh	7.453	Maharashtra	5.063
Arunachal Pradesh	0.292	Manipur	0.367
Assam	3.277	Meghalaya	0.376
Bihar	11.173	Mizoram	0.242
Chhattisgarh	2.689	Nagaland	0.266
Goa	0.262	Orissa	5.229
Gujarat	3.616	Punjab	1.316
Haryana	1.089	Rajasthan	5.683
Himachal Pradesh	0.529	Sikkim	0.230
Jharkhand	3.405	Tamil Nadu	5.374
Karnataka	4.518	Tripura	0.433
Kerala	2.700	Uttar Pradesh	19.517
Madhya Pradesh	6.799	Uttaranchal	0.952
		West Bengal	7.150
		All States	**100.000**

Endnotes

1 Report of the Seventh Finance Commission, Chapter 9, para 22 p81-82.

2 "We have fixed the states' share with reference to the amount which, in our scheme as a whole, we consider it appropriate should be transferred to the states by the division of excise duties." (Report of the First Finance Commission, Chapter V, p82).

3 "Considering their size, the Union excise revenues must have a predominant role in the transfer of financial resources to the states. We have also decided, as mentioned earlier, that the bulk of the fiscal transfers to the states should be by way of tax shares, reducing the elements of grants-in-aid under article 275 to a residual position on the one hand and leaving surpluses on revenue account with as large a number of states as possible on the other" [para 31 of the Report of the Seventh Finance Commission, centre state financial relations and our scheme of transfers].

4 Report of the Tenth Finance Commission: Share of states in Aggregate Central Tax Revenues, Table 2.

5 Annexure VI.1 Chapter 7 of the Report of the Eleventh Finance Commission.

6 National Common Minimum Program of the UPA Government, New Delhi, May 27, 2004

7 Report of the Eleventh Finance Commission, Table 6.2, p 58.

8 13.34 per cent, that is, 2/3rd of 20 per cent

9 Report of the Fifth Finance Commission, p36.

10 Mention may be made here of another criterion that uses the per capita income was the Income Adjusted Total Population (IATP) which was the inverse of per capita income of a state. The share of a state is determined by the percentage of IATP of the state to the aggregate IATP of all states. The Seventh and Eighth Commissions, and the Ninth Commission in its first report, used this method. But in view of certain technical flaws the use of this criterion was discontinued since the Tenth Finance Commission.

11 Since Area = (Area/Population) ×Population.

Chapter 8

Local Bodies

8.1 Para 4(iii) of the terms of reference enjoins upon the Commission to make recommendations as to the following matter:

> "the measures needed to augment the Consolidated Fund of a State to supplement the resources of the Panchayats and Municipalities in the State on the basis of the recommendations made by the Finance Commission of the State."

This is a consolidated reproduction of the provisions contained in article 280(3)(bb) and (c) of the Constitution of India, as amended in 1993.

Approach of the Previous Commissions

8.2 For the first time, it was the Eleventh Finance Commission (EFC), which was required to suggest, as per its terms of reference (TOR), the measures to augment the consolidated fund of the states to enable them to supplement the resources of the local bodies. However, earlier, the Tenth Finance Commission had also made recommendations in this regard, as article 280 had been amended before the expiry of its term and the Commission felt that it was obliged to deal with the issue in terms of the amended article 280 even though it was not included in its TOR. The Commission expressed the view that the measures to augment the consolidated funds of the states for supplementation of the resources of the panchayats and the municipalities need not necessarily involve transfer of resources from the centre to the states. It observed that once the state finance commissions (SFCs) completed their task, the central finance commission was duty bound to assess and build into the expenditure stream of the states, the funding requirements for supplementing resources of the panchayats and the municipalities. Measures needed for augmentation of the consolidated funds of the states could be determined accordingly. The transfer of duties and functions listed in the eleventh and twelfth schedules of the constitution would also involve concomitant transfers of staff and resources. Transfer of duties and functions should, therefore, not entail any extra financial burden. Nevertheless, the Commission recommended a grant of Rs.100 per capita of rural population as per the 1971 census for the panchayats and Rs.1,000 crore for the municipalities to be distributed amongst the states on the basis of the inter-state ratio of slum population derived from 1971 census. The state governments were required to prepare suitable schemes and prepare detailed guidelines for the utilization of the grants. The local bodies were required to raise 'suitable' matching contributions for the purpose. No amount was to be used for expenditure on salaries and wages.

8.3 The TOR of the EFC clearly required it to make recommendations to augment the consolidated fund of the states to supplement the resources of local bodies on the basis of SFC recommendations. The EFC was, however, asked to make its own assessment, if the recommendations of the SFCs were not available, either because they had not been constituted or they were yet to submit their reports. In making its own assessment of the resources of the local bodies, the EFC was required to keep in view (i) the emoluments and terminal benefits of the employees of the local bodies including teachers; (ii) existing powers of these local bodies to raise financial resources; and (iii) powers, authority and responsibility transferred to the local bodies under articles 243G and 243W of the Constitution.

8.4 The EFC found itself unable to adopt the SFC reports as the basis for its recommendations because of:

a) non-synchronization of the period of the recommendations of the SFCs and the central finance commission;
b) lack of clarity in respect of the assignment of powers, authority and responsibilities of the local bodies;
c) absence of a time frame within which the state governments are required to take action on the recommendations of the SFCs; and
d) non-availability of the reports of the SFCs.

In view of these constraints, the EFC went so far as to recommend an amendment to the Constitution to delete the words "on the basis of the recommendations made by the Finance Commission of the State".

8.5 The EFC, while dealing with the issue of local body finances recommended a number of measures which could be taken by the state governments and the local bodies for augmenting the consolidated funds of the states to supplement the resources of panchayats and municipalities. These included assignment of land tax, profession tax and surcharge/cess on state taxes for improving the basic civic services and taking up schemes of social and economic development. Reforms had been recommended in respect of property tax/ house tax, octroi/entry tax and user charges. The EFC observed that while assessing the revenue and expenditure of the states, it had already taken into account the additional burden falling on their financial resources due to implementation of the SFCs reports and no additional provision, therefore, need be made on this account. But, considering the fact that certain critical areas get overlooked in the normal flow of funds from the states, the EFC recommended *ad hoc* annual grant of Rs.1600 crore for panchayats and Rs.400 crore for municipalities and mandated certain activities such as maintenance of accounts, development of data base and audit to be the first charge on this grant. Amount remaining thereafter was to be utilized by the local bodies for maintenance of core civic services.

Views of the States

8.6 The memoranda received from the states are a mix of demands and suggestions.

Some of the major suggestions made by the states are as follows: (i) a formula based approach, need to be followed for grants from the central finance commission; which may include a minimum level of own revenue generation by the local bodies as one of the conditions; (ii) the *inter se* distribution should take into account the rural capital assets rather than the population; (iii) frequent occurrence of natural calamities should be taken into account; (iv) grants-in-aid should be provided to support an incentive fund for the panchayat samitis and zila parishads; (v) the system of grants should be linked to the level of reforms undertaken by the states; (vi) the central grants should be conditional upon the implementation of the SFC recommendations by the state government; (vii) funds should be made available to meet the revenue account gap, as estimated by the SFC, as also for upgradation of services; (viii) the divisible pool of central taxes should be expanded by 10 per cent for devolution to local bodies; (ix) central support is required to bridge the resource gap of local bodies for upgrading the infrastructure to provide services as per norms; (x) the Twelfth Finance Commission should follow the approach of the EFC and make an independent assessment of the resources required by the local bodies; (xi) an allocation of 5 per cent of the funds may be made for the newly created states; (xii) states, which have truly discharged their constitutional mandate in letter and spirit of the 73rd/74th amendment, should be rewarded; (xiii) 50 per cent of the transfers from the state government to the local bodies should be funded by the centre; (xiv) the transfers recommended by the SFC should be treated as committed expenditure of the state government while reassessing the expenditure forecasts.

8.7 Some states have sought compensation for the loss of revenue on account of abolition of octroi. Grants have been sought for improving the training infrastructure and for continuing the efforts to streamline the data base and maintenance of accounts. Several states have suggested the withdrawal of the condition, which requires either the state government or the local bodies to provide matching contribution.

8.8 We have taken due note of these suggestions and kept them in view while arriving at the quantum of central grants that could be set apart for the purpose of supplementing the resources of the local bodies.

Views of the Ministry of Rural Development

8.9 The Ministry of Rural Development (MRD) has raised the following issues related to panchayati raj institutions (PRIs) in its memorandum:

i) poor revenue efforts by the PRIs; their internal revenue mobilization (IRM) of the PRIs constituted only 4.17 per cent of their total revenue as per a study done on behalf of the EFC;

ii) inefficiencies arising because of reluctance to charge fees, low rates thereof even when imposed and non revision for long periods;

iii) state governments prescribing minimum and maximum rates of tax thereby encroaching into the financial autonomy of the PRIs;

iv) lack of administrative machinery for collection of taxes;

v) limited capacity of the people to pay taxes in the villages, especially in those affected by drought and other disasters;

vi) inability of the central government to intervene in a substantial manner, local bodies being a state subject;

vii) lack of synchronization in the award periods of the central finance commission and the SFCs;

viii) part acceptance/implementation of SFC recommendations by state governments;

ix) release of funds meant for panchayats to line departments which operate independent of panchayats;

x) inability of the system to regularly collect, compile and monitor the status of panchayat finances;

xi) lack of information on the initiatives that were taken by panchayats towards data base building for which funds were earmarked by EFC;

xii) poor quality of the SFC reports;

xiii) the casual manner in which SFCs are constituted.

8.10 MRD had initially suggested grants amounting to Rs.22,250 crore for the PRIs at the rate of Rs 300 per capita of the rural population as per 2001 census for 2005-10, as against Rs.8000 crore given by EFC for 2000-05. Subsequently, MRD submitted a supplementary memorandum wherein it recommended a grant of Rs 23468 crore at the rate of Rs.2 lakh per gram panchayat per annum mainly for operation and maintenance (O&M) activities related to assets like water supply system, canal system, buildings, roads, drains etc. MRD expressed the view that if a decentralization index is to be used, it should comprise parameters which are simple, transparent and objective. It may include (i) constitution and functioning of district planning centres as required under article 243ZD; (ii) assignment of all the 29 functions given in eleventh schedule along with funds and all functionaries (iii) implementation of the SFC recommendations.

8.11 We received a memorandum from the Department of Drinking Water Supply (DDWS), Ministry of Rural Development regarding the requirements of the water supply and sanitation sector. Drinking water and sanitation are among the state subjects that can be entrusted to the panchayats under the eleventh schedule of the constitution. As per 2001 census, while 94.2 per cent of the rural inhabitants have access to potable drinking water with a norm of 40 litres per capita per day, only 22 per cent have basic sanitation facilities. Government of India has been supplementing the efforts of the states in the areas of drinking water supply and sanitation in villages through two centrally sponsored programmes namely, the Accelerated Rural Water Supply Programme (ARWSP) since 1972-73 and the Central Rural Sanitation Programme (CRSP) since 1986.

8.12 Looking at the gaps in the two sectors and the need to encourage PRIs to take over assets created in the past, DDWS suggested a grant of Rs.29,200 crore with the break-up as follows:

(i) financial assistance to PRIs for major

repairs and replacement of existing water supply schemes – Rs 9000 crore;

(ii) financial assistance to state government for repair/rejuvenation of existing rural water supply schemes – Rs 5200 crore;

(iii) one-time incentive contribution to O&M fund of PRIs for new schemes to be transferred to them under Swajaldhara – Rs 1000 crore;

(iv) creation of water quality monitoring and surveillance infrastructure in states- Rs 440 crore;

(v) state share in water quality mitigation programme – Rs 1500 crore;

(vi) completion of ongoing drinking water supply schemes - Rs 6700 crore;

(vii) O&M cost of sanitation services – Rs 3600 crore;

(viii) states' share in the Rural Sanitation Programme – Rs 1400 crore;

(ix) capacity building of PRIs – Rs.350 crore;

Views of the Ministry of Urban Development and Poverty Alleviation

8.13 The Ministry of Urban Development and Poverty Alleviation (MUD&PA) has estimated a resource gap of Rs.76896 crore for all the states during the period 2005-10 in the matter of operation and maintenance of various civic services in urban areas. It has suggested that this gap should be bridged through a grant-in-aid by Twelfth Finance Commission (TFC).

8.14 MUD&PA has suggested the following to improve the functioning of the urban local bodies:—

i) it should be made obligatory for the state governments to take a final decision on the recommendations of the finance commission within a specified period preferably within 6 months;

ii) urban local bodies should be assigned a separate list of taxes and any exemption from levy of property tax should be avoided. They should be adequately compensated if any exemption are given by the state government;

iii) unproductive and non-viable taxes should be abolished and new sources of revenue should be explored;

iv) urban local bodies should explore the possibility of issue of municipal bonds;

v) the accounting procedure should be modernized and use of computer should be facilitated;

vi) performance budgeting and social auditing should be introduced;

vii) the cost of public utility services should be recovered by charging appropriate fees from the user of the services;

viii) municipalities must progressively recover full costs covering operation and maintenance, billing and collection and capital;

ix) inter-governmental transfers including share in state taxes and grants-in-aid should be formula based and not amenable to negotiation;

x) borrowings can be one of the primary sources of capital funding for municipalities; and

xi) grants given for development of infrastructure should be utilized to leverage additional financial resources.

8.15 In another memorandum, MUD&PA drew the Commission's attention to the deficiencies in urban waste management arising out of poor financial health of the urban local bodies and inadequacies in the solid waste management systems in the country. It has been stated that about 42 million tonnes of municipal solid waste is produced annually in urban India with a per capita generation varying between 0.2 to 0.6 kg per day. The waste generation is expected to grow at the rate of 5 per cent per annum. On an average, the urban local bodies spend about 60 to 70 per cent of their budget on this important activity. Following the out break of plague in 1994 in Surat and the intervention of the Supreme Court of India, detailed guidelines for municipal solid waste management (MSW) were issued and the Ministry of Environment and Forests notified rules for managing municipal solid waste, laying down deadlines for completion of various activities by the urban local bodies. Since adequate budgetary support has not been made available for this purpose during the Tenth Plan, MUD&PA has suggested devolution of sufficient funds by TFC to assist urban local bodies for solid waste management. According to the scheme prepared by MUD&PA, a total outlay of Rs.3763 crore at an average per capita cost of Rs.220 would be required for implementing it in 400 class I towns. The inter se allocation among the states has been worked out on the basis of the urban population of the class – I towns, as per 2001 census. The scheme, however, focuses on funding of capital expenditure including the cost of construction of sanitary landfills and compost plants based on wastes. The capital cost of equipment and machinery required for collection, transportation and disposal and their replacement cost for five years are proposed to be provided to the urban local bodies as grants-in-aid.

8.16 The shortcomings of the present solid waste management systems in the urban local bodies extend well beyond the lack of capital infrastructure. Most of the urban local bodies are over-staffed and have to pay for a large, but idle workforce. A lot could be achieved by productively deploying the existing resources and making use of the available infrastructure. However, in view of obvious constraints in this regard, we expect the scheme to emphasize out-sourcing of the services connected with the solid waste management in order to achieve efficiency gains. Investing in capital infrastructure without addressing the issue of labour productivity would turn out to be wasteful.

8.17 Composting and waste to energy initiatives would be economically viable in the private sector provided the municipalities can assure regular supply of solid waste (segregated, if necessary). The role of the municipalities should, therefore, be restricted to ensuring proper collection, segregation (if necessary) and transportation. If these activities are out-sourced, there would be no need for the capital expenditure on machinery, equipments, etc. It is, therefore, necessary that the scheme for solid waste management provides for grants-in-aid to support the minimum revenue expenditure (including cost of outsourcing) required to be incurred by the municipalities to ensure its success through public-private partnership.

Studies/Seminars sponsored by the TFC

8.18 The National Institute of Rural Development (NIRD) was commissioned to study the innovative/best practices being adopted by different states to augment the resources of the PRIs with a view to exploring the scope for their replication in others. The detailed study was confined to three major states viz., Kerala, Gujarat and Madhya Pradesh which in the opinion of NIRD exhibit some distinct features in the system of their PRIs. An attempt was also made to cull out important features of panchayati raj in other major states. The study reported that the obligatory/mandatory provisions of the 73rd amendment have largely been complied with by almost all the states.

8.19 In regard to replicating the best practices, the study suggested the following:

i) levy of certain major taxes and exploitation of non-tax revenue sources be made obligatory for the panchayats. The minimum rates for all such levies be fixed by the state government;

ii) a minimum revenue collection from the panchayat taxes be insisted;

iii) incentive grants related to revenue collection beyond a prescribed minimum be introduced by the state government;

iv) user charges be made obligatory levies;

v) all common property resources vested in the village panchayats may be identified, listed and made productive of revenue;

vi) valuation of taxable lands and buildings should be done by a separate cell in the panchayati raj department of the state government and not left to the panchayats;

vii) powers to levy a tax/surcharge/cess on agricultural holdings should be given to the intermediate or district panchayats;

viii) revenue transfers from the states to panchayats in the form of revenue sharing/revenue assignment be made statutory in nature;

ix) state governments should desist from unilaterally taking decisions in regard to revenues whose proceeds are to be transferred either in full or in part to the panchayats;

x) the quantum of revenue that a panchayat can reasonably expect under the revenue sharing mechanism should be predictable;

xi) state government should adhere to its commitment in regard to the grants-in-aid; all untied grants to the panchayats should be made statutory in nature;

xii) SFC should be constituted for a lifespan of 18 months and a time limit of six months be prescribed for a state government to act on the SFC recommendations;

xiii) the maintenance of accounts by the panchayats be standardized;

panchayat department officials should not be made statutory auditors of the village panchayats; the accounts of the intermediate and district panchayats be subjected to audit by Comptroller and Auditor General (C&AG);

xiv) a performance audit system be adopted.

We are in broad agreement with these recommendations and commend them for adoption by the state governments.

8.20 The NIRD was also asked to study the recommendations of the SFCs with a view to assessing their impact on state finances so that the required augmentation of the consolidated fund could be known. The findings of the study are summarized below:

(i) states have not made any progress in mobilizing additional resources exclusively for supplementing the resources of panchayats;

(ii) together with village panchayats, the intermediate and district panchayats have been granted some revenue powers;

(iii) the data deficiencies observed four years ago have not been corrected by the states as yet;

(iv) the size of the own resources of the panchayats are extremely limited in relation to their needs. During 1990-91 to 1997-98, the internal revenue mobilization (IRM) of the panchayats at all levels in 23 states constituted 4.17 per cent of the total revenue. In Bihar, Rajasthan, Manipur and Sikkim there was virtually no IRM. The annual per capita IRM of the panchayats in some states was only around Rs.8;

(v) there has been a phenomenal dependence of panchayats on revenue transfer from both the Union and the state governments. In 1997-98, the panchayats mobilized 0.04 per cent of the GDP and incurred an expenditure of 1.38 per cent of GDP;

(vi) assistance to the panchayats from the state government takes the form of revenue sharing, revenue assignments and grants-in-aid. State government grants account for not less than 80 per cent of the total resources of the panchayats, but most of them are tied grants. The system of grants has not been rationalized in many states and the quantum to be made available is often not predictable;

(vii) in some states, there were delays in constituting the second SFC whereas in others the second SFC was not constituted at all. Only 19 states constituted the second SFC, of which 10 had submitted their reports. Of these, only six have been laid before the state legislature along with action taken report;

(viii) with regard to implementation of the SFC reports which were accepted, the following issues were highlighted:-

a) several states did not take follow up action in terms of legislative/administrative measures;

b) recommendations marked

"under examination" met with "natural death";

c) very few states have honoured their commitment for the release of additional resources against these recommendations;

d) budgetary provisions regarding these recommendations have "fallen short".

The study has admitted that it could not succeed in assessing the net additional resource flow from the states to the panchayats consequent to the implementation of the SFC recommendation.

8.21 The National Institute of Public Finance and Policy (NIPFP) was commissioned to undertake similar studies in respect of urban local bodies. The NIPFP conducted the study in respect of 23 states. The study observed that municipal finance statistics were fragile and posed problems in interpreting the data. It noted that the size of municipal sector, measured in terms of what the municipalities raised and spent was 1 per cent of GDP with large inter-state disparities. Performance of municipalities on revenue mobilization and spending levels varied across states. States with high per-capita income were also the ones taking major reform initiatives and were better performing. Transfers constituted an important source of municipal revenue, but were just 3.8 per cent of states' own resources.

8.22 A study was commissioned on "Management of Solid Waste in Indian Cities". The report submitted by the Infrastructure Professional Enterprises (IPE) brought out some of the best practices followed in India as well as around the world. It also listed certain technology options available to convert waste into compost or energy in India and abroad. The IPE worked out the costs for integrated solid waste disposal relating to one sample city, Burdwan (West Bengal). While conducting another study on the costs of provision of sewerage, waste water treatment and drainage, IPE selected five towns of different size classes of population. The case study took into account the urban infrastructure available as well as the coverage of population and worked out the per capita cost in respect of sewerage, waste water treatment and drainage separately. The gaps were estimated separately on each item to arrive at the overall gap. The estimates so provided could at best be a benchmark for a particular class of town. The actual requirement of funds would depend on the availability of infrastructure and population size of each town and need to be estimated independently.

8.23 The task of looking into the qualitative and quantitative measures needed to augment the consolidated funds of the states for supplementing the resources of local bodies based on the recommendations of the SFC reports was assigned to an expert. The focus of the study was the areas that required action on the part of the central government. The report estimated the uncovered gap of the local bodies at Rs.74,000 crores over a five year period. Some of the measures suggested by the SFCs which require action on the part of the central government were listed. These are the following:

(i) raising the ceiling on the professional tax;

(ii) enhancement of rates of royalty on mineral resources;

(iii) constitutional amendment for empowering states/local bodies to levy service taxes;

(iv) transferring centrally sponsored schemes along with funds and functionaries to the state government/local bodies;

(v) continuation of fiscal reforms incentive scheme;

(vi) review of Gadgil formula to enhance the ratio of grants in the plan transfers from the centre to the non-special category states, with a view to reducing their burden of interest payments;

(vii) writing off old debts of the state governments to the central government, to enable such states to make a clean start while embarking upon fiscal reforms;

(viii) larger weight to be given by the TFC in its devolution formula to factors like;

(a) extent of functional and fiscal decentralization;

(b) backwardness of states; and

(c) incentive for tax efforts;

(ix) possibility of setting up of Municipal Finance Corporation and Panchayat Finance Corporation through direct funding by the central government or through merger of existing financial institutions at the central/state level.

We have commented on these issues at different places in our report and hope that the central government will take due note of our views while formulating or revising various policy measures. In particular, we endorse the suggestion for raising the ceiling on professional tax.

8.24 In order to understand the precise role of the central finance commission in the light of the constitutional provisions and to gain an insight into the felt needs of the third tier of the government, the TFC sponsored two seminars, one for urban local bodies and the other for the PRIs, organized by the Indian Institute of Public Administration (IIPA) and the NIRD respectively. A list of the speakers and the papers presented by them is placed at annexure 8.1. Some of the views expressed in the seminars were as follows:

(i) PRIs can realize higher taxes provided they improve administrative capacities by correct evaluation of tax base, cutting out exemptions etc. Financial needs of panchayats far outweigh the resources at their disposal;

(ii) the transfers from the TFC should be linked to effective fiscal decentralization, meaning thereby transfer of administrative and financial powers to PRIs by states;

(iii) measures for restructuring of public finances would be complete only if the third tier of the government is also taken into account;

(iv) the phrase "on the basis of recommendations by SFCs" in the terms of reference of the TFC should be replaced by "after considering the recommendations of SFCs";

(v) there is a crucial need for incentivising local revenue collection. The revenue potential of the panchayats can be assessed using secondary sources such as SDP from non plantation agriculture sector ;

(vi) the only cost-effective way to incentivise revenue collection is to have a system of norm-based closed-ended grants from the state governments, where allocations for a panchayat are made after deducting baseline calculations of local revenue potential;

(vii) the initial fixation of the total kitty for distribution to the local bodies should be made on the basis of a decentralization target based on local expenditure as a percent of total government expenditure, instead of an arbitrary per capita allocation for the local bodies. This should be met from central tax sharing; in the global revenue sharing for devolution to the states, the share of the local bodies should be decided simultaneously;

(viii) there should be a 'Local List' in the Constitution covering both local functions and taxes;

(ix) the centre and state transfers should be transparent and predictable with rewards for better performances;

(x) resources should flow to the local governments as a matter of right rather than a concession or a consideration.

Data collected by the Commission

8.25 The Commission collected detailed information from each state in respect of local bodies in five schedules which are placed at annexure 8.2 to 8.6. The states were requested to send notes on the following topics with a view to assessing the requirement of each state for augmentation of their consolidated fund in the light of the SFC reports:

I. status of setting up of SFCs – award periods of SFCs – principles laid down by SFCs for assignment of taxes/devolution/grants-in-aid to PRIs and ULBs – implementation of SFC recommendations – recommendation not accepted-reasons therefor;

II. details of transfers made to PRIs/ULBs before the setting up of SFCs - growth rate of such transfers – amounts recommended by SFCs under different categories of transfers (such as assignments of taxes, devolution, grants-in-aid) – actual transfers effected –difference between the projected amount for each year based on the average growth rate (in the previous five years) and amounts recommended by SFCs for the same functional responsibilities;

III. details of additional functional responsibilities assigned to PRIs/ULBs consequent on 73rd/74th amendment-expenditure incurred by state government on the functions before such transfers –growth rate of such expenditure in five years before such transfer-resources transferred to PRIs /ULBs to carry out additional responsibilities – transfer of man power from the state to PRIs/ULBs for such functions/ adequacy of transfer of resources compared to responsibilities – approach of SFCs on the issue – recommendations by SFCs – financial implications thereof for the state government;

IV. the impact on the consolidated fund of the state on account of implementation of SFC recommendations - details of recommendations –annual financial implication of accepting each of the recommendations – efforts made to raise revenues to meet the additional requirement – results thereof;

V. status of implementation of EFC recommendations – efforts made to raise resources of local bodies for pursuance and results thereof-utilization of grants recommended by EFC-arrangements for maintenance of accounts of village level panchayats and intermediate level panchayats-creation of data base relating to the finances of local bodies-arrangements made for audit of panchayat and urban local bodies and status thereof;

VI. market borrowing by local bodies-whether permitted – if so, borrowings and outstanding liabilities during the last five years may be furnished.

It was expected that there would be a system of collection and compilation of such information at the state headquarters not only for the purpose of monitoring by the state government but also for the use of the SFCs and, therefore, the information would be updated and made available within a reasonable time. However, even after considerable persuasion, the response received from different states, barring a few exceptions was found to be rather sketchy. The data furnished by the states did not facilitate quantification of the required augmentation of the consolidated fund on the basis of the SFC recommendations. Information could, however, be compiled regarding (a) the number of rural and urban local bodies at different tiers in each state, and (b) the details of own revenues and transfers from the states to their local bodies. These have been placed at annexures 8.7 to 8.9. These data show that the share of own revenues of the panchayats (all tiers) was 6.40 per cent of their total revenues for the period 1998-99 to 2002-03 which is a definite improvement over 4.17 percent estimated for the period 1990-91 to 1997-98 but is still low.

8.26 The EFC had set apart Rs.200 crore for creation of data base relating to the finances of local bodies and Rs. 98.61 crore per annum for maintenance of accounts of village and intermediate level panchayats. It was recommended that a database on the finances of the panchayats and municipalities should be developed at the district, state and central government levels and be easily accessible by computerising it and linking it through V-SAT. The authority prescribed for conducting the audit of accounts of the local bodies was to be made responsible for this task and the data were to be collected and compiled in standard formats, prescribed by the C&AG. This would have facilitated comparison of performance and state of development of local bodies among the states.

8.27 The progress in respect of implementation of the EFC recommendations relating to accounts, as reported by the C&AG, is as under:

i. **Entrustment of technical guidance and supervision (TGS) over proper maintenance of accounts and audit of all 3 tiers of PRIs and ULBs to C&AG of India** – As of now, 19 states have entrusted the TGS over local bodies to the C&AG. Leaving out the states where the 73rd & 74th amendments are not applicable, five major states viz. Punjab, Haryana, Andhra Pradesh, Gujarat and Arunachal Pradesh have not yet implemented this recommendation;

ii. **Documents prescribed by C&AG for providing TGS** – The C&AG has prescribed auditing standards for PRIs and ULBs, guidelines for certification audit of the account of PRIs, budget and accounts formats for PRIs and ULBs and list of codes for programmes, functions and activities for PRIs;

iii. **Acceptance of Budget and Accounts formats for PRIs and ULBs** – 18 states have agreed to accept the formats prescribed for PRIs and 6 states of Bihar, Tamil Nadu, Himachal Pradesh, Uttar Pradesh, Kerala and Orissa have issued formal orders in this regard. For ULBs, the report of the task force set up by C&AG for devising the budget and accounts formats has been accepted by all states for uniform implementation;

iv. **Arrears in accounts maintenances** – As per the guidelines issued by the Ministry of Finance, the C&AG has to lay down the qualifications and experience for the person/agency to whom the work of maintenance of accounts wherever in arrears, could be awarded. Accordingly, the C&AG has approved the parameters for engaging the outside agencies in the states of Bihar, Tamil Nadu, Kerala and Rajasthan based on the request from the state government. The Accountants General concerned are in touch with the remaining state governments to assess the extent of arrears and send proposals accordingly;

v. **Capacity Building, Training Initiative by C&AG** – Comprehensive training programmes to upgrade the skills of the staff of local fund audit department and PRIs in the states are being conducted by the C&AG through the Institute of Public Auditors of India as nodal agency. This training is to be provided in two phases wherein the first phase would be the training of trainers and in the second phase, these trainers would impart training to the remaining staff. The first phase which is being funded by the C&AG has been completed in 9 states of Bihar, Uttar Pradesh, Orissa, Chhatisgarh, Uttaranchal, Assam, Kerala, Himachal Pradesh and Gujarat. It is being taken up in the remaining states;

vi. **Creation of Central Database on Finances of Local Bodies** – The C&AG has formulated draft standard formats for creation of a networked database on finances of PRIs at the district and state levels. As of now, 10 states have agreed to adopt of the formats and 7 states have initiated action to set up the infrastructure for collection, transmission and maintenance of the database.

It is hoped that these initiatives would make further progress and in future, it would be possible for the state to make the data required by the central finance commission available on a certified basis.

Role of the State Finance Commissions

8.28 In terms of articles 243(I) and 243(Y) of the Constitution, the state finance commissions are to recommend (a) the principles that should govern the distribution between the state on the one hand and the local bodies on the other of the net proceeds of taxes etc. leviable by the state and the inter-se allocation between different panchayats and municipalities; (b) the determination of the taxes, duties, tolls and fees which may be assigned to, or appropriated by the local bodies; and (c) grants in aid from the consolidated fund of the state to the local bodies. The SFCs are also required to suggest measures needed to improve the financial position of the panchayats and the municipalities. We have collected information regarding the number of SFCs set up by different states in pursuance of their constitutional obligation, the status of submission of reports by the SFCs and the action taken by the state governments thereon. We are placing the information at annexure 8.10.

8.29 The importance of the SFCs in the scheme of fiscal decentralization is that besides arbitrating on the claims to resources by the state government and the local bodies, their recommendations would impart greater stability and predictability to the transfer mechanism. The convention established at the national level of accepting the principal recommendations of the finance commission without modification, however, is not being followed in the states. Often, even the accepted recommendations are not fully implemented, citing resource constraints and this defeats the very purpose of constituting the SFCs. This situation needs a change.

8.30 If the SFCs follow the procedure adopted by the central finance commission for transfer of resources from the centre to the states, their reports would contain an estimation and analysis of the finances of the state government as well as the local bodies at the pre and post transfer stages along with a quantification of the revenues that could be generated additionally by the local bodies by adopting the measures recommended therein. The gaps that may still remain would then constitute the basis for the measures to be recommended by the central finance commission.

8.31 While estimating the resource gap, the SFCs should follow a normative approach in the assessment of revenues and expenditure rather than make forecasts based on historical trends. Per capita norms for revenue generation must take into account the data relating to the tax bases and the avenues for raising non tax income by the municipalities and the panchayats, assuming reasonable buoyancies and the scope for additional resource mobilization. Per capita expenditure norms could be evolved on the basis of the average expenditure incurred by some of the best performing municipalities and panchayats in the provision of core services. The gap between the aggregate revenue and the aggregate expenditure calculated in this manner, after adjusting for the resource transfers recommended by the SFC, will provide the basis for the approach of the central finance commission.

8.32 A careful scrutiny of the SFC reports reveals that few SFCs have followed this approach. This has made it impossible for us to adopt the reports as the basis for our recommendations. We strongly recommend that in future, all SFCs including those which are already set up but are yet to submit their recommendations, follow the above procedure so as to enable the central finance commission to do full justice to its constitutional mandate.

8.33 To make this possible, it is necessary that the states constitute SFCs with people of eminence and competence, instead of viewing the formation of SFCs as a mere constitutional formality. We find that most states are yet to appreciate the importance of this institution in terms of its potential to carry the process of democratic decentralization further and evolve competencies at the cutting edge level by strengthening the PRIs and the municipalities. The delays in the constitution of the SFCs, their constitution in phases, frequent reconstitution, the qualification of the persons chosen, delayed submission of reports and delayed tabling of the action taken report (ATR) in the legislature have in many cases defeated the very purpose of this institution. This cannot, but, be a matter of concern for the central finance commission, which has to adopt their reports as the basis for its recommendations.

8.34 In the matter of composition of the SFCs, states may be well advised to follow the central legislation and rules which prescribe the qualifications for the chairperson and members and frame similar rules. It is important that experts are drawn from specific disciplines such as economics, public finance, public administration and law. In order that the concerns of both rural and urban local bodies are adequately addressed, it is suggested that at least one member with specialization and/or experience in matters relating to the PRIs and another similarly well versed in municipal affairs must be appointed in the SFC. The number of members including the chairperson may not exceed five excluding a serving officer who may act as the secretary. Since the SFCs are temporary bodies and dedicated efforts are called for to discharge their functions within the time limit, all members and chairman should be full time. Frequent reconstitution of the SFCs should be avoided, as it disturbs the continuity of approach and thought. The main reason for reconstitution appears to be the routine transfers of serving officials. This situation will not arise if the SFC comprises non official experts.

8.35 The compilation of disaggregated data in the formats suggested by C&AG in a time series is the need of the hour for the SFCs to be able to assess the income and expenditure requirements of the local bodies. Both the EFC as well as this Commission were hampered by the absence of credible data. It is with a view to overcome this problem that the EFC had made provision for the creation and maintenance of data as well as for an improvement in the accounting standards. We are happy to note that the formats prescribed by the C&AG have been accepted by most states and hope that the remaining states will also follow suit. As the collection and collation of data would need to be done constantly and data would need to be made available to the SFC as and when it is constituted, it may be desirable to set up a permanent SFC cell in the finance department of each state. This cell may be headed by a secretary level officer, who will also function as secretary of the SFC, as and when constituted.

8.36 The other issues are the time span to be prescribed for the setting up of a new SFC, the time allowed for submission of its report, the time limits for ATR and synchronization of its award period with that of the central finance commission. The time taken by the SFCs to submit their reports ranges from less than three months to more than three years. There are also instances of a state abandoning the first SFC without receiving a report and setting up the second SFC. The problem with the delayed submission of reports is that quite often the time period for which they are to make recommendations passes out. It is desirable that SFCs are constituted at least two years before the required date of submission of their recommendations, and the deadline should be so decided as to allow the state government at least three months' time for tabling the ATR, preferably along with the budget for the ensuing financial year. Synchronization of the award periods of the SFC with the central finance commission does not mean that they should be co-terminus. What is necessary is that the SFC reports should be readily available to the central finance commission, when the latter is constituted so that an assessment of the state's need could be made by the central finance commission on the basis of uniform principles. This requires that these reports should not be too dated. As the periodicity of constitution of the central finance commission is predictable, the states should time the constitution of their SFCs suitably. In order to fulfill the overall objective, the procedure and the time limits would need to be built into the relevant legislation.

Role of the Central Finance Commission

8.37 An attempt was made to understand fully the scope of the constitutional provisions requiring the central finance commission to recommend measures for the augmentation of the consolidated fund of the states. Although the dominant view that emerged from the papers presented in the seminars and the meetings held with the state governments, was that these are meant only to be a mechanism for additional resource transfers from the centre to the states, we feel that there may be more to it than this. To us the purport of the relevant provision of the Constitution appears to be two-fold:- (a) there may be a case to augment the consolidated fund of the states through additional grants from the centre keeping in view the special circumstances of the states, which may justify such assistance; and (b) certain recommendations of the SFCs for augmenting the revenues of the state may require decision making by the central government as they may have centre-state and/or inter-state ramifications. The central government may benefit from the expert advice of the central finance commission, while acting on the issues taken up by the state governments with the centre on the basis of such SFC recommendations. For example, the centre can act in respect of matters such as (a) revision of the rates of taxes/duties wherever the proceeds of such taxes/duties are to be appropriated by or assigned to the state; the stamp duty and duties of excise on medicinal and toilet preparations under article 268 and the central sales tax under article 269 fall in this category; (b) revision of rates for certain categories of non-tax revenues, which are determined by the central government, such as the royalty from minerals wherever a part of such revenues have been recommended to be shared with the local bodies; (c) issues concerning central public sector undertakings, railways etc. including the property and other local taxes payable by them, return of land in their possession in excess of requirement etc.; and (d) upward revision of ceiling on profession tax requiring a constitutional amendment. These are but an illustrative list of issues which do require central intervention and where the decisions of the central government would influence the flows into the consolidated fund of a state. Measures that a central finance commission may choose to recommend on these and other issues of a similar nature after taking into account the views of the SFCs would, therefore, be a substantial fulfillment of its constitutional mandate. In view of this, we recommend that in future, the SFCs must clearly identify the issues which require action on the part of the central government to augment the consolidated fund of the state and list them out in a separate chapter for the consideration of the central finance commission.

Recommendations

8.38 Keeping in view the spirit of the 73rd and 74th amendments and the clear need to provide an impetus to the decentralization process, we have decided to recommend a sum of Rs.25000 crore for the period 2005-10 as grants-in-aid to augment the consolidated fund of the states to supplement the resources of the municipalities and the panchayats. This will be equivalent to 1.24 per cent of the sharable tax revenues and 0.9 per cent of gross revenue receipts of the centre as estimated by us during the period 2005-10.

8.39 The EFC had recommended that the division of the grants in aid should be in the ratio 80:20 for the panchayats and the municipalities respectively. It was reasoned that the urban local bodies had a greater access to tax and non-tax resources of their own and, therefore, it is the PRIs which require substantial support. The urban population of 28 states as per 2001 census is 26.8 per cent. We have separately recommended grants for maintenance of roads and buildings which include the roads maintained by the local bodies. The municipalities will be major beneficiaries of these grants. Looking at the capacity as well as the need to encourage the municipalities to augment their own revenues, a share at 20 per cent, appears to be in order. We accordingly recommend that the amount of Rs.25000 crore may be divided between the panchayats and the municipalities in the ratio of 80:20. The amounts of Rs.20,000 crore for the PRIs and Rs.5,000 crore for the municipalities thus worked out, are a substantial increase over the levels recommended by the previous commissions and will go a long way in improving the standards of civic services performed by the local governments.

8.40 We would like the grants for the PRIs to be utilized to improve the service delivery by the panchayats in respect of water supply and sanitation. We have been informed that an amount of over Rs.45,000 crore has been invested in the rural water supply schemes over several years. The schemes being taken up under Swajaldhara are provided a grant of 10 per cent of capital costs as incentive for the O&M along with a matching contribution by the state government after it is run successfully for 12 months. There is no provision for O&M for the schemes completed previously. The panchayats need to be encouraged to take over and maintain all such schemes. Some of the existing schemes may require special repairs to make them fully functional. The PRIs may take over the assets and utilize these grants for repairs/rejuvenation and maintenance to make them fully operational. Even after this, the PRIs may not be able to bear the entire cost of O&M of water supply for an initial period of five years. They should, however, recover at least 50 per cent of the recurring costs in the form of user charges.

8.41 The Department of Drinking Water Supply has informed us that panchayats do not get any financial assistance under the total sanitation campaign (TCS) for disposal of solid waste, cleaning of drains etc., until there is basic sanitation coverage. Once they achieve basic sanitation coverage, they qualify for the Nirmal Gram Puraskar ranging from Rs.2 lakh to 4 lakh depending on their population. Till such time as they qualify they could be provided assistance to maintain environmental sanitation for a hand holding period of five years. Against this background we recommend that of the grants in aid allocated by us for the PRIs in each state, priority should be given to expenditure on the O&M costs of water supply and sanitation. This will facilitate panchayats to take over the schemes and operate them.

8.42 In the case of the urban local bodies, we have already stressed the importance of public-private partnership to enhance the service delivery in respect of solid waste management. The municipalities should concentrate on collection, segregation and transportation of solid waste. State governments may require the municipalities of towns of population over 100,000 by 2001 census to prepare a comprehensive scheme including composting and waste to energy programmes to be undertaken in the private sector for appropriate funding from the grants in aid recommended by us. Grants-in-aid shall, however, be available to support the cost of collection, segregation and transportation only, as the activities to be taken up by the private sector should be commercially viable once the municipality is able to discharge its role effectively. We suggest that at least 50 per cent of the grants provided to each state for the urban local bodies should be earmarked for these schemes. The six mega cities of Delhi, Mumbai, Kolkata, Chennai, Bangalore and Hyderabad may be excluded for the purpose of grants-in-aid, as it should be possible for them to generate their own resources for this important service.

8.43 The EFC allocated Rs.200 crore for creation of database by local bodies, but only Rs.93 crore could be utilized, as per information received from the Ministry of Finance. Out of the allocation of Rs.483 crore for maintenance of accounts, only Rs.113 crore was utilized. The total utilization has, thus, been hardly 30 per cent of the allocation. While the reasons for such gross under utilization are far from clear, there is no doubt that the data quality at the grass-roots level is poor. Most states do not have accurate information on the finances of their local bodies. A proper accounting system has to be put in place at the grass-roots level to facilitate realistic assessment of the needs of the panchayats and municipalities for basic civic and developmental functions. Resource gap estimation for core services is central to the process of a fiscal transfer that would encourage equalization. The absence of data necessary for a rational determination of the gap between the cost of service delivery and the capacity to raise resources makes the task of recommending measures for achieving equalization of services almost impossible. It is, therefore, imperative that high priority should be accorded to creation of database and maintenance of accounts at the grass-roots level. Some of the modern methods like GIS (Geographic Information Systems) for mapping of properties in urban areas and computerization for switching over to a modern system of financial management would go a long way in creating strong local governments, fulfilling the spirit of the 73rd and 74th constitutional amendments. It is, therefore, recommended that besides expenditure on the O & M costs of water supply and sanitation in rural areas and on the schemes of solid waste management in urban areas, as indicated in paras 8.41 and 8.42 above, PRIs and municipalities should give high priority to expenditure on creation of database and maintenance of accounts through the use of modern technology and management systems, wherever possible. In the absence of credible costing data, we refrain from making specific allocation for individual items of expenditure and leave it to the states to assess the requirement of each local body on the basis of the principles stated above and earmark funds accordingly out of the total allocation recommended by us.

8.44 As for the *inter se* allocation of the grants in aid among the states, the EFC had adopted the following factors and weights for working out the inter-se allocation of the grants-in-aid among the states:

	Criterion	Weight (per cent)
I.	Population	40
II.	Geographical area	10
III.	Distance from highest per capita income	20
IV.	Index of decentralization	20
V.	Revenue effort	10

We note that the criteria of population and geographical area being neutral meet general acceptance. We have, therefore, decided to retain the weights recommended by the EFC for these two factors. We have used population as per 2001 census for this purpose. We have also decided to retain the criteria of 'distance from the highest per capita income' as evolved by the EFC with a weight of 20 per cent. We have used the average per capita GSDP from primary sector (at comparable prices) derived on the basis of the GSDP figures supplied by the CSO for the years 1999-2000, 2000-01 and 2001-02. The population figures were interpolated/projected for these three years on the basis of census data on rural population for the year 1991 and 2001. The interpolation/projection have been made on the basis of exponential growth in population between 1991 and 2001. Since state wise rural/urban population estimates were not available based on the census 2001 results, these were first derived for the calendar year and thereafter interpolated for the financial years 1999-00, 2000-01 and 2001-02. The distance of each state was measured from the state with the highest average per capita GSDP, plus half of the standard deviation. The distances were then weighted by the rural population (2001) of the respective state to arrive at its share for the panchayats.

8.45 In the case of the urban local bodies, we have used the average per capita GSDP excluding primary sector (at comparable prices) on the basis of the GSDP data supplied by the CSO and the population figures interpolated/projected for three years; viz. 1999-00, 2000-01 and 2001-02 based on 1991 and 2001 census data on urban population. The distance of each state was measured from the state with the highest average per capita GSDP, plus half of the standard deviation. The distances were then weighted by the urban population (2001) of the respective state to arrive at its share.

8.46 We have in addition attempted to construct an index of deprivation to take into account intra–state disparities on the basis of data relating to certain minimum needs of the population. Drinking water and sanitation are the two core services performed by the local bodies, both rural and urban. State-wise census 2001 data are available with a break up between rural and urban areas regarding the number of households fetching water from a distance (over 100 metres in the case of urban and 500 metres in the case of rural households), households with no latrines within the house premises and households with no drainage facilities for flow of waste water. These have been used to construct this index. The formula used is $D.I=0.5x+0.25(y+z)$ where D.I is the Deprivation Index, x is the percentage of households fetching water from a distance, y is the percentage of households without latrines and z, the percentage of households without drainage. The distance from the minimum deprived state was then weighted by the census 2001 population for rural and urban areas to derive the state-wise share. A standard deviation of 0.5 has been allowed so as to enable the least deprived state also to get a share. We assign a weight of 10 per cent to this criterion.

8.47 The EFC had selected the following 10 parameters for the purpose of arriving at the index of decentralization: -

(i) enactment/amendment of the state/ panchayats/municipal legislation;

(ii) intervention/restriction in the functioning of the local bodies;

(iii) assignment of functions to the local bodies by state legislation;

(iv) actual transfer of functions to these bodies by way of rules, notification and orders;

(v) assignment of power of taxation to the local bodies;

(vi) extent of exercise of taxation powers;

(vii) constitution of the SFCs and the submission of action taken on their reports;

(viii) action taken on the major recommendations of the SFC;

(ix) elections to the local bodies; and

(x) constitution of the district planning committees as per the letter and spirit of article 243ZD.

Considering that almost all states have by now taken effective steps for the implementation of the 73rd and 74th amendments and have enacted legislations, held elections, constituted the state finance commissions and taken action on their reports, most of the factors mentioned above may not be of much relevance in the present context. We have decided to drop this criterion in this form.

8.48 In order to assess the 'revenue effort', the EFC had linked the ratio of own revenues of the local bodies to the state's own revenue and the SDP separately and assigning a 5 per cent weight to each. While in the case of panchayats, the SDP from primary sector excluding mining & quarrying was taken into account, in the case of municipalities the SDP net of primary sector was taken as the basis. These were suitably weighted by the rural and urban population as the case may be. We have decided to modify this criterion by including the mining and quarrying in case of panchayats, with a weight of 10 per cent to each of the elements. The period taken was 2000-01 to 2002-03 in the case of the own revenues of local bodies related to states own revenue and 1999-2000 to 2001-02 in case of own revenues of local bodies related to SDP. Since the newly created states of Jharkhand, Uttaranchal and Chattisgarh were created in November 2000, the fiscal data relating to states own revenue were available from November only. In view of this, the data relating to 2001-02 and 2002-03 only were taken to compute revenue efforts of local bodies vis-à-vis state's own resources in respect of the states of Bihar, Jharkhand, Chattisgarh, Madhya Pradesh, Uttar Pradesh and Uttaranchal. This approach had to be followed for the residual states of Bihar, Uttar Pradesh and Madhya Pradesh, as the data for 2000-01 were a combination of composite state till November and the divided states after November, 2000. The significance of the ratio of own resources of local bodies to states own revenues is that it also serves as a proxy of revenue decentralization.

8.49 The criteria used for inter-se allocation of grants are summarized below:

	Criterion	Weight (per cent)
i)	Population	40
ii)	Geographical area	10
iii)	Distance from highest per capita income	20
iv)	Index of deprivation	10
v)	Revenue effort	20
of which	(a) with respect to own revenue of states	10
	(b) with respect to GSDP	10

The shares of the states derived on the basis of the above criteria were rounded off to the nearest whole number in rupees crore. The results of this exercise in terms of state-wise allocation of the grants in aid are given in Table 8.1. The amounts to be released annually to each state for panchayats and municipalities are given in annexures 8.17 and 8.18 respectively.

The data used in respect of each of the factors and the pro rata shares of each state under each of the indicators are shown in annexures 8.11 to 8.18.

8.50 The issue of exclusion of certain areas from the provision of the 73rd and 74th

Table 8.1

Shares of States in Allocation (2005-10)

Sl.No	State	Panchayats		Municipalities	
		Per cent	(Rs Crore)	Per cent	(Rs Crore)
1.	Andhra Pradesh	7.935	1587	7.480	374
2.	Arunachal Pradesh	0.340	68	0.060	3
3.	Assam	2.630	526	1.100	55
4.	Bihar	8.120	1624	2.840	142
5.	Chhattisgarh	3.075	615	1.760	88
6.	Goa	0.090	18	0.240	12
7.	Gujarat	4.655	931	8.280	414
8.	Haryana	1.940	388	1.820	91
9.	Himachal Pradesh	0.735	147	0.160	8
10.	Jammu & Kashmir	1.405	281	0.760	38
11.	Jharkhand	2.410	482	1.960	98
12.	Karnataka	4.440	888	6.460	323
13.	Kerala	4.925	985	2.980	149
14.	Madhya Pradesh	8.315	1663	7.220	361
15.	Maharashtra	9.915	1983	15.820	791
16.	Manipur	0.230	46	0.180	9
17.	Meghalaya	0.250	50	0.160	8
18.	Mizoram	0.100	20	0.200	10
19.	Nagaland	0.200	40	0.120	6
20.	Orissa	4.015	803	2.080	104
21.	Punjab	1.620	324	3.420	171
22.	Rajasthan	6.150	1230	4.400	220
23.	Sikkim	0.065	13	0.020	1
24.	Tamil Nadu	4.350	870	11.440	572
25.	Tripura	0.285	57	0.160	8
26.	Uttar Pradesh	14.640	2928	10.340	517
27.	Uttaranchal	0.810	162	0.680	34
28.	West Bengal	6.355	1271	7.860	393
		100.000	**20000**	**100.000**	**5000**

amendments still remains. The fifth and the sixth schedule areas stood excluded from the operation of the 73rd and 74th amendments. The states of Meghalaya, Mizoram and Nagaland have been specifically excluded from the operation of the 73rd amendment, but the legislatures of these states have been given the power to extend this amendment to their states by law, except in respect of the sixth schedule areas. Autonomous district councils have been constituted under the sixth schedule in the states of Assam, Meghalaya, Mizoram and Tripura. For extension of the provisions of the 73rd amendment to the fifth schedule areas, legislation was passed by Parliament in 1996. In the case of the sixth schedule areas, no action has yet been taken by the Parliament to make these amendments applicable to these areas. The EFC had segregated the grants for normal and excluded areas and hoped that the latter would become 'eligible' through necessary administrative and legislative measures.

8.51 We have been informed that the

state governments as the collection and collation of data would need to be done constantly and data would need to be made available to the SFC as and when it is constituted.

xi) A sum of Rs.20000 crore for the panchayats and Rs.5000 crore for the municipalities may be provided as grants-in-aid to augment the consolidated fund of the states for the period 2005-10 to be distributed with inter-se shares as indicated in table 8.1.

xii) The PRIs should be encouraged to take over the assets relating to water supply and sanitation and utilize the grants for repairs/rejuvenation as also the O&M costs. The PRIs should, however, recover at least 50 percent of the recurring costs in the form of user charges.

xiii) Of the grants allocated for panchayats, priority should be given to expenditure on the O&M costs of water supply and sanitation. This will facilitate panchayats to take over the schemes and operate them.

xiv) At least 50 per cent of the grants-in-aid provided to each state for the urban local bodies should be earmarked for the scheme of solid waste management through public-private partnership. The municipalities should concentrate on collection, segregation and transportation of solid waste. The cost of these activities whether carried out in house or out sourced could be met from the grants.

xv) Most states do not have credible information on the finances of their local bodies. Local bodies would continue to need funding support for building data base and maintenance of accounts. States may assess the requirement of each local body in this regard and earmark funds accordingly out of the total allocation recommended by us.

xvi) Separate grants-in-aid for the normal and the excluded areas are not proposed. It is for the state concerned to distribute the grants recommended for the state among the local bodies including those in the excluded areas in a fair and just manner.

xvii) No conditionality over and above those recommended by us need be imposed by the central government for releasing the grants-in-aid.

Chapter 9

Calamity Relief

9.1 Para 10 of the TOR requires us to review the present arrangements as regards financing of disaster management with reference to the National Calamity Contingency Fund and the Calamity Relief Fund and make appropriate recommendations thereon.

Calamity Relief Fund (CRF)

9.2 The problem of funding relief expenditure has been recognized by every finance commission since the second. Successive finance commissions since then have made recommendations with regard to provision for relief expenditure out of the revenues of the states and the extent of support to be extended by the centre to the states. The earlier arrangement made in this regard, at the behest of the Second Finance Commission, was commonly called the 'margin money scheme'. This arrangement, which involved setting apart a specified sum by the states as margin for relief expenditure, with centre meeting excess requirement, continued to be endorsed by the later finance commissions upto the eighth, with some minor changes.

9.3 The present scheme of CRF is essentially based on the recommendations of the Ninth Finance Commission. While determining the size of the CRF the Ninth Finance Commission did not restrict itself to the margin money, as was done by the earlier (fourth to the eighth) finance commissions but took into consideration the average of ceilings of expenditure, which included margin money, advance plan assistance (grant and loan), special central assistance and the state's own share of 25 per cent over the ten year period ending in 1988-89. On this basis, the total amount of CRF for all states was worked out to Rs.804 crore per year. While determining the size of the CRF, the Tenth Finance Commission considered the average of the aggregate of ceilings of expenditure for the years 1983-84 to 1989-90 and the amount of CRF for the years 1990-91 to 1992-93 The amount so worked out for all the states was adjusted for inflation up to 1994-95 and thereafter, at graduated rates with the same elasticity as for other non-plan revenue expenditure, upto 1999-2000. The total amount of CRF for all states for the period 1995-2000 was thus worked out to Rs.6304.27 crore.

9.4 The salient features of the present scheme of the CRF, which is based on the recommendations of the Eleventh Finance Commission (EFC), are as under:

(i) The CRF should be used for meeting the expenditure for providing immediate relief to the victims of cyclone, drought, earthquake, fire, flood and hailstorm.

(ii) The size of the CRF of the states was fixed after taking into account the average expenditure incurred by the states under the major head 2245 for 12 years ending on 1998-99 at 1998-99 prices, after fully adjusting for inflation on the basis of consumer price index for industrial workers. The amount so worked out has been projected up to 1999-2000 on the basis of estimated inflation, and provision for each year up to 2004-05 has been made after assuming the current rate of inflation. Where the average expenditure worked out to be less, the allocation for the year 2000-01 was maintained at the level of 1999-2000, to ensure that no state got less than what it was getting earlier. In the case of the poorer states, such as Assam, Bihar, Orissa, Madhya Pradesh, Uttar Pradesh and West Bengal, the size of their CRF was strengthened by an additional provision of ten per cent of the aggregate size of the CRF, allocated among these six states in the same ratio in which these states had their own CRF.

(iii) The contributions from the centre and the states to the CRF are to be in the ratio of 75:25.

(iv) The share of the central government is remitted to the state governments in two installments on 1st May and 1st November of each financial year. Likewise the state governments also transfer the total contribution (including their own share) to the fund in two installments in May and November of the same year. Before an installment is released, the state should give a certificate indicating that the amount received earlier has been credited to the CRF. The certificate is to be accompanied by a statement giving the up-to-date expenditure and the balance amount available in the CRF. In order to ensure that the CRF funds are not diverted to meet expenditure not approved as per the items/norms laid down by the expert committee, the central government has now prescribed a detailed proforma in which the states are to report item-wise expenditure.

(v) The money drawn from the CRF is to be utilized for the purpose of providing immediate relief to the affected area and population only on items of expenditure and as per norms contained in the guidelines issued by the Ministry of Home Affairs, which has substituted the Ministry of Agriculture as the nodal ministry for the scheme of CRF.

(vi) Expenditure on restoration of infrastructure and other capital assets, except those which are intrinsically connected with relief operations and connectivity with the affected area and population, should be met from the plan funds on priority.

(vii) If in a particular year, the amount required to be spent on the natural calamity is more than the sum available in the CRF, the state should be able to draw 25 per cent of the funds due to the state in the following year from the centre, to be adjusted against the dues of the subsequent year.

(viii) The CRF is administered by the respective state level committees, headed by the chief secretary of the state and consisting of other officials, who are normally connected with the relief work and experts in various fields in the state. The committee decides on all matters connected with the financing of the relief expenditure, arranges to obtain the contributions from the concerned governments; administers the fund and invests the accretions to the fund as per the norms approved by the central government. The committee ensures that the money drawn from the CRF is actually utilized for the purposes for which the fund has been set up and only on items of expenditure and as per norms contained in the guidelines issued by Ministry of Home Affairs.

(ix) The investment of the funds is carried out by the branch of the Reserve Bank of India (RBI), having a banking department at the headquarters of the state. In the case of states in which there is no such branch of the RBI at state headquarters, the investment is to be carried out by the bank designated by RBI and in the case of governments of Jammu & Kashmir and Sikkim, these functions are carried out by their bankers. The accretions to the fund together with the income earned on the investment is to be invested in one or more instruments, such as (i) central government dated securities, (ii) auctioned treasury bills, (iii) interest earning deposits and certificates of deposits with scheduled commercial banks and (iv) interest earning deposits in co-operative banks. If for some reason, it is not possible to invest in the manner prescribed in the scheme, the periodic contributions to the fund as well as other income of the fund may be kept in the public account, on which the state government should pay interest on half-yearly basis to the fund at one and half times the rate applicable to overdrafts under Overdraft Regulation Scheme of the RBI.

(x) The balance in the fund at the end of the five-year plan period is made available to the state for being used as a resource for the next plan.

National Calamity Contingency Fund (NCCF)

9.5 Successive finance commissions have acknowledged the need for quick response and direct intervention of the central government in cases of calamities of rare severity and made recommendations in this regard. The seventh and eighth finance commissions recommended that in case the calamity is of rare severity, the centre should provide special assistance to the affected state over and above its prescribed share. The Ninth Finance Commission expected that, if any region faced a calamity of such dimensions and severity as to warrant its handling at the national level, the centre would take appropriate action as the situation demanded and incur the necessary expenditure. The Tenth Finance Commission, for the first time, formulated a distinct funding mechanism for taking care of calamities of rare severity. The Commission observed that any definition of the term 'rare severity' would bristle with insurmountable difficulties and is likely to be counter-productive. The Commission was of the view that a calamity of rare severity would necessarily have to be adjudged on a case-to-case basis taking into account, inter alia, the intensity and magnitude of the calamity, level of relief assistance needed, the capacity of the state to tackle the problem, the alternatives and flexibility available with the plans to provide succour and relief, etc. The Commission recommended setting up of a 'National Fund for Calamity Relief' (NFCR) to be managed by a National Calamity Relief Committee (NCRC). Both the centre and the states were to be represented in NCRC, which was to be chaired by the Union Minister of Agriculture and had members including the Deputy Chairman, Planning Commission and some chief ministers. The NFCR was to have a corpus of Rs. 700 crore to be contributed by the centre and the states in the ratio 75:25 over a period of 5 years.

9.6 While deliberating on the issue of calamities of rare severity, the EFC observed that under the scheme of NFCR the states had to go through a long-drawn procedure before they were allocated any relief from the committee. It was also pointed out that there had been occasions when the recommendations made by the central teams and the Inter-Ministerial Group for providing relief were either not accepted or were modified and the amount of relief was reduced. The EFC further observed that the corpus of the NFCR was not adequate to last for the full five years; it was exhausted in the first three years i.e. 1995-98 and had to be supplemented. The Commission recommended discontinuation of the fund, as it had not resulted in making funds readily available for meeting the calamity of rare severity. The EFC was, however, of the view that in the case of occurrence of calamity of rare severity, the states can not be left to fend for themselves and that the centre and other states are also expected to come forward to provide relief to the distressed state. The Commission, therefore, felt that there was a need to develop a system in which it should be possible to take suo motu cognizance of the occurrence of calamities of rare severity by the central government, without waiting for any memorandum from the state government or for the deputation of a central team for getting on-the-spot assessment of the damage and of the extent of relief required. The EFC recommended setting up of National Calamity Contingency Fund.

9.7 The salient features of the present scheme of the NCCF, based on the recommendations of the EFC, are as under:

(i) A National Centre for Calamity Management (NCCM) under the Ministry of Home Affairs has been established to monitor natural calamities relating to cyclone, drought, earthquake, fire, flood and hailstorm. The NCCM is expected to monitor such occurrences on a regular basis and assess their impact on the area and the population and to assess whether the state would be in a position to provide relief in a specific case of calamity of severe nature from the CRF and its own resources. It should then make a recommendation to the central government, on its own, as to whether the calamity is of a severe nature, and therefore, eligible for assistance from the central government and other state governments. The centre should then take appropriate action on such recommendation.

(ii) Any financial assistance provided by the central government to the states in this regard, should be recouped by levy of a special surcharge on central taxes. Collections from such a surcharge/cess should be kept in a separate fund created in the public account of the central government, to which it should contribute Rs. 500 crore as the initial core amount. Outgo from this fund should be recouped by levy of the surcharge.

(iii) The unspent balance in the National Fund at the end of the financial year 2004-05 will be available to the central government for being used as resource for the next plan.

Views of the States

9.8 The states have expressed their views on various issues related to the schemes of CRF and NCCF. Their views on some of the key issues are given below:

(a) On the issue of the size of the CRF, Andhra Pradesh, Punjab, Uttar Pradesh and Himachal Pradesh have urged that the size of the fund may be raised at least by 10 per cent per annum. Arunachal Pradesh and Assam have requested for raising the corpus of CRF by twice and thrice respectively. Kerala has suggested that the CRF may be enhanced to 10 per cent of the amount of the annual state plan size of the state concerned. Some of the states have represented that the size of the CRF should not be fixed on the basis of average annual expenditure only. While Andhra Pradesh and Orissa want the Twelfth Finance Commission to consider the proneness of the states to calamities and their severity, Madhya Pradesh has suggested for considering the drought prone area, duration, periodicity and other related factors. Bihar has submitted that the size of CRF be fixed on the basis of population affected, as per norms of relief and provision for restoration of infrastructural facilities. It further added that whatever be the size of the CRF, inflation should be fully provided for. Uttar Pradesh has also suggested for taking into consideration the intensity, regularity and duration of relief required, while determining the size of the CRF.

(b) Andhra Pradesh, Bihar, Haryana, Kerala, Maharashtra, Meghalaya, Orissa, Punjab, Tamil Nadu and Rajasthan have suggested that the contribution of the states to the CRF be reduced to 10 per cent, while Uttar Pradesh has suggested for keeping it at 15 per cent. Assam, Nagaland, Sikkim and Manipur are of the view that the entire funding should be done by the centre. Madhya Pradesh has suggested that backward states should not be made to contribute to the fund or alternatively, their contribution may be limited to 10 per cent. Tripura wants special category states to be relieved of making any contribution to the fund. Similarly, Uttaranchal has suggested that, for a disaster prone state like Uttaranchal, which is also fiscally disadvantaged, the entire relief should come from the centre as 100 per cent grant. Manipur has urged that, in view of the fiscal constraints being faced by the state, entire contribution to the CRF in its case should be made by the centre.

(c) A large number of calamities have been suggested by the states for providing relief. Most of these are area specific and have only been suggested by states, which get affected by these calamities. The calamities that have been suggested, apart from the existing six calamities under the CRF, (names of the states shown in the parenthesis), are landslides (Arunachal Pradesh, Assam and Tamil Nadu), soil erosion (Assam), heat and cold waves (Bihar, Haryana, Orissa), lightening (Haryana), pest attacks (Punjab, Tamil Nadu), water logging (Punjab), bamboo flowering (Mizoram) and changes in the course of rivers (Bihar).

(d) Andhra Pradesh, Assam, Himachal Pradesh, West Bengal and Uttar Pradesh have requested for allowing the states to meet expenditure on restoration of damaged infrastructure and bring it to pre-calamity level. On the issue of norms fixed for relief expenditure to be met out of the CRF, states have represented for their relaxation for the sake of flexibility of the scheme. According to Andhra Pradesh, in severe drought conditions norms may be relaxed for expenditure on capital works like digging of bore wells, installation of pumps etc. Gujarat and Uttar Pradesh have suggested that the expenditure on establishment to oversee the relief work should also be a valid charge on the CRF.

(e) Chhattisgarh and Gujarat have suggested that the states be allowed full freedom in the matter of investment of the accretion to the fund on the ground of liquidity. While Gujarat has suggested for keeping the fund in the public account of the states, Chhattisgarh is for complete freedom to the states on this issue, including the freedom to keep it in public account of the states. Uttar Pradesh has represented that for the sake of liquidity and sufficient return on the investment of funds, the investment pattern should be left to the discretion of state level committees.

(f) The states have suggested for the continuance of the NCCF, but with enhanced corpus. The states of Andhra Pradesh, Arunachal Pradesh and West Bengal are of the view that corpus of the NCCF is inadequate and should be suitably increased. Kerala has suggested that the corpus of the fund may be enhanced to the level of 10 per cent of the aggregate amount transferred as the central share of the CRF to the states. As per Maharashtra, the initial core amount of Rs. 500 crore for NCCF should be increased to Rs. 1000 crore.

(g) Kerala is of the view that the disaster of rare severity may be defined very clearly with parameters for different kinds of disasters and scales of intensity so as to minimize discretion and delay. Orissa has expressed the view that the funding and rehabilitation during the natural calamities of rare severity should be flexible and adequate and it should be free from any bias.

Views of the Central Government

9.9 The Ministry of Home Affairs has, in its memorandum, made a case for shifting focus from post-disaster relief to pre-disaster preparedness and mitigation. The Ministry has suggested setting up of a special fund called Disaster Mitigation Fund to be created for the preparedness and mitigation aspects, and to be placed at the disposal of the Ministry of Home Affairs. It has also been brought out in the memorandum of the Ministry of Home Affairs that, based on the recommendations of an expert group set up by the Ministry, the norms of expenditure have been revised. Now the states are permitted to use 10 per cent of the inflows into the CRF each year for the procurement of search and rescue equipment for the search and rescue teams to be set up by the states. The Ministry of Home Affairs considers this, alongwith the provision of permitting use of CRF for training specialists' teams as a change in orientation – permitting use of CRF for preparedness. On the other hand, the Ministry of Finance is of the view that it is important to keep the focus of CRF/NCCF primarily on calamity relief and disaster mitigation; reconstruction and like activities should be funded separately as distinct plan schemes. The Ministry of Home Affairs is of the view that the present system of determining the size of CRF on the basis of average expenditure incurred in the past is heavily loaded against poorer states and the states which incur expenditure from CRF more cautiously. The Ministry has therefore, recommended that factors like vulnerability/hazard profile, poverty status of the states, amount of losses due to disasters in last ten years, etc. should be taken into consideration in addition to the existing criteria for determining the size of CRF. Other suggestions made by the Ministry of Home Affairs are with regard to inclusion of land slides and avalanches in the list of calamites eligible for relief from CRF/NCCF and making provision for relief to union territories from the NCCF, as no contribution is made by the states to the corpus of NCCF.

Recommendations

9.10 Having considered the views of the states and the central ministries, we find that the CRF scheme has by and large fulfilled the objective of meeting the immediate relief needs of the states. Accordingly, we recommend continuance of the scheme of CRF in its present form with some minor changes as suggested hereafter.

9.11 In order to determine the size of the CRF, relief expenditure incurred under the major head 2245 for the years 1993-94 to 2002-03 has been taken into account, as the figures for 2003-04 were available as revised estimates only. For this purpose, allocations from the NCCF have been excluded. Thereafter, we have followed the methodology of the EFC for fixing the size of the CRF. The average of the total expenditure incurred during these years has been adopted as the projected figure for 2003-04 and an annual rate of inflation of 5 per cent has been added for each year up to 2009-10. It was noticed that in some years, the expenditure of some of the states increased considerably, because of certain events (like earthquake in Gujarat or super cyclone in Orissa), which may not recur during our award period. It is also recognized that taking expenditure as the criterion for providing relief may not do justice to states, which could not afford to spend because of low fiscal capacity, despite the need. The EFC had made an additional provision of ten per cent of the aggregate size of the CRF to be allocated among 'low-income' states of Assam, Bihar, West Bengal, Orissa, Uttar Pradesh and Madhya Pradesh. In our view, the problem of low income states persists and we have taken care of this aspect by making an additional allocation of 25 per cent to undivided Uttar Pradesh, Madhya Pradesh and Bihar alongwith those for Orissa, West Bengal and the special category states. Allocations to the newly created states of Jharkhand, Chhattisgarh and Uttaranchal have been made on the basis of the proportion of area. We noticed that in case of Uttaranchal, reckoning of average relief expenditure on the basis of area and making of additional provision on account of its being a special category state, have not done full justice to the state. This is for the first time that the size of the CRF of Uttaranchal is being determined. Uttaranchal, although comparable to Himachal Pradesh in area, terrain and climatic conditions, has more population. Therefore, to bring some degree of parity to the CRF of Uttaranchal as compared to that of Himachal Pradesh, its allocation is enhanced by a sum of Rs. 144 crore. Taking all these into consideration, the size of the CRF of each state has been determined for each year from 2005-06 to 2009-10. The size of the CRF, thus, gets enhanced from Rs.11007.59 crore in the EFC period to Rs.21333.33 crore under our allocation. The centre's contribution increases from Rs.8255.69 crore to Rs. 16,000 crore. It may be noted that the size of CRF for each state as recommended by us, is larger than what was recommended by the EFC even after indexation for inflation. This takes care of the demand of the states to enhance the size of the CRF and for providing for inflation. We are, however, not inclined to agree to the suggestions of the states and of the Ministry of Home Affairs to take into account other factors like the proneness of the states to calamities and their severity and amount of losses due to disasters in last ten years. We endorse the views of the EFC on the issue, that all these factors are reasonably captured by data on relief expenditure incurred under the major head 2245 over a period of time. We are also not inclined to agree to the suggestion of the states with regard to reducing the contribution of the states to the CRF. States' own contribution to the CRF instills a sense of responsibility in the states and curbs the tendency to incur wasteful expenditure from the fund. We, therefore, recommend that the centre and the states will continue to contribute to the CRF to the extent of 75 per cent and 25 per cent respectively.

9.12 We find considerable justification in widening the list of calamities, which may be covered by our recommendations. The definition of natural calamity, as applicable at present, may be extended to cover land slides, avalanches, cloud burst and pest attacks. Although our terms of reference include the term "disaster", we do not consider it feasible to expand the scope of the term further. Other disasters, chemical and industrial, as also air/railway accidents may continue to be taken care of by the respective ministries.

9.13 Expenditure on restoration of infrastructure and capital assets will continue to be excluded, as any expenditure other than that incurred for the purpose of providing immediate relief to the states on the occurrence of a calamity, will not only put a very heavy burden on the CRF but will also lead to wasteful expenditure on the part of the states to the detriment of the scheme of CRF. The restoration of damaged infrastructure has to be planned very often to new standards, arrived at after detailed analysis of the phenomena that caused the damage and also it has to be done by following the prescribed procedure, which, obviously, is not possible as part of any immediate relief programme.

9.14 Several states as well as the Ministry of Home Affairs have referred to the requirements relating to disaster preparedness and mitigation. We agree that this is an important area, which requires consideration. But, this needs to be built into the state plans, as has been the practice. The focus of CRF/NCCF must be primarily on calamity relief. In relation to disaster preparedness, a suggestion that has been made is for hazard mapping for different types of calamities. In this context, it will be useful to set up a committee consisting of scientists, flood control specialists and other experts to study the hazards to which several states are subject to, given the geo-physical and agro-meteorological heterogeneity of the country.

9.15 We also decline to interfere with the present arrangements with regard to investment of unspent funds lying in the CRF and items/norms for incurring relief expenditure from the CRF. We, however, suggest that the Ministry of Finance may have a re-look at the issue of investment of the funds lying in the CRF and give necessary guidelines to the states, provided that such guidelines do not contravene the broad framework of the present scheme.

9.16 We are in agreement with the suggestions of the states with regard to continuance of the scheme of NCCF. We, therefore, recommend that the present scheme of the NCCF should continue in its present form. The scheme has stood the test of Gujarat earthquake and in addressing other situations, which were beyond the control of the states. On the front of raising funds also, the scheme has stood the test of time, as the fund gets replenished each year, in the absence of any special time-bound surcharge, by way of National Calamity Contingent Duty imposed on cigarettes, pan masala, biris and other tobacco products. This duty is exclusively for replenishing the NCCF and is estimated to yield Rs. 1769 crore for the year 2004-05. This yearly accretion to the NCCF enables build-up of its corpus.

9.17 We have considered the views of the states with regard to the inadequacy of the funds in NCCF and enhancement of the core corpus of Rs. 500 crore. As the funding mechanism of the scheme of the NCCF provides for immediate and simultaneous replenishment of the fund on account of any outgo, the corpus of Rs.500 crore appears to be a reasonable amount to take care of any eventuality that may arise as a result of occurrence of a calamity of rare severity. We, therefore, do not see any justification for enhancing the core corpus of the NCCF.

9.18 The Commission has noted the allocation of foodgrains by the central government particularly to meet the drought situations in the states in recent years. The Ministry of Rural Development has formulated a scheme of its own, of a financial magnitude comparable with the CRF. The scheme has assured grain, free of cost, as well as cash to sustain employment. The programmes of rural employment announced by the Ministry under the Sampoorna Grameen Rozgar Yojna (SGRY) were integrated with the relief programmes in a number of states, particularly in Andhra Pradesh, Rajasthan and Karnataka. The SGRY was announced on 15.8.2001 and under the scheme, 50 lakh tonnes of foodgrains, worth Rs.5000 crore, were to be provided every year to the states/union territories, free of cost. In the recent years, Rajasthan has been the most notable beneficiary of the scheme of Ministry of Rural Development, as it was able to generate work for seven million people in 2003. Andhra Pradesh is another state which got substantial benefit from the scheme of the Ministry. The allocation to other states under the scheme, although not substantial, has still been comparable to the annual allocation under the CRF. The expenditure on the allocation of food grains to the affected states by the central government is essentially relief expenditure for mitigation in the aftermath of drought or other calamities and the central government can continue to make such allocations, putting in place a transparent policy in this regard.

9.19 Earlier commissions had explored the possibility of mitigating the effect of calamites by evolving a suitable insurance scheme. The terms of reference of the Ninth Finance Commission required it to examine the feasibility of establishing a national insurance fund to which the states may contribute a percentage of their revenue receipts. The Commission, however, observed that the concept of an insurance fund for disaster relief was neither viable nor practicable on the ground that the process of making the assessment of loss by an external agency was bound to be complicated and time consuming, which would defeat the very purpose, that is, of providing timely succour to the affected people. The EFC too did not find the concept of an insurance cover in which the premium is paid fully by the centre and the states, workable. The Commission, however, felt that the crop insurance scheme would help individual farmers, especially at the time of natural calamities and therefore, suggested for strengthening of the scheme. Andhra Pradesh, Kerala and Tamil Nadu have requested the Twelfth Finance Commission to recommend an insurance scheme for providing relief to the affected population.

9.20 We endorse the views of the Ninth and Eleventh Finance Commissions on this issue, as any insurance scheme, the premium for which is to be paid by the centre or the state governments will put a very heavy burden on them, year after year, without providing any substantial benefit to the affected population. The centre and the state governments can, however, play a vital role in encouraging insurance of private assets in vulnerable zones. Strengthening of the crop insurance scheme and loan-linked insurance schemes in rural areas is one such measure. Besides, micro-insurance seems to be the need of the hour. Micro-insurance refers to protection of assets and lives against insurable risks of the target populations, such as micro-entrepreneurs, small farmers and the landless, women and low-income people through formal institutions i.e. insurers and semiformal/ informal institutions, such as NGOs, self-help groups etc. The concept is still at a nascent stage in the country and the Insurance Regulatory and Development Authority (IRDA) is in the process of finalization and notification of the micro-insurance regulations. Since formal institutions serve but a fraction of the population, which typically lies within the upper quartile of the social hierarchy, any initiative to involve the NGOs and self-help groups, which are directly accessible to all segments of the population, can be best done at the behest of the state governments.

9.21 We have been informed by the IRDA that the General Insurance Company has decided to create an "earthquake pool", which will enable all the insurance companies to share the burden of risk in case of huge losses arising out of earthquakes. A working group has already been constituted to look into the modalities for constitution of the "earthquake pool". Under this concept, the insurers will divert the earthquake premia to the "pool". Such a scheme can prove useful in providing social security to the public in the unfortunate event of a catastrophe. It is hoped that an insurance solution like this may result in orderly distribution of disaster relief to the affected population.

9.22 To sum up, our recommendations are as follows:

(a) The scheme of CRF be continued in its present form with contributions from the centre and the states in the ratio of 75:25.

(b) The size of the CRF for our award period is worked out at Rs. 21333.33 crore.

(c) Besides cyclone, drought, earthquake, fire, flood and hailstorm, the definition of natural calamity, as applicable at present, may be extended to cover land slides, avalanches, cloud burst and pest attacks.

(d) The provision for disaster preparedness and mitigation needs to be built into the state plans, and not as a part of calamity relief.

(e) A committee consisting of scientists, flood control specialists and other experts be set up to study and map the hazards to which several states are subject to.

(f) The scheme of NCCF may continue in its present form with core corpus of Rs. 500 crore. The outgo from the fund may continue to be replenished by way of collection of National Calamity Contingent Duty and levy of special surcharge.

(g) The centre may continue to make allocation of foodgrains to the needy states as a relief measure, but a transparent policy in this regard is required to be put in place.

□□

Chapter 10

Grants-in-aid to States

10.1 Para 4(ii) of the TOR requires us to make recommendations on the principles which should govern the grants-in-aid of the revenues of the states out of the consolidated fund of India, and the sums to be paid to the states, which are in need of assistance by way of grants-in-aid of their revenues under article 275 of the Constitution for purposes other than those specified in the proviso to clause (1) of the article.

Principles governing grants-in-aid

10.2 As the system of grants has evolved in India, grants flow from the centre to the states in three ways. The first consists of grants-in-aid given under the recommendations of the finance commission. The second category consists of plan grants covering central assistance for state plans as decided by the Planning Commission, as well as the plan grants given by the central ministries for implementation of plan schemes. The third type of grants, which is much smaller in magnitude, essentially consists of discretionary grants given by the central ministries to states on the non-plan side.

10.3 The finance commission has the mandate to recommend the principles and the amounts of grants-in-aid of revenues for states which are in need of assistance in accordance with the provisions of article 275 of the Constitution. Needs require to be assessed in relation to services provided by the states, the standard of these services in relation to the average or other desirable norms, and the extent to which these requirements can be met by own revenues. As discussed in chapters 2 and 6, a normative approach is required to be adopted to assess the expenditure requirements as well as the own revenues of the states. In making these assessments, one issue is whether the requirements of the states on their plan accounts should also be considered. We have decided to make an assessment of the needs of the states to the extent of their requirements on the non-plan account. This is because plan requirements are best determined on an annual basis, and the states determine their plans in consultation with the Planning Comm-ission, which is charged with deter-mining the plan grants.

10.4 As discussed in Chapter 4, we have made one recommendation with respect to the principles governing central assistance for state plans. At present, the normal central assistance and the additional central assistance are given to the general category states by the centre in the form of

70 per cent loan and 30 per cent grant (10 per cent loan and 90 per cent grant in the case of special category states). This means that if a general category state wants a grant of Rs.30 from the centre, it must necessarily borrow Rs.70 from the same, and that, too, at a rate of interest which is often higher than the open market rate. It is also well known that the existing plan process inherently encourages ever larger plan sizes. All these result in states getting deeper into debt on account of structurally mandated borrowings. There is indeed no reason why plan grants to states should be linked to compulsory loans from the centre. The considerations that go into deciding the grants are, and should be, different from those relating to loans. Since almost the entire expenditure on plan is met by the centre from borrowed funds, central loans as part of the plan assistance unnecessarily increase the fiscal deficit of the centre (on a stand-alone basis). Under the circumstances, we recommend that the system of imposing a 70 : 30 ratio between loans and grants for extending plan assistance to general category states (10:90 in the case of special category states) should be done away with. Instead, the Planning Commission should confine itself to extending plan grants to the states, and leave it to the states to decide how much they wish to borrow and from whom, i.e., from the centre or from the open market. This "dis-intermediation" of the centre in the borrowing process of the states would go a long way in ensuring greater fiscal discipline on the part of the states by removing the structural obligation to borrow from the centre. This would, of course, benefit the centre as well, because it would bring down its own fiscal deficit.

Finance Commission Grants

10.5 While making recommendations regarding grants-in-aid of the revenues of the states, the suggestions received from the states as well as those received from experts in the field have been carefully considered. During the discussions with the state governments, it was noticed that they generally favoured a larger part of finance commission transfers as tax devolution, rather than as grants-in-aid. The states feel that tax devolution is a matter of entitlement, and by its very nature, unconditional.

10.6 While this is so, grants have several unique characteristics as an instrument of fiscal transfer. First, these are determined in absolute terms and the amounts are, therefore, known. Secondly, these can be targeted better. Thirdly, in determining these, better account can be taken of cost disabilities and redistributive considerations that are not adequately captured in the tax devolution formula. For these reasons, we have allowed a greater role for grants in overall finance commission transfers. As would emerge from the discussions later in the chapter, the relative share of grants to tax devolution in our recommendations has been increased as compared to previous Commissions. This can be seen from Table 10.1.

10.7 Based on the assessment of needs and developmental concerns of the states, grants-in-aid of the revenues of the states for the award period 2005-10 have been

Table 10.1

Transfers Recommended by Finance Commissions

(Rs.in crore)

Commission	Period	Grants-in-aid		Share in Taxes		Total Amount
		Amount	% Share	Amount	% Share	
Seventh	1979-84	1609.92	7.72	19233.05	92.28	**20842.97**
Eighth	1984-89	3769.43	9.55	35682.58	90.45	**39452.01**
Ninth*	1989-95	11030.38	9.96	99667.64	90.04	**110698.02**
Tenth	1995-00	20300.30	8.96	206343.00	91.04	**226643.30**
Eleventh	2000-05	58587.39	13.47	376318.01	86.53	**434905.40**
Twelfth	2005-10	142639.60	18.87	613112.02	81.13	**755751.62**

* **Ninth Finance Commission covered six years, and in addition also provided plan grants of Rs.9000.83 crore (not included above).**

recommended, as indicated below:

(i) Post-devolution non-plan revenue deficit: Rs.56,856 crore.
(ii) Health sector : Rs.5887 crore.
(iii) Education sector : Rs.10,172 crore.
(iv) Maintenance of roads & bridges : Rs.15,000 crore.
(v) Maintenance of buildings : Rs.5000 crore.
(vi) Maintenance of forests : Rs.1000 crore.
(vii) Heritage conservation : Rs.625 crore.
(viii) State-specific needs : Rs.7100 crore.
(ix) Local bodies : Rs.25,000 crore.
(x) Calamity relief : Rs.16,000 crore.

Total Finance Commission Grants : Rs.142640 crore.

The first eight items have been dealt with in this chapter, and the remaining two have already been covered in chapters 8 and 9 respectively.

Post-Devolution Non-Plan Revenue Deficit

10.8 The grants-in-aid to cover non-plan revenue deficit have generally been the largest component of the finance commission grants. The objective has been to give grants to those states which are projected, on a normative basis, to have post-devolution non-plan revenue deficit in any year, so that the normatively assessed deficit can be provided for. It needs to be emphasised here that this approach is different from a pure gap filling approach. In the latter case, deficits are assessed without making any corrections in the fiscal behaviour of the states. We have, as has been done by the previous commissions, followed a normative approach, which ensures that deficiency in fiscal capacity is corrected, but inadequate revenue effort or excessive expenditure is not encouraged.

10.9 The pre-devolution non-plan revenue surplus/deficit of each state has been assessed in a normative manner under chapter 6. Table 10.2 provides the result of that exercise.

10.10 As seen from Table 10.2, all special category states are to have, on the basis of normative projection, non-plan revenue deficit in each of the five years of the award period in the pre-devolution scenario. In the case of non-special category states, Goa, Gujarat, Haryana, Karnataka and Maharashtra have been assessed as having

Table 10.2

Pre-Devolution Non-Plan Revenue Surplus/Deficit(-)

(Rs. in crore)

State	2005-06	2006-07	2007-08	2008-09	2009-10	2005-10
1	2	3	4	5	6	7
Andhra Pradesh	-2252.29	-1171.68	-2815.30	-1407.41	287.30	**-7359.38**
Arunachal Pradesh	-535.21	-564.47	-639.05	-671.81	-714.68	**-3125.22**
Assam	-3263.86	-3356.94	-3730.26	-3794.54	-3838.37	**-17983.97**
Bihar	-8327.27	-8623.72	-9412.75	-9719.92	-10130.36	**-46214.02**
Chhattisgarh	-196.11	-60.14	-545.04	-380.84	-170.77	**-1352.90**
Goa	70.76	196.17	306.34	502.52	746.19	**1821.98**
Gujarat	99.15	1447.25	1872.02	3945.18	6371.47	**13735.07**
Haryana	2172.96	2948.57	3385.95	4484.74	5791.17	**18783.39**
Himachal Pradesh	-2641.47	-2653.65	-2748.04	-2712.79	-2649.65	**-13405.60**
Jammu & Kashmir	-3576.54	-3722.12	-4010.51	-4181.68	-4304.32	**-19795.17**
Jharkhand	-531.12	-457.31	-1416.60	-1357.60	-1360.13	**-5122.76**
Karnataka	2612.70	4517.46	5194.17	7956.95	11267.78	**31549.06**
Kerala	-2907.35	-2415.69	-3137.66	-2444.79	-1562.85	**-12468.34**
Madhya Pradesh	-1979.58	-1463.29	-2008.59	-1336.55	-468.17	**-7256.18**
Maharashtra	73.08	2604.01	4367.63	8009.66	12262.34	**27316.72**
Manipur	-1139.43	-1220.17	-1323.99	-1418.62	-1511.21	**-6613.42**
Meghalaya	-715.93	-747.43	-838.93	-868.32	-902.86	**-4073.47**
Mizoram	-755.73	-806.72	-892.27	-964.16	-1025.43	**-4444.31**
Nagaland	-1234.13	-1312.98	-1440.34	-1531.46	-1631.26	**-7150.17**
Orissa	-5207.47	-5272.97	-6117.81	-6190.06	-6300.37	**-29088.68**
Punjab	-2744.68	-2282.59	-2213.66	-1506.75	-619.22	**-9366.90**
Rajasthan	-5098.50	-4666.61	-5046.73	-4396.04	-3461.81	**-22669.69**
Sikkim	-274.39	-284.71	-325.56	-335.53	-360.02	**-1580.21**
Tamil Nadu	-785.96	539.66	1095.37	3229.94	5874.47	**9953.48**
Tripura	-1433.25	-1512.35	-1637.01	-1723.12	-1814.56	**-8120.29**
Uttar Pradesh	-12448.30	-11744.71	-12338.20	-11072.60	-9624.16	**-57227.97**
Uttaranchal	-1971.60	-2047.40	-2243.08	-2289.28	-2325.54	**-10876.90**
West Bengal	-8892.12	-7993.98	-7309.07	-5679.90	-3626.73	**-33501.80**
Total States (Deficit)	**-68912.29**	**-64381.63**	**-72190.45**	**-65983.77**	**-58402.47**	**-329870.61**
Total States (Surplus)	**5028.65**	**12253.12**	**16221.48**	**28128.99**	**42600.72**	**104232.96**

pre-devolution surplus in each of the five years. Tamil Nadu would have surpluses from 2006-07 onwards, while Andhra Pradesh is expected to have surplus in the last year.

10.11 The share of each state in tax devolution during the award period has been assessed in chapter 7. The post-devolution position of states is indicated in Table 10.3.

Table 10.3

Post Tax Devolution Non-Plan Revenue Surplus/Deficit(-)

(Rs. in crore)

State	2005-06	2006-07	2007-08	2008-09	2009-10	2005-10
1	2	3	4	5	6	7
Andhra Pradesh	4474.35	6529.51	6021.40	8754.77	11999.27	37779.30
Arunachal Pradesh	-271.84	-262.94	-293.07	-273.92	-256.11	-1357.88
Assam	-305.67	29.83	155.86	674.49	1312.21	1866.72
Bihar	1757.18	2921.76	3835.05	5515.02	7428.01	21457.02
Chhattisgarh	2230.82	2718.40	2643.18	3285.61	4054.85	14932.86
Goa	307.58	467.30	617.45	860.28	1158.51	3411.12
Gujarat	3362.80	5183.73	6159.42	8875.68	12053.91	35635.54
Haryana	3155.98	4074.00	4677.32	5969.82	7502.73	25379.85
Himachal Pradesh	-2164.12	-2107.14	-2120.96	-1991.64	-1818.52	-10202.38
Jammu & Kashmir	-2458.56	-2446.64	-2552.18	-2510.64	-2385.44	-12353.46
Jharkhand	2542.31	3061.39	2620.92	3285.53	3991.11	15501.26
Karnataka	6690.21	9185.72	10550.74	14117.00	18367.27	58910.94
Kerala	-470.37	374.36	63.77	1236.85	2680.26	3884.87
Madhya Pradesh	4157.22	5562.61	6053.24	7934.53	10216.81	33924.41
Maharashtra	4642.56	7835.51	10370.49	14912.94	20218.41	57979.91
Manipur	-808.39	-841.17	-889.10	-918.50	-934.82	-4391.98
Meghalaya	-376.67	-359.02	-393.24	-355.78	-312.15	-1796.86
Mizoram	-537.19	-556.52	-605.17	-634.00	-644.91	-2977.79
Nagaland	-993.65	-1037.66	-1124.44	-1168.17	-1212.58	-5536.50
Orissa	-488.04	130.22	82.05	939.76	1916.80	2580.79
Punjab	-1556.83	-922.64	-653.20	287.78	1448.99	-1395.90
Rajasthan	30.61	1205.60	1691.32	3352.69	5468.65	11748.87
Sikkim	-66.81	-47.06	-52.86	-21.94	1.40	-187.27
Tamil Nadu	4065.11	6093.55	7468.14	10558.61	14320.81	42506.22
Tripura	-1041.91	-1064.30	-1122.91	-1131.90	-1133.18	-5494.20
Uttar Pradesh	5167.48	8423.22	10803.39	15540.17	21047.22	60981.48
Uttaranchal	-1112.91	-1064.30	-1115.02	-992.02	-830.43	-5114.68
West Bengal	-2438.90	-605.82	1168.44	4069.21	7609.18	9802.11
Total States (Deficit)	**-15091.86**	**-11315.21**	**-10922.15**	**-9998.51**	**-9528.14**	**-56855.87**
Total States (Surplus)	**42584.21**	**63796.71**	**74982.18**	**110170.74**	**152796.4**	**444330.24**

10.12 It is seen from Table 10.3 that all the special category states, except Assam and Sikkim are expected to have normatively determined post-devolution non-plan revenue deficit during the entire award period. Assam is assessed to have revenue surplus from the second year onwards and Sikkim is expected to have revenue surplus in the last year of the award period. Most of the non-special category states, except

Kerala, Orissa, Punjab and West Bengal have post-devolution non-plan revenue surplus during the entire award period. Kerala and Orissa are projected to have a deficit only in the first year of the award period, whereas West Bengal is assessed to be in deficit in the first two years and Punjab in the first three years, before a surplus emerges. In order to cover the assessed non-plan revenue deficit states, we recommend year-wise grants-in-aid as indicated in Table 10.4.

10.13 During the first year of the award period, fifteen states are recommended for non-plan revenue deficit grant amounting to Rs.15091.86 crore. By the last year of the award period, only nine states would get non-plan revenue deficit grants amounting to Rs.9528.14 crore. In all, we recommend total non-plan revenue deficit grant of Rs.56855.87 crore during the award period.

Education and Health Sectors

10.14 In the normative approach, as applied to the own tax revenues of the states, a correction was made in the case of states, where the tax-GSDP ratio was less than the group average. This is consistent with the equalisation approach, although only to a limited extent. There is a need to follow a similar approach on the expenditure side. Per capita expenditures of many states are much below the average per capita expenditure of the relevant group of states. While the amount of transfer required for a full application of the equalisation approach would be too large, we have decided to focus on two critical areas of deficiencies, namely, education and health. But, only a partial correction could be made, because of large disparity between the relevant group average and the actual per capita expenditure

Table 10.4

Grant-in-aid for Non-Plan Revenue Deficit (2005-10)

(Rs. in crore)

State	2005-06	2006-07	2007-08	2008-09	2009-10	2005-10
1	2	3	4	5	6	7
Arunachal Pradesh	271.84	262.94	293.07	273.92	256.11	1357.88
Assam	305.67	Nil	Nil	Nil	Nil	305.67
Himachal Pradesh	2164.12	2107.14	2120.96	1991.64	1818.52	10202.38
Jammu & Kashmir	2458.56	2446.64	2552.18	2510.64	2385.44	12353.46
Kerala	470.37	Nil	Nil	Nil	Nil	470.37
Manipur	808.39	841.17	889.10	918.50	934.82	4391.98
Meghalaya	376.67	359.02	393.24	355.78	312.15	1796.86
Mizoram	537.19	556.52	605.17	634.00	644.91	2977.79
Nagaland	993.65	1037.66	1124.44	1168.17	1212.58	5536.50
Orissa	488.04	Nil	Nil	Nil	Nil	488.04
Punjab	1556.83	922.64	653.20	Nil	Nil	3132.67
Sikkim	66.81	47.06	52.86	21.94	Nil	188.67
Tripura	1041.91	1064.30	1122.91	1131.90	1133.18	5494.20
Uttaranchal	1112.91	1064.30	1115.02	992.02	830.43	5114.68
West Bengal	2438.90	605.82	Nil	Nil	Nil	3044.72
Total States	**15091.86**	**11315.21**	**10922.15**	**9998.51**	**9528.14**	**56855.87**

of some of the constituent states, particularly those having low fiscal capacity and large population. In the estimation of grants, care is taken of those states, who have not been able to allocate on education and health an amount equal to the group average, as measured in relation to the aggregate revenue expenditure, including both plan and non-plan. Aggregate expenditure for this purpose is taken net of interest payments, pensions, and some other adjustments, as explained below. This consideration has been called 'preference correction' in the ensuing discussion.

10.15 Even though considerable funds are made available by the central government to the states on the plan side, the availability of funds still falls short of the requirements in view of the magnitude of the problem. In many plan schemes in these two sectors, the inability to meet the requirement of counterpart funding by the state governments also becomes a handicap in fully utilising the funds. To cite an example, under the scheme of Sarva Shiksha Abhiyan (**SSA**), the states are required to provide 25 per cent of the scheme outlay from their resources in order to avail of the central grant fully. Many states have been unable to meet this requirement. It was, therefore, felt that we should provide specific grants-in-aid for these two sectors to those states which are unable to spend adequately in these sectors because of deficiencies in fiscal capacity.

10.16 In estimating the extent of grants for these two sectors, a two-step normative approach has been adopted. In the first instance, low expenditure preferences of the states in these sectors have been corrected. In other words, it is expected that all states should spend normatively a certain minimum percentage of their total revenue expenditure (both plan and non-plan) on education and health. The second step involves identification of those states which, even after spending the required percentage, fall short of a normative level of per capita expenditure in these two sectors.

10.17 For this purpose, the expenditure data (both plan and non-plan) of each of the states for 2002-03 were examined. In the case of education, the ratio of revenue expenditure under the major head 2202 (plan and non-plan) was worked out for each state with reference to its "adjusted" total revenue expenditure (plan and non-plan). While working out this ratio, expenditure relating to pensions, interest payments and other adjustment items (as already described in the chapter 6) were excluded from non-plan revenue expenditure for arriving at the "adjusted" total revenue expenditure. Thereafter, average ratios were worked out for special and non-special category states. Those states, whose ratio was less than their respective group average, were deemed as having low expenditure preference in regard to the education sector, in the sense that these states were not spending (as a percentage of revenue expenditure) what other states in their group were able to do. This low expenditure preference, therefore, was corrected by normatively assigning the respective group average ratio to those states which were below the average. After this adjustment, the corrected per capita revenue expenditure relating to education (both under plan and non-plan put together) for each state for 2002-03 was worked out. Thereafter, average per capita expenditure was worked out for the two groups of special and non-special category states. Those states, whose per capita expenditure was less than their group average, were reckoned as needing financial assistance, because their lower expenditure could be on account of low fiscal capacity. We worked out the amount of grant required for covering 15 per cent of the distance by which a below-average state was lagging behind its group average of per capita expenditure (after having adjusted for low expenditure preference). It may be noted here that this grant is equal to 15 per cent of the distance with reference to both plan and non-plan revenue expenditure, and it would constitute a much larger proportion if seen against the non-plan revenue expenditure only. The extent of equalisation is, however, limited by the availability of resources. Having thus determined the amount of grant required in 2002-03 for education, a growth rate equal to the group's TGR for 1993-2003 for non-plan revenue expenditure on education was applied on this amount in order to estimate the quantum of grant in the base year. Thereafter, a growth rate of 9.5 per cent was assigned during the forecast period. This is the rate at which the normal expenditure stream on education has been estimated to grow for determining the pre-devolution non-plan revenue surplus/deficit of each state. As a result of this exercise, we recommend that eight states be given grants-in-aid of Rs.10171.65 crore over the award period 2005-10 for the education sector, with a minimum of Rs.20 crore in a year for any eligible state. Details are given in Table 10.5.

10.18 As far as the grant for health sector (major head 2210 & 2211) is concerned, the same methodology, as that for education sector discussed above, was followed. There are, however, two important differences. In the case of health, we have assigned a higher percentage, i.e., 30 per cent, of the distance from group's average per capita expenditure for determining the additional grant for 2002-03, as against 15 per cent in the case of education. This is because while there has been a major initiative in the form of Sarva Shiksha Abhiyan recently in the education sector for which substantial funds are being provided by Government of India, the health sector lacks such increases in central funding. The other difference relates to the assigned growth rate for the forecast period. It is 11.5 per cent for the health

Table 10.5

Grants-in-aid for Education Sector (major head 2202)

(Rs. in crore)

State	2005-06	2006-07	2007-08	2008-09	2009-10	2005-10
1	2	3	4	5	6	7
Assam	183.20	200.60	219.66	240.53	263.38	**1107.37**
Bihar	443.99	486.17	532.36	582.93	638.31	**2683.76**
Jharkhand	107.82	118.06	129.28	141.56	155.01	**651.73**
Madhya Pradesh	76.03	83.25	91.16	99.82	109.30	**459.56**
Orissa	53.49	58.57	64.13	70.22	76.89	**323.30**
Rajasthan	20.00	20.00	20.00	20.00	20.00	**100.00**
Uttar Pradesh	736.87	806.87	883.52	967.45	1059.36	**4454.07**
West Bengal	64.83	70.99	77.73	85.11	93.20	**391.86**
Total States	**1686.23**	**1844.51**	**2017.84**	**2207.62**	**2415.45**	**10171.65**

sector in keeping with the growth rate adopted for working out the normal expenditure stream for health for purposes of determining pre-devolution non-plan revenue surplus/deficit. As a result of this exercise, we recommend that seven states be given grants amounting to Rs.5887.08 crore over the award period 2005-10, for the health sector (major head 2210 & 2211), with a minimum of Rs.10 crore a year for any eligible state. Details are given in Table 10.6.

10.19 These grants are being provided for the education and health sectors as an additionality, over and above the normal expenditure by the states in these sectors. These grants should be utilised only for the respective sectors (non-plan), i.e., major head 2202 in the case of education and major heads 2210 & 2211 in the case of health. Conditionalities governing the releases and utilisation of these grants have been specified in annexures 10.1 to 10.3. No further conditionalities should be imposed by the central government for the release of these grants. Monitoring of the expenditure relating to these grants will rest with the state government concerned.

Maintenance of Roads and Buildings

10.20 We are required under para 6(vi) of the TOR to take into consideration the expenditure on non-salary component of maintenance of capital assets and recommend specific amounts for this purpose. The Eleventh Finance Commission did not recommend separate grants for maintenance of roads and buildings. Instead, the projections regarding the maintenance expenditure were subsumed in the overall projection of non-plan revenue expenditure and the requirement for this purpose was embedded in the non-plan revenue deficit grant. We, however, notice that maintenance of roads and buildings has not been given adequate importance by the states. We are, therefore, recommending additional grants separately for maintenance of roads and bridges, and for maintenance of buildings.

10.21 In the case of roads and bridges, the requirement of funds for maintenance in the base year was assessed normatively by adopting, with some modifications, the norms for plains and for hilly areas furnished by the Ministry of Road Transport & Highways. While normal repairs have been fully provided for, the provision for

Table 10.6

Grants-in-aid for Health Sector (major head 2210 & 2211)

(Rs. in crore)

State	2005-06	2006-07	2007-08	2008-09	2009-10	2005-10
1	2	3	4	5	6	7
Assam	153.58	171.24	190.93	212.89	237.38	**966.02**
Bihar	289.30	322.57	359.66	401.02	447.14	**1819.69**
Jharkhand	57.39	63.99	71.35	79.55	88.70	**360.98**
Madhya Pradesh	28.88	32.20	35.90	40.03	44.63	**181.64**
Orissa	31.22	34.81	38.81	43.28	48.25	**196.37**
Uttar Pradesh	367.63	409.90	457.04	509.60	568.21	**2312.38**
Uttaranchal	10.00	10.00	10.00	10.00	10.00	**50.00**
Total States	**938.00**	**1044.71**	**1163.69**	**1296.37**	**1444.31**	**5887.08**

periodical repairs has been restricted to 20 per cent of the norms. The norm-based requirement of funds for maintenance expenditure has been worked out for the base year 2004-05, as well as for the forecast period, by adopting the road length data received from the states. The expenditure stream for the forecast period based on TGR for each state has also been worked out. Taking into account these two estimates, we have decided to provide an amount of Rs.15,000 crore over the period 2006-10. This amount is in addition to the normal expenditure, which the states would be incurring on maintenance of roads and bridges. It has been distributed among the states on the basis of road lengths. For this purpose, the length of local body roads has been given a weightage of 0.5, and the hilly roads a weightage of 1.2, before being added to the length of roads other than those of local bodies and hill areas. Further, we have decided to provide this amount in equal instalments over the last four years (i.e., 2006-07 to 2009-10) of the forecast period, so that the states get a year for making preparations to absorb these funds. State-wise amounts recommended as grants-in-aid for maintenance of roads and bridges are shown in Table 10.7.

Table 10.7

Grants-in-aid for Maintenance of Roads & Bridges

(Rs. in crore)

State	2005-06	2006-07	2007-08	2008-09	2009-10	2005-10
1	2	3	4	5	6	7
Andhra Pradesh	0.00	245.03	245.03	245.03	245.03	**980.12**
Arunachal Pradesh	0.00	11.09	11.09	11.09	11.09	**44.36**
Assam	0.00	82.53	82.53	82.53	82.53	**330.12**
Bihar	0.00	77.34	77.34	77.34	77.34	**309.36**
Chhattisgarh	0.00	65.60	65.60	65.60	65.60	**262.40**
Goa	0.00	9.87	9.87	9.87	9.87	**39.48**
Gujarat	0.00	223.80	223.80	223.80	223.80	**895.20**
Haryana	0.00	45.68	45.68	45.68	45.68	**182.72**
Himachal Pradesh	0.00	65.41	65.41	65.41	65.41	**261.64**
Jammu & Kashmir	0.00	29.42	29.42	29.42	29.42	**117.68**
Jharkhand	0.00	102.26	102.26	102.26	102.26	**409.04**
Karnataka	0.00	364.53	364.53	364.53	364.53	**1458.12**
Kerala	0.00	160.58	160.58	160.58	160.58	**642.32**
Madhya Pradesh	0.00	146.72	146.72	146.72	146.72	**586.88**
Maharashtra	0.00	297.42	297.42	297.42	297.42	**1189.68**
Manipur	0.00	19.24	19.24	19.24	19.24	**76.96**
Meghalaya	0.00	21.60	21.60	21.60	21.60	**86.40**
Mizoram	0.00	10.53	10.53	10.53	10.53	**42.12**
Nagaland	0.00	30.22	30.22	30.22	30.22	**120.88**
Orissa	0.00	368.77	368.77	368.77	368.77	**1475.08**
Punjab	0.00	105.24	105.24	105.24	105.24	**420.96**
Rajasthan	0.00	158.33	158.33	158.33	158.33	**633.32**
Sikkim	0.00	4.66	4.66	4.66	4.66	**18.64**
Tamil Nadu	0.00	303.60	303.60	303.60	303.60	**1214.40**
Tripura	0.00	15.37	15.37	15.37	15.37	**61.48**
Uttar Pradesh	0.00	600.79	600.79	600.79	600.79	**2403.16**
Uttaranchal	0.00	81.14	81.14	81.14	81.14	**324.56**
West Bengal	0.00	103.23	103.23	103.23	103.23	**412.92**
Total States	**0.00**	**3750.00**	**3750.00**	**3750.00**	**3750.00**	**15000.00**

10.22 With respect to public buildings, the maintenance norms were obtained from the Central Public Works Department (CPWD). These norms are elaborate and highly differentiated, covering buildings of different types and age, separately for civil and electrical works. While the states were able to provide aggregate plinth area of all the public buildings in the state, they found it difficult to furnish differentiated data, which were required for the application of the CPWD norms. Even the plinth area reported by some of the states was found to be abnormally high, and had to be adjusted by comparing it with states of similar size. We recommend an amount of Rs.5000 crore as grant for maintenance of public buildings. This has been distributed as shown in Table 10.8 among the states based on the plinth area.

Table 10.8

Grants-in-aid for Maintenance of Public Buildings

(Rs. in crore)

State	2005-06	2006-07	2007-08	2008-09	2009-10	2005-10
1	2	3	4	5	6	7
Andhra Pradesh	0.00	60.64	60.63	60.63	60.63	242.53
Arunachal Pradesh	0.00	14.35	14.35	14.36	14.36	57.42
Assam	0.00	57.66	57.66	57.66	57.66	230.64
Bihar	0.00	89.90	89.90	89.91	89.90	359.61
Chhattisgarh	0.00	45.78	45.77	45.77	45.77	183.09
Goa	0.00	6.05	6.05	6.04	6.04	24.18
Gujarat	0.00	50.90	50.90	50.90	50.91	203.61
Haryana	0.00	37.95	37.95	37.95	37.95	151.80
Himachal Pradesh	0.00	36.90	36.90	36.90	36.90	147.60
Jammu & Kashmir	0.00	41.14	41.14	41.13	41.13	164.54
Jharkhand	0.00	39.90	39.90	39.90	39.91	159.61
Karnataka	0.00	51.28	51.28	51.28	51.28	205.12
Kerala	0.00	25.88	25.88	25.87	25.87	103.50
Madhya Pradesh	0.00	110.76	110.76	110.75	110.75	443.02
Maharashtra	0.00	55.90	55.90	55.90	55.91	223.61
Manipur	0.00	9.42	9.43	9.43	9.43	37.71
Meghalaya	0.00	8.75	8.76	8.75	8.76	35.02
Mizoram	0.00	5.82	5.82	5.82	5.83	23.29
Nagaland	0.00	11.54	11.55	11.54	11.54	46.17
Orissa	0.00	97.28	97.28	97.29	97.29	389.14
Punjab	0.00	37.95	37.95	37.95	37.95	151.80
Rajasthan	0.00	53.27	53.27	53.27	53.28	213.09
Sikkim	0.00	8.04	8.03	8.04	8.04	32.15
Tamil Nadu	0.00	60.64	60.63	60.63	60.63	242.53
Tripura	0.00	12.53	12.53	12.53	12.52	50.11
Uttar Pradesh	0.00	150.07	150.07	150.08	150.06	600.28
Uttaranchal	0.00	24.40	24.40	24.40	24.40	97.60
West Bengal	0.00	45.30	45.31	45.32	45.30	181.23
Total States	**0.00**	**1250.00**	**1250.00**	**1250.00**	**1250.00**	**5000.00**

10.23 The grants for maintenance of roads & bridges as also for buildings are expected to be an additionality, over and above the normal maintenance expenditure to be incurred by the states. These grants should be released and spent in accordance with the conditionalities indicated in annexures 10.4 to 10.6. Monitoring of the expenditure relating to these grants would rest with the state governments concerned.

Additional Grants-in-aid for States

10.24 It is seen that the formula used for horizontal distribution of sharable taxes among the states, by its nature, cannot take care of all dimensions of the fiscal needs of a state. It is, therefore, necessary to look at certain common as well as specific needs of the states. Previous finance commissions, starting with the Sixth Commission, have been providing separate grants-in-aid for special needs of the states, even when the TOR did not make any specific reference to special problems. Based on our discussions and visits to the states, we have also decided to recommend grants for certain common and specific needs of the states. These are discussed in the following paragraphs.

Maintenance of Forests

10.25 Several states have represented that subsequent to the restrictions placed by the Supreme Court on exploitation of forest wealth, the forests have become a net liability for the states rather than a source of revenue. The Eleventh Finance Commission had recommended preparation and implementation of scientific work plans for management of forests for the country as a whole. Some of the states have already got work plans approved and have started implementing them. They have, however, pointed out that maintenance of the forest area as per the working plan has become a problem due to financial constraints. They have pleaded that separate grants should be provided to them for maintenance of forests. We recognise that forests are a national wealth, and the country as a whole has a responsibility in preserving it. Accordingly, we have decided to recommend a grant of Rs.1000 crore spread over the award period 2005-10 for maintenance of forests. This would be an additionality over and above what the states have been spending through their forest departments. This amount has been distributed among the states based on their forest area, and it should be spent for preservation of forest wealth. It should also result in increased expenditure to the extent of this grant, in addition to the normal expenditure of the forest department. Table 10.9 indicates the state-wise break-up of this grant.

Heritage Conservation

10.26 During our visits to the states, we had occasion to see several historical monuments and archaeological sites. It was noticed that many of these were poorly maintained. Several state governments have sent proposals for providing funds for their maintenance. These requests have been considered carefully. We are of the view that these historical monuments and archaeological sites constitute our non-renewable cultural resource, and there is a definite need to preserve them and to encourage people to visit them. Accordingly, we have decided to

Table 10.9

Grants-in-aid for Maintenance of Forests

(Rs. in crore)

State	Forest Area (Sq.Km.)	2005-06	2006-07	2007-08	2008-09	2009-10	2005-10
1	2	3	4	5	6	7	8
Andhra Pradesh	44637	13.00	13.00	13.00	13.00	13.00	65.00
Arunachal Pradesh	68045	20.00	20.00	20.00	20.00	20.00	100.00
Assam	27714	8.00	8.00	8.00	8.00	8.00	40.00
Bihar	5720	1.00	1.00	1.00	1.00	1.00	5.00
Chhattisgarh	56448	17.00	17.00	17.00	17.00	17.00	85.00
Goa	2095	0.60	0.60	0.60	0.60	0.60	3.00
Gujarat	15152	4.00	4.00	4.00	4.00	4.00	20.00
Haryana	1754	0.40	0.40	0.40	0.40	0.40	2.00
Himachal Pradesh	14360	4.00	4.00	4.00	4.00	4.00	20.00
Jammu & Kashmir	21237	6.00	6.00	6.00	6.00	6.00	30.00
Jharkhand	22637	6.00	6.00	6.00	6.00	6.00	30.00
Karnataka	36991	11.00	11.00	11.00	11.00	11.00	55.00
Kerala	15560	5.00	5.00	5.00	5.00	5.00	25.00
Madhya Pradesh	77265	23.00	23.00	23.00	23.00	23.00	115.00
Maharashtra	47482	14.00	14.00	14.00	14.00	14.00	70.00
Manipur	16926	6.00	6.00	6.00	6.00	6.00	30.00
Meghalaya	15584	6.00	6.00	6.00	6.00	6.00	30.00
Mizoram	17494	5.00	5.00	5.00	5.00	5.00	25.00
Nagaland	13345	5.00	5.00	5.00	5.00	5.00	25.00
Orissa	48838	15.00	15.00	15.00	15.00	15.00	75.00
Punjab	2432	0.40	0.40	0.40	0.40	0.40	2.00
Rajasthan	16367	5.00	5.00	5.00	5.00	5.00	25.00
Sikkim	3193	1.60	1.60	1.60	1.60	1.60	8.00
Tamil Nadu	21482	6.00	6.00	6.00	6.00	6.00	30.00
Tripura	7065	3.00	3.00	3.00	3.00	3.00	15.00
Uttar Pradesh	13746	4.00	4.00	4.00	4.00	4.00	20.00
Uttaranchal	23938	7.00	7.00	7.00	7.00	7.00	35.00
West Bengal	10693	3.00	3.00	3.00	3.00	3.00	15.00
Total States	**668200**	**200.00**	**200.00**	**200.00**	**200.00**	**200.00**	**1000.00**

recommend an amount of Rs.625 crore spread over the award period for this purpose. In distributing this amount among the states, we have been guided by the requirements indicated by them. This grant will be used for preservation and protection of historical monuments, archaeological sites, public libraries, museums and archives, and also for improving the tourist infrastructure to facilitate visit to these sites. Table 10.10 indicates the grants-in-aid earmarked for each state.

Table 10.10

Grants-in-aid for Heritage Conservation

(*Rs. in crore*)

State	2005-06	2006-07	2007-08	2008-09	2009-10	2005-10
1	2	3	4	5	6	7
Andhra Pradesh	0.00	10.00	10.00	10.00	10.00	40.00
Arunachal Pradesh	0.00	1.25	1.25	1.25	1.25	5.00
Assam	0.00	5.00	5.00	5.00	5.00	20.00
Bihar	0.00	10.00	10.00	10.00	10.00	40.00
Chhattisgarh	0.00	2.50	2.50	2.50	2.50	10.00
Goa	0.00	5.00	5.00	5.00	5.00	20.00
Gujarat	0.00	6.25	6.25	6.25	6.25	25.00
Haryana	0.00	3.75	3.75	3.75	3.75	15.00
Himachal Pradesh	0.00	2.50	2.50	2.50	2.50	10.00
Jammu & Kashmir	0.00	2.50	2.50	2.50	2.50	10.00
Jharkhand	0.00	2.50	2.50	2.50	2.50	10.00
Karnataka	0.00	12.50	12.50	12.50	12.50	50.00
Kerala	0.00	6.25	6.25	6.25	6.25	25.00
Madhya Pradesh	0.00	5.00	5.00	5.00	5.00	20.00
Maharashtra	0.00	12.50	12.50	12.50	12.50	50.00
Manipur	0.00	1.25	1.25	1.25	1.25	5.00
Meghalaya	0.00	1.25	1.25	1.25	1.25	5.00
Mizoram	0.00	1.25	1.25	1.25	1.25	5.00
Nagaland	0.00	1.25	1.25	1.25	1.25	5.00
Orissa	0.00	12.50	12.50	12.50	12.50	50.00
Punjab	0.00	2.50	2.50	2.50	2.50	10.00
Rajasthan	0.00	12.50	12.50	12.50	12.50	50.00
Sikkim	0.00	1.25	1.25	1.25	1.25	5.00
Tamil Nadu	0.00	10.00	10.00	10.00	10.00	40.00
Tripura	0.00	1.25	1.25	1.25	1.25	5.00
Uttar Pradesh	0.00	12.50	12.50	12.50	12.50	50.00
Uttaranchal	0.00	1.25	1.25	1.25	1.25	5.00
West Bengal	0.00	10.00	10.00	10.00	10.00	40.00
Total States	**0.00**	**156.25**	**156.25**	**156.25**	**156.25**	**625.00**

State-specific Needs

10.27 All the states, in their memoranda, have asked for grants for tackling certain state-specific issues. For obvious reasons, it has not been possible to consider all such requests. An assessment of the more pressing needs of the states was made on the basis of the representations made by the states in meetings as well as during Commission's visits to the states. State-wise details of grants-in-aid recommended for state-specific needs are given ahead.

Andhra Pradesh

(i) *Drinking water supply to fluoride-affected areas*: The state government has requested for a special package for installation of de-fluorination plants in Nalgonda and neighbouring districts to supply safe drinking water by complete removal of fluorosis, at an estimated cost of Rs.500 crore. We have provided Rs.325 crore for this purpose.

(ii) *Improving the socio-economic conditions of the people living in the remote areas*: The state government has requested for a grant of Rs.300 crore for construction of roads in remote and tribal areas. An amount of Rs.175 crore has been provided for this purpose.

Arunachal Pradesh

Treasury buildings: For its 12 treasury and 5 sub-treasury buildings, which are in a dilapidated condition, the state government has requested for an assistance of Rs.10 crore, which is being provided.

Assam

(i) *Development of urban areas*: The state government has requested for a provision of Rs.924 crore for construction of road side drains and for clearing storm water drains in Guwahati city. An assistance of Rs.121 crore is being provided as seed money for construction of road side drains in Guwahati city.

(ii) *Health infrastructure*: For expanding and improving eye care facilities in the high-tech hospital set up at Guwahati with the assistance of the state government, a sum of Rs.9 crore has been requested for. This is being provided to the state government.

Bihar

(i) *Technical education*: As major technical institutions have gone to Jharkhand after the bifurcation, an amount of Rs.108.33 crore has been requested by the state to improve and expand the existing technical institutions like Muzaffarpur Institute of Technology, Bhagalpur College of Engineering, Lok Nayak Jayaprakash Institute of Technology and six government polytechnics. A grant of Rs.50 crore is being provided for this purpose.

(ii) *Establishment of Administrative Training Institute*: The Administrative Training Institute of Bihar was located at Ranchi and it is now with Jharkhand government. Bihar government now proposes to establish a new institute at an estimated cost of Rs. 110.17 crore. A grant of Rs.50 crore is being provided for this purpose.

(iii) *e-Governance*: The state has formulated a project, Bihar Revenue Administration Intra Net (BRAIN), with an estimated cost of Rs.47.95 crore. The project aims at collecting and using on-line data relating to commercial taxes, registration, treasuries and sub-treasuries and the Directorate of Provident Fund, with the data centre located in the finance department. The project covers not only internal computerization of the above offices, but also their district level offices across the state. We have provided Rs.40 crore for this project.

(iv) *Construction of homes under Juvenile Justice Act and improvement of remand home, after-care home and residential school for the handicapped*: A proposal in this regard has been submitted by the state at an estimated cost of Rs.21.20 crore. An amount of Rs.20 crore has been provided for this project.

(v) *Improvement of urban water supply and drainage*: A project for augmentation of water supply, sewerage and drainage facilities in major towns has been formulated by the state. It is estimated to cost Rs.180 crore. The same amount has been provided.

(vi) *Fire services*: In order to strengthen the infrastructure of fire service, the state government has prepared a development plan at an estimated cost of Rs.10.65 crore. The proposal includes construction of fire station buildings, replacement of old fire engine equipments, purchase of new equipments and setting-up of a fire service training school. A provision of Rs.10 crore has been made for this purpose.

(vii) *Construction of residential schools and hostels for SC/ST/OBC*: With a view to improving the educational levels of the children of SC/ST and other weaker sections of the society, the state government has proposed construction of residential schools and hostels for boys and girls at a cost of Rs.124.22 crore. A sum of Rs.50 crore has been provided for construction of such residential schools and hostels, preferably for girls.

Chhattisgarh

(i) *Development of the state capital at Raipur*: The state has requested for an amount of Rs.1000 crore for development of the state capital at Raipur. We have provided Rs.200 crore for creating state level infrastructure including construction of secretariat, legislative assembly and other buildings at Raipur on land to be made available by the state government.

(ii) *Improving the police infrastructure*: The state has requested for a grant of Rs.237 crore for upgrading and improving arms/ ammunition, equipments, vehicles, training and communication infrastructure of the police force. We have provided Rs.100 crore for this purpose.

Goa

Health infrastructure: As against an assistance of Rs.150 crore sought by the state, a grant of Rs.10 crore is being provided for the improvement of primary health centres.

Gujarat

Salinity ingress: The State has made a request for an amount of Rs.1000 crore to tackle salinity ingress problem, particularly in the Saurashtra coastal area. Gujarat has a long sea coastline of 1600 kms., which is about one third of the total coastline of India. About seven lakh hectare of coastal land in the state has lost its fertility due to ingress of salinity, which in turn has affected the economic prosperity of the coastal region. Given the urgency of tackling the problem, we have provided Rs.200 crore for such projects.

Haryana

Water logging/salinity and declining water table: The state government has stated that in some parts of Haryana, large scale introduction of canal irrigation has resulted in higher water table with brackish water underneath. The problem of water-logging and salinity is threatening the agricultural production in the state. Further, due to over-drawal in sweet water zone, there is considerable decline in the ground water table in such zones. The state government has requested for a grant of Rs. 523 crore to address these problems. We have provided Rs. 100 crore for this purpose.

Himachal Pradesh

Development of urban areas: A sum of Rs.13.46 crore has been requested for construction of Sanjuali bye-pass. We have provided Rs.12 crore for the purpose. The state has also prepared a project for augmenting water supply in Shimla at a cost of Rs.39.37 crore. We have provided Rs.38 crore for the purpose. In all, the state is being provided grants amounting to Rs.50 crore for development in and around Shimla.

Jammu & Kashmir

(i) *Tourism related schemes*: The state government has sought an assistance of Rs.136.33 crore to upgrade its tourism facilities. An assistance of Rs.90 crore is being provided for this purpose.

(ii) *Construction of Public Service Commission building in Jammu*: As against an assistance of Rs. 15.85 crore sought by the state government, a sum of Rs.10 crore is being provided.

Jharkhand

(i) *Development of the state capital at Ranchi*: The State has requested for an amount of Rs.5000 crore for development of the state capital at Ranchi. We have provided Rs.200 crore for creating state level infrastructure including construction of secretariat and other buildings at Ranchi on land to be made available by the state government.

(ii) *Special needs of the police force*: The state government has requested for a grant of Rs.181.90 crore to set up new police stations and for modernising and improving the effectiveness of the police force. We have provided Rs.130 crore for this purpose.

Karnataka

(i) *General administration*: The state has requested for an amount of Rs.250 crore for improving the general administration including state-wide WAN and for upgradation of training institutes. We have provided the amount sought by the state for these purposes.

(ii) *Youth services and sports facilities*: An amount of Rs. 100 crore has been requested for improvement of youth services and sports facilities including construction of multi-gyms and sports complexes at Taluka levels. We have provided the amount sought by the state for this purpose.

(iii) *Improvement of police administration*: The state has requested for a grant of Rs.100 crore to modernise police administration and improve its effectiveness. We have provided the amount sought by the state for this purpose.

(iv) *Improvement of health services*: The state government has requested for a grant of Rs.350 crore for improving health services by providing ambulance services at local level. We have provided Rs.150 crore for the purpose.

Kerala

(i) *Inland waterways and canals*: The state government has stated that inland water transport, which was an important part of transport system until a few decades ago, has fallen into disuse. This system of transport has attained great importance again for bulk transport of goods and for tourism. The state government has requested for a grant of Rs.237.49 crore for improving the existing main canals and feeder canals. We have provided Rs.225 crore for this purpose.

(ii) *Coastal zone management*: The state government has asked for a grant of Rs.199.43 crore for construction, maintenance and reformation of the sea walls in the state. It has been pointed out that Kerala Coast is subject to severe erosion, which undermines the valuable coastal eco-system and affects the lives of millions of people. Nearly 100 kilometres of coastal zone, prone to severe sea erosion, needs to be urgently protected on a long-term basis. We have provided Rs.175 crore for this purpose.

(iii) *Improvement of quality of school education*: The state government has requested for a grant of Rs.258 crore for improving the quality of standards of education in 416 schools by constructing laboratories and libraries, and for providing computers. We have provided Rs.100 crore for this purpose.

Madhya Pradesh

(i) *Development of tourism*: The state government has requested for a grant of Rs.90 crore for development of tourism infrastructure for promoting religious tourism, heritage tourism, wildlife and adventure tourism, development of the Jain circuit and development of new tourist destinations at Burhanpur, Asirgarh and Seoni. We have provided Rs. 67 crore for this purpose. The grant should not be used for payment of salaries, construction of tourist bungalows and purchase of vehicles.

(ii) *Development of road infrastructure*: The state government has made a request for a grant of Rs.1000 crore to improve the road infrastructure in the state. It has been mentioned that the state has a very low density of roads and consequently very poor connectivity. We have already made a provision of Rs.586.88 crore as grants-in-aid for maintenance of roads and bridges (vide table 10.7) and Rs.67 crore for development of tourism infrastructure in the state (sub-para (i) above). Considering the needs of the state in this sector, we recommend additional grant of Rs.208 crore for improvement of the existing roads and for extending the road network to remote areas. With this additional grant, the total allocation for the road sector for the state will be more than Rs.800 crore.

(iii) *Development of urban areas*: A grant of Rs. 29.71 crore has been requested for improvement of the existing water supply system, construction/widening of road network and improvement of drainage facilities in Dewas, which serves as the satellite town of two important cities of Indore and Ujjain. We have provided Rs.25 crore for the purpose of development of this important urban area.

Maharashtra

(i) *Infrastructure for women and child development programme*: The state government has requested for a grant of Rs.93 crore to improve the infrastructure for women and child development. We have provided Rs.50 crore for the purpose, with the stipulation that the grant should not be spent on manpower and vehicles.

(ii) *Coastal and eco-tourism*: The state government has requested for a grant of Rs.1000 crore for integrated tourism development in coastal areas. We have provided Rs.250 crore for the purpose.

Manipur

(i) *Secretariat complex*: For the construction of the fourth and fifth floors of Manipur secretariat, the state government has requested for an assistance of Rs.3.50 crore. We have provided the amount sought for by the state government for this purpose.

(ii) *Sports complex*: In order to upgrade the facilities of its sports complex, the state government has indicated a capital expenditure requirement of Rs.16.07 crore. We have provided Rs 15 crore for this purpose.

(iii) *Loktak lake*: For improving the water management at the lake, the state has requested an assistance of Rs.32.88 crore. We have provided Rs 11.50 crore for this purpose.

Meghalaya

(i) *Zoological park*: For protecting endangered species, the state government has requested for an assistance of Rs.30 crore to establish a zoological park. We have provided the amount sought for by the state for this purpose.

(ii) *Botanical garden*: In order to conserve flora, the state government has requested for a provision of Rs.5 crore for establishment of a botanical garden. We have provided the same.

Mizoram

(i) *Bamboo flowering*: The state has sought an assistance of Rs.566 crore to meet its project cost for tackling the problem of rodents arising out of impending bamboo flowering, which leads to large scale losses in agriculture and forestry. We have provided Rs.40 crore for this purpose to the state for commencing the project.

(ii) *Sports complex*: The state government has requested for an assistance of Rs.50 crore for the construction of a sports complex in Aizwal. We have provided Rs.25 crore for this purpose.

Nagaland

(i) *Health facilities*: For upgradation of its health facilities, the state government has sought an assistance of Rs.17.92 crore towards capital expenditure. An assistance of Rs. 15 crore is being provided for the same.

(ii) *Assembly secretariat*: As against the capital expenditure requirement of Rs.34.60 crore for the construction of the assembly secretariat, a provision of Rs.30 crore is being made.

Orissa

(i) *Consolidation and strengthening eco-restoration work in the Chilika lake*: The Eleventh Finance Commission had provided Rs.30 crore for undertaking consolidation measures for eco-restoration works in the Chilika lagoon. Given the vastness of the lagoon, the state has requested for an additional support of Rs.30 crore from the Twelfth Finance Commission for consolidating and further expanding the scope of eco-restoration works and improving the socio-economic conditions of the fishermen dependent on the lagoon. We have provided the amount sought by the state for this purpose.

(ii) *Sewerage system for Bhubaneswar*: The state government has made a request for Rs.150 crore during 2005-10, being 25 per cent of the estimated project cost of Rs.600 crore, for providing a comprehensive sewerage system with necessary branch sewers, trunk sewers and treatment units in the capital city of Bhubaneswar. Absence of comprehensive sewerage system has been causing pollution of major river systems and hence calls for timely action. We have provided Rs.140 crore for this purpose.

Punjab

Stagnant agriculture: Agriculture in Punjab is beset with a number of problems, which include continuous deterioration in the soil health, depletion of water table, ecological degradation, and inadequacy of post harvest infrastructure. The state government had constituted an advisory committee on agriculture which submitted its report titled 'Agriculture Production Pattern Adjustment Programme in Punjab for Productivity and Growth'. The state government has requested the Twelfth Finance Commission to provide adequate funds for implementing programmes, which aim at weaning away farmers from rice-wheat-rotation. We are providing Rs.96 crore for this purpose. The sum may be used for initiating appropriate programmes in a few districts on a pilot project basis.

Rajasthan

(i) *Indira Gandhi Nahar Pariyojana*: The state government has stated that Indira Gandhi Nahar Pariyojana is still incomplete due to paucity of funds. The project involves transfer of surplus water of Ravi and Beas rivers to desert and border districts of the state with a view to eliminating drought, irrigating desert areas and providing drinking water. An amount of Rs. 411 crore has been requested by the state for undertaking remaining works of the project. As accelerated completion of the project will mitigate the adverse effects of desertification and hostile climatic condition, we have provided Rs.300 crore for the purpose.

(ii) *Meeting drinking water scarcity in border and desert districts*: Rajasthan is amongst the most water deficient states in the country. The state government has drawn the attention of the Commission to the problem of drinking water, which has assumed alarming proportions in the desert and border districts. Additional funds amounting to Rs.295 crore have been requested by the state government for augmentation of water from existing sources, improving the distribution system and setting up of fluoride and salinity treatment plants in the border and desert districts. We have provided Rs. 150 crore for augmentation of water from existing sources and setting-up of fluoride and salinity treatment plants in the border and desert districts.

Sikkim

Construction of airport: The state government has sought an assistance of Rs.174 crore for this purpose. The Eleventh Finance Commission had provided Rs.50 crore. We are now providing an amount of Rs.100 crore.

Tamil Nadu

(i) *Development of urban areas*: The state government has drawn our attention to the continuing problem of slums in some of the urban areas of the state. We have provided Rs.250 crore for this purpose, as against a request of Rs.1107 crore.

(ii) *Sea erosion and coastal area protection works*: The state has requested for an amount of Rs.169 crore for tackling the problem of sea erosion in various parts of the state. We have provided Rs. 50 crore for this purpose.

Tripura

(i) *Construction of capital complex*: The state government has requested assistance for the construction of capital complex which includes :(a) completion of new assembly building: Rs.4.40 crore, (b) new secretariat building: Rs. 5.13 crore, (c) state high court building: Rs. 8.65 crore, (d) state guest house at new capital complex: Rs.6.73 crore and (e) seismic retrofitting and renovation of Ujjyanta palace: Rs.4 crore. We have provided Rs 28 crore for this purpose.

(ii) *Establishment of a 150 bedded hospital for Dhalai district at Kulai*: The state has requested

Rs.11.99 crore against which an amount of Rs.11 crore is being provided.

(iii) *Construction of a model prison at Bishalgarh*: The state has requested Rs.11 crore, against which an amount of Rs.10 crore is being provided.

Uttar Pradesh

(i) *Renovation of more than 100 year old collectorate buildings*: The state has requested for Rs. 180.25 crore to renovate and reconstruct 29 collectorate buildings, which are more than 100 years old and in a very bad condition. We have provided Rs.60 crore for this purpose.

(ii) *Accelerating development of Bundelkhand and eastern regions*: The State has requested for a grant of Rs.5044.56 crore for accelerating the development of Bundelkhand and eastern regions, which are relatively underdeveloped due to lack of social and economic infrastructure facilities. With a view to bridging the regional disparities existing within the state, we have provided Rs.700 crore for the purpose. The grant may be utilised for schemes pertaining to improvement of water supply and sanitation facilities, rehabilitation of distressed dams, construction of roads and bridges and ground water recharge/ rain water harvesting.

(iii) *Development of urban areas*: A request of Rs.52.47 crore has been made for improving the physical infrastructure of Allahabad city, which is an important pilgrimage centre receiving lakhs of pilgrims every year. The grant is required for various developmental activities like water supply, drainage, sewerage, cattle colony, slaughter houses, parks etc. We have provided Rs.40 crore for this purpose.

Uttaranchal

(i) *Development of the state capital*: The state government has requested for an amount of Rs.398 crore for development of the state capital. We have provided Rs.200 crore for creating state level infrastructure including construction of secretariat, assembly, public service commission and other buildings on the land to be made available by the state government.

(ii) *Promotion of tourism*: The state government has submitted a number of proposals to promote tourism by improving physical infrastructure in tourist destinations, improving access to tourist places, and developing new tourist destinations. The cost of these proposals comes to about Rs.325 crore. We have provided Rs.35 crore for this purpose.

(iii) *Health infrastructure*: The state government has requested for a grant of Rs.6 crore for establishment of a 50 bed speciality eye hospital at Dehradun to provide high quality tertiary eye care to people of Uttaranchal and neighbouring areas of other states. The state government has stated that the hospital would give free treatment to the poor, as presently there is no such facility in the state. We have provided Rs.5 crore for this purpose.

West Bengal

(i) *Arsenic contamination of ground water*: Arsenic contamination of ground water is a serious problem affecting certain areas in West Bengal. To provide arsenic free water to about 77.76 lakh population in 4,747 habitations, the state government has projected its requirement of funds at about Rs. 964 crore. Given the serious threat to the health of the community due to arsenic contamination of ground water, we have provided Rs.600 crore for this purpose.

(ii) *Problems relating to erosion by Ganga-Padma river in Malda and Murshidabad districts*: The state government has drawn attention to the problem posed by severe bank erosion of the river Ganga-Padma in Malda and Murshidabad districts. The severity of the problem has been increasing over time. The Eleventh Finance Commission had provided Rs.60 crore for tackling this problem. The State government has requested for additional grant amounting to Rs.500 crore for the critical anti-erosion schemes in the two districts. We have provided Rs.190 crore for this purpose.

(iii) *Development of Sundarbans Region*: The state government has requested for a grant of Rs. 150 crore for accelerating the development of the Sundarbans region. It has stated that Sundarbans is a predominantly riverine area, which is not easily accessible. The bulk of the population in the region is dependent on agriculture. This region needs focused attention for development of agriculture, strengthening of embankments, development of communication facilities, provision of power supply etc. We have provided Rs. 100 crore for the purpose.

10.28 Table 10.11 sums up the grants-in-aid recommended by us for state-specific needs. While these grants have been phased out equally over the last four years, this phasing should be taken as indicative in nature. The states may communicate the required phasing of grants to the central government.

10.29 A statement indicating total transfers to the states is given in Table 10.12.

Table 10.11

Grants-in-aid for State-specific needs

(Rs. in crore)

State	2005-06	2006-07	2007-08	2008-09	2009-10	2005-10
1	2	3	4	5	6	7
Andhra Pradesh	0.00	125.00	125.00	125.00	125.00	500.00
Arunachal Pradesh	0.00	2.50	2.50	2.50	2.50	10.00
Assam	0.00	32.50	32.50	32.50	32.50	130.00
Bihar	0.00	100.00	100.00	100.00	100.00	400.00
Chattisgarh	0.00	75.00	75.00	75.00	75.00	300.00
Goa	0.00	2.50	2.50	2.50	2.50	10.00
Gujarat	0.00	50.00	50.00	50.00	50.00	200.00
Haryana	0.00	25.00	25.00	25.00	25.00	100.00
Himachal Pradesh	0.00	12.50	12.50	12.50	12.50	50.00
Jammu & Kashmir	0.00	25.00	25.00	25.00	25.00	100.00
Jharkhand	0.00	82.50	82.50	82.50	82.50	330.00
Karnataka	0.00	150.00	150.00	150.00	150.00	600.00
Kerala	0.00	125.00	125.00	125.00	125.00	500.00
Madhya Pradesh	0.00	75.00	75.00	75.00	75.00	300.00
Maharashtra	0.00	75.00	75.00	75.00	75.00	300.00
Manipur	0.00	7.50	7.50	7.50	7.50	30.00
Meghalaya	0.00	8.75	8.75	8.75	8.75	35.00
Mizoram	0.00	16.25	16.25	16.25	16.25	65.00
Nagaland	0.00	11.25	11.25	11.25	11.25	45.00
Orissa	0.00	42.50	42.50	42.50	42.50	170.00
Punjab	0.00	24.00	24.00	24.00	24.00	96.00
Rajasthan	0.00	112.50	112.50	112.50	112.50	450.00
Sikkim	0.00	25.00	25.00	25.00	25.00	100.00
Tamil Nadu	0.00	75.00	75.00	75.00	75.00	300.00
Tripura	0.00	12.25	12.25	12.25	12.25	49.00
Uttar Pradesh	0.00	200.00	200.00	200.00	200.00	800.00
Uttaranchal	0.00	60.00	60.00	60.00	60.00	240.00
West Bengal	0.00	222.50	222.50	222.50	222.50	890.00
Total States	**0.00**	**1775.00**	**1775.00**	**1775.00**	**1775.00**	**7100.00**

Table 10.12

Total Finance Commission Transfers to States

(*Rs.in crore*)

States	Share in Central Taxes & Duties (2005-10)	Grants-in-aid: Non-Plan Revenue Deficit (2005-10)	Health Sector (2005-10)	Education (2005-10)	Maintenance of Roads & Bridges (2006-10)	Maintenance of Buildings (2006-10)	Maintenance of Forests (2005-10)	Heritage Conservation (2006-10)	State Specific Needs (2006-10)	Local Bodies (2005-10)	Calamity Relief (2005-10)	Total (Col. 3 to Col. 12)	Total Transfers (Col. 2 + Col. 13)
1	2	3	4	5	6	7	8	9	10	11	12	13	14
Andhra Pradesh	45138.68				980.12	242.53	65.00	40.00	500.00	1961.00	1425.93	5214.58	50353.26
Arunachal Pradesh	1767.34	1357.88			44.36	57.42	100.00	5.00	10.00	71.00	112.56	1758.22	3525.56
Assam	19850.69	305.67	966.02	1107.37	330.12	230.64	40.00	20.00	130.00	581.00	767.89	4478.71	24329.40
Bihar	67671.04		1819.69	2683.76	309.36	359.61	5.00	40.00	400.00	1766.00	592.37	7975.79	75646.83
Chhattisgarh	16285.76				262.40	183.09	85.00	10.00	300.00	703.00	444.45	1987.94	18273.70
Goa	1589.14				39.48	24.18	3.00	20.00	10.00	30.00	8.73	135.39	1724.53
Gujarat	21900.47				895.20	203.61	20.00	25.00	200.00	1345.00	1019.47	3708.28	25608.75
Haryana	6596.46				182.72	151.80	2.00	15.00	100.00	479.00	515.46	1445.98	8042.44
Himachal Pradesh	3203.22	10202.38			261.64	147.60	20.00	10.00	50.00	155.00	400.52	11247.14	14450.36
Jammu & Kashmir	7441.71	12353.46			117.68	164.54	30.00	10.00	100.00	319.00	343.89	13438.57	20880.28
Jharkhand	20624.02		360.98	651.73	409.04	159.61	30.00	10.00	330.00	580.00	501.46	3032.82	23656.84
Karnataka	27361.88				1458.12	205.12	55.00	50.00	600.00	1211.00	475.16	4054.40	31416.28
Kerala	16353.21	470.37			642.32	103.50	25.00	25.00	500.00	1134.00	354.32	3254.51	19607.72
Madhya Pradesh	41180.59		181.64	459.56	586.88	443.02	115.00	20.00	300.00	2024.00	1011.27	5141.37	46321.96
Maharashtra	30663.19				1189.68	223.61	70.00	50.00	300.00	2774.00	923.77	5531.06	36194.25
Manipur	2221.44	4391.98			76.96	37.71	30.00	5.00	30.00	55.00	22.11	4648.76	6870.20
Meghalaya	2276.61	1796.86			86.40	35.02	30.00	5.00	35.00	58.00	44.88	2091.16	4367.77
Mizoram	1466.52	2977.79			42.12	23.29	25.00	5.00	65.00	30.00	26.19	3194.39	4660.91
Nagaland	1613.67	5536.50			120.88	46.17	25.00	5.00	45.00	46.00	15.19	5839.74	7453.41
Orissa	31669.47	488.04	196.37	323.30	1475.08	389.14	75.00	50.00	170.00	907.00	1199.37	5273.30	36942.77
Punjab	7971.00	3132.67			420.96	151.80	2.00	10.00	96.00	495.00	605.16	4913.59	12884.59
Rajasthan	34418.56			100.00	633.32	213.09	25.00	50.00	450.00	1450.00	1722.50	4643.91	39062.47
Sikkim	1392.94	188.67			18.64	32.15	8.00	5.00	100.00	14.00	69.74	436.20	1829.14
Tamil Nadu	32552.74				1214.40	242.53	30.00	40.00	300.00	1442.00	866.46	4135.39	36688.13
Tripura	2626.09	5494.20			61.48	50.11	15.00	5.00	49.00	65.00	51.12	5790.91	8417.00
Uttar Pradesh	118209.45		2312.38	4454.07	2403.16	600.28	20.00	50.00	800.00	3445.00	1177.11	15262.00	133471.45
Uttaranchal	5762.22	5114.68	50.00		324.56	97.60	35.00	5.00	240.00	196.00	369.28	6432.12	12194.34
West Bengal	43303.91	3044.72		391.86	412.92	181.23	15.00	40.00	890.00	1664.00	933.64	7573.37	50877.28
Total States	**613112.02**	**56855.87**	**5887.08**	**10171.65**	**15000.00**	**5000.00**	**1000.00**	**625.00**	**7100.00**	**25000.00**	**16000.00**	**142639.60**	**755751.62**

Chapter 11

Fiscal Reform Facility

11.1 Para 8 of our terms of reference requires us to "review the Fiscal Reform Facility introduced by the Central government on the basis of the recommendations of the Eleventh Finance Commission, and suggest measures for effective achievement of its objectives".

Background

11.2 As a part of its additional term of reference, which was notified on April 28, 2000, the Eleventh Finance Commission (EFC) was asked to draw a monitorable fiscal reform programme aimed at reduction of revenue deficit of the states and recommend the manner in which the grants to the states to cover the assessed deficit in their non-plan revenue account may be linked to progress in implementing the programme. In its interim report submitted in January 2000, the EFC had recommended a lumpsum provision of Rs. 11000 crore in the central budget 2000-01 for revenue deficit grants to states. Thereafter, in its main report submitted in July 2000, the EFC recommended a revenue deficit grant of Rs. 35359 crore during 2000-2005 for 15 states. The remaining 10 states were assessed to be in revenue surplus.

11.3 With regard to the mandate assigned through the April, 2000 notification, the EFC submitted a supplementary report on 30th August, 2000. Although only 15 states were assessed to be in revenue deficit and consequently, the fiscal reforms programme could have covered these states, the majority view in the EFC favoured making fiscal performance based grants available to all (then 25) states through an incentive fund. The incentive fund was recommended to be set up in two parts, one by withholding 15 per cent of the Rs. 35359 crore deficit grants for 15 states and the other, by an equal matching contribution by government of India, with year-wise phasing as shown in Table 11.1.

Table 11.1

Composition of the Incentive Fund

(Rs. in crore)

Year	Withheld Portion of the Revenue Deficit Grants	Contribution of the Centre	Total Fund
2000-01	1523.06	598.48	2121.54
2001-02	1080.43	1041.11	2121.54
2002-03	994.64	1126.91	2121.55
2003-04	861.74	1259.81	2121.55
2004-05	843.99	1277.55	2121.54
Total	**5303.86**	**5303.86**	**10607.72**

11.4 In view of the overall objective of bringing down the revenue deficit of all states at the aggregate level to zero by 2004-05, the EFC identified five indicators as a measure of the fiscal performance of the states and recommended weights for each, as indicated below :

S.No.	Indicator	Weight (per cent)
(i)	Growth of tax revenue	30
(ii)	Growth of non-tax revenue	20
(iii)	Growth of non-plan revenue expenditure on salaries and allowances	30
(iv)	Interest payments	10
(v)	Reduction of subsidies	10

It was stated that the areas indicated for monitoring were only suggestive and so were the weights. These could be suitably modified, while drawing state specific programmes. For assessing the overall performance, excess achievement in some areas could be balanced against shortfall in others, keeping the broad contents of the reform, indicated in the EFC's main report, in view.

The Scheme of Fiscal Reform Facility

11.5 As recommended by the EFC, an incentive fund in the form of Fiscal Reform Facility (FRF) was set up by the Ministry of Finance leaving 85 per cent of the revenue deficit grant recommended by the EFC to be released to the states without linking it with performance. The remaining 15 per cent, which constituted part A, has been linked with the improvement in fiscal performance. As far as part B is concerned, the initial share of the states was worked out pro rata, on the basis of the population, as per the 1971 census. The amount was to be made available to a state on achieving an improved level of performance in regard to various fiscal indicators.

11.6 While introducing the scheme of FRF, government of India prescribed a single monitorable indicator for the purpose of making releases from the incentive fund. The indicator expected each state to achieve a minimum improvement of 5 per cent in the revenue deficit/surplus as a proportion of its revenue receipts each year till 2004-05 measured with reference to the base year 1999-2000. The revenue deficit was to be inclusive of:

(i) contingent liabilities such as guarantees and letters of comfort due in that year, which would directly constitute budget liabilities; and

(ii) subsidies due to public sector enterprises (PSEs), whether or not the state pays such a subsidy upfront; thus, a budget subsidy payable to a state electricity board (SEB) would be "recognized" as a revenue expenditure, for the purpose of computing revenue deficit.

11.7 Under the scheme, if a state was unable to get the amount initially earmarked for it in any year, this amount would not lapse but would continue to be carried forward upto the fourth year i.e. upto 2003-04. If the state was still not able to draw in full the amount indicated on the basis of the performance of the first four years, the undisbursed amount would become a part of the common pool, to be shared by the performing states in the fifth year on a pro rata basis, in addition to the amounts to which they would otherwise be entitled.

11.8 The EFC also recommended that in addition to the incentive for better performance, central government was also to consider a fiscal reform programme linked assistance, by way of extended ways and means advance and additional open market borrowings. The scope and dimension of these facilities were to be decided by the central government, bearing in mind their macro-economic implications and the centre's fiscal position. The facilities were to be linked to the monitorable fiscal reform programme drawn up by the states.

11.9 The EFC recommended setting up of a monitoring agency to review the progress in the utilization of EFC grants. Accordingly, a monitoring committee headed by Secretary (Expenditure) was set up in the Ministry of Finance. In terms of the guidelines issued by the Ministry of Finance, each state was expected to take effective steps for revenue augmentation and expenditure compression over the five-year period so as to broadly achieve the following objectives with reference to the base year 1999-2000, as laid down in the main report of the EFC :

(i) gross fiscal deficit of the states as an aggregate to reduce to 2.5 per cent of GSDP;

(ii) revenue deficit of all states, in an aggregate, to fall to zero;

(iii) interest payments as a percentage of revenue receipts of the state sector as a whole to remain between 18 to 20 per cent.

The supplementary report of the EFC had also recommended that the increase in wages and salaries should not exceed 5 per cent or the increase in consumer price index whichever is higher, increase in interest payments should be limited to 10 per cent per year and explicit subsidies should be brought down by 50 per cent over the next five-year period, with a view to eliminating subsidies completely by 2009-10. Given the contours of these fiscal objectives, state governments were asked to dovetail time bound action points covering fiscal objectives and reforms, power sector reforms, public sector restructuring and budgetary reforms. Based on these guidelines, each state was to draw up a Medium Term Fiscal Reform Programme (MTFRP) and enter into a Memorandum of Understanding (MOU) with the central government.

11.10 The scheme mentioned above was subjected to certain changes after its inception. For states that were already in revenue surplus, it was felt that it would be adequate, if, with improving revenue balance, the state shows a commensurate improvement in its balance from current revenue (BCR). It was, therefore, decided that the revenue surplus states would be expected to achieve a minimum improvement of three percentage points in the BCR, as a percentage of non-plan revenue receipts in each year. Further, in the case of special category states, a two percentage point improvement in the ratio of revenue deficit to total revenue receipts with effect from 2002-03 entitled them to releases from the incentive fund. With effect from September 2003, government of India also decided to finance the cost of reforms, such as voluntary retirement scheme (VRS) etc. in states through a blend of grants and open market borrowings. In the case of the special category states, government of India would finance 80 per cent of such costs. For non-special category states, 60 per cent of such costs would be met by the centre. Counter-part funds for these measures are to be provided by the states from their own revenues. This facility is not available to states which are beneficiaries of any structural adjustment loans from multilateral/bilateral agencies in that particular year. For different reform initiatives, the assistance extended by government of India has a different composition of grants and additional open market borrowings. The assistance of the government of India has also been made available to the states for restructuring of debt with financial institutions, to take advantage of the low interest regime. The "debt restructuring" included `debt re-schedulement' or 're-financing' but not 'debt pre-payment' or exercise of any put option. Re-schedulement or re-financing could involve payment of premium on account of lower interest on the new debt vis-a-vis the old debt. It was decided that government of India, through the FRF, would share a part of a state's share of the premium cost of the restructuring by allocation of additional open market borrowing. We have been informed that Nagaland and Himachal Pradesh have been assisted under this facility.

11.11 As of 31st August, 2004, the Medium Term Fiscal Reforms Programme of 25 states has been finalized by the monitoring committee and memoranda of understanding have been signed with 19 states. MOUs of two states – Uttaranchal and Madhya Pradesh are in final stages of discussion and are expected to be signed soon. Uttar Pradesh and Sikkim have asked for amendments in their MOUs and are yet to furnish the revised ones. The total amount released from the incentive fund of Rs. 10607.72 crore till mid-November, 2004 was Rs. 5029.51 crore. This included an amount of Rs. 40.65 crore released for voluntary retirement schemes (VRS) etc. The releases pertained to the years 2000-01 to 2002-03 except for Tripura, Orissa, Rajasthan and Karnataka, which have been granted the releases for 2003-04 also. The performance of individual states in terms of the ratio of revenue deficit/surplus to total revenue receipts and the total releases made from the fund to individual states is indicated in annexure 11.1. Annexure 11.2 indicates the year-wise releases made to states from part A and part B of the fund.

11.12 The guidelines issued by the Ministry of Finance on states' FRF envisage that if the state sector, on an average achieves a five percentage point reduction in revenue deficit (RD) as percentage of revenue receipt (RR) consistently each year, by the financial year 2005-06, the sector as a whole would come into revenue balance. Against this objective, the performance of the states as reported by the Ministry of Finance has been as shown in Table 11.2.

Table 11.2

Ratio of Revenue Deficit/Surplus to Total Revenue Receipts (TRR)

RD/TRR ratio	1999-00	2000-01	2001-02	2002-03	2003-04 BE/RE	2004-05 BE
FRF objective	-27.40	-22.40	-17.40	-12.40	-7.40	-2.40
Performance	-27.23	-23.85	-24.49	-21.00	-22.89*	-

Source : Ministry of Finance

*** : RE for 24 states/BE for 4 states**

It is observed from this table that states have achieved a 6.23 percentage point reduction in RD/RR ratio by 2002-03 as against the targeted 15 percentage point reduction over the base year, 1999-00. In 2003-04, the position deteriorated by 1.89 percentage points. The data collected by the Commission, however, show a slightly different outcome in each year with the ratio (including net lotteries) of revenue deficit/ surplus to total revenue receipts for states declining by 6.24 percentage points from 1999-00 to 2002-03, as indicated in the Table 11.3. There was a further deterioration of the order of 2.05 percentage points in 2003-04.

11.13 We have been informed that, as per the scheme envisaged by the EFC for fiscal reform programme linked assistance by way of extended ways and means advances and additional open market borrowings, additional amounts by way of open market borrowings are being allocated to the states for (i) meeting a structural adjustment burden, necessitating voluntary retirement/ severance payments for downsizing public sector enterprises and core civil service and (ii) steps linked to fiscal reforms programme, if these have an initial 'reform cost' that impacts upon the budget. Seven states, namely, Nagaland, Kerala, Mizoram, Andhra Pradesh, Tamil Nadu, Orissa and Sikkim were allowed additional open market borrowings to the tune of Rs. 2363 crore to fund ongoing reform initiatives. Medium term loans of Rs. 3151 crore were extended to six fiscally stressed states, namely, Manipur, Orissa, Assam, Rajasthan, West Bengal and Nagaland, to fund 66 per cent of their opening deficit for 2002-03 after they had drawn up MTFRPs and entered into MOUs with government of India. An amount of Rs. 40.65 crore has so far been released as grant from Part B of the incentive fund for the purpose of structural reforms. This includes Rs. 29.91 crore released during the financial year 2003-04 to Jammu and Kashmir, Manipur and Kerala and Rs. 10.74 crore released during the current financial year to Nagaland and Punjab. During the financial year 2003-04, an amount of Rs. 255.99 crore has been allocated as additional open market borrowings to Manipur (Rs. 5.20 crore), Kerala (Rs. 200.00 crore), Nagaland (Rs. 0.81 crore) and Himachal Pradesh (Rs. 49.98 crore).

Mid Term Review by the Ministry of Finance

11.14. Ministry of Finance has carried out a mid term review of the facility in early 2004. Some of the points, highlighted in the review and relevant to our terms of reference, are as follows :

(i) On both tax and non-tax revenues, the performance of the states has been in line with the projections of the EFC. The problem lies with the trends for revenue expenditure, particularly on account of the rising interest burden;

Table 11.3

Ratio of Revenue Deficit/Surplus to Total Revenue Receipts

All States	1999-00	2000-01	2001-02	2002-03	2003-04 RE	2004-05 BE
RD/TRR ratio	-27.53	-23.59	-25.19	-21.29	-23.34	-13.99

(ii) On the basis of performance, 5 states could be classified as consistently improving (Kerala, Uttar Pradesh, Goa, Sikkim, and Chhattisgarh), 4 States as consistently deteriorating (Gujarat, Himachal Pradesh, Uttaranchal and Jharkhand), 12 states as showing initial improvement and then deterioration (West Bengal, Rajasthan, Punjab, Bihar, Tamil Nadu, Manipur, Madhya Pradesh, Assam, Haryana, Karnataka, Tripura and Meghalaya) and the remaining states as showing initial deterioration and then improvement (Maharashtra, Jammu and Kashmir, Andhra Pradesh, Mizoram, Nagaland, Arunachal Pradesh and Orissa);

(iii) There was 'admittedly' a design failure in prescribing a uniform five percentage point improvement in the ratio for all states. At the beginning of the reform period, 1999-2000, states had different magnitudes of revenue deficits as a percentage of revenue receipts. While the average revenue deficit as a percentage of revenue receipts was 27 per cent, individual states had much higher ratios ranging from 10 per cent (Tripura) to (West Bengal) 90 per cent. A design alternative could have been to prescribe an 18 percentage point improvement for West Bengal annually, and a 2 percentage point improvement for Tripura. If states start off with larger base year deficits, it is relatively easier for them to make huge improvements in the initial years. West Bengal, for example, was able to reduce the ratio to 52 per cent in one year, a 38 percentage point improvement. The state has thus achieved in one year, what it was expected to achieve in 5 years;

(iv) Although the gross fiscal deficit (GFD) and revenue deficit (RD) have come down and are projected to improve further, the "strong reforms" objectives of a GFD at 2.5 per cent of GDP and a zero revenue deficit by 2004-05 are not likely to be achieved. A programme that does not fully address the problem of a plan revenue deficit will not be able to eradicate revenue deficit altogether;

(v) The facility has largely failed to address the need for a steady convergence to a stable, sustainable debt path. The ultimate aim of any medium term fiscal reforms is to bring down debt to sustainable levels. The stock of consolidated debt (including guarantees) to total revenue receipts should not exceed 300 per cent. It must be the aim of every state to ultimately reach this objective through its MTFRP;

(vi) Corrective measures in regard to states' debt such as debt-swap arrangement, special relief for severely debt stressed states etc. need to be considered.

Views of the States

11.15 States have submitted divergent views regarding the FRF including suggestions to discontinue the facility, to increase the size of the incentive fund and to change the criteria. The views, as submitted by the states in their memoranda are summarized as follows :

(i) The scheme goes against the spirit of article 275 of the Constitution, as it extends the facility to even states which are not in deficit, and hence not in need of grants.

(ii) The scheme should be reviewed in the light of the provisions under article 275 of the Constitution. If the Commission feels that conditional release of grants is constitutionally tenable, the scheme should have a built-in flexibility and due allowance be given for external factors over which the states have no control.

(iii) The single monitorable factor should be removed and a medium-term-matrix-based program instituted.

(iv) There has been a significant shortfall in devolution of central taxes as compared to the estimates by the Eleventh Finance Commission. As such, states have not been able to achieve the prescribed target due to centre's poor performance in revenue collection.

(v) The size of the fund is insignificant and does not provide a proper incentive.

(vi) Assistance should be given as a proportion of the level of correction.

(vii) In case of states that achieve a reduction in the ratio of revenue deficit to revenue receipt by more than 25 per cent before five years, the year to year reduction clause should be modified.

(viii) The assessment of performance of a state in the fiscal reforms programme should be primarily based on its achievement with regard to the reduction of the primary revenue deficit, wherein the policy variables (such as state's own revenue, non-plan revenue expenditure excluding interest payment on account of past loans, etc.) are within the control of the state government.

(ix) The monitorable objective (i.e. reduction of revenue deficit as percentage of revenue receipt by 5 per cent every year) in terms of which the performance of a state under the medium term fiscal reform programme is judged needs to be reviewed and reduced to 2 per cent.

(x) The incentive fund should be discontinued and all the criteria laid down as a precondition to the release from the fund, should be in-built into the performance parameters on which the formula for devolution will be based.

(xi) The FRF in its present form should be scrapped and all the withheld revenue deficit grants should be released forthwith to the states.

(xii) Separate central funds should be earmarked as incentive funds for fiscal reforms. Another scheme which takes into account the inherent backwardness and circumstances of the special category states should be framed for such states.

Views of the Ministry of Finance

11.16 The Commission called for the specific views of the Ministry of Finance on the functioning of the facility. The Ministry of Finance has drawn our attention to some of the key lessons learnt from the implementation of the facility, as summarized below:

(i) The facility encouraged the states to draw MTFRPs for the first time. It is an important development in managing state finances inasmuch as the states have started thinking about fiscal matters on a medium-term framework.

(ii) As fifty per cent of the incentive fund was contributed from the withheld portion of the non-plan revenue deficit grant of 16 states and the remaining 50 per cent from government of India, the revenue deficit states contributed disproportionately to the fund and the remaining 12 states made no contribution. In a way, while 16 revenue deficit states stood to lose fiscal resources to cover their non-plan deficits, in case they did not bring about the necessary correction, other states only had to gain from the Fiscal Reform Facility and there was no negative incentive for them.

(iii) The size of the incentive fund at Rs. 10600 crore over a period of 5 years and Rs. 2120 crore per annum was relatively small, considering the fact that the total transfers to the states including tax devolution, grants (plan and non-plan) and small savings transfers/plan loans average Rs. 60000 crore, Rs. 40000 crore and Rs. 90000 crore respectively per annum. Some other reforms facilities like Accelerated Power Development and Reforms Programme (APDRP) have larger financial allocation.

(iv) The states were expected to draw up an MTFRP, which was expected to have fiscal projections, factoring in the effect of various measures suggested by the Eleventh Finance Commission and the measures which, in the opinion of the states and the central government were required to be taken to achieve the necessary correction of reduction in revenue deficit of 5 percentage points per annum on an average. For making reforms scenario projections, the states should have drawn a baseline scenario, on the basis of the trend and the operating policy framework in 1999-2000. An assessment of the fiscal impact of various measures, suggested by the Eleventh Finance Commission and agreed to be taken by the states would have given the programme of reforms. The states did not prepare either baseline or reform based projections. The MTFRP of many states did not even project achievement of 25 per cent revenue deficit reduction/improvement, leading to the inference that the states did not have any plan/programme to enable them to achieve the target.

(v) Initially, a uniform criterion of 5 percentage points improvement in RD ratio was prescribed for every state, including the special category states. For the revenue surplus states, a 3 percentage point annual improvement in the balance from current revenue as a percentage of their non-plan revenue receipt was adopted as the criterion for the release from the incentive fund. In the third year, guidelines were amended to provide that special category states could achieve a minimum improvement of 2 percentage points (from 2002-03 onwards). This criterion for special category states could further be modified to link their performance to their own revenues and expenditures, as the overall fiscal performance of these states depended disproportionately on the central transfers.

(vi) The definition of revenue deficit presented problems. Some states argued for consolidated revenue deficit including the deficit of the power sector utilities. Some states wanted revision of the definition of revenue deficit, mid-stream. This led to adoption of different definitions of revenue deficits for different states. Release criteria also led some states to resort to window dressing in numbers.

(vii) The reform programme and conditionalities, agreed to by the states in their MOUs, were not linked to the release of incentive. There was no effective way of monitoring the achievements or lack of that for states in relation to the agreed reforms. Moreover, the disconnection between reform conditionality and any reward/punishment framework based thereon, made the structure of MOUs quite weak. MOUs were neither disclosed for public information nor were they shared with other states.

(viii) The facility of financing reforms was not available to those states which were beneficiaries of any structural adjustment loans from multilateral/bilateral agencies in that particular year. There has been very limited use of the window that provides for structural adjustment costs, which is a part of the FRF.

11.17 The Ministry of Finance has suggested that the incentive from the central government through the FRF could be a two-part facility, with part A of the incentive fund (comprising 60 per cent of the total fund) being released on achievement of agreed path/targets of fiscal correction based on multiple but separate criteria, and part B (comprising the remaining 40 per cent of the total fund) of the incentive fund, being released on the states taking certain agreed reforms action. It has further been stated that there are five most prominent indicators of fiscal performance, namely,

(i) ratio of interest and pensions to total tax revenues of the state (comprising own tax revenues and share in central taxes), indicating clearly what part of the tax revenues of the states go in funding currently unproductive expenditure;

(ii) ratio of salaries, wages and other costs of personal benefits to employees to states' total tax revenues, which captures current personnel delivery cost of government;

(iii) ratio of present debt and liabilities of the state to states' acceptable level of debt and liabilities; the acceptable level of debt and liabilities should be determined by working out what debt at currently effective rate of interest can be supported by assuming an ideal interest to tax revenues ratio of 20 per cent in Indian situation;

(iv) ratio of consolidated revenue deficit (inclusive of deficits/losses of all state owned entities) to revenue receipts; and

(v) ratio of fiscal deficit to GDP.

Part A of the incentive fund could be linked to performance vis-à-vis these five indicators, each of which may be given a weight. The states should be asked to draw a medium-term reform programme for closing the gap between the base year (2004-05) ratio and the target ratios (to be recommended by the TFC) expected to be achieved. Proportionate releases can be made on the basis of annual achievements every year. Part B of the incentive fund should be meant for incentivising specific fiscal reforms action. Certain key reforms actions, which have been suggested as part of the reforms programme are :

a) enactment of fiscal responsibility legislation;

b) eliminating access to overdrafts from RBI;

c) streamlining of pensions by converting unfunded pensions into a pensions fund;

d) mandatory financial viability analysis of every project and upfront provision of the viability gap;

e) delinking wage and inflation increases for the state employees from the central system;

f) adoption of VAT; and

g) full computerization of treasuries, fiscal transactions management and debt recording and management.

Every specific action could be incentivised by providing a specified amount of fiscal grant. If the state does achieve the same, incentive can be released.

Our Analysis and Approach

11.18 We have analyzed in detail the functioning of the facility from the point of view of assessing whether it has met its objectives. While doing so, we have considered the points brought out in the mid term review of the Ministry of Finance and the submissions of the central and state governments to the Commission. We note that as per the stated objectives of the facility, the fiscal targets mainly relate to reduction in GFD of states, revenue deficit of states, interest payments, wages and salaries, and subsidies together with the achievement of reform objectives in the power sector, public sector etc.

11.19 The mid term review has termed the various fiscal reform initiatives and reform initiatives in public sector restructuring, power sector and budgetary reforms taken by states as a positive outcome of the facility. Although the introduction of the scheme seems to have imparted a certain measure of discipline in the states in that they have been persuaded to draw up MTFRPs and sign MOUs and has sensitized them to the need for fiscal consolidation, in terms of actual fiscal performance the scheme has not been as effective. The percentage of revenue deficit to total revenue receipts of all states in the aggregate was to be reduced to 7.40 per cent in 2003-04 based on an annual 5 percentage point improvement. Data provided by Ministry of Finance, however, indicates that the percentage in 2003-04 was 22.89 per cent. Further, an amount of Rs. 2121.54 crore was expected to be released from the fund in each of the 5 years starting from 2000-01. The amounts actually released are Rs. 2006.67 crore for 2000-01, Rs. 1691 crore for 2001-02, Rs. 1037.52 crore for 2002-03 and Rs. 253.67 crore for 2003-04. The releases actually made in respect of the years 2000-03 work out to 74.4 per cent of the expected releases. This comprises 87.88 per cent of the expected releases from part A and 56.85 per cent of expected releases from part B.

11.20 As part of the reform scenario, the EFC had projected that the fiscal deficit of states in the aggregate would be 2.94 per cent in 2003-04 and fall further to 2.5 per cent of GDP by 2004-05. Similarly, the revenue deficit in the aggregate was to fall to 0.59 per cent of GDP in 2002-03 and become zero in 2004-05. The mid term review states that out of 28 states, 12 have been either consistently improving or have shown an improvement after initial deterioration. The remaining states have not shown an improvement. As far as the aggregate position of all states is concerned, Table 11.4 brings out the actual performance vis-à-vis the projections made by the EFC. It may be noted that the actual fiscal deficit in 2003-04 (RE) is higher than that in 1999-2000.

11.21 The performance of all states with reference to interest payments (which were to be 18-20 per cent of revenue receipts of the states as a whole and were to grow at rates limited to 10 per cent per year) and expenditure on salaries (whose growth was to be limited to 5 per cent per annum in

Table 11.4

Revenue and Fiscal Deficit of States

(per cent of GDP)

		1999-2000	2000-01	2001-02	2002-03	2003-04
(i)	**Fiscal Deficit**					
	Eleventh Finance Commission Projections	4.71	4.27	3.83	3.38	2.94
	Actual position	**4.64**	**4.16**	**4.09**	**3.94**	**4.97**
(ii)	**Revenue Deficit**					
	Eleventh Finance Commission Projections	2.96	2.37	1.78	1.18	0.59
	Actual position	**2.82**	**2.61**	**2.68**	**2.29**	**2.67**
(iii)	**Outstanding debt (including reserve funds and deposits)**					
	Eleventh Finance Commission Projections	25.07	26.46	27.24	27.49	27.27
	Actual position	**25.20**	**27.42**	**29.37**	**31.15**	**31.23**

Table 11.5

Profile of Expenditure on Interest Payments and Salaries of States

	1999-00	2000-01	2001-02	2002-03	2003-04
Interest payment as a % of total revenue receipts	22.46	22.42	25.23	26.04	26.07
Annual growth rate of interest payments (%)	24.06	15.95	18.31	13.09	19.27
Annual growth rate of salaries and allowances (%)	18.44	2.36	3.23	5.64	12.58

terms of the objectives of the facility), has been indicated in Table 11.5. Clearly, the objectives set out by EFC and envisaged in the MTFRP in regard to the fiscal deficit, revenue deficit and the targets relating to growth of interest payments and salaries have not been and are not likely to be met.

11.22 The primary objective around which the facility has been structured is the elimination of the revenue deficit of states, so that surpluses are available for creation of capital assets. We have suggested elsewhere in our report that each state must enact a fiscal responsibility legislation so as to eliminate the revenue deficit by 2008-09. Our terms of reference require us to suggest measures for the effective achievement of the objectives of the Facility. In our view, the major drawbacks of the present scheme are : (a) the scheme does not provide an adequate incentive for prudent fiscal behaviour, as the size of the fund is relatively small; (b) the withholding of deficit grant itself leads to a deterioration in the finances of the states inasmuch as the additional gap so left open is bridged through borrowings with implications for future; and (c) prescription of a uniform target does not invariably reward prudent behaviour, as it provides a soft and easily achievable target for states with large deficits and a difficult one for the more prudent states.

11.23 In order to provide an adequate incentive for prudent fiscal behaviour, the size of the fund would need to be substantially larger than the present size. The central government may, however, not be able to find resources to create an incentive fund of the required magnitude, particularly in the context of the additional resource transfers recommended by the Commission elsewhere. We are not in favour of setting up of a facility by withholding deficit grants which have been assessed on a normative basis. Further, we find that that the central government has not been able to strictly adhere to the terms and conditions of the facility. For example, the definition of the revenue deficit has not been uniform for all states. Releases have not always been based on credible data such as the finance accounts. Changes seem to have also been made on a selective basis to accommodate states when they faced a fiscal crisis. A scheme which lends itself to such arbitrary flexibility is, in our view, not desirable.

11.24 We have taken note of the observation made by the Ministry of Finance that the facility has failed to address the problem of lack of convergence to a stable and sustainable debt path. A scheme, which incentivises prudent behaviour and simultaneously tackles the problem of debt burden of states, appears to us to be more conducive to the achievement of the objective of elimination of the revenue deficit. We have, in chapter 12, devised an incentive scheme based on fiscal performance, which will meet the objectives prescribed for the FRF and at the same time provide debt relief to states.

Conclusion

11.25 The Commission notes the efforts made by a number of states to undertake an improvement of their respective medium-term fiscal situations in the period 1999-2000 to 2003-04. There is undoubtedly a need to encourage states to draw up a medium-term programme for fiscal reforms and consolidation. But, after carefully weighing the various arguments and considerations on both sides of the issue, the Commission does not recommend continuation of the FRF over the period 2005-10. As discussed earlier, the following major reasons underlie the Commission's recommendation.

11.26 First, despite the operations of the FRF, the aggregate fiscal deficit of states actually increased from 4.64 per cent of GDP in 1999-2000 to 4.97 per cent in 2003-04 (RE), as compared to the Eleventh Finance Commission reform scenario projection of 2.9 per cent of GDP by 2003-04. Similarly, the states' revenue deficit declined only marginally from 2.82 per cent of GDP in 1999-2000 to 2.67 per cent in 2003-04. Also, the outstanding debt of the states rose substantially from 25.20 per cent of GDP in 1999-2000 to 31.23 per cent in 2003-04. While many other factors were also at work during this period, it is difficult to avoid the conclusion that the FRF did not play a significant role in bringing about an improvement in the states' fiscal position in the past five years.

11.27 Second, it appears that the scale of the incentive fund of the FRF was not able to provide adequate incentives to counter the short-term "rewards" of imprudent fiscal behaviour by the states.

11.28 Third, the operation of such a reform facility necessarily requires judgment and discretion in the application of broad parameters of conditionality. This leads to several dilemmas in a federal fiscal structure. On balance, the Commission takes the view that the finance commission transfers should be as free of subjective and discretionary dimensions as is practically feasible.

11.29 Finally, recognizing the paramount importance of improving the states' medium-term fiscal situation, the Commission has decided to reflect these considerations in the scheme of debt relief, as described in chapter 12. This obviates the need for a separate fiscal reform facility.

Chapter 12

Debt Position of States: Relief and Corrective Measures

12.1 Para 9 of our terms of reference (TOR) requires us to make an assessment of the debt position of the states as on the 31st March 2004, and suggest such corrective measures, as are deemed necessary, consistent with macro-economic stability and debt sustainability. While making recommendations, weightage is to be given to the performance of the states in the fields of human development and investment climate.

Approach of Earlier Finance Commissions

12.2 The Second Finance Commission was the first one to handle the issue of state debt and was required to make recommendation on rates of interest and terms of repayment of central loans made to states after independence and upto 31st March, 1956. Thereafter, a review of the state debt has been a term of reference from the Sixth Commission onwards. Till the Eighth Commission, the TOR of finance commissions required them to make an estimation of the non-plan capital gap of the states and to undertake a review of the debt position with particular reference to the central loans to states. These commissions were asked to suggest debt relief measures having regard to the overall non-plan capital gap and the purposes for which loans had been utilized and the requirements of the centre. From the Ninth Finance Commission onwards, finance commissions were mandated to review the debt position of the states as a whole and suggest corrective measures. The Ninth Commission was required to suggest corrective measures with particular reference to investments made in infrastructure projects and to link them to improvements in financial and managerial efficiency. While the Tenth Finance Commission had the mandate to suggest corrective measures keeping in view the financial requirements of the centre, the Eleventh Finance Commission (EFC) was required to consider the long-term sustainability of debt for both the centre and the states. Our TOR are at a slight variance with that of the EFC in that, apart from debt sustainability, the measures are to be consistent also with macro-economic stability. In addition, there is a reference to linking the recommendations to performance of the states in the fields of human development and investment climate.

12.3 We have examined the manner in which the finance commissions in the past have approached the problem of states' debt and the fiscal measures necessary for maintaining debt at sustainable levels. The finance commissions had commented on the need to consider the cost of debt, the use and the productivity of borrowed funds and the arrangements for amortization of debt while resorting to borrowings. In particular, the Ninth Finance Commission was of the view that the solution to the problem of public debt lay in borrowed funds (a) not being used for financing revenue expenditure and (b) being used efficiently and productively for capital expenditure so as to either earn returns or increase the productivity of the economy resulting in increased governmental revenues. The Tenth Finance Commission had, similarly, commented that the disturbing features of the debt profile of states were the diversion of borrowed funds for meeting revenue expenditure, use of loans in unproductive or non-performing enterprises and non-provision of depreciation or amortization of funds in respect of government owned assets. This led to repayments being made out of fresh borrowings. The EFC observed that the determination of stable and sustainable levels of debt would depend critically upon the rate of growth of (nominal) GDP/GSDP, the effective interest rate on borrowing by the concerned governments (centre/states), the rate of growth of revenue receipts and the proportion of primary expenditure (expenditure other than interest payments) relative to GDP/GSDP that may be considered desirable. Given other things, a state which had a higher growth rate relative to interest rate, would be able to sustain debt at a higher level relative to GSDP. The EFC also identified the steps desirable for reducing the debt burden of states as the following :- (i) incremental revenue receipts should meet the incremental interest burden and the incremental primary expenditure, (ii) a surplus should be generated on revenue account to go into a sinking fund to meet future repayment/obligation, and (iii) state should have and maintain balance in its revenue account.

12.4 As required by our TOR, we have already suggested in chapter 4 a restructuring plan that would restore budgetary balance and enable the states and the centre to achieve macro-economic stability and debt reduction along with equitable growth. We have analyzed the reasons for the mounting debt and the revenue and fiscal deficits of states. We have also looked at the various conditions for macro-economic stability. Our approach to debt sustainability and the fiscal discipline required for macro-economic stability have been outlined in that chapter. The suggestions contained therein provide the overall context for the corrective measures in regard to the existing debt to be considered in this chapter.

Debt Position of the States

12.5 We have made an assessment of the debt position of the states as on 31st March, 2004. We have also collected data from the states on their estimates of outstanding debt as on 31st March, 2005. The public debt of states comprises internal debt [(including market borrowings, loans from banks and financial institutions, special securities issued to the National Small Savings Fund (NSSF)], loans from the centre, and small savings and provident funds, etc. The total outstanding debt of states, including short term borrowings, is estimated at Rs 865859 crore at the end of March 2004 and is expected to rise to Rs 963870 crore by the end of March 2005 as per data collected from states. The share of market borrowings (including loans from banks and ways and means advances) and provident funds and deposits was 35.60 and 14.94 per cent respectively at the end of 2003-04 and is likely to be 37.23 and 14.74 per cent respectively at the end of 2004-05. The state-wise composition of debt at the end of 2003-04 and 2004-05 are at annexures 12.1 and 12.2.

12.6 Previous finance commissions had followed the practice of excluding the short-term components of debt viz. ways and means advances and reserve funds and deposits, while looking at the debt position of states. Table 12.1 shows the results of a similar exercise carried out on the basis of information provided to us by the states in regard to estimated debt of state governments, excluding ways and means advances and reserve funds and deposits.

Table 12.1

Total Outstanding Debt of State Governments

(Rs. in crore)

	At the end of Financial Year	2003-04	2004-05
1)	Market Loans	200690	230292
2)	Loans from Banks etc.	102531	124236
3)	Loans from Centre*	252809	261416
4)	Provident Funds & Deposits etc.	129376	142103
5)	Others@	97906	123303
	TOTAL	**783312**	**881350**

Source : State governments
*** May include NSSF loans also.**
@ Includes NSSF loans for some states

12.7 In recent years, market borrowings have emerged as the cheapest source of funds for state governments, with interest rates declining continuously from 14 per cent in 1995-96 to around 6 per cent by 2003-04. The states' access to market borrowings is, however, regulated by the central government keeping in view its own requirements and the liquidity in the market. The central loans to states form the largest component of the states' debt. These are often market loans raised by the centre at the prevailing interest rates but onlent to states at rates of interest very different from the market rates. The practice of the central government providing loans to the states enables the centre to exercise control over the borrowings of states, as under article 293 of the Constitution, a state cannot raise any loan without the consent of government of India, if any part of a loan which has been made to a state by the central government or a guarantee is still outstanding.

12.8 The loans given by the central government to states comprise :

a) loans for state plan schemes as a part of normal central assistance, additional central assistance for state projects funded by external agencies and the loan component of the schematic portion of several state plan schemes (state plan loans), which are consolidated as one loan on October 1 every year, carrying the same rate of interest and other terms of conditions;

b) small savings loans comprising of loans given prior to April 1, 1999, when the National Small Savings Fund was created;

c) loans for centrally sponsored schemes/central plan schemes and other miscellaneous loans provided through central ministries;

Table 12.2

Profile of Central Loans to States

(Rs in crore)

At the end of	1999-2000	2000-01	2001-02	2002-03	2003-04	2004-05
Central loans outstanding*	209882	218380	228902	227343	193034	196346
Total outstanding debt @	415142 (50.48)	489768 (44.59)	576171 (39.73)	667891 (34.04)	788401 (24.48)	885700 (22.17)

* Source : Receipts Budget, government of India 2004-05
@ Source : States' finance accounts/state government data (excludes reserve funds and deposits but includes W&M Advances)
Figures in parenthesis are percentage share of central loans to total outstanding debt for all states.

d) medium term loans given by the Ministry of Finance; and

e) ways and means advance loans by the Ministry of Finance.

12.9 The outstanding central loans to states at the end of each year from 1999-2000 onwards, as indicated in the Receipts Budget 2004-05 of the government of India, are shown in Table 12.2. It would be observed that there has been a gradual reduction in the dependence of the states on the centre for borrowing requirements. While central loans constituted over 50 per cent of outstanding loans of states in 1999-2000, in 2002-03 this figure has declined to 34.04 per cent and is expected to come down further to 22.17 per cent at the end of 2005. One of the reasons for the decline is that the central loans no longer include the borrowings against small savings as the investments made in special securities of states against collections in the NSSF are maintained in the public account with effect from 1.4.99. The other reason for the decline is the debt-swap allowed by the central government. This has been dealt with later in this chapter.

12.10 The rates of interest on central loans to states have varied from 7.5 per cent to 13 per cent in respect of plan and non-plan loans (other than small savings loans) from the years 1984 to 2004. In regard to loans against small savings collections given before the NSSF was formed, the rate of interest had varied from 6.25 per cent from 1.8.74 to 31.5.81 to a maximum of 15 per cent from 1.6.93 to 1.9.93, after which it was 14.5 per cent from 2.9.93 to 31.12.98 and 14 per cent from 1.1.99 to 31.3.99. Since central loans formed the largest component of the state debt in the past, increasing interest rates on central loans has contributed, to a large extent, to the growing burden of debt servicing of states. Annexure 12.3 indicates details of the rates of interest applicable on central loans from time to time.

12.11 The standard criterion for determining the sustainability of debt of states has been to arrive at the acceptable levels of debt-GSDP ratios and the ratio of interest payments to total revenue receipts. An analysis of the relative position of the debt-GSDP ratios of states and the percentage share of each state in the total outstanding debt of states for the year 2002-03, which is the latest year for which the finance accounts are available, shows the results indicated in Table 12.3.

Table 12.3

Debt-GSDP Ratios and Percentage Share of States in Overall Debt in 2002-03

Sl. No.	State	Debt GSDP ratio	Share in total debt of states	Sl. No.	State	Debt GSDP ratio	Share in total debt of states
General Category States							
1	Andhra Pradesh	28.85	7.50	16	Uttar Pradesh	39.08	11.90
2	Bihar	55.33	4.79	17	West Bengal	41.15	10.46
3	Chhattisgarh	25.46	1.20	**Special Category States**			
4	Goa	28.15	0.45				
5	Gujarat	33.93	6.61	18	Arunachal Pradesh	55.45	0.18
6	Haryana	27.85	2.70	19	Assam	33.91	1.94
7	Jharkhand	24.28	1.29	20	Himachal Pradesh	63.25	1.71
8	Karnataka	25.12	4.72	21	Jammu & Kashmir	53.80	1.65
9	Kerela	36.34	4.65	22	Manipur	43.08	0.31
10	Madhya Pradesh	32.28	4.07	23	Meghalaya	32.17	0.22
11	Maharashtra	21.56	9.51	24	Mizoram	81.56	0.27
12	Orissa	62.93	4.23	25	Nagaland	52.10	0.38
13	Punjab	48.51	5.52	26	Sikkim	60.27	0.13
14	Rajasthan	45.38	6.31	27	Tripura	37.78	0.46
15	Tamil Nadu	26.80	6.02	28	Uttaranchal	32.37	0.80

Debt excludes reserve funds and deposits

The aggregate Debt-GSDP ratio for all states works out to 34.21 per cent. At the end of 2002-03, all states, except Maharashtra and Jharkhand, have debt-GSDP ratios exceeding 25 per cent. Year-wise figures of debt-GSDP ratios upto 2002-03 are at annexure 12.4.

12.12 In the context of sustainable levels of debt, the EFC had recommended that the proportion of interest payments to revenue receipts, including tax devolution and grants, should be reduced to about 18 per cent compared to the then average of 22 per cent. We, however, find that from 2000-01 to 2002-03, the average ratio in respect of 17 states has been above 18 per cent and in respect of 11 states has been above 22 per cent. In terms of this criterion, therefore, 17 out of 28 states have unsustainable levels of debt. The relative position of states is indicated in Table 12.4.

Table- 12.4

Interest Payments as a percentage of Revenue Receipts

Percentage of Interest Payments to Revenue Receipts (Average of 2000-01 to 2002-03)	States
Above 35 %	Orissa, Punjab, West Bengal
28-35%	Himachal Pradesh, Rajasthan, Uttar Pradesh
22-28%	Andhra Pradesh, Bihar, Gujarat, Haryana, Kerala
18-22%	Goa, Jharkhand, Karnataka, Madhya Pradesh, Maharashtra, Tamil Nadu
10-18%	Assam, Arunachal Pradesh, Chhattisgarh, Jammu & Kashmir, Manipur, Meghalaya, Mizoram, Nagaland, Sikkim, Tripura, Uttaranchal

State-wise and year-wise data on the ratio of interest payments to total revenue receipts are at annexure 12.5. The aggregate position of the ratio of interest payments to revenue receipts for all states for the year 2003-04 (RE) is found to be 26.07 per cent and in the year 2004-05 it is estimated at 25.19 per cent.

12.13 The deteriorating debt situation of states is reflected both in terms of the debt-GSDP ratio and the ratio of interest payments to revenue receipts. The position seems particularly grim for the states with high debt-GSDP ratios (i.e. over 35 per cent) coupled with high ratios of interest payments to revenue receipts (over 22 per cent). These states are Bihar, Himachal Pradesh, Kerala, Orissa, Punjab, Rajasthan, Uttar Pradesh and West Bengal.

12.14 The Ministry of Finance, in its review of the Fiscal Reform Facility, has worked out sustainable levels of debt as a percentage of total revenue receipts. In its formulation, debt has been defined as inclusive of guarantees. It considers non-special category states as 'highly stressed' in terms of debt and debt servicing, if this ratio exceeds 300 per cent. In the case of special category states, the threshold is 200 per cent. The ratio in respect of 20 states considered in the review, in the year 2002-03, ranges from 96.09 per cent for Sikkim to 500.93 per cent for West Bengal. The corresponding figures are estimated at 98.26 per cent to 529.69 per cent for the year 2004-05. In 2002-03, out of 20 states, 7 non-special category states and 2 special category states were highly stressed.

12.15 An examination of the debt profile of states indicates that the total outstanding debt of states (excluding reserve funds and deposits) has risen steadily from 18.62 per cent of GDP in 1993-94 to 27.04 per cent of GDP in 2002-03. The corresponding figures for 2003-2004 and 2004-05 are 28.43 per cent and 28.53 per cent respectively. The rising debt of states is a reflection of the deterioration in the fiscal performance of states and signifies a long- term mismatch between the growth of revenues and expenditures of the states. It is the consequence of persistent increases in non-plan revenue expenditure, such as interest payments, subsidies, salaries and pensions, together with sluggish growth in tax-GDP ratios, inadequate returns from public investments and insufficient growth in central transfers. Large revenue deficits have led to large fiscal deficits and spiraling debt, resulting in the emergence of a vicious cycle of deficit, debt and debt service payments.

Debt-Swap Scheme

12.16 In the context of the debt of states, a mention needs to be made of the recent initiatives taken by the government of India to tackle the high level of interest payments. Taking advantage of the falling interest regime, the central government introduced the debt-swap scheme in September, 2002 to give relief to the states on the 'high-cost debt' owed by the states to the central government. High-cost debt was defined as the debt which carried interest rate of 13 per cent or above. Only state plan loans and small savings loans given upto 31.3.99 qualified for debt-swap. We have been informed that on March 31, 2002, such high-cost debt amounted to Rs 114325 crore. Two borrowing sources were identified for swapping the 'high-cost' central government loans - additional open market borrowings and state governments' investment in small savings securities. It was expected that additional market borrowings could be raised at around 7 per cent. As the states had over Rs 65000 crore of small savings debt, which carried interest in excess of 14.5 per cent, this swap was expected to give the state governments a clear interest savings of over 6 to 8 per cent in respect of small savings loan swapped with additional market borrowings. The states' investments in the NSSF securities carried an interest obligation of 9.5 per cent. This stream was expected to result in interest savings of 3.5 per cent to 5.5 per cent. The scheme envisaged that during the year 2002-03, 20 per cent of net small savings loans payable to states from September, 2002, would be used to pre-pay the past debt. Use of 30 per cent of net small savings in the year 2003-04 and 40 per cent of net small savings in the year 2004-05 were envisaged for effecting debt-swap. The small savings are supplemented with additional market borrowings by the state governments depending upon the liquidity position.

12.17 The Ministry of Finance has informed us that the total debt-swap has so far been Rs 87672 crore, the year-wise details of which are indicated in Table 12.5.

Table 12.5

Position of Debt-Swap Already Effected

(Rs. in crore)

	With Small Savings	With Additional Open Market Borrowings	Total
2002-03	3766	10000	13766
2003-04	17943	26623	44566
2004-05 upto Sept.04	15559	13781	29340

12.18 In the year 2004-05, the total debt expected to be swapped is approximately Rs 46000 crore. The debt-swap is expected to provide a total interest relief of Rs 31000 crore over its lifetime and Rs 14500 crore and Rs 28000 crore respectively in the first five and ten years. We have been informed that these calculations of savings in interest payments are based on the assumption that high cost of loans of Rs 1.14 lakh crore have equal amortization schedule of 20 years and annual payment of Rs 6017 crore and that the average interest on swapped loans is 7 per cent for additional open market borrowings and 9.5 per cent for small savings. The Ministry of Finance has calculated the savings in the revenue expenditure of states as a result of the scheme as 0.75 per cent per annum.

12.19 The central government has used the proceeds of debt-swap for pre-paying its debt to the NSSF assumed at the time of its creation in 1999. There would, however, be a loss of revenue for the centre as the high cost loans were effectively yielding an average annual interest of 14 per cent, whereas even where the centre uses the entire debt-swap proceeds to effect pre-payment of its debt to the NSSF, carrying a rate of interest of 10.5 per cent, there would be an interest rate differential of 3.5 per cent per annum. For the states, the debt-swap scheme results only in a change in the composition and maturity profile of debt, but not the overall stock of debt. The benefits, however, are that over a period of time, savings by way of lower interest payments would reduce the pressure on the states' revenue account and, consequently, the overall borrowing requirements. Further, the role of the central government as an intermediary in respect of loans to state governments gets reduced.

Debt Relief by Earlier Finance Commissions

12.20 Before formulating our approach to debt relief, we have looked into the measures of debt relief provided to states by successive commissions. We find that debt relief has been granted in the form of (i) consolidation of loans on common terms and with reduction in the interest rates for the future, (ii) revision in the terms of repayment of loans given to states without a lowering of interest rates, (iii) moratorium on interest payments and repayment of principal due in certain years, (iv) write-off of loans or repayments falling due during a specified period, (v) introduction of schemes of debt relief linked to fiscal performance etc. While the Second, Seventh and Eighth Finance Commissions consolidated some of the earlier loans and rescheduled them at lower rates of interest, the Sixth Finance Commission revised the terms of repayment of outstanding loans. The Seventh Finance Commission also recommended that small savings loans outstanding at the end of 1978-79 be converted into loans in perpetuity. This recommendation was, however, not accepted by the central government. Write- off of specific loans also constituted a part of the recommendations of these commissions. We would, however, like to delve in greater detail on the recommendations of the three immediately preceding commissions in regard to debt relief as these are considered to be more relevant to us. The Ninth Finance Commission, in its second report, recommended write-off of loans given to states on account of drought during 1986-89 and outstanding on 31st March, 1989 and those given to Madhya Pradesh during 1984-89 in connection with the Bhopal Gas Leak Tragedy with the stipulation that repayment on account thereof, already made by the state government by way of principal and interest shall be adjusted against other payments due from the state government. The commission also suggested a moratorium of two years on repayment of principal and payment of interest in respect of special loans given to Punjab during 1984-89. Further, the state plan loans advanced during the five-year period of 1984-89 and outstanding as on 31st March, 1990 were recommended for consolidation and reschedulement for 15 years in the case of all states. During the first five years i.e. 1990-95, repayments were to be less than those due on the then existing basis to the extent of 10 per cent in the case of Andhra Pradesh, Karnataka, Madhya Pradesh, Maharashtra, Orissa, Tamil Nadu, Goa and special category states, 7.5 per cent in the case of Gujarat, Rajasthan and Uttar Pradesh and 5 per cent in the case of Bihar, Haryana, Kerala, Punjab and West Bengal.

12.21 The Tenth Finance Commission stated that, since many of the relief measures recommended by previous commissions continued to operate, any future relief should be viewed only as incremental. The Commission recommended a debt relief scheme in two parts, namely, (i) a scheme for general debt relief for all states linked to fiscal performance and (ii) specific relief for states with high fiscal stress, special category states and states with debt problems warranting special attention. This was in addition to a scheme for encouraging retirement of debt from proceeds of disinvestment and equity holding of state governments. The general debt relief scheme of the Tenth Finance Commission measured improvement in fiscal performance by comparing the ratio of revenue receipts (including devolution and grants from the centre) to total revenue expenditure in a given year with the average of the corresponding ratio in the three immediately preceding years. The performance of each state was measured against its own past performance. Twice the excess of the ratio over the average ratio of fiscal improvement during the preceding three years was recommended for relief on loans contracted during the period 1989-95 and falling due for repayment after 31st March, 1995. The relief was admissible only to the extent of ten per cent of the amount due for repayment from these loans in any year. We observe that the actual relief sanctioned to states based on the Tenth Finance Commission recommendations was Rs. 212 crore during the period 1995-2000 compared to the relief of Rs. 565.51 crore (assuming increase in performance by 2.5 percentage points) estimated by the Tenth Finance Commission. A specific relief in the form of write-off of 5 per cent of repayments due in regard to fresh central loans given during 1989-95 and outstanding as on 31.3.95 was also recommended by the Tenth Finance Commission for special category states and three other states (Orissa, Bihar and Uttar Pradesh), considered to have high fiscal stress, as their average ratio of interest payments to revenue expenditure exceeded 17 per cent during 1989-90 to 1993-94. In the case of Punjab, one-third of repayment of principal on special term loans falling due during 1995-2000 was recommended to be waived.

12.22 The EFC did not consider any special debt relief for the fiscally stressed states, but continued the general debt relief scheme of the Tenth Finance Commission with the following modifications :-

(i) instead of a factor of 2, a factor of 5 was applied on the ratio of fiscal improvement in terms of revenue receipts to total revenue expenditure

(ii) the ceiling of stipulated relief was set at 25 per cent of repayment due in any one year instead of 10 per cent and

(iii) in the calculation of revenue receipts, the revenue deficit grants recommended by the EFC under article 275 were to be excluded.

This relief was to be available in respect of fresh loans granted during 1995-2000 and outstanding on March, 2000. Although the estimated debt relief was Rs. 600 to Rs. 700 crore, we have been informed by the Ministry of Finance that till September, 2004, the states qualified for a relief of Rs. 131.77 crore only. The states which have benefited under the scheme are Andhra Pradesh (Rs. 77.52 crore), Arunachal Pradesh (Rs. 1.72 crore), Manipur (Rs. 2.47 crore), Tamil Nadu (Rs. 7.89 crore) and Punjab (Rs. 42.11 crore).

Views of State Governments

12.23 We have considered the suggestions made by the state governments in their memoranda in regard to debt relief. A large number of states have pleaded that interest rates on central loans to states may be brought down. Suggestions have been made for waiver of interest, consolidation of loans, writing-off of principal, rescheduling and moratorium on repayments. Many states have requested for a consolidation and reschedulement of loans with or without moratorium on interest and repayment. Some states have also suggested that a portion of the consolidated loans may be written-off. The continuation of the debt-swap scheme is another demand of states with some states suggesting that the scheme should be extended to all outstanding high-cost loans including those from financial institutions. Some states have suggested modifications to the scheme of debt relief linked to fiscal performance recommended by the EFC. The other suggestions made by states are summarized below:

a) External assistance received by the government of India as grant-in-aid should be passed on to the states as grant and a fee may be collected from the states for covering the transaction cost.

b) The repayment of the borrowings from external agencies, passed on to states, should be on the same terms and conditions as prescribed by the external agency and the central government should charge only a fee for meeting the transaction cost.

c) In respect of small savings, central government may recover from the states only the amount which is to be paid to the investor plus a nominal cost not exceeding half per cent for administration of the schemes.

d) Debt-swap scheme should be applicable to all high-cost loans and states should be allowed to raise low-cost loans from the market, both internal and external, to repay high-cost loans within certain limits to be imposed by the central government.

e) Plan assistance given in the form of special term loans for meeting emergencies like insurgency or natural calamities should be converted into grant. In future, such assistance should come in the form of grants-in-aid only.

f) Additional plan assistance given to special category states under Accelerated Irrigation Benefit Programme and Rural Electrification Programme should, like other plan schemes, be converted into 90 per cent grant and 10 per cent loan, instead of 100 per cent, loan as is the case at present.

g) The Non-Lapsable Central Pool of Resources, which consists of the unspent balance of funds earmarked in various ministries for the north-eastern states should be given to the states concerned as 100 per cent grant as against the current pattern of 90 per cent grant and 10 per cent loan.

h) The rate of interest charged by the government of India on loans granted to the states should be reviewed every year and should be closely aligned to the prevailing market rate of interest.

i) The central plan assistance should generally be in the form of grants and the states should have the option to contract the loan component from the open market.

j) Financial institutions should be advised to extend loans to public sector undertakings on the basis of the viability of a project without insisting on the state guarantee.

Views of the Central Government

12.24 The central government in its memorandum has stated that an appropriate fiscal management plan for bringing down the ratio of state debt to GDP during the award period is an imperative. It has further been stated that, while the central government has been making efforts to reduce burden of states through debt-swap and reduction in interest rates on plan loans and small savings transfers, state debt to the centre should not be written-off or rescheduled, as the centre is no longer in a position to bear any additional burden on this count. In any case, debt relief to states should not be unconditional and across the board.

12.25 The memorandum also states that guarantees given by state governments have risen sharply over the years and at the end of March 2002, stood at Rs. 166116 crore, constituting 7.2 per cent of GDP for 17 major states. While steps, administrative and legislative, have been initiated by some state governments to cap the level of guarantees, it may be appropriate if the Commission recommends an appropriate level of guarantees that may be given by an individual state government. In so far as the central government is concerned, efforts will be made to limit fresh guarantees to 0.5 per cent of GDP each year, as provided in the Fiscal Responsibility and Budget Management Bill.

12.26 In a subsequent reference, it has been stated that in the case of states, the issue of debt sustainability is being addressed through the medium-term fiscal reform framework. Many states have also been working towards fiscal correction through adoption of fiscal responsibility legislation, ceilings on guarantees etc. and it is believed that these will favourably impact on their future borrowing requirement and thereby on their overall stock of debt.

12.27 On the issue of linking debt relief to progress in human development index, the Commission has been urged to balance the considerations of efficiency with equity so that the concerns of states with lower than India's average human development indices, are taken care of. In any case, debt relief should specifically address the issues related to cost of debt rather than write-off, which the centre is not in a position to bear, given the restraints being put into effect by the Fiscal Responsibility and Budget Management Act.

12.28 In a further submission on the issue of linkage of debt relief to progress in human development index (HDI), the Ministry of Finance expressed the view that, given the diverse methodologies, incomplete coverage of states and infrequency of data, it may not be appropriate to link HDI to debt relief to states. There is merit in adhering to pure "financial" and "fiscal" indicators in the matter of debt relief.

12.29 Since the central government stated that the problem of debt sustainability is being addressed through the medium-term fiscal reform framework, we specifically studied the features of the fiscal reform facility (FRF) related to debt. The mid term review of the FRF by the Ministry of Finance has noted that, instead of the conventional definition of sustainable debt based on the Domar principle, the assessment of debt as a percentage of total revenue receipts has been found more appropriate, as there is a methodological problem in using state GSDP as a denominator. Since there is a correspondence between GSDP growth and growth in states' revenues, anchoring of debt as a percentage of total revenue receipts (TRR) was not inappropriate. In the formulation contained in the mid term review, the definition of debt includes guarantees. Sustainable debt (including guarantees) to TRR ratio has been worked out as 300 per cent for non-special category states, keeping in view the need for the gross fiscal deficit to stabilize at 3 per cent of GSDP. The review states that general category states can be considered as highly stressed, if the ratio is greater than 300 per cent. For special category states, if the ratio is more than 200 per cent, they can be classified as highly stressed. It has been estimated that by 2004-05, the number of highly stressed states is likely to be to eight (special category – Assam and Himachal Pradesh and non-special category – Kerala, Maharashtra, Orissa, Punjab, Rajasthan and West Bengal).

12.30 The mid term review of the FRF further suggests that a practical approach would be to divide states in three categories, viz., (a) severely debt stressed, (b) moderately debt stressed, and (c) non-stressed. For severely debt stressed, a modified form of IMF-World Bank HIPC Initiative covering all loans should be conceptualized. Further, the debt-swap scheme must continue and for meeting reform costs, a blend of loans and grants should be adopted where the loan part should not exceed 50 per cent of the mix.

12.31 We are given to understand that assistance has been made available to states for restructuring of debt with financial institutions to take advantage of the low interest regime. The assistance is for debt reschedulement or refinancing and government of India, through the FRF, shares a part of the premium cost of restructuring by allocation of additional open market borrowings. Nagaland and Himachal Pradesh have availed the benefit of this assistance till now. Further, under the scheme for financing the cost of reforms like voluntary retirement scheme (VRS) etc. through a blend of grants and open market borrowings, Jammu and Kashmir, Manipur, Himachal Pradesh, Kerala and Nagaland have benefited.

12.32 We also note that the Medium Term Fiscal Policy Strategy of the government of India placed before Parliament in July, 2004 intends to encourage states to approach the market directly rather than routing state debt through central budget and to consider on-lending external loans to states on a back-to-back basis. Further, in the National Common Minimum Programme, it has been stated that a structured and transparent approach to alleviate the burden of debt on states will be adopted to enable them to increase social sector investments and that the interest rates on loans to states will be reduced.

Studies Assigned by the Commission

12.33 A study was assigned by the Commission to the Indian Institute of Management, Ahmedabad to develop a suitable methodology for assessing the fiscal sustainability of debt of the states in India and identifying the major factors that have led to the deterioration of the debt profile in the recent past. Using case studies in respect of six states, the study was required to suggest a model programme of reforms and policy interventions for resolving the debt related issues. The study has recommended linking of the resource transfers (tax and grants) from the centre to the states to states' own revenue generation and their own account primary deficit. Once the finance commission determines the level of transfers to a state on whatever basis, its ratio to states' own revenues stands determined and should form the basis of an incentive scheme. It has further been recommended that all high interest loans given for calamity/disaster relief should be considered separately for either writing them off fully or partially or giving a five-year moratorium, apart from reducing interest rates thereon. It has been concluded that four states would need restructuring of about 15 per cent of their debt through a five-year moratorium on interest payments and for two of the states, this level would be 30 per cent and 50 per cent respectively. All this should be subject to strict adherence to the achievement of targeted growth in states' own revenues and in primary expenditure of 13.5 per cent and 10 per cent per annum respectively, failing which, the interest should be added back with penal interest of additional 2 per cent. It has been suggested that since loans from the centre have the highest effective interest rate compared to other sources of funds for a state, there should be at least a 200 basis points reduction in the effective interest rate charged by the centre and over a five-year period, it should be brought in line with the market rate of interest. It has further been suggested that the existing cap on market borrowing by states should be reviewed and more freedom should be given to states based on their credit rating and overall economic performance. Regarding small savings, which carry a higher interest cost, the centre should give an option to states in the matter of availing of these loans. The centre can supply excess of small savings from one state to another in need of such loans. Alternatively, the centre could bear the difference in the interest cost of these loans and the market rate of interest. The study has also suggested that the central government should facilitate the pre-payment negotiations of loans by state governments to the public sector financial institutions, since they carry a very high effective interest rate due to their loan vintage.

12.34 A paper on Debt Sustainability/Debt Relief was also outsourced by the Commission. The paper covered various aspects of debt sustainability, measures of debt relief and the suggested policy for future borrowings. It stresses the importance of the elimination of the revenue deficit with an additional limit on the size of the fiscal deficit. A fiscal deficit target of 3 per cent of GSDP for every state and a targeted debt ratio of 25 per cent of GSDP has been suggested. The achievement of this would, inter alia, require three different forms of debt relief in the case of central loans to states, namely (a) reduction of interest liability by lowering the interest rate on central loans to states to an appropriate level, (b) write-off of debt owed by states to the centre, eliminating future budgetary outflows on amortization and interest payment together with modification of the policy of central lending to states, and (c) reschedulement of debt over a longer period to reduce the annual budgetary outgo for states in terms of amortization. In order to explore the possibility of linking debt relief to performance in human development, we examined the reports prepared by the

Planning Commission and UNDP. For measuring inter-state differences in investment climate, two indices, namely, index of investment attractiveness and index of investment climate were developed by M/s Indicus Analytics using a number of variables. 20 states were ranked on the basis of percentage change between 1996-2001.

Our Approach

12.35 We have taken into account the existing levels of debt of states, their fiscal situation, the corrective measures recommended by previous finance commissions, the suggestions made by the central government and the submissions of the state governments while formulating our views. We have also taken into account the suggestions made by the two studies assigned by us as well as other studies. Considering all these factors, we are of the view that unless concrete and immediate measures are taken to tackle the debt of states, fiscal sustainability of states cannot be achieved. We agree with the approach of the EFC that the incremental revenue receipts should meet incremental interest burden and incremental primary expenditure. We, however, feel that the pre-requisite to this is the achievement of revenue balance by instituting measures for augmenting revenue receipts and compressing expenditure. As such, debt relief measures will need to be recommended by us in the context of debt considered sustainable and with a view to eliminating the revenue deficit of the states. Apart from providing for specific debt relief, qualitative and quantitative measures also need to be prescribed to restrict the future growth of debt stock of states beyond sustainable levels. Specifically, the debt relief measures recommended in regard to central loans to states need to be substantial and need to encourage better fiscal performance. The role of the centre vis-à-vis the debt of states needs to be re-determined by prescribing a rational lending policy for the future. This should include a rational computation of interest rates for future loans to the states. In addition, the future requirements in regard to repayments, particularly on open market borrowings, needs to be catered for in a manner that bunching or bullet payments do not cause undue fiscal stress.

12.36 As debt is the aggregate of borrowings made to finance fiscal deficits over the years, higher revenue and fiscal deficits lead to larger accretions in the stock of debt. We feel that states should make efforts to eliminate their revenue deficits so that borrowings are not used to finance revenue expenditure but are utilized for generating capital assets. We note that five states, namely, Karnataka, Kerala, Punjab, Tamil Nadu and Uttar Pradesh have enacted fiscal responsibility legislations to safeguard fiscal discipline and impose a statutory limit on the size of state's debt and/or borrowings (including guarantees). A fiscal responsibility bill had also been introduced in the state assembly of Maharashtra. We find that the fiscal responsibility legislations of these six states have specified targets for the fiscal and revenue deficits. In regard to total liabilities, ceilings have been prescribed by Karnataka, Punjab and Uttar Pradesh. Maharashtra proposes to put a restriction on borrowings. Capping of guarantees is provided for in the legislation of Karnataka, Tamil Nadu, Punjab, Uttar Pradesh (ceiling to be laid down under the rules or the law) and Maharashtra. We recommend that in the first instance, as a measure of fiscal discipline, all states should enact fiscal responsibility legislations prescribing specific annual targets for reducing their revenue and fiscal deficits and providing for a ceiling alongwith a path for reduction of borrowings and guarantees. We further recommend that the legislation should provide that the revenue deficit of states be brought down to zero by 2008-09, coinciding with similar targets prescribed for the central government. Enacting the fiscal responsibility legislation on the lines indicated in chapter 4 will be a necessary pre-condition for availing of debt relief, as recommended in this chapter.

12.37 Our TOR require us to recommend corrective measures giving weightage to performance of states in the fields of human development and investment climate. We have considered the matter keeping in view the suggestions of the central and state governments and the feasibility of providing such a linkage. While some state governments have supported the inclusion of these as a criterion for debt relief, other states are not in favour of linking debt relief to progress in human development or investment climate stating that the poor performance or the relatively low ranking of states in these fields are largely attributable to fiscal imbalance including unsustainable debt burden. Such a linkage would also widen the gap between the developing and backward states. Further, preparing an index of HDI and judging the performance of a state as on a particular cut-off date may render the assessment subjective. Similarly, defining what constitutes improvement in investment climate could also prove contentious. As far as the central government is concerned, their view is that it may not be appropriate to link debt relief to improvements in HDI.

12.38 The feasibility of linking debt relief to performance of states in the fields of human development and investment climate has been examined by us. We note that our TOR do not clarify whether such performance should be given a positive or negative weight in the scheme of relief. After a careful examination of the issues involved including the methodology and the outcome of the study assigned by us, we are unable to establish any direct link between debt relief and performance in the field of either human development or investment climate. Even the central government has not favoured such a linkage, suggesting that there is merit in adhering to pure financial and fiscal indicators in the matter of debt relief. Besides, given the diverse methodologies, incomplete coverage of states and infrequent availability of data, the linkage of performance in human development with debt relief would not be appropriate. The formulation of an index of investment climate suffers from even greater constraints, as it involves considerable subjective judgement based on perception with no accepted or standard methodology for formulating the index. We have, therefore, decided not to link debt relief with performance in human development or investment climate.

12.39 We have, in paras 12.20 to 12.22 referred to the manner in which previous commissions have sought to provide debt relief to states. In formulating our scheme of debt relief, we have taken into account the schemes recommended by the tenth and eleventh finance commissions. The debt-swap scheme of the central government has provided substantial relief to the states. Our focus, as far as fiscal reforms are concerned, is on the states achieving revenue balance by 2008-09. We have, therefore, followed a two-pronged approach to debt relief- firstly, a general scheme of debt relief applicable to all states and secondly, a write-off scheme linked to fiscal performance with a view to providing an incentive for the achievement of revenue balance by 2008-09. We have, however, excluded the loans given to the states from the NSSF from 1.4.99 onwards from the scope of the debt relief as the Fund is maintained in the public account.

12.40 As already noted, the debt-swap scheme of the government of India covers central loans which have an interest rate of 13 per cent and above and is expected to close by 2004-05. States have requested for alignment of interest rates on central loans with interest rates applicable to market borrowings. It is seen from the receipts budget 2004-05 that the weighted average cost of market borrowings of the centre during 2003-04 was 5.74 per cent. As per data collected from the Ministry of Finance, the weighted average cost of the total borrowings in 2003-04 works out to 6.04 per cent as indicated in Table 12.6. The interest rate charged from the states by the centre in 2003-04 was, however, 10.5 per cent. The marginal cost of borrowing by the centre is, therefore, much lower than the interest rate charged from states. Large interest payments have been a major factor leading to increase in the outstanding debt of state governments. In our view, therefore, the reduction of interest payments is integral to attaining debt sustainability. We requested the central and state governments to provide loan-wise details containing outstanding balances as on 31.3.04 and the quantum of repayments and the interest payments due from the central loans during our award period. Data provided reveal that a large number of loans for each state are being administered by Ministry of Finance and that consolidation of these loans would lend simplicity to the management of these loans. A consolidation exercise in respect of central loans to states outstanding as on 31.3.04, except the loans given by central ministries for which data were not available, has, therefore, been carried out by us.

12.41 For the purpose of consolidation of outstanding central loans to states as on

Table 12.6

Weighted Average Interest Rate of Central Government Borrowings in 2003-04

Net Borrowings	Amount	Interest Rate (percentage)
Market borrowings	86797	5.74
NSSF	13765	7
NSSF	32602	6
NSSF	13608	5.95
Provident Funds	5000	8
Others (tax-free)	4520	6.5
Others (taxable)	1588	8
Total	157880	
Weighted Average Interest Rate		6.04 %

31.3.04, we have relied on the statement of outstanding central loans supplied to us by the Ministry of Finance for the reason that, (a) the Ministry of Finance data have taken into account the debt-swap expected to take place by the end of 2004-05 and determines the repayments accordingly and (b) the data of central loans supplied by states in many cases include loans from NSSF. The balance of outstanding central loans to states, as on 31.3.04, consolidated by us works out to Rs. 184268 crore. These loans do not include loans given by ministries/departments for central plan/centrally sponsored schemes. The break-up of these outstanding loans is shown in Table 12.7.

Table 12.7

Break-up of Outstanding Central Loans to States as on 31.03.2004

Balance of loans on 31.3.04	(Rs. in crore)
Block Loans	146198
Mid Term Loans	2431
Small Savings Loans granted upto 31.3.99	30638
Pre-1979-80 Consolidated Loans (30 years)	475
Pre-1979-80 Re-Consolidated Loans (30 years)	1441
1979-84 Consolidated Loans (20 years)	27
1979-84 Consolidated Loans (25 years)	550
1979-84 Consolidated Loans (30 years)	1562
1984-89 Consolidated Loans (15 years)	942
Others	4
GRAND TOTAL	**184268**

12.42 A debt-swap of about Rs. 44000 crore has been indicated as expected to take place in 2004-05 in the data provided. The balance of these consolidated loans, which will remain as on 31.3.05 after taking into account normal repayments in 2004-05 and the expected debt-swap, is Rs. 128795 crore. The state-wise details of the repayments due on the loans mentioned in Table 12.7 above during our award period are in annexure 12.6. We observe that even after the debt-swap scheme closes, the effective interest rate on the outstanding loans would be around 11.5 per cent. In our view, a relief in interest payments is called for by way of adjustment of the difference between the marginal cost of borrowing of the central government and the effective interest rates charged by the centre on loans. Keeping in view the fact that some premium in the form of transaction costs should be available to the centre, we recommend that the central loans to states contracted till 31.3.04 and outstanding on 31.3.05 (amounting to Rs. 128795 crore) may be consolidated and rescheduled for a fresh term of 20 years (resulting in repayment in 20 equal installments), and an interest rate of 7.5 per cent be charged on them. The consolidated loans include some loans which had been consolidated by earlier commissions at interest rates lower than 7.5 per cent. We have, however, included them in the present exercise so that management of loans becomes simpler for the central government. States would get benefit in repayment on account of reschedulement of these loans. In terms of these recommendations relating to consolidation, reschedulement and lowering of interest rate, the debt relief during the award period for all states put together, works out to Rs. 21276 crore in interest payments and Rs. 11929 crore in repayments. Thus, the proposed scheme provides benefit both in terms of interest rate reduction and a reschedulement of loans which will ease the liquidity position of states. The state-wise details of debt relief are indicated in annexure 12.7. In the debt consolidation exercise, we have not taken into account the fresh loans to be granted by the centre in the year 2004-05, as state-wise details of such loans were not available. The central government has, however, lowered the rate of interest on loans to states from 10.5 per cent to 9 per cent in 2004-05. This general debt relief comprising consolidation, reschedulement and lowering of interest rate to 7.5 per cent shall be available to all states with effect from the year they enact the fiscal responsibility legislation as recommended by us at para 12.36.

12.43 In addition to providing general debt relief by consolidating and rescheduling at substantially reduced rates of interest the central loans granted to states before 31.3.04 and outstanding as on 31.3.05, we have devised a scheme of debt write-off based on fiscal performance. We have already stressed the need for each state to enact a fiscal responsibility legislation prescribing the fiscal adjustment path for reduction of the revenue deficit to zero by 2008-09. We have, in chapter 11 of our report, suggested discontinuation of the states' Fiscal Reform Facility on the ground that the present design of the facility is not conducive to achievement of its objectives. In our opinion, instead of a multiplicity of incentive schemes to reward fiscal performance, incentives for fiscal performance should be built into the debt write-off package. We feel that states will be provided a tangible incentive if a reduction of the revenue deficit also entitles them to a write-off of debt. A scheme of this nature would further the efforts at eliminating the revenue deficit of states. We, therefore, recommend the introduction of a debt write-off scheme linked to the reduction of revenue deficit of states. Under the scheme, the repayments due on central loans from 2005-06 to 2009-10 after consolidation and reschedulement as recommended in paras 12.40 to 12.42 will be eligible for write-off. The quantum of write-off of repayment will be linked to the absolute amount by which the revenue deficit is reduced in each successive year during our award period. In effect, if the revenue deficit is brought down to zero, the entire repayments during the period will be written-off. The scheme of write-off shall be available for all states from the year they have qualified for the general debt relief by enacting the fiscal responsibility legislation.

12.44 The manner in which the scheme will operate is outlined below:

(a) Fiscal performance will be measured with reference to the revenue deficit/ revenue surplus, as worked out in absolute numbers by taking an average of three years, viz., 2001-02 (Actuals), 2002-03 (Actuals), and 2003-04 (RE). This average will be taken as the base year figure for 2003-04.

(b) For states which were in revenue surplus, as per the base year figure (calculated in the manner indicated above), and continue to remain so in the subsequent years till the end of our award period, the installment of repayment due on the central loans (after consolidation and re-schedulement) may be written-off in each of the years from 2005-06 onwards so long as the revenue surplus of the states does not go below the base year level in absolute terms. In the year the revenue surplus is less than that in the base year figure, no write-off will be permitted.

(c) As for the states which were in revenue deficit as per the base year figure, the revenue deficit is expected to be eliminated by 2008-09, i.e. over a five year period. Fiscal performance will be measured by the absolute amount by which the revenue deficit is reduced in each year compared to the deficit in the previous year starting from the base year figure. For the purpose of determining the scale at which the relief will be provided, the ratio of the repayment due by a state during the period 2005-10 (of central loans after consolidation and re-schedulement) to the base year revenue deficit figure has been worked out. This determines the amount of write-off of repayment that will be allowed to each state for the reduction of each rupee of revenue deficit. Annexure 12.8 contains the ratios which will be applicable to the states for determining the quantum of write-off.

(d) The actual reduction in the revenue deficit in each year over the immediately preceding one would determine the amount of write-off for the state in the repayment due in the immediately succeeding year. This is calculated by multiplying the above mentioned ratio by the amount of reduction of the revenue deficit. The total amount of write-off in a year will, however, be restricted to the repayments due on the consolidated loans in that year. Further, the write-off will only be admissible if the state reduces the revenue deficit to a level lower than the base year figure.

(e) It may be noted that, other things remaining the same, a reduction of revenue deficit is inherent from 2005-06 onwards as a result of the debt relief due to the lowering of the interest rate recommended in para 12.42. Reduction in revenue deficit which is at least equal to the interest rate relief shall be treated as an eligibility requirement. Each state will, therefore, be required to achieve, in each year of our award period, a reduction in the revenue deficit, which, compared to the base year figure, is cumulatively higher than the cumulative reduction attributable to the interest relief recommended by us. Details of the year-wise relief in interest payments and the cumulative reduction in revenue deficit arising out of lowering of interest rate for each state during 2005-10 are at annexure 12.9.

(f) If the reduction in revenue deficit in a year is more than the minimum required for the write-off of the entire repayment due in that year, the excess will be carried forward fully to the next year, provided the revenue deficit continued to follow a downward trend in the next year and is lower than the base year figure. On the other hand, if there is an increase in the revenue deficit in the next year, but the revenue deficit is still lower than the base year figure, the entitlement to write-off shall be determined on the basis of improvement from the minimum revenue deficit figure of the previous year that would have given full relief in the previous year.

(g) To provide an illustration of our scheme, if state A has the base year revenue deficit figure of Rs 2000 crore and the repayments due from 2005-2010 are Rs 1000 crore (or say Rs 200 crore in each year), the ratio for determining the quantum of write-off will be 0.50 i.e. the state will be eligible for write-off of debt equal to 50 per cent of the amount of reduction in revenue deficit. If the state reduces its deficit by Rs 300 crore in 2004-05, compared to the base year level, it will qualify for a debt write-off of Rs 150 crore in 2005-06. If, however, the reduction in deficit is of the order of Rs 600 crore, although the state will be eligible for a write-off of Rs 300 crore, the debt write-off in that year will be restricted to the instalment of repayment due (i.e. Rs 200 crore) in the year, the remaining amount (i.e. Rs 100 crore) qualifying for write-off in the next year subject to the state maintaining or further reducing its revenue deficit in the next year. If on the other hand, in the year 2005-06, the revenue deficit increases by say Rs.100 crore from 2004-05 level, the net improvement over the base year level would only be Rs 500 crore. In that event, since an amount of Rs 400 crore has already been utilized for debt relief in the previous year, the state will qualify for a relief in repayment amounting to fifty per cent of the balance of Rs 100 crore i.e., a relief of Rs.50 crore only in 2006-07.

(h) If the performance of a state deteriorates in a year, with the revenue deficit registering a higher level over the previous year for which relief in repayment has been availed of, any improvement in the succeeding year will be measured, not with reference to that year, but the performance level in the previous year up to which relief has been availed of. If the revenue deficit reduction in that previous year was more than the minimum reduction required to qualify for 100 per cent write-off of repayment, the revenue deficit in that year may be re-determined notionally keeping in view the minimum revenue deficit reduction that would have qualified the state for 100 per cent relief in repayment. To illustrate in continuation of sub para (g) above, if the revenue deficit of state A goes up to Rs.1800 crore in 2005-06 after being reduced to Rs 1400 crore in 2004-05, it will not qualify for relief in repayment in 2006-07. Also, its performance in 2006-07 for relief in 2007-08 will be measured from the notional level of 2004-05. The notional level in this case would be Rs 2000 crore minus Rs.400 crore i.e. Rs 1600 crore. This would ensure that no state will be able to avail of relief more than once for the same level of improvement over the base. Nor would any state stand penalized for performing better than the minimum required level in any year.

(i) One criticism against the debt relief scheme of the Tenth and Eleventh Commissions has been the time lag involved in granting the benefit. We, therefore, recommend that for the purpose of determining the write-off, the revenue deficit indicated in the revised estimates of the preceding year may be used provisionally, so that the relief in respect of a year is available in the immediately succeeding year. Necessary adjustment may be carried out subsequently once the finance accounts become available.

(j) Looking at the necessity of containing the fiscal deficit, we further recommend that the benefit of write-off would be available only if the fiscal deficit of the state is contained to the level of 2004-05. If, in any year, the fiscal deficit exceeds this level, the benefit of write-off, even if eligible otherwise, would not be given.

12.45 In terms of our debt write-off package, if a state achieves through a consistent performance, a zero revenue deficit by 2008-09, it will have the facility of having all the repayments due from 2005-10 on central loans contracted upto 31.3.04 and consolidated by us written-off. The total amount which would be written-off if all states achieve revenue balance by 2008-09 is approximately Rs 32200 crore in a period of five years.

Future lending policy

12.46 In the context of the debt burden of states, the direction in which future lending policy of the centre should move was considered by us. While there might have been some justification for the centre to act as a banker to states when market rates of interest were high and in the process of on-lending to states, an indirect subsidy was granted to states by way of concessional interest, this is no longer valid in a low interest rates regime. In some ways, central lending to states, which is done at much higher rates of interest than the marginal cost of borrowing, results in a reverse subsidy from the states to the centre. In most federal countries, the federal government's loan intermediation role has been discontinued over the years, subjecting the states to market discipline. Such a dispensation allows the constituent units to borrow on terms that reflect their credit risk. While fiscally prudent states manage to borrow at rates lower than those offered by the federal government, the fiscally imprudent states would find their access to loan finance curtailed. We feel that it would be appropriate for states to take advantage of the market rates and avoid the spread charged by the centre. We, therefore, recommend that, in future, the central government should not act as an intermediary and allow the states to approach the market directly. If, however, some fiscally weak states are unable to raise funds from the market, the centre could resort to lending, but the interest rates should remain aligned to the marginal cost of borrowing for the centre.

External Assistance Loans

12.47 A large number of states have suggested that external loans should be passed on to states on the same terms and conditions as granted by the lending agency. External assistance to India is project based, except for structural adjustment assistance. The financing terms for externally aided projects and programmes vary according to projects and lending agencies. There are grants, soft loans and non-concessional loans, provided by lending agencies, depending upon the nature, the financial viability of the project and the revenue earning potential of a project. The external assistance received for states' projects is, however, passed on as 70 per cent loan and 30 per cent grant (10 per cent and 90 per cent respectively in case of special category states). Interest rates applied are those applicable to block loans.

12.48 While the external assistance from some sources and for some projects is highly concessional, in other cases it may be expensive. In the process of pooling and fixing a uniform interest rate in rupee terms, an element of cross-subsidization occurs at two levels : between centre and all states, and among the states. In the case of cross-subsidization between the centre and the states, the gain/loss to one side vis-à-vis another depends on the rate of depreciation of the Indian rupee against major foreign currencies. In the case of states, the cross-subsidization takes place, when states having a relatively larger share of grants and soft loans (which may offer relief to social welfare and long gestation, low return type of projects) in their assistance portfolio, are required to pay a higher rate of interest to help sustain the relatively larger share of high cost loans, which may often relate to commercial projects, used by some states.

12.49 We have examined the recommendations of the EFC in this regard and the policy enunciated in the medium term fiscal policy strategy statement of the government of India. Since the transfer of external assistance on back-to-back basis will enable states to participate on an equal footing in concessional external assistance, we recommend that external assistance be transferred to states on the same terms and conditions as attached to such assistance by external funding agencies, thereby making government of India a financial intermediary without any gain or loss. States would get the same maturity, moratorium and amortization schedule, as the government of India gets from the external lender. As per our information, no loan from the external agency is for less than 20 years, and as such the states would get the benefit of higher maturity (35 years in case of International Development Association (IDA) loans, 25 years in case of Asian Development Bank (ADB) loans and 20 years for International Bank for Reconstruction and Development (IBRD) loans). The states would also get a longer moratorium of 10 years in case of IDA credits. Although the states would gain on interest payments, they would be subject to the risk of foreign exchange fluctuations. We further feel that it would be easier to operate the external assistance outside the Consolidated Fund of India and it will result in faster disbursement of external assistance to the states. We, therefore, recommend that the external assistance pass through to states should be managed through a separate fund in the public account. The Fund could also be utilized for taking care of the foreign exchange risk.

Special Term Loans of Punjab

12.50 Special term loans amounting to Rs. 5799.92 crore were given to Punjab by the government of India during 1984-85 to 1988-89 for combating insurgency and militancy. The Ninth Finance Commission had granted a moratorium of two years (1990-92) on the repayment of principal and payment of interest in respect of these special term loans. The Tenth Finance Commission had recommended that one-third of the repayment of principal, amounting to Rs. 490.63 crore falling due during the period 1995-2000, be waived in view of the special circumstances prevailing when these loans were advanced, and also keeping in view the need for the state to reinvigorate its developmental efforts. The EFC recommended a moratorium on payment of installments of debt and interest during the period 2000-05 on the outstanding special term loans amounting to Rs. 3772 crore, stating that the expenditure incurred on security be worked out by Ministry of Home Affairs in consultation with the Punjab government and Ministry of Finance and relief of debt to the extent the state is entitled to reimbursement on account of security related expenditure be given after the period of moratorium is over and after taking into account waiver already given.

12.51 In its submissions to us, the state government has requested that the outstanding special term loan of Rs. 3772 crore as on 31st March, 2000 plus the interest thereon may be waived by the government of India. The state has cited article 355 of the Constitution, the assurance by the then Prime Minister of India and the poor financial condition of the state in support of its request. We understand that the quantum of the security related expenditure out of the special term loans and, the consequent debt relief to be given after the moratorium period (2000-05) has not yet been worked out. An account of the security related expenditure has now been submitted by the government of Punjab to the Ministry of Home Affairs. This is still to be examined by the Ministries of Home Affairs and Finance. Pending finalization of the amount in respect of which debt relief is to be allowed in terms of the recommendations of the EFC, we recommend that the moratorium on repayments and interest payments on these loans may continue for another two years i.e. upto 2006-07, by which time the central government must finalize the quantum of debt relief to be allowed.

Relief and Rehabilitation Loan for Gujarat Earthquake

12.52 Government of Gujarat had taken a loan of Rs. 5478 crore from ADB and World Bank through the central government for relief, rehabilitation and reconstruction work in the wake of the earthquake of 2001. This amount was passed on by the central government on the pattern of normal central assistance, namely 30 per cent grant and 70 per cent loan. The request of the government of Gujarat is that the entire amount may be treated as a grant.

12.53 In order to consider the request, we called for detailed information from the Ministry of Finance on this loan. We have been informed that the IDA credit was passed on to the state on the standard terms applicable to additional central assistance with 1 per cent reduction in interest rate on the undisbursed amount of the loan with effect from 27.05.2003. The disbursement under the project till September, 2004 was

US$ 200 million, while the outstanding loan amount is US$ 242.8 million. As per the amortization schedule, repayment by the central government starts from 15th October, 2012 i.e. no payment needs to be made during the award period of the Commission. The interest charges due from 31.3.04 to 15.4.2010 are US$ 6984432.39 and the commitment charges paid till now are US$ 1.779 million.

12.54 The government of Gujarat has informed us that the total estimated cost of earthquake rehabilitation and reconstruction was Rs. 8087 crore of which Rs. 2244 crore was to be received as grant and Rs. 5843 crore was to be raised as loan from all sources including external aid from World Bank and ADB. The government of India approved external aid of US$ 699.80 million (Rs. 3219 crore at an exchange rate of Rs. 46 per US dollar) from World Bank and US$ 350 million (Rs. 1610 crore at Rs. 46 per US$) from ADB. Out of this, the Gujarat government has received Rs. 2920.94 crore. These loans have been treated as loan for externally aided projects by government of India. Repayments to the extent of Rs. 621.03 crore and interest payment as Rs. 1158.67 crore are to be made to the central government during our award period.

12.55 We have examined the request of the Gujarat government keeping in view the terms on which the external agencies have extended the loans and those on which the loans have been passed on to Gujarat. While we are unable to recommend a write-off or a conversion of these loans into grants, we feel that considerable relief will be available to Gujarat, if the loan is passed on to the state on the same terms and conditions as agreed to between the government of India and the external agencies. We, therefore, recommend that if the government of Gujarat so desires, the central government may alter the terms and conditions of these loans so that these are available to Gujarat on a back-to-back basis.

12.56 Apart from Punjab and Gujarat, some of the other states have also suggested a write-off or waiver of specific loans. We have examined these demands but are unable to recommend further write-off over and above the debt relief package already recommended by us.

Setting up of Sinking Funds

12.57 Some of the states have recommended setting up of sinking funds for amortization of debt. We have recommended earlier that in future, the role of the central government as intermediary should be re-defined and the centre should not lend to states. Instead, states should be allowed to access the market directly. In this context, we have noted that the Ninth Finance Commission had observed that loans should be repaid out of amortization/ sinking funds. The Tenth Finance Commission had recommended the establishment of sinking funds as being desirable for overall fiscal discipline. The EFC had also emphasized the need for setting up of a sinking fund in each state for amortization of debt.

12.58 We further understand that a consolidated sinking fund has been set up in 1999-2000 by the Reserve Bank of India to meet redemption of market loans of states. So far, eleven states, viz. Andhra Pradesh, Arunachal Pradesh, Assam, Chhattisgarh, Goa, Maharashtra, Meghalaya, Mizoram,

Tripura, Uttaranchal and West Bengal have set up sinking funds.

12.59 In the context of the debt-swap scheme, we have been informed that the old debts had a residual life of less than 20 to 25 years (block loans/small savings loans). The additional open market borrowings used for the purpose of swap are bullet payments, with maturity of ten years/twelve years for some tranches raised in 2003-04. This maturity structure requires the states to make less principal repayments in first ten years and would leave the states with higher cash. As per the Ministry of Finance, there would be bunching of payments in the period 2013-2015 when all the additional open market borrowings (expected to be over Rs. 45000 crore) would mature in a short span of three to five years. The states would experience lumps in their servicing profile. This necessitates the constitution of a fund for repayment of debt. This would improve the credit rating of states when they apply for loans. We, therefore, recommend that all states should set up sinking funds for amortization of all loans including loans from banks, liabilities on account of NSSF etc. The fund should be maintained outside the consolidated fund of the states and the public account and should not be used for any other purpose, except for redemption of loans.

Guarantee Redemption Fund

12.60 The outstanding guarantees of state governments have shown a rising trend during the 1990s. Although contingent liabilities do not directly form a part of the debt burden of the states, the states will be required to meet the debt service obligations in the event of default by the borrowing agency. The outstanding guarantees of state governments increased from Rs. 132029 crore (6.8 per cent of GDP) as at the end of March, 2000 to Rs. 168712 crore (8.1 per cent of GDP) as at the end of March, 2001. These are estimated to be lower at Rs. 166116 crore at the end of March, 2002 (7.2 per cent of GDP). In view of the fiscal implication of rising level of guarantees, many states have taken initiative to place a ceilings on guarantees. While statutory ceilings on guarantees have been imposed by Goa, Gujarat, Karnataka, Sikkim and West Bengal, some other states viz., Assam, Orissa and Rajasthan have imposed ceilings through administrative orders. It is also understood that Andhra Pradesh, Orissa, Haryana and Gujarat have set up guarantee redemption funds. We have recommended elsewhere that all states should impose a ceiling on guarantees through the mechanism of their fiscal responsibility legislation. In order to provide for sudden discharge of the states' obligations on guarantees, we further recommend that states should set up guarantee redemption funds through earmarked guarantee fees. This should be preceded by risk weighting of guarantees. The quantum of contribution to the fund should be decided accordingly.

Recommendations

12.61 To sum up, our recommendations are as follows:

(i) Each state must enact a fiscal responsibility legislation prescribing specific annual targets with a view to eliminating the revenue deficit by 2008-09 and reducing fiscal deficits based on a path for reduction of borrowings and guarantees. Enacting the fiscal responsibility legislation on the lines indicated in chapter 4 will be a necessary pre-condition for availing of debt relief.

(ii) Debt relief may not be linked with performance in human development or investment climate.

(iii) The central loans to states contracted till 31.3.04 and outstanding on 31.3.05 (amounting to Rs. 128795 crore) may be consolidated and rescheduled for a fresh term of 20 years (resulting in repayment in 20 equal installments), and an interest rate of 7.5 per cent be charged on them. This is, however, subject to the state enacting the fiscal responsibility legislation and will take effect prospectively from the year in which such legislation is enacted.

(iv) A debt write-off scheme linked to the reduction of revenue deficit of states may be introduced. Under the scheme, the repayments due from 2005-06 to 2009-10 on central loans contracted upto 31.3.04 and recommended to be consolidated will be eligible for write off. The quantum of write off of repayment will be linked to the absolute amount by which the revenue deficit is reduced in each successive year during our award period. In effect, if the revenue deficit is brought down to zero, the entire repayments during the period will be written-off. The enactment of the fiscal responsibility legislation would be a necessary pre-condition for availing the debt relief under this scheme also with the benefit accruing prospectively. Details of the scheme have been outlined in para 12.44.

(v) As regards the future lending policy, the central government should not act as an intermediary and allow the states to approach the market directly. If, however, some fiscally weak states are unable to raise funds from the market, the centre could borrow for the purpose of on-lending to such states, but the interest rates should remain aligned to the marginal cost of borrowing for the centre.

(vi) External assistance may be transferred to states on the same terms and conditions as attached to such assistance by external funding agencies, thereby making government of India a financial intermediary without any gain or loss. The external assistance pass through to states should be managed through a separate fund in the public account.

(vii) The moratorium on repayments and interest payments on the outstanding special term loan amounting to Rs. 3772 crore as on 31.3.2000 given to Punjab may continue for another two years i.e. upto 2006-07, by which time the central government must finalize the quantum of debt relief to be allowed in terms of the recommendations of the EFC.

(viii) In respect of relief and rehabilitation loans given to Gujarat from ADB and World Bank through the central government, if the government of Gujarat so desires, the central government may alter the terms and conditions of these loans so that these are available to Gujarat on the same terms on which the external agencies have extended these loans.

(ix) All states should set up sinking funds for amortization of all loans including loans from banks, liabilities on account of NSSF etc. The fund should be maintained outside the consolidated fund of the states and the public account and should not be used for any other purpose, except for redemption of loans.

(x) States should set up guarantee redemption funds through earmarked guarantee fees. This should be preceded by risk weighting of guarantees. The quantum of contribution to the fund should be decided accordingly.

□□

Chapter 13

Sharing of Profit Petroleum

13.1 The issue of sharing of profit petroleum was added to the terms of reference of the Commission *vide* Presidential notification dated 31st October, 2003. This notification requires the Commission to make recommendations on the following :

(i) "Whether non-tax income of profit petroleum to the Union, arising out of contractual provisions, should be shared with the states from where the mineral oils are produced; and,

(ii) If so, to what extent".

Profit Petroleum

13.2 Profit petroleum is in the nature of non-tax revenue receivable by the central government out of the profit generated on account of production of crude oil and natural gas from the fields awarded by the government under a production sharing contract (PSC). Central government becomes entitled to a share in profit if, in the event of commercial production, a project generates profit. The formula for sharing of the profit is specified in the relevant PSC.

Background

13.3 The "regulation and development of oil fields and mineral oil resources; petroleum and petroleum products; other liquids and substances declared by Parliament by law to be dangerously inflammable" is included as entry 53 in the Union List of the Seventh Schedule to the Constitution of India. Accordingly, the Oil-fields (Regulation and Development) Act, 1948 (ORDA) was enacted by the Parliament. The Petroleum and Natural Gas Rules, 1959 (P&NGR), framed under this Act, lay down the terms and conditions for grant of exploration licenses and mining leases in respect of petroleum and natural gas. But, the central government is at liberty under the Act to authorize granting of mining lease on terms and conditions different from those laid down in the rules.

13.4 In terms of articles 294-296 of the Constitution, the ownership rights on all land and mineral resources located within the territory of the state, rest with the state. It is in recognition of this constitutional right that the P&NGR provide that a license or lease in respect of any land vested in a state government shall be granted by the state government, albeit with the previous approval of the central government. In addition, section 6A of the ORDA specifically creates a liability on the holder of a mining lease for payment of royalty in respect of any mineral oil mined, quarried, excavated or collected by the holder from the leased area at the rate specified in the Schedule in respect of that mineral oil. As regards the authority to whom royalty is to be paid, rule 14 (1) of P&NGR states that:

"(1) (a) Notwithstanding anything in any agreement, a lessee shall

(i) where the lease has been granted by the central government, pay to that Government

(ii) where the lease has been granted by the state government, pay to that Government

a royalty ....".

It is, therefore, clear that the royalty is payable to the state for on-shore areas and to the centre, for off-shore areas. But, under the ORDA, the central government has the authority to enhance or reduce the rates of royalty.

13.5 Keeping in view the ownership rights of the states over the land within their territory, the exploration blocks in the on-land areas are offered to national oil companies or to others by the central government after obtaining the concurrence of the respective state governments.

Mining Lease/Licence for Oil and Gas Exploration

13.6 The Ministry of Petroleum and Natural Gas (MOP&NG) has informed us that at present there are five different regimes in the matter of mining lease/ licenses for exploration of oil and gas, namely :

a) Petroleum Exploration License (PEL) and Petroleum Mining Lease (PML) granted to national oil companies [Oil and Natural Gas Commission (ONGC) and Oil India Ltd. (OIL)],

b) Mining Licences granted under small size discovered field PSCs,

c) Mining Licences granted under medium size discovered field PSCs,

d) Petroleum Exploration License and Petroleum Mining Lease granted under pre-NELP PSCs, and

e) Exploration Licences granted under the New Exploration Licensing Policy (NELP).

13.7 Under the first regime, exploration blocks were offered to national oil companies on nomination basis. These companies are required to pay full statutory levies viz. royalty to the state government/ central government for on-land/off-shore areas and cess to the central government. The combined burden of royalty and cess on the national oil companies at present works out to more than Rs 3000 per metric tonne. National oil companies pay customs duties in the nomination fields, in case of petroleum mining licenses granted prior to 1.4.1999. ONGC and OIL have also incurred substantial exploration costs in discovering oil and gas in on-land and off-shore areas.

13.8 Some of the small and marginal fields discovered by ONGC and OIL were offered to other parties for rapid development under two rounds of bidding in the year 1992 and 1993. In the PSCs relating to those fields, the rates of royalty and cess were frozen with a view to providing fiscal stability i.e. a stable tax regime to the contractors. In order to ensure that the states get royalty from on-land blocks at full rates i.e. 20 per cent, the difference is paid to the states through Oil Industry Development Board. The central government has exempted the imports from customs duties and has frozen the cess for the life of the contract at the rate of Rs 900 per metric tonne as against the normal rate of Rs 1800 per metric tonne effective from 1st March, 2002.

13.9 Prior to 1997, in the pre-NELP exploration blocks, the two national oil companies as licensees, were required to bear all the liability of statutory levies, namely royalty and cess, but the exploration blocks were offered to various companies in order to attract private investments in exploration and production of oil. The private companies were selected through a bidding process. As per the PSCs under this regime, the share of the national oil companies could be up to a maximum of 40 per cent and the parties to the contract are to share profit oil and profit gas separately from each field on the basis of post-tax returns. Royalty is paid to the state for on-land areas at the same rate as applicable in the nomination blocks/fields i.e. at the rate of 20 per cent. Further, central government forgoes its revenues by granting customs duty exemption on imports required for exploration, development and production. At present, two fields are on production under this regime, and ONGC has so far incurred an expenditure of about Rs 250 crore towards statutory levies. This way, ONGC and OIL are carrying an additional burden, for which there are no provisions in the PSCs.

13.10 The system of offering exploration blocks to various parties was modified in 1997 with the introduction of the NELP, under which the national oil companies and private players are treated at par and are required to compete with each other for acquiring exploration acreages under uniform contractual and fiscal framework. As regards PSCs entered into under NELP, the policy was announced by the government in 1997 and it became effective in 1999, after completion of relevant requirements, including concurrence from state governments. Under NELP, ONGC and OIL compete for obtaining the petroleum exploration license instead of being nominated. The net revenue remaining after deduction of royalty and costs (i.e. pre-tax profit) is to be shared between the contractor and the government of India on the basis of an investment multiple system. The contractor is allowed full cost recovery on all costs incurred in an exploration block. All companies are required to pay royalty at the rate of 12.5 per cent on crude oil to the state governments for on-land areas and at 10 per cent to central government for shallow water areas. Royalty is payable at half the rate i.e., at 5 per cent, to the central government for deep water areas for the initial seven years of commercial production. Half the royalty from off-shore areas is credited to a hydrocarbon development fund to promote and fund exploration related activities. Under NELP, government has exempted companies from payment of cess on crude oil. Further, imports have been exempted from custom duties and a seven year tax holiday is available from the date of commencement of commercial production. In forgoing the revenues, the objective of the central government is to encourage exploration of oil and gas and find more reserves to meet economic growth and strategic requirements of the country.

13.11 Apart from Gujarat and Assam, which are the two major oil and gas producing states, blocks have, at present, been offered under NELP in nine other states, namely Andhra Pradesh, Bihar, Himachal Pradesh, Madhya Pradesh, Mizoram, Nagaland, Rajasthan, Tripura and West Bengal.

The Issue

13.12 The MOP&NG has informed us that, after approval of NELP by the cabinet, the matter was taken up with the state governments for obtaining their concurrence. While concurring with the New Exploration Licensing Policy, which reduces the rate of royalty from 20 per cent to 12.5 per cent, government of Gujarat maintained that the central government should share at least 50 per cent of the profit petroleum under the PSCs with the state government. Similar requests were also made by the governments of Assam and Madhya Pradesh. The claims of the state governments were referred to the Ministry of Law, which opined that the legal issues raised were not quite sustainable, as the regulation and development of oil fields and mineral oil resources is a subject of the central government under entry 53 of the Union List and is clearly outside the purview of states. However, since the state governments have been given the benefit of certain arrangements/practices under P&NGR for the areas falling in the states, such as the authority to grant license, lease etc. and receive rents, fees and royalties, there would not be any constitutional or legal objection if, in the same spirit, the central government decided to share profit petroleum under the PSCs with the state concerned in the interest of cordial centre-state relationship.

Views of States

13.13 The Commission sought the views of the states on the basic issue of sharing of profit petroleum as well as the criteria for distribution of the profit. States have sent varied responses on the issue of sharing of profit petroleum. Andhra Pradesh, Assam, Jharkhand, Manipur, Nagaland and Rajasthan support the sharing of profit petroleum with the producing states. While Assam, Nagaland, Rajasthan have favoured a sharing between the centre and the states in the ratio of 50:50, Manipur has suggested sharing with mineral oil producing states in the same proportion as other taxes/duties. Assam has referred to the proprietary rights of states over the petroleum reserves and has added that when the state consented to the NELP, it clearly stated that the state should get a share of the profit, especially in view of the lower rates of royalty fixed under the NELP. Rajasthan has also made a similar submission in the context of the rights of the state by virtue of its ownership of the land and minerals, the power given to the state to grant leases and the inadequacy of rates of royalty. Assam, Nagaland and Rajasthan have also referred to the expenditure incurred by them on development of infrastructure, provision of essential public services and to environmental costs in order to facilitate oil exploration and development. Jharkhand has suggested a share of 15 per cent of profit for the petroleum producing states. Andhra Pradesh has suggested sharing of profit petroleum to the extent of 50 per cent according to the present procedure of collection and 25 per cent if states are permitted to collect royalty from off-shore and provided a share in the oil development cess. Maharashtra has suggested that the states' share of 'profit petroleum' in respect of petroleum produced in the state or in contiguous high seas be fixed at 50 per cent. The same logic must be extended in respect of other minerals being mined by central public sector undertakings in the state.

13.14 Haryana, Himachal Pradesh, Orissa, Punjab, Uttaranchal and Uttar Pradesh have suggested that profit petroleum should be shared not only with the producing states but with all the states. While Haryana has recommended determination of the share of each state on the basis of per capita consumption, Punjab would like this income to be part of the divisible pool with at least 40-50 per cent of profit petroleum devolved to all the states. The *inter se* distribution may be made as per the same formula as for the share of Union taxes/duties. Orissa has also suggested that the profit from petroleum should be brought into the divisible pool to be shared with all states, but in proportion to the consumption of petroleum products. Chhattisgarh is of the view that the central government cannot raise revenues for itself from on-shore mineral oil, which vest in the state concerned. The revenues from petroleum, whether accruing from on-shore or off-shore oilfields, should be in the nature of receipts under Union excise duty and form part of the shareable pool of taxes and apportioned on the same basis as other receipts in the shareable pool of taxes. Himachal Pradesh has suggested that any profit income, that has accrued to the Union government, should be made part of the total shareable pool, because the profits arise from sales across the country and not in the state of origin alone. Profit income is not and should not be made specific to the state of origin.

13.15 Chhattisgarh, Madhya Pradesh, Orissa and Tamil Nadu have represented that if it is accepted that mineral oil producing states have a right on profit petroleum arising out of contractual provisions entered into by the Union government, the same principle should be recognized in the case of other minerals.

13.16 Goa, Jammu and Kashmir, Karnataka, Meghalaya and Sikkim have no comments on the matter, as mineral oils are not produced in these states.

13.17 Kerala has suggested that if non-tax revenue is to be shared, sharing should not be confined to any particular item and instead, the entire non-tax revenue of the Union government should be shared with the states as per formula arrived at by the Finance Commission. However, if only profit petroleum is to be shared, it should be given to the concerned states only after factoring in the receipts from the Union government as projected to the Finance Commission.

13.18 The stand of Gujarat is somewhat different from other states. The contention of Gujarat is that as per article 296 of the Constitution, the states have ownership rights on all lands and minerals located within the territory of the state. Under article 297, all lands, minerals and other things of value underlying the ocean within the territorial water or the continental shelf or exclusive economic zone of India vest in the Union and are held for the purpose of Union. These provisions clearly establish ownership rights of the state government as well as government of India. All petroleum resources located within the territory of the state are, therefore, the property of the state. Under the constitutional provisions, government of India has only legislative competence for regulation and development of oil fields and mineral oil resources, petroleum and petroleum products etc. Under the P&NGR, petroleum exploration license or mining lease is to be issued by the state government in on-shore areas after prior approval of government of India. Further, the royalty on production from on-shore areas is to be paid to the respective state governments. Special conditions, if any, on exploration license or mining lease by government of India, can be imposed only in consultation with the respective state government for on-shore areas. A reference has also been made to the rates of royalty, stating that these are lower than the maximum rate of 20 per cent indicated in the rules and that in the non-NELP oil fields also the royalty rate would decrease to 12.5 per cent. The state has also referred to environmental costs and to the costs incurred by it for development of infrastructure and public services.

13.19 In the opinion of the government of Gujarat, the constitutional provisions do not confer on the central government, ownership rights of the petroleum resources located in on-shore areas. The issue regarding ownership of petroleum resources for on-shore areas is further clarified by the fact that royalties are payable to the state government and the royalty payments, by their nature, are required to be made to the owners. Government of Gujarat has stressed that sharing of profit in any commercial activity is a right, which only the owner can exercise. Since the government of India is not the owner of on-shore hydrocarbon resources, it cannot exercise such rights.

13.20 Government of Gujarat has, therefore, suggested that the central government's claims to future profit petroleum should be devolved to respective state governments. Tripura has also expressed a similar view and stated that the entire profits derived under PSCs should go to the state concerned. Government of Gujarat has, however, further submitted that past receipts of the central government from on-shore production should also be reimbursed to respective state governments. The profit petroleum arising from ONGC's operations (not covered under NELP) should also be made available to the state government by applying the profit petroleum formula and by making retrospective payments to the state.

Views of the Ministry of Petroleum and Natural Gas

13.21 MOP&NG is of the view that for the acceleration of exploration efforts in the on-land areas, the support and cooperation of the state governments is critical. State governments grant PELs and PMLs for the on-land areas located in the states. Without the grant of these licenses, no legal right can flow for exploration and production of crude oil and natural gas. State governments also give approvals for land acquisition, laying of pipeline etc. In the absence of full cooperation of state governments, exploration and production would suffer. As these are high risk activities, no estimation of recoverable costs and profits can be made with certainty. Actual accruals of profit petroleum from the NELP blocks may start only after 8 to 10 years of operations during which period costs are expected to be recovered by the contractors. There are, however, uncertainties not only regarding the time by which revenue flow would commence but even the quantum of receipts.

13.22 MOP&NG has further expressed the view that from a harmonious construction of the provisions of the Constitution, ORDA and P&NGR, it would appear that the central government is not prohibited from considering the claim of state governments regarding sharing of profit petroleum on "equity considerations". Hence, in order to promote centre-state relations and to seek maximum cooperation from state governments, sharing of profit petroleum between the centre and the respective states could be agreed to. MOP&NG would, however, like this arrangement to apply only in respect of the PSCs signed under the NELP and not under those signed prior to that.

13.23 Regarding the claims made by the government of Gujarat, MOP&NG has stated that the memorandum submitted by the government of Gujarat needs to be seen from the point of view of the requirement to attract investment for exploration and production of oil and gas, balancing the interest of the state government with national/public interest. It is also necessary that the states and the centre get reasonable shares from the development and production of hydrocarbon resources. As for profit petroleum from ONGC in particular, it has been stated that the concept of profit petroleum under the PSC is a different concept, where the contractors are first given the right to recover the entire cost incurred in exploration, appraisal, development and production after payment of all statutory levies. ONGC, on the other hand, has taken a risk and invested huge resources in the exploration of oil and gas all over the country, as well as in off-shore areas, which includes Gujarat. Irrespective of profit or losses, it is required to pay all statutory levies and taxes as may be specified from time to time. The state government gets royalty as per the P&NGR. In addition, ONGC pays local taxes and its operations add to the benefit of the local economy. ONGC has been working in Gujarat for over forty years and is governed by the arrangement applicable to the nomination regime. The demand of the state government for profit petroleum from ONGC on notional basis is not justified, as ONGC operates under a different regime. ONGC, being a national oil company, is also required to incur certain liabilities in public interest from time to time. Recently, this liability involved bearing a portion of subsidy on kerosene and LPG, the fuels for mass consumption, the benefit of which has flowed to all people including those in Gujarat. In view of these factors, the ministry is of the view that the question of ONGC giving profit petroleum to the state should not arise inasmuch as the central government also does not receive any profit petroleum from ONGC or OIL from nomination areas/fields.

13.24 With respect to the demand of the government of Gujarat for sharing of profit petroleum for the oil and gas fields located in Gujarat under the PSCs for small size fields (all PSCs for discovered fields in Gujarat relate to small size fields), it has been stated that the government of India has provided fiscal stability to the contractor in the respective PSCs, whereby they are required to pay statutory levies at the rates specified in the respective PSCs, which have been frozen for the entire contract period.

Further, in order to promote development of marginal/small fields, the central government has also provided certain fiscal incentives, such as nil customs duty on imports for petroleum operations. The central government has also undertaken the liability to compensate the states including Gujarat for additional royalty as may be decided from time to time under the P&NGR and which is over and above the rate provided in the PSCs. The interests of the state governments are thus fully protected, as far as royalty is concerned. As such, in this case also, there is little justification for sharing profit petroleum.

13.25 As regards the PSCs under the pre-NELP regime, it has been stated that ONGC as a nominee has undertaken to pay royalty to the state as is applicable for its own nomination blocks/fields. In these exploration blocks, considerable liability has been passed on to national oil companies and the profit petroleum, which may accrue under the PSCs in case of commercial production, gets eroded by the liability of the national oil companies in respect of these PSCs. There is also a proposal to compensate national oil companies for the statutory levies borne by them on behalf of private companies. The issue of profit petroleum should not, therefore, be raised in isolation by Gujarat government. As for profit petroleum under NELP, it has been stated that the state has concurred with the terms of NELP. It had, however, separately demanded that the centre shares at least 50 per cent of the profit petroleum accruing to it under the PSCs. Under NELP, the royalty rate for on-land area for crude oil is 12.5 per cent as compared to the rate of 20 per cent applicable for nomination blocks to ONGC. In view of the lower rate of royalty under NELP and the over all scenario, the profit petroleum under NELP PSCs could be shared with the state in the ratio of 50:50. MOP&NG has concluded by stating that the demand for a share in profit petroleum by the state should be seen in the context of the overall fiscal regime, the impact on the revenues of the central government, overall public interest/national interest as well as the need for a reasonable share to the state government from its national resources.

Views of the Ministry of Finance

13.26 The Ministry of Finance has stated that the profit petroleum is a new source of non-tax revenue for the government and is likely to become important after a few years. Keeping in view the long term implications, in case the Commission feels it necessary to provide a certain share of this non-tax revenue to states, it should be within the overall ceiling to be prescribed for the transfers to states from the gross revenue receipts of the centre. The Ministry has also requested the Commission to keep in view the implication of sharing one particular stream of non-tax revenue with states as this may lead to requests for sharing of other sources of non-tax revenue of the centre, as well.

Our Approach

13.27 We have examined the suggestions made by the states, the Ministry of Petroleum and Natural Gas and the Ministry of Finance, keeping in view the specific constitutional provisions in this regard as well as the overall context of centre-state fiscal relations.

13.28 As far as regulation and

development of oilfields are concerned, we are inclined to agree with the view expressed by the Ministry of Law that it is a subject given to the Union under the Constitution. Parliament has given the powers of licensing and earning of royalties to the states through the ORDA. Even in the matter of additional conditions to be put on a license, the central government is required to consult the state government concerned but not necessarily take its consent. The central government is also entitled to fix the rate of the royalty, keeping in view the overall interests of development of the industry. Further, while the Act and rules provide for payment of royalty, there is no mention of profit petroleum, which flows from the arrangements between the central government and the contractor. The payment of royalty to the state recognizes adequately the ownership of the state over its land and mineral resources. The contention that the profit petroleum should accrue exclusively to the states of origin is, therefore, not tenable.

13.29 The next issue is whether the profit petroleum accruing to the central government as per contractual arrangements could be shared with the mineral oil producing states. In our view, the ownership of the land and mineral clearly confers a right on the state to revenues arising out of the exploitation of the minerals. It is in view of this that the state is entitled to a royalty. When the rates of royalty are reduced from existing levels for speedier development of the sector, it is natural that the states would expect to be compensated at a later date, once the uncertainties are over and profits start accruing.

13.30 We have been informed that the NELP provides for a reduction in the rate of royalty from the existing 20 per cent to 12.5 per cent with a view to encouraging petroleum exploration and mining. To this extent, there is a sacrifice involved on the part of the state concerned in respect of revenues that would otherwise be due to it. The states, where mineral oil is produced, have obviously consented to the NELP in the expectation that profit petroleum would be shared. It would, therefore, be appropriate for the central government to agree for a certain share in profit petroleum for the states in which the exploration blocks are offered under the NELP. The share of the state concerned should, however, be commensurate with the sacrifice made in terms of loss of revenue from royalty. We are also conscious of the fact that profit petroleum from the blocks offered after introduction of the NELP will only accrue after our award period. In the meantime, states may suffer a revenue loss on account of lower royalty rates.

13.31 MOP&NG has drawn our attention to substantial revenues forgone by the central government by exempting companies from payment of customs duty on imports for exploration, development and production activities as well as granting seven year tax holiday for discoveries made after 1998. These fiscal incentives have been granted by the central government in order to attract risk capital in the country to explore areas for oil and gas. Even in the case of NELP blocks, although the state governments have been persuaded to agree to a lower royalty rate for on-land areas for crude at 12.5 per cent compared to 20 per cent applicable for the earlier regime, the central government is forgoing its revenues by exempting companies from payment of cess on crude oil as well as customs duty on imports. Keeping these factors in view, the MOP&NG has suggested sharing to the extent of 50 per cent of the profits earned by the central government. Most of the states that produce mineral oil and gas have agreed to this suggestion. In the circumstances, we recommend that the non-tax income of profit petroleum to the Union, arising out of contractual provisions in the case of NELP blocks, may be shared in the ratio of 50:50 with the states from where the mineral oils are produced.

13.32 The additional term of reference given to us does not distinguish between the profit petroleum from NELP blocks and those under PSCs signed prior to the adoption of the NELP. However, the MOP&NG has suggested sharing of profits in respect of the PSCs under the NELP only. Profit sharing has not been recommended in respect of nomination fields held by the national oil companies on the ground that the burden of royalties as well as other taxes and duties, including local taxes is discharged by the national oil companies under the prevalent fiscal regime. In the case of PSCs signed for discovered fields, the Ministry, while not supporting sharing, has pointed out that although these contracts provided for freezing of royalty rates for the duration of the contract in the interest of fiscal stability for the contractor, states are entitled to a compensation by the centre, if the royalty rate fixed under the P&NGR is higher than the rate agreed to in the PSC. We, therefore, agree with the MOP&NG that the question of sharing of profits in respect of nomination fields and non-NELP blocks does not arise.

13.33 While submitting its views to the Commission, the MOP&NG had informed us that the claims of states in respect of non-tax revenue relating to 'Production Level Payments' and 'Commercial Discovery Bonus' on contracts signed under the coal bed methane policy would also be referred to this Commission. But this has not been done. It is, however, felt that the approach to sharing of the revenues with the states concerned would have to be uniform for petroleum and coal bed methane. We, therefore, recommend that revenues earned by the central government on contracts signed under the coal bed methane policy may also be shared with the producing states in the same manner as profit petroleum.

13.34 Some states have contended that if profit petroleum is to be shared with the producing states, profits on other minerals should also be shared with the producing states. We have recommended sharing of profit petroleum only in the case of NELP contracts, where the states are likely to lose revenues from royalty due to lower royalty regime. Our intention is not to recommend sharing of non-tax revenues with the states as a general principle. But, recognizing the need for equitable treatment in respect of all minerals, we recommend that wherever loss of revenue is anticipated for a state in the process of implementation of a policy, which involves production sharing, a similar compensation scheme must be put in place by the central government.

Recommendations

13.35 To sum up, our recommendations are as follows :

(i) The Union should share the profit petroleum from NELP areas with the states from where the mineral oil and natural gas are produced;

(ii) The share should be in the ratio of 50:50;

(iii) There need not be sharing of profits in respect of nomination fields and non-NELP blocks;

(iv) The revenues earned by the central government on contracts signed under the coal bed methane policy may also be shared with the producing states in the same manner as profit petroleum; and

(v) In respect of any mineral, if a loss of revenue is anticipated for a state in the process of implementation of a policy, which involves production sharing, a similar compensation mechanism should be adopted by the central government.

❑❑

Chapter 14

Institutional Changes and Reforms

14.1 For effective functioning of the finance commission and for proper implementation of the recommendations made, certain institutional changes, as mentioned below, are necessary. The observations made in this chapter must be read along with the suggestions that we have made in other chapters.

A Permanent Secretariat for the Finance Commission

14.2 Finance commissions are set up as temporary bodies every five years or so for a specific duration and are wound up as soon as they submit their recommendations. The temporary character of finance commissions necessitates that each time a finance commission is constituted, all administrative and infrastructural arrangements such as hiring of office building, appointment of personnel, procurement of equipment etc. are made afresh. It also necessitates that each commission collects data and information afresh due to which considerable time lapses before the commission can start functioning in an effective manner.

14.3 The process of setting up of the Twelfth Finance Commission commenced with the creation of an advance cell under an Officer on Special Duty in a small rented portion of Lok Nayak Bhawan with effect from 01.06.2002 for making preparatory arrangements for setting up of the Commission. The orders sanctioning posts to provide personnel for the Commission took some time and were issued on 12.4.02, 12.7.02 and 26.02.03. Two floors measuring approximately 16000 sq.ft. were hired in the Jawahar Vyapar Bhawan (STC building) at Tolstoy Marg, New Delhi to house the Commission. The process of appointment of staff and of furnishing and interior decoration of the hired premises was started by the advance cell more or less simultaneously. The Commission was constituted vide the Presidential notification dated 1.11.2002. By the end of 2002, however, it had been possible to fill up only 19 out of the 141 posts sanctioned for the Commission and only about 4000 sq.ft. of space was available for occupation in Jawahar Vyapar Bhawan. It took another six months till the end of June 2003 for the work of furnishing and interior decoration of the premises to be completed. Thus, there was a time lag of about nine months between hiring of the space and its becoming fully operational. Further, the Commission was constrained by rigid and elaborate government rules for appointment/deputation and lack of flexibility in offering higher pay scales or incentives to attract the right personnel for essentially short period appointments, as a result of which only 111 out of the 141 sanctioned posts could be filled up even by March 2004. The first eight months after constitution of the Commission were, therefore, spent on setting up administrative and infrastructural facilities during which little attention could be paid to the substantive functions of the Commission.

14.4 The finance commission division (FCD) set up in Ministry of Finance is expected to provide support to the new finance commission in the form of continuity of data, as soon as it is set up. The Eleventh Finance Commission (EFC) observed that the sole job of the FCD had been to monitor the expenditure and release of upgradation grants to the states and that it had not devoted itself to building a database on central/state finances or been a conduit for research in specified areas. It had only been keeping the records left over by previous finance commissions, without proper referencing. The Commission recommended that there should be a permanent secretariat with core research staff placed under an officer of the level of an additional secretary to government of India and that this would facilitate coordination with the ministries/ departments of the government of India as also with the state governments at appropriate levels. This would also ensure an up-to-date building of data base on centre-state finances and documentation, which could be used by the commission when it is constituted. Unfortunately, the recommendations of the EFC in regard to creation of a permanent secretariat have not been taken seriously. In spite of successive finance commissions stressing the importance and need for constant upgradation of data and organizing studies relevant to the working of the future commissions, not much attention seems to have been paid by the Ministry of Finance to this pressing need. The FCD remains a small cell in the Ministry of Finance and does not appear to be capable of providing the necessary assistance to the commission. It continues to maintain a separate identity even after the constitution of a new finance commission and is only accountable to the Ministry of Finance. In relation to our work, it was noticed that the division had not compiled data relating to debt due to which we not only faced major difficulties but spent considerable time in collection of such data. Further, the division had not undertaken any compilation of data or analysis of the working of state undertakings. Even the information regarding union finances in the prescribed proforma and notes on issues could only be received from the Ministry of Finance after considerable delay and constant persuasion, raising questions over the precise role of the FCD. Considering that the division has not been strengthened, as recommended by the previous commissions and heavy responsibilities were expected to be discharged by the division, these failures were understandable.

14.5 The terms of reference of the finance commission were initially confined to its role under the Constitution viz., the distribution between the Union and the states of the net proceeds of taxes and the grants-in-aid to the revenues of the states. However, over time, more and more items have been added to the terms of reference of finance commissions. The most notable among these are the additional terms arising from the 73rd and 74th amendments of the Constitution as a result of which finance commissions are required to make recommendations on the measures needed to augment the consolidated fund of the states to supplement the resources of panchayats and municipalities. Even the other issues referred to the commission at the discretion of the President have become more numerous and complex. For example, the Twelfth Finance Commission, like the Eleventh Finance Commission, has been required to make recommendations on the restructuring of the finances of the Union and the state governments. Like earlier commissions, it has also been required to address issues relating to the debt position of the states and the financing of calamity relief. The Twelfth Finance Commission has also been required to review the Fiscal Reform Facility introduced by the central government on the basis of the recommendations of the Eleventh Finance Commission and suggest measures for effective achievement of its objectives. An additional term of reference was also made in regard to sharing of non-tax revenue of the central government from profit petroleum with the states. The expanding scope of the terms of reference and the need to have a mechanism to monitor implementation of the recommendation of the finance commission, place enormous demands on the preparatory and continuing work of the commission that may not have been envisaged by the framers of the Constitution. While we consider updating of data and carrying out of relevant studies on a continuous basis in the interregnum between two finance commissions a minimum essential requirement, some of the additional requirements that have emerged due to the expanding scope of the terms of reference of finance commissions are equally important.

14.6 In our view, bulk of problems faced by successive finance commissions can be overcome by providing for a permanent secretariat for the purpose of doing the preliminary work both in terms of collecting data and organizing research. We, therefore, recommend that the finance commission division should be converted into a full fledged department serving as the permanent secretariat for finance commission. Legally and constitutionally, there is no infirmity in putting such an arrangement in place.

14.7 Another important issue which needs attention is the lack of financial autonomy for finance commissions. All their financial needs have to be cleared by the Ministry of Finance, which acts as the nodal ministry in the government in respect of the finance commission. This results in references, back references, and delays, especially due to finance commission's work receiving a relatively low priority. The effect of delays in the sanctioning of posts, entrustment of studies, etc., is felt more acutely since the finance commissions are appointed only for a limited time. Another major difficulty experienced by the commission, working to a tight time schedule, has been inadequate delegation in financial matters. For example, the Member-Secretary had only been designated the Head of a Department for exercise of financial powers. Sanctions issued by him were subject to the concurrence of FA (Finance) and Secretary (Expenditure). The need for frequent and repeated references to the Department of Expenditure or Economic Affairs proved to be a great hindrance to the smooth functioning of the Commission. Although the Twelfth Finance Commission was ultimately granted the powers of a government department, it came too late and only towards the end of our tenure, by which time most of our work had already been completed. As such, the declaration could not contribute to the effectiveness of the Commission in any manner. We, therefore, recommend that the secretariat of the finance commission should be vested with the powers of a full-fledged department of the government with Ministry of Finance only as its nodal ministry for the purpose of linkage with the Parliament.

14.8 We also recommend the setting up of a research committee with adequate funding to organize studies relevant to fiscal federalism. The data collected and updated by the secretariat would require careful analysis under expert guidance in a manner relevant to the issues concerning public finance and this process being time consuming, it is suggested that the finance commission should have a tenure of at least three years to do its work adequately. The next finance commission should, therefore, be set up at the beginning of 2007. Further, in order that the commission's time is not wasted in routine administrative matters, appropriate and adequate arrangements for the office and residence of the chairman and members of the commission must be made before the appointment of the commission. This work will be greatly facilitated, if the decision to have a permanent secretariat for the commission is taken quickly and the secretariat is in position much before the Thirteenth Finance Commission is constituted.

14.9 The Finance Commission, as envisaged under the Constitution, is an independent body arbitrating the claims of the centre and the states to shareable taxes. It is, therefore, felt that, as in the case of the Union Public Service Commission and Supreme Court, the expenditure of finance commissions should be treated as expenditure "charged" on the consolidated fund of India, instead of being treated as "voted" expenditure. This will provide a great deal of autonomy to the functioning of the commission.

Monitoring Mechanism

14.10 In our scheme of transfers, we have envisaged a greater role for grants in the overall finance commission transfers, so as to ensure better targeting of expenditure in certain important areas. Our recommendations include specific grants for education and health sectors, for maintenance of roads and buildings, as also for maintenance of forest and for heritage conservation. Grants have also been recommended, within the constraints of available resources, for state-specific needs. We have increased the grants to support local bodies. We have no doubt that the states themselves would be committed to timely and qualitative implementation of the projects / schemes for which we have provided grants, as these have been on the priority list of the states, having been selected out of the demands received from them. That is why, we have specifically mentioned in chapter 10 that no conditionalities, other than what we have prescribed, should be imposed by the central or state governments in respect of release or utilization of the grants. The states must have flexibility in deciding the basket of projects to be undertaken within each sector, in framing the time schedule for various stages of these projects and in reprioritizing within this basket of projects, if necessary.

14.11 To ensure that the end objectives, for which the grants have been recommended, are achieved, it is desirable that the states put a robust monitoring mechanism in place. We suggest that every state should constitute a high level committee for monitoring proper utilization of grants. The committee should be responsible for monitoring both financial and physical targets and for ensuring adherence of the specific conditionalities in respect of each grant, wherever applicable. In the beginning of the year, the committee may approve the projects to be undertaken in each sector, quantify the targets, both in physical and financial terms, and lay down the time period for achieving specific milestones.

14.12 The high level monitoring committee may be headed by the Chief Secretary with the Finance Secretary and the secretaries / heads of departments concerned as members. The committee should meet at least once in every quarter to review the utilization of the grants and to issue directions for mid-course correction, if considered necessary.

Accounting Procedure

14.13 Under the present system of cash based system of accounting, followed by the central and state governments, transactions are recognized, when the cash is paid out or received in. In the books of accounts, expenditures are recorded at the time of payment, i.e. when a cheque is issued, and receipts are recorded when these are reported by the collecting bank. Movements in the government cash balance kept with RBI as a result of such payments and receipts are also simultaneously recorded in the account books. Thus, the government accounts are a record of cash flows into and out of consolidated fund and public account, and the effect of these cash flows reflect on government's liquidity position.

14.14 The cash based system of accounting lays emphasis on transactions vis-à-vis the budget. It does not record and report complete financial information required for management of resources. It does not provide a full picture of the government's financial position at any given point and the changes that take place over time as a result of government policy. The system fails to reflect government's liabilities such as accrued liabilities arising due to unfunded pensions and superannuation benefits and current liabilities arising from a disconnect between commitments and payments. Similarly, the present system is unable to track current assets as well as non-financial assets. It does not provide information on the assets held by the government, much less the cost of holding and operating these assets and the impact of current consumption on the stock of assets. Another major limitation is its inability to record the full cost of providing services by the government's departments or the commitments made by the government regarding payment in future years. The cash based system of accounting provides room for fiscal opportunism, as tax revenues can be collected in excess during a period followed by high incidence of refunds, payments can easily be deferred and passed on to future periods, revenues due in the future could be compromised by providing for one time payments, etc. To quote some other examples, it takes no note of transformation of indebted government agencies into autonomous legal entities outside government through suitable state guarantees, and on the expenditure side, omit existing net liabilities of public enterprises and agencies outside the government, though the latter cannot escape such liabilities.

14.15 Compared to the cash based system, the system of accrual accounting recognizes financial flows at the time economic value is created, transformed, exchanged, transferred or extinguished, whether or not cash is exchanged at that time. It is different from cash based system in that it records flow of resources. Expenses are recorded when the resources (labour, goods and services and capital) are consumed, and income when it is earned, i.e. when the goods are sold or the services rendered. The associated cash flows generally follow the event after some time and may or may not take place during the same accounting period. Thus, in addition to cash flow, unpaid consumptions (payables) and unrealized income (receivables) are also recorded. Resources acquired but not fully consumed during an accounting period are treated as assets (inventory and fixed assets). Payments made for acquisition of inventory are included in the operating cost for the period in which it is consumed. Payments made for acquisition of physical assets, that have future service potential, are amortized over the entire useful life of the asset by charging depreciation.

14.16 The system of accrual accounting, thus, inter alia, allows better cost – price calculations, records capital use properly, distinguishes between current and capital expenditures, presents a complete picture of debt and other liabilities and focuses policy attention on financial position, as shown in the whole balance sheet not just cash flows or debts. It gives a complete measure of cost of various services, takes care of disinvestment receipts and provides adequate information of both fiscal balance and net worth and their changes over time. Information, as would be available under accrual accounts, constitutes an essential input for bodies like finance commissions, not only in assessing the revenue requirements of the centre and states vis-à-vis the available resources, but also in appraising their fiscal performance with a view to assigning due credit to the governments, which have performed well and providing disincentives to those, which fail to measure upto expectations. We understand that some action has been initiated by the central government to move towards accrual basis of accounting. However, the transition would occur in stages, as this is a time consuming process. While we are in favour of a changeover to the accrual based system of accounting in the medium term, we suggest that in the interim, some additional information as mentioned below in the form of statements should be appended to the present system of cash accounting to enable more informed decision making. An illustrative list of statements, which could be included are:

(i) a statement of subsidies given, both explicit and implicit;

(ii) a statement containing expenditure on salaries by various departments/ units;

(iii) detailed information on pensioners and expenditure on government pensions;

(iv) data on committed liabilities in the future;

(v) statement containing information on debt and other liabilities as well as repayment schedule;

(vi) accretion to or erosion in financial assets held by the government including those arising out of changes in the manner of spending by the government;

(vi) implications of major policy decisions taken by the government during the year or new schemes proposed in the budget for future cash flows; and

(vii) statement on maintenance expenditure with segregation of salary and non-salary portions.

14.17 While introducing these statements, the ultimate goal of switching over to the accrual based system of accounting may be kept in view and proformae designed in a manner that facilitates a smooth and effective transition. We have, while dealing with the Fiscal Reform Facility in chapter 11, noted the absence of a standard definition of revenue deficit with states being allowed selectively to include/exclude the deficits of major state government entities like the state electricity board, road transport undertakings etc. for the purpose of measuring performance. We have also noticed that some states have started classifying the grants to local bodies as capital expenditure. Some states are already meeting the deficit of their electricity boards by granting loans or investing in equity rather than providing transparent subsidies. Our scheme of debt relief in respect of repayment of loan during 2005-10 is linked to reduction in revenue deficit so as to eliminate it by 2008-09. It is necessary to guard against any attempts to defeat the objectives of the scheme through creative accounting. We, therefore, recommend that the definition of revenue and fiscal deficits etc. be standardized and instructions for a uniform classification code for all states down to the object head are issued. Unauthorized changes in accounting policies and arbitrary reclassification of expenditure should be viewed seriously by the monitoring agency while granting relief under the scheme.

14.18 The change over to the accrual based system of accounting will place considerable demands on the accounting personnel in various government organizations, particularly at the lower and middle levels of the accounting hierarchy, consisting of accounts clerks, accountants, assistants, treasury officials and others. Although a few of these functionaries would have a formal background in finance and accounts, majority of them may not possess professional qualifications. Even those who have professional qualifications often need to upgrade their skills during their career. In most countries, accountants are required to acquire recognized vocational qualifications in public sector accounting and audit. In the United States of America, for instance, the Association of Government Accountants and Government Financial Officers' Association train accountants to become accounting technicians. Similar arrangements for providing continuing professional education are also in place in the UK, Malaysia, Singapore, South Africa,

Behrain, etc. through chartered institutes. The absence of professionalized accounting personnel in the public sector in India has also been commented on by several analysts. Considering the need for qualified and professional accounts staff and training for capacity building particularly in the context of our recommendation for changeover to the accrual based system of accounting, we recommend that a National Institute of Public Financial Accountants be set up by the government of India and its charter be decided in consultation with the C&AG.

❑❑

Chapter 15

Concluding Observations

15.1 The Commission has recommended a scheme of fiscal transfers that can serve the objectives of equity and efficiency within a framework of fiscal consolidation. The effort needed to achieve fiscal consolidation should be seen as the joint responsibility of the central and state governments. For achieving vertical and horizontal balance, consistent with the responsibilities of the two levels of governments in respect of providing public and merit goods and services, both the centre and the states need to raise the levels of revenues relative to their respective revenue bases, and exercise restraint in undertaking unwarranted expenditure commitments.

15.2 The finances of the central and state governments, individually and in the aggregate, have evinced large and persistent imbalances in the period preceding the Commission's award period. Four factors have accounted for the continuing deterioration: fall in centre's tax-GDP ratio compared to the peak levels achieved in the late eighties, substantial increase in the level of salary and pension payments, particularly for the states, in the wake of the recommendations of the Fifth Central Pay Commission, high levels of nominal interest rates in the late nineties combined with the subsequent fall in inflation rates, and the low growth rates in the first three years of the new decade. While these reasons account for the acuteness of the ailment, there are also underlying structural reasons for the persistence of fiscal deterioration because of the tax structure and expenditure pattern.

15.3 In the scheme of fiscal transfers, the correction of vertical imbalance is, to some extent, based on judgment. An assessment has to be made of the gap between resources and responsibilities at the two levels of government. Taking into account a variety of factors including the historical trends, we have recommended an increase in the share of states in the divisible pool of taxes to 30.5 per cent from the current level of 29.5 per cent. We believe that this increase can be accommodated by the central government by pruning their activities that fall in the domain of the states. We have raised the indicative limit of overall transfers out of the gross revenue receipts of the centre from 37.5 per cent to 38 per cent.

15.4 In the context of horizontal imbalance, we feel that the equalization approach to transfers is appropriate as it is consistent with both equity and efficiency.

It has not, however, been possible to implement this approach fully, as the extent of disparities in the per capita fiscal capacities of the states is too large and some of the better-off states are also in serious fiscal imbalance. In the devolution scheme recommended by us, we have endeavored to strike a balance among different criteria reflecting deficiency in fiscal capacities, cost disabilities, and fiscal efficiency. Apart from following a normative approach in assessing own resources and expenditures of the states with a view to estimating the resource gap, we have focused on education and health as the two critical merit services, where highest priority must be accorded in reducing disparities in the level of service provision, and have recommended conditional grants, within the framework of the equalization approach. We have also increased the proportion of grants to tax-devolution in the scheme of transfers. It is therefore necessary that in judging the transfer to a state, both tax devolution and grants should be taken into account. The coefficient of correlation between comparable GSDP per capita (average of 1999-00 to 2001-02) and the recommended per capita transfers, comprising tax devolution and all the grants, among the general category states excluding Goa, is estimated at -0.89, which emphasises the redistributive character of the transfers.

15.5 We have laid emphasis on strengthening the local bodies in keeping with the constitutional mandate for effective and autonomous local self-governance, recognizing that local bodies must be supported by a scheme of transfers that encourages decentralization and own effort for raising revenues. The recommended transfers for the local bodies constitute about 1.24 per cent of the shareable taxes and 0.9 per cent of centre's gross revenue receipts.

15.6 We have recognized that the debt burden of the states is currently heavy. We have provided a scheme of debt relief, which is in two parts. First, there is the relief that comes from consolidating the past debt and rescheduling it, along with interest rate reduction. The second part consists of a debt write-off, which is linked to the reduction in the absolute levels of revenue deficits. Both reliefs will be available, only if states enact appropriate legislations to bring down the revenue deficit to zero by 2008-09 and commit to reducing the fiscal deficit in a phased manner. With the relief that we have recommended, it should be possible for states to pursue their developmental goals with fiscal prudence.

15.7 We have argued that important institutional changes are required to tackle some of the structural problems in managing government finances. One central change relates to the regime of government borrowing. We have recommended that states, like the centre, must decide their annual borrowing programme, within the framework of their respective fiscal responsibility legislations. There is also a need to let the states access the market directly for their borrowing requirements. The overall limit to their annual borrowing from all sources should be supervised by an independent body like a Loan Council with representatives from the Ministry of Finance, Planning Commission, Reserve Bank of India, and the state governments. This Council may, at the beginning of each year, announce borrowing limits for each state, taking into account the sustainability considerations into account. Our suggestion for de-linking grants and loans in plan assistance, as these need to be determined on different principles, is part of the reform of the borrowing regime.

15.8 In our plan for restructuring government finances, we expect a positive growth dividend, as revenue deficits relative to GDP progressively fall, implying a fall in government dis-savings, and an increase in the overall savings relative to GDP. A higher tax-GDP ratio combined with higher growth on a sustained basis, and fall in interest payments, create the necessary space for increasing government capital expenditure, and productivity enhancing non-interest, non-salary revenue expenditure. The virtuous cycle of reforms, robust government finances, and an equalizing system of fiscal transfers, should help establish a sound federal fiscal system in India.

Chapter 16

Summary of Recommendations

Plan for Restructuring Public Finances

1. By 2009-10, the combined tax-GDP ratio of the centre and the states should be increased to 17.6 per cent, primary expenditure to a level of 23 per cent of GDP and capital expenditure to nearly 7 per cent of GDP

(Para 4.52)

2. The combined debt-GDP ratio with external debt measured at historical exchange rates should, at a minimum, be brought down to 75 per cent by the end of 2009-10.

(Para 4.45)

3. The system of on-lending should be brought to an end over time and the long term goal for the centre and states for the debt-GDP ratio should be 28 per cent each.

(Para 4.45)

4. The fiscal deficit to GDP ratio targets for the centre and the states may be fixed at 3 per cent of GDP each.

(Para 4.45)

5. The centre's interest payment relative to revenue receipts should reach about 28 per cent by 2009-10. In the case of states, the level of interest payments relative to revenue receipts should fall to about 15 per cent by 2009-10.

(Para 4.54)

6. The revenue deficit relative to GDP for the centre and the states, for their combined as well as individual accounts should be brought down to zero by 2008-09.

(Para 4.51)

7. States should follow a recruitment and wage policy, in a manner such that the total salary bill relative to revenue expenditure net of interest payments and pensions does not exceed 35 per cent.

(Para 4.63)

8. Each state should enact a fiscal responsibility legislation, which should, at a minimum, provide for

   (a) eliminating revenue deficit by 2008-09;

   (b) reducing fiscal deficit to 3 per cent of GSDP or its equivalent, defined as the ratio of interest payment to revenue receipts;

   (c) bringing out annual reduction targets of revenue and fiscal deficits;

(d) bringing out annual statement giving prospects for the state economy and related fiscal strategy; and

(e) bringing out special statements along with the budget giving in detail the number of employees in government, public sector, and aided institutions and related salaries.

(Para 4.79)

Sharing of Union Tax Revenues

9. The share of the states in the net proceeds of shareable central taxes shall be 30.5 per cent. For this purpose, additional excise duties in lieu of sales tax are treated as a part of the general pool of central taxes. If the tax rental arrangement is terminated and the states are allowed to levy sales tax (or VAT) on these commodities without any prescribed limit, the share of the states in the net proceeds of shareable central taxes shall be reduced to 29.5 per cent.

(Para 7.22)

10. If any legislation is enacted in respect of service tax after the eighty eighth Constitutional amendment is notified, it must be ensured that the revenue accruing to a state under the legislation should not be less than the share that would accrue to it, had the entire service tax proceeds been part of the shareable pool.

(Para 7.22)

11. The indicative amount of over all transfers to states may be fixed at 38 per cent of the central gross revenue receipt.

(Para 7.22)

12. The states should be given a share as specified in the following table in the net proceeds of all the shareable Union taxes in each of the five financial years during the period 2005-06 to 2009-10.

(Paras 7.35, 7.36)

State	**Share (all shareable taxes excluding service tax) (per cent)**	**Share of Service Tax (per cent)**
1	**2**	**3**
Andhra Pradesh	7.356	7.453
Arunachal Pradesh	0.288	0.292
Assam	3.235	3.277
Bihar	11.028	11.173
Chhattisgarh	2.654	2.689
Goa	0.259	0.262
Gujarat	3.569	3.616
Haryana	1.075	1.089
Himachal Pradesh	0.522	0.529
Jammu & Kashmir	1.297	nil
Jharkhand	3.361	3.405
Karnataka	4.459	4.518
Kerala	2.665	2.700
Madhya Pradesh	6.711	6.799
Maharashtra	4.997	5.063
Manipur	0.362	0.367
Meghalaya	0.371	0.376
Mizoram	0.239	0.242
Nagaland	0.263	0.266
Orissa	5.161	5.229
Punjab	1.299	1.316
Rajasthan	5.609	5.683
Sikkim	0.227	0.230
Tamil Nadu	5.305	5.374
Tripura	0.428	0.433
Uttar Pradesh	19.264	19.517
Uttaranchal	0.939	0.952
West Bengal	7.057	7.150
All states	**100.000**	**100.000**

Local Bodies

13. A total grant of Rs.20000 crore for the panchayati raj institutions and Rs.5000 crore for the urban local bodies may be given to the states for the period

2005-10 with *inter-se* distribution as indicated in Table 8.1.

(Para 8.38)

14. The PRIs should be encouraged to take over the assets relating to water supply and sanitation and utilize the grants for repairs/rejuvenation as also the O&M costs. The PRIs should, however, recover at least 50 percent of the recurring costs in the form of user charges.

(Para 8.40)

15. Out of the grants allocated for the panchayats, priority should be given to expenditure on the O&M costs of water supply and sanitation. This will facilitate panchayats to take over the schemes and operate them.

(Para 8.41)

16. At least 50 per cent of the grants provided to each state for the urban local bodies should be earmarked for the scheme of solid waste management through public-private partnership. The municipalities should concentrate on collection, segregation and transportation of solid waste. The cost of these activities, whether carried out in house or out sourced, could be met from the grants.

(Para 8.42)

17. Besides expenditure on the O&M costs of water supply and sanitation in rural areas and on the schemes of solid waste management in urban areas, PRIs and ULBs should, out of the grants allocated, give high priority to expenditure on creation of data base and maintenance of accounts through the use of modern technology and management systems, wherever possible. Some of the modern methods like GIS (Geographic Information Systems) for mapping of properties in urban areas and computerization for switching over to a modern system of financial management would go a long way in creating strong local governments, fulfilling the spirit of the 73rd and 74th Constitutional amendments.

(Para 8.43)

18. The states may assess the requirement of each local body on the basis of the principles stated by us and earmark funds accordingly out of the total allocation re-commended by us.

(Para 8.43)

19. Grants have not been recommended separately for the normal and the excluded areas under the fifth and sixth schedule of the Constitution. The states having such areas may distribute the grants recommended by us to all local bodies, including those in the excluded areas, in a fair and just manner.

(Para 8.51)

20. The central government should not impose any condition other than those prescribed by us, for release or utilization of these grants, which are largely in the nature of a correction of vertical imbalance between the centre and the states.

(Para 8.52)

21. The normal practice of insisting on the utilization of amounts already released before further releases are considered, may continue and the grants may be released to a state only after it certifies that the previous releases have been

passed on to the local bodies. The amounts due to the states in the first year of our award period i.e. 2005-06 may be released without such an insistence.

(Para 8.52)

22. State governments should not take more than 15 days in transferring the grants to local bodies after these are released by the central government. The centre should take a serious view of any undue delay on the part of the state.

(Para 8.53)

23. The central government should take note of our views on the issues listed in para 8.23, while formulating or revising various policy measures. In particular, action may be taken to raise the ceiling on profession tax.

(Para 8.23)

24. The state should adopt the best practices listed in para 8.19 to improve the resources of the panchayats.

(Para 8.19)

25. The suggestions made by us in respect of state finance commissions in paras 8.29 to 8.37 and 8.54 should be acted upon with a view to strengthening the institution of SFCs, so that it may play an effective role in the system of fiscal transfers to the third tier of government.

(Paras 8.29 to 8.37, 8.54)

Calamity Relief

26. The scheme of CRF be continued in its present form with contributions from the centre and the states in the ratio of 75:25.

(Paras 9.10, 9.11)

27. The size of the CRF for our award period is worked out at Rs.21333.33 crore.

(Para 9.11)

28. The scheme of NCCF may continue in its present form with core corpus of Rs.500 crore. The outgo from the fund may continue to be replenished by way of collection of National Calamity Contingent Duty and levy of special surcharges.

(Paras 9.16, 9.17)

29. The definition of natural calamity, as applicable at present, may be expanded to cover landslides, avalanches, cloud burst and pest attacks.

(Para 9.12)

30. The centre may continue to make allocation of foodgrains to the needy states as a relief measure, but a transparent policy in this regard is required to be put in place.

(Para 9.18)

31. A committee consisting of scientists, flood control specialists and other experts be set up to study and map the hazards to which several states are subject to.

(Para 9.14)

32. The provision for disaster preparedness and mitigation needs to be built into the state plans, and not as a part of calamity relief.

(Para 9.14)

Grants-in-aid to States

33. The system of imposing a 70:30 ratio between loans and grants for extending plan assistance to non-special category states (10:90 in the case of special

category states) should be done away with. Instead, the centre should confine itself to extending plan grants to the states, and leave it to the states to decide how much they wish to borrow and from whom.

(Para 10.4)

34. A total non-plan revenue deficit grant of Rs.56855.87 crore is recommended during the award period for fifteen states (*vide* Table 10.4).

(Paras 10.12, 10.13)

35. Eight states have been recommended for grants amounting to Rs.10171.65 crore over the award period for the education sector, with a minimum of Rs.20 crore in a year for any eligible state (*vide* Table 10.5).

(Para 10.17)

36. Seven states have been recommended for grants amounting to Rs.5887.08 crore over the award period for the health sector (major heads 2210 and 2211), with a minimum of Rs.10 crore a year for any eligible state (*vide* Table 10.6).

(Para 10.18)

37. The grants for the education and health sectors are an additionality, over and above the normal expenditure to be incurred by the states in these sectors. These grants should be utilised only for the respective sectors (non-plan), i.e., major head 2202 in the case of education and major heads 2210 and 2211 in the case of health. Conditionalities governing the releases and utilisation of these grants have been specified in annexures 10.1 to 10.3. No further conditionalities should be imposed by the central or the state government for the release or utilisation of these grants. Monitoring of the expenditure relating to these grants will rest with the state government concerned.

(Para 10.19)

38. A grant of Rs.15,000 crore over the award period is recommended for maintenance of roads and bridges. This amount will be in addition to the normal expenditure which the states would be incurring on maintenance of roads and bridges. This amount will be provided in equal instalments over the last four years (i.e., 2006-07 to 2009-10) of the award period, so that the states get a year for making preparations to absorb these funds.

(Para 10.21)

39. An amount of Rs.5000 crore is recommended as grants for maintenance of public buildings.

(Para 10.22)

40. The maintenance grants for roads and bridges, and for buildings, are an additionality, over and above the normal maintenance expenditure to be incurred by the states. These grants should be released and spent in accordance with the conditionalities indicated in annexures 10.4 to 10.6.

(Para 10.23)

41. A grant of Rs. 1000 crore spread over the award period 2005-10 is recommended for maintenance of forests. This would be an additionality over and above what the states would be spending through their forest departments. It should also result in increased expenditure to the extent of this grant, in addition to the

normal expenditure of the forest department.

(Para 10.25)

42. A grant of Rs.625 crore spread over the award period is recommended for heritage conservation. This grant will be used for preservation and protection of historical monuments, archaeological sites, public libraries, museums and archives, and also for improving the tourist infrastructure to facilitate visits to these sites.

(Para 10.26)

43. An amount of Rs.7100 crore has been recommended as grant for state specific needs. While these grants have been phased out equally over the last four years, this phasing should be taken as indicative in nature. The states may communicate the required phasing of grants to the central government (*vide* Table 10.11).

(Para 10.28)

Fiscal Reform Facility

44. The scheme of Fiscal Reform Facility may not continue over the period 2005-10, as the scheme of debt relief, as described in chapter 12 obviates the need for a separate Fiscal Reform Facility.

(Para 11.25)

Debt Relief and Corrective Measures

45. Each state must enact a fiscal responsibility legislation prescribing specific annual targets with a view to eliminating the revenue deficit by 2008-09 and reducing fiscal deficits based on a path for reduction of borrowings and guarantees. Enacting the fiscal responsibility legislation on the lines indicated in chapter 4 will be a necessary pre-condition for availing of debt relief.

(Para 12.36)

46. Debt relief may not be linked with performance in human development or investment climate.

(Para 12.38)

47. The central loans to states contracted till 31.3.04 and outstanding on 31.3.05 (amounting to Rs 128795 crore) may be consolidated and rescheduled for a fresh term of 20 years (resulting in repayment in 20 equal instalments), and an interest rate of 7.5 per cent be charged on them. This will be subject to the state enacting the fiscal responsibility legislation and will take effect prospectively from the year in which such legislation is enacted.

(Para 12.42)

48. A debt write-off scheme linked to the reduction of revenue deficit of states may be introduced. Under the scheme, the repayments due from 2005-06 to 2009-10 on central loans contracted up to 31.3.04 and recommended to be consolidated will be eligible for write off. The quantum of write off of repayment will be linked to the absolute amount by which the revenue deficit is reduced in each successive year during the award period. The reduction in the revenue deficit must be cumulatively higher than the cumulative reduction attributable to the interest relief recommended by us. Also, the fiscal deficit of the state must be contained at least to the level of 2004-05. In effect, if the revenue deficit is brought

down to zero, the entire repayments during the period will be written off. The enactment of the fiscal responsibility legislation would be a necessary pre-condition for availing the debt relief under this scheme also with the benefit accruing prospectively. Details of the scheme have been outlined in para 12.44.

(Para 12.43)

49. The central government should not act as an intermediary for future lending and allow the states to approach the market directly. If some fiscally weak states are unable to raise funds from the market, the centre could borrow for the purpose of on lending to such states, but the interest rates should remain aligned to the marginal cost of borrowing for the centre.

(Para 12.46)

50. External assistance may be transferred to states on the same terms and conditions as attached to such assistance by external funding agencies, thereby making government of India a financial intermediary without any gain or loss. The external assistance passed through to states should be managed through a separate fund in the public account.

(Para 12.49)

51. The moratorium on repayments and interest payments on the outstanding special term loan amounting to Rs. 3772 crore as on 31.03.2000 given to Punjab may continue for another two years i.e. up to 2006-07, by which time the central government must finalize the quantum of debt relief to be allowed in terms of the recommendations of the EFC.

(Para 12.51)

52. In respect of relief and rehabilitation loans given to Gujarat from ADB and World Bank through the central government, the central government may, if the government of Gujarat so desires, alter the terms and conditions of these loans, so that these are available to Gujarat on the same terms on which the external agencies have extended these loans.

(Para 12.55)

53. All states should set up sinking funds for amortization of all loans including loans from banks, liabilities on account of NSSF etc. The fund should be maintained outside the consolidated fund of the states and the public account and should not be used for any other purpose, except for redemption of loans.

(Para 12.59)

54. States should set up guarantee redemption funds through earmarked guarantee fees. This should be preceded by risk weighting of guarantees. The quantum of contribution to the fund should be decided accordingly.

(Para 12.60)

Profit Petroleum

55. The Union should share the profit petroleum from NELP areas with the states from where the mineral oil and natural gas are produced. The share should be in the ratio of 50:50.

(Para 13.31)

56. There need not be sharing of profits in respect of nomination fields and non-NELP blocks.

(Para 13.32)

57. The revenues earned by the central government on contracts signed under the coal bed methane policy may be shared with the producing states in the same manner as profit petroleum.

(Para 13.33)

58. In respect of any mineral, if a loss of revenue is anticipated for a state in the process of implementation of a policy, which involves production sharing, a similar compensation mechanism should be adopted by the central government.

(Para 13.34)

A Permanent Secretariat for the Finance Commission

59. The finance commission division of the Ministry of Finance should be converted into a full-fledged department, serving as the permanent secretariat for the finance commissions. This secretariat should be vested with the powers of a full-fledged department of the government, with Ministry of Finance only as its nodal ministry for the purpose of linkage with the Parliament.

(Paras 14.6, 14.7)

60. The expenditure of finance commissions should be treated as expenditure "charged" on the consolidated fund of India.

(Para 14.9)

61. A research committee should be set up with adequate funding to organize studies relevant to fiscal federalism.

(Para 14.8)

62. The finance commissions should have a tenure of at least 3 years to enable them to do their work adequately.

(Para 14.8)

63. The Thirteenth Finance Commission should be set up at the beginning of 2007 and appropriate and adequate arrangements for the office and residence of the chairman and members of the Commission must be made before the appointment of the Commission, so that Commission's time is not wasted in routine administrative matters.

(Para 14.8)

Monitoring Mechanism

64. Every state should set up a high level monitoring committee headed by the Chief Secretary with the Finance Secretary and the Secretaries / heads of departments as members for monitoring proper utilization of finance commission grants.

(Paras 14.11, 14.12)

65. The monitoring committee should meet at least once in every quarter to review the utilization of the grants and to issue directions for mid-course correction, if considered necessary.

(Para 14.12)

66. The monitoring committee should be responsible for monitoring both financial and physical targets and for ensuring adherence to the specific conditionalities in respect of each grant, wherever applicable.

(Para 14.11)

67. In the beginning of the year, the monitoring committee should approve finance commission assisted projects to be undertaken in each sector,

quantify the targets, both in physical and financial terms and lay down the time period for achieving specific milestones.

(Para 14.11)

Accounting Procedure

68. Central government should gradually move towards accrual basis of accounting.

(Para 14.16)

69. In the interim period, additional information in the form of statements should be appended to the present system of cash accounting to enable more informed decision making. The additional information may relate to subsidies, expenditure on salaries, expenditure on pensions, committed liabilities, maintenance expenditure, segregation of salary and non-salary portions and liabilities and repayment schedule on outstanding debts.

(Para 14.16)

70. The definition of revenue and fiscal deficits be standardized and instructions for a uniform classification code down to the object head may be issued to all the states.

(Para 14.17)

71. A National Institute of Public Financial Accountants be set up by the government of India and its charter be decided in consultation with the Comptroller and Auditor General.

(Para 14.18)

C. Rangarajan
Chairman

Shankar N. Acharya
Member

T.R. Prasad
Member

D.K. Srivastava
Member

G.C. Srivastava
Member Secretary

New Delhi
November 30, 2004

I am happy to record my deep appreciation of the unstinted cooperation and support provided by Members of the Commission. The Report is a joint effort and has benefited from the wealth of knowledge and experience brought to bear on it by each Member. I also wish to thank Shri Som Pal, who was a Member of the Commission till May, 2004. He articulated his views with great clarity and sincerity in the various discussions that the Commission had. I must place on record the exemplary services rendered by the Member Secretary, Dr. G.C. Srivastava, who, besides making a substantive contribution to the Report, provided effective leadership to the Secretariat and organized meticulously the multifarious work related to the Commission. His experience at the various levels of government was a great asset to the Commission.

New Delhi
November 30, 2004

C. Rangarajan
Chairman